PELICAN BOOKS

THE FREE
AND THE UNFREE

Peter N. Carroll was born in New York City in 1943. After his graduation from Queens College in 1964, he went on to earn his M.A. and Ph.D. degrees at Northwestern University. He has taught at Northwestern, the University of Illinois at Chicago Circle, and the University of Minnesota, and he is currently a lecturer at San Francisco State University. Books by him include *Puritanism and the Wilderness: The Intellectual Significance of the New England Frontier* and *The Restless Centuries: A History of the American People,* the latter also written with David W. Noble.

David W. Noble was born on a farm near Princeton, New Jersey, in 1925. He was graduated from Princeton University in 1948 and received his M.A. and Ph.D. degrees at the University of Wisconsin in 1949 and 1952. Since 1952 he has taught at the University of Minnesota, where he is now Professor of History and American Studies. Among several books to his credit are *The Paradox of Progressive Thought, Historians against History,* and *The Progressive Mind.*

The Free and the Unfree

★ ★

A NEW HISTORY OF THE UNITED STATES

Peter N. Carroll

and

David W. Noble

PENGUIN BOOKS

Penguin Books Ltd, Harmondsworth, Middlesex, England
Penguin Books, 625 Madison Avenue, New York, New York 10022, U.S.A.
Penguin Books Australia Ltd, Ringwood, Victoria, Australia
Penguin Books Canada Limited, 2801 John Street, Markham, Ontario,
Canada L3R 1B4
Penguin Books (N.Z.) Ltd, 182–190 Wairau Road, Auckland 10, New Zealand

First published 1977
Reprinted 1979

LIBRARY OF CONGRESS CATALOGING IN PUBLICATION DATA
Carroll, Peter N.
The free and the unfree.
Bibliography: p. 425.
Includes index.
1. United States—History. I. Noble,
David W., joint author. II. Title.
E178.1.C28   973   76–30412
ISBN 0 14 02.2038 0

Printed in the United States of America by
Offset Paperback Mfrs., Inc., Dallas, Pennsylvania
Set in Linotype Times Roman

Lines from "If We Must Die" from *Selected Poems of Claude McKay* by Claude McKay reprinted by permission of Twayne Publishers, A Division of G. K. Hall & Co., Boston. Copyright 1953 by Twayne Publishers, Inc.

Lines from "Yet Do I Marvel" from *On These I Stand* by Countee Cullen reprinted by permission of Harper & Row, Publishers, Inc.

Lines from "Ma Rainey" by Sterling Brown from *Folk-Say: A Regional Miscellany,* edited by B. A. Botkin, reprinted by permission of Gertrude Botkin. Copyright © B. A. Botkin, 1958.

Lines from "Howl" from *Howl and Other Poems* by Allen Ginsberg reprinted by permission of City Lights Books. Copyright © Allen Ginsberg, 1956, 1959.

Lines from "Kaddish" from *Kaddish and Other Poems* by Allen Ginsberg reprinted by permission of City Lights Books. Copyright © Allen Ginsberg, 1961.

Lines from "The Change" from *Planet News* by Allen Ginsberg reprinted by permission of City Lights Books. Copyright © Allen Ginsberg, 1968.

Lines from "Mid-August at Sourdough Mountain Lookout" and "Water" from *Riprap, and Cold Mountain Poems* by Gary Snyder reprinted by permission of the author.

Lines from "Song of the Taste" from *Regarding Wave* by Gary Snyder reprinted by permission of New Directions Publishing Corporation and Fulcrum Press. Copyright © Gary Snyder, 1968. "Song of the Taste" was first published in *Poetry*.

Excerpt from *The Big Sea* by Langston Hughes reprinted by permission of Harold Ober Associates Incorporated. Copyright 1940 by Langston Hughes.

Excerpt from *The Great Gatsby* by F. Scott Fitzgerald reprinted by permission of Charles Scribner's Sons.

For
Jeannette Ferrary
and
Lois Noble

Contents

Acknowledgments

This book had its inception in 1973 in a conversation at one of F. Scott Fitzgerald's watering grounds, The Commodore Hotel in St. Paul, Minnesota. Since then, we have depended upon more immediate inspiration from numerous friends. From the beginning, the late Alex Fraser encouraged us to undertake this project. Michael Batinski, Robert Divine, Bruce Irvine, and Jennifer Williams read various drafts of the manuscript and offered many suggestions for its improvement. John Y. Simon generously shared his thoughts about Lincoln, and Louis Carroll, "The Old Timer," contributed his knowledge of early American clocks and watches. Susan Zuckerman, our editor at Penguin, vastly improved the original manuscript and turned our separate efforts into one book.

Jeannette Ferrary and Lois Noble supported us in so many ways that even dedicating this book to them can be only a token acknowledgment; presumably, they already know this.

PETER N. CARROLL
DAVID W. NOBLE

Preface

"In the beginning," wrote the philosopher John Locke in 1689, "all the World was *America,* and more so than that is now." To seventeenth-century Europeans, America symbolized some mythical state of nature, virtually uncorrupted by civilization and practically devoid of government and laws, arts and sciences. Locke's statement also implied that this unblemished condition already had been altered by the introduction into the wilderness of European civilization; colonization had introduced social institutions into what previously had been a natural world of God's Creation.

To Locke's contemporaries, these changes seemed entirely advantageous and demonstrated the obvious blessings of European expansion. Since Europe epitomized human civilization, then Europe must transform the remainder of the earth into its own image. This grandiose vision provided a powerful impetus for overseas expansion that enabled the relatively small nations of Western Europe to conquer the entire world and, to a large extent, to impose their values and institutions upon the other inhabitants of the globe.

It is from the perspective of European expansion that this history is written. About five hundred years ago, a small but aggressive European culture burst its traditional geographic bounds and began extending its influence around the world. Africans and Asians felt the effects of Western expansion first, succumbing to the blandishments of European traders and the force of European arms. But the European conquest achieved its greatest successes in another part of the globe, the apparently simple state of nature called America. The Europeanization of the New World had profound effects upon the American continent, upon the native inhabitants, and ultimately upon Europe itself.

The expansion of European culture represented more than political domination. Renaissance Europeans themselves were not many centuries away from a premodern peasant mentality that passively accepted the natural state of the world and believed in preserving traditional values and institutions. Yet the driving force of European expansion depended upon a modern technological vision which insisted that rational secular improvements should be imposed upon the irrationality of nature and traditional societies. These assumptions enabled Europeans to define themselves as a

15

superior people and to believe earnestly that the process of Europeanization was good for everyone.

During the past century, however, some of the victims of Europeanization have begun to challenge their ethnocentric oppressors. In international terms, liberation movements in the so-called Third World have attacked the political and economic power of the Western empires and have resisted new modes of exploitation. No less important has been the movement for liberation within the modern Europeanized societies. In the United States, such movements as Black Power, Red Power, Woman's Liberation, and the youthful counterculture represent fundamental resistance to the culture of the dominant elite. From this perspective, the history of the American people may be seen as the attempt by transplanted Europeans to impose Western values on nature and society in the face of spreading opposition from within—from Native Americans, blacks, ethnics, women, and, most recently, young people.

Historians tend to group themselves according to their interpretive biases. Early in the twentieth century, "progressive" historians viewed the history of the United States as a story of evolutionary progress in which democratic principles struggled against the forces of reaction. In the 1950s, a school of "consensus" historians placed the American past in the context of the cold war and emphasized the uniqueness and superiority of American ideals. By the 1960s, this optimism gave way to historical revisionists who again described an American history based on ethnic, racial, and class conflict.

In these terms, *The Free and the Unfree* may be described as a "counterculture" interpretation of American history. Though it recognizes the political preeminence of a ruling elite—which for the most part consisted of male white Anglo-Saxon Protestants—it also examines the historical experiences of some of the outgroups— Native Americans, Afro-Americans, ethnic Americans, and female Americans. This discussion avoids both the simplifications of "consensus" historians as well as the polarities of "conflict" historians. Instead, it emphasizes a *dynamic* relationship between established groups and outgroups. To explore this dynamic, *The Free and the Unfree* describes not only the American political system but also the cultural milieu upon which it was based.

In structure, *The Free and the Unfree* is divided into four historical eras: (1) pre-Columbian settlement to the adoption of the United States Constitution; (2) the founding of the republic through the Civil War; (3) Reconstruction through World War I; (4) 1920 to Watergate. Each historical era is treated in a series of interrelated, overlapping chapters that examine social, economic, and political events.

This structure replaces the familiar political chronology that tends to emphasize the history of established groups. The thematic arrangement of chapters also illuminates aspects of American culture usually ignored in standard works. The analyses of "American space" and "American time" for example, uncover broad cultural trends that affected all people, not merely those who happened to control political power.

The last chapter of each historical section recapitulates the relationship between the free and the unfree at a specific point in time. These discussions focus on the changing American identity as expressed in the lives of four national leaders: Jefferson, Lincoln, Wilson, and Nixon. Jefferson represented the values of the ruling elite in the Revolutionary era, just as Lincoln, Wilson, and Nixon did in their own epochs. The changing stature of these Presidents and their changing relationships to the outgroups reveals a fundamental alteration in the national identity during the past three centuries. If these trends continue, perhaps the outgroups in the United States may yet transform the home of the brave into the land of the free.

It may be that some little root of the sacred tree still lives. Nourish it then, that it may leaf and bloom and fill with singing birds.

—Black Elk

Part One

★ ★

AMERICAN SOCIETIES:
FROM SETTLEMENT TO NATION

"The course of humanity was orderly"

* * * * * * * * * * * * * * * * * * * *

1

Native Americans
Meet Native Europeans

Native American cultures and their lands

The first contact: Columbus and European exploration

The European background: Protestant Reformation,
political nationalism, economic change, Renaissance curiosity

Race for empire: early exploration, conquest, and colonization

Five hundred years ago, on the warm, windswept islands known today as the Greater Antilles and the Bahamas, there existed a people called the Arawak. They had emigrated from the South American mainland about five hundred years earlier in rough dugout boats. Though peaceful and friendly, the Arawak had displaced the indigenous peoples, who were smaller in number and lived without agriculture or pottery, to the more northern regions of present-day Haiti and Cuba. Now, however, the Arawak themselves were being pressed by their bellicose neighbors, the Caribs, and lived in fear of invasion.

Neither the Arawak nor the Caribs nor the other smaller groups of the region possessed written alphabets or calendars. They relied for continuity, like other preliterate peoples, upon oral traditions that, along with the people themselves, have become extinct. We must reconstruct their lives from fragments of pottery, burial remains, and other artifacts that have endured the passage of centuries. It is an imprecise operation, to be sure, but it provides sufficient information to glimpse these peoples on their own terms. And there is also the testimony of their literate conquerors, the Spanish, who began invading the area nearly five centuries ago.

As in other premodern societies, the peoples of the Caribbean lived in harmony with nature, adjusting their existence to the natural rhythms of life. For food, they cultivated a variety of crops, particularly maize, beans, and yams, and made cassava bread from yuccas. Skilled as fishermen, they supplemented this diet with shellfish, rich in proteins. They wore scant clothing, preferring to go naked in the tropical sun, and probably did no weaving. But they twisted various wild fibers, including cotton, into nets, bags, and hammocks. Their salubrious environment enabled them to flourish, and it is now estimated that the population of the region, at the time of the first European contacts, numbered about eight million.

The density of population—far greater than previously believed —reflected not simply the abundance of food, but also the ecological balance of the area. For these people, nature and humanity did not exist in opposition but interacted both in material and in spiritual ways. Their rituals and taboos brought them closer to the natural flow of the sun and the tides, to the heavens as well as the earth.

The Arawak believed in a world of spirits, some human in shape, some animals or totems, which protected each person and, together, the group. These spirits formed a hierarchy that paralleled the social organization of the people, thus linking the human world with the supernatural. The leaders' personal spirits, in other words, constituted the gods of the entire group. Today, there is no one left to practice their worship, but we know that at ceremonial times they displayed their idols on large ball courts and propitiated the spirits of their gods with elaborate rituals. Apparently, such spiritual forces could not protect them from invaders. For within one century of the Spanish arrival, the peaceful Arawak and most of their neighbors became extinct, victims of European disease, maltreatment, and cultural upheaval.

While the Arawak fished and planted around their sun-blanched islands, other complex cultures flourished in other parts of the Americas. These peoples varied enormously, ranging from poor nomadic food gatherers of the interior plains of North America to opulent fishing societies of the Pacific Northwest, from the woodland hunting tribes of what is now the northern United States to the wealthy and powerful peoples of Central America. Together, depending upon population estimates reconstructed in our own times, they constituted somewhere between fifty and one hundred million people, of which about ten million lived in North America. Many areas in the western hemisphere contained denser populations than regions of Western Europe in the age of Christopher Columbus. America was not a vacant wasteland awaiting the arrival of "civilized" Europeans.

Consider, for example, the chiefdoms of the Pacific Northwest, which included, among others, such groups as the Tlingits of southern Alaska, the Nootka on Vancouver Island, and the Yurok of northern California. Like the Arawak of the Caribbean, these peoples were blessed with an incredibly rich environment based on the vast stock of fish, especially salmon, and abundant edible plants. The large succulent fish annually make their way upstream to spawn and then return to the sea, and the indigenous peoples learned to make nets and weirs to harvest this crop. The natives of the region also developed techniques to preserve their fish, thus assuring sufficient food in seasons of scarcity. The natural abundance encouraged the formation of a sedentary society even though agriculture remained generally undeveloped.

The ecological patterns of the Pacific Northwest influenced the social organization of the local peoples. Since the acquisition of food was no problem, wealth and status within society became more serious concerns. One way of demonstrating wealth was to acquire more slaves than anyone else, a social consideration that encouraged sporadic warfare among the tribes as a way of obtaining slaves. Such servants possessed the lowest position in these status-conscious groups.

The desire for prestige also produced a periodic mass feast known as a "potlatch" (a corruption of the Nootka word meaning "to give"), in which a host demonstrated his affluence by giving away property. Such generosity might result in the emancipation or murder of slaves and the destruction or distribution of blankets and copper, as well as the lavish provisioning of guests. Such conspicuous consumption, to use a modern phrase, reinforced the elaborate distinctions within the social hierarchy.

The concern for visible symbols of wealth also led to the acceptance of sumptuary laws, which defined appropriate dress and ornamentation for certain social groups. The chief enjoyed the most opulent accouterments, including the most expensive costume and the largest house. Such patterns, similar to the policies established by the monarchies of Europe, reflect a people living well above the minimal needs of subsistence. The introduction of Western technology, however, soon undermined this social order by bringing mass-produced goods and epidemic diseases.

Halfway across the continent, from the Great Lakes to the Atlantic seaboard, lived groups of interrelated cultures. Speaking such languages as Siouan, Algonquian, and Iroquoisan, they formed complicated societies that often differed markedly from one another. Relying upon agriculture, as well as on fishing, hunting, and trapping, the peoples of the Eastern Woodlands built stable villages, some of them with as many as five thousand inhabitants. Living either in birch-covered wigwams or in rectangular longhouses, they usually palisaded their villages with log stockades. They also possessed, in their light birchbark canoes, a reliable means of commerce and communication with other tribes.

As the ecological patterns of this large geographic area varied enormously, each native group adjusted its lifestyle to benefit from

nature intimately attached to spirit world in Indian culture

the available resources. Such patterns reflected not so much economic prudence as a spiritual relationship with nature. Regardless of regional variations, the native peoples viewed the world as a balanced system in which all creation, animate and inanimate, existed harmoniously. Thus the biological world of edible plants or fish or game remained intimately attached to a spirit world. Humanity was but one part of that system. The acquisition of food, clothing, or shelter therefore depended upon maintaining spiritual relations with the rest of creation. From this perspective, the idea of owning parcels of land, bits of creation, was unthinkable.

The native cultures recognized the importance of preserving the ecological balance and protecting the wildlife and the land. This attitude partly reflected the seasonal shifts in available resources. Equally important was the need to palliate the spirit world for the appropriation of material goods. Thus hunting followed explicit spiritual rules or taboos, lest the destruction of certain living creatures undermine the cosmic unity. Among the Micmac, an Algonquian tribe of eastern Canada, the moose and beaver, both indispensable for life, received careful treatment after being killed. Their bones were never burned, nor thrown into the rivers, nor given to the dogs. Such taboos reflected a fear that the animal spirits would inform the living animals of their fates and thus prevent their further capture by the native hunters. These spiritual concerns structured the natives' relationship to the entire natural world. Only after the appearance of Europeans did the system begin to disintegrate, and with it, the ecological balance of the continent.

Perhaps the most famous of the Eastern Woodlands peoples were the Iroquois, a powerful tribal group that lived between the Adirondack Mountains and the Great Lakes in what is now central New York. Scattered through the forest, the Iroquois formed communal societies in which all property was shared. In this culture the men were responsible for hunting and fishing, both spiritually endowed enterprises, while the women cultivated the sacred soil of the Mother Earth. Since the fruits of these labors were shared, the division of tasks along sexual lines worked to strengthen communal bonds.

The Iroquois peoples, called by the Europeans the League of the Iroquois, embraced five major tribes: the Mohawks, Oneidas, Senecas, Cayugas, and Onondagas; later, a sixth tribe, the Tuscaroras, entered the union. According to oral tradition, the League originated about four hundred years ago, shortly after European explorers began to penetrate the coastal areas of North America. Perhaps there was a causal relationship between the two events, for the Iroquois League, by successfully terminating the internecine wars between the tribes, enabled the natives to present a fairly united front to the Europeans.

The Iroquois peoples had previously been badly divided by persistent blood feuds and wars of revenge. Amid this general unrest, the arrival of Europeans, or perhaps simply the growth of the native population, heightened the desirability of tribal unity. These unarticulated needs achieved spiritual importance when a Huron prophet named Deganawidah, perhaps a supernatural apparition, inspired a vision of a Great Peace. Appearing before Hiawatha, a Mohawk sachem, Deganawidah proposed a union among the Iroquois tribes, based primarily upon the cessation of warfare and the creation of an intertribal council of chiefs. The Iroquois must bind their hands together so firmly and form a circle so strong, declared Deganawidah, "that if a tree should fall upon it, it could not shake or break it, so that our people and grandchildren shall remain in the circle of security, peace, and happiness."

Captivated by this dream, Hiawatha traveled from village to village, appealing for tribal unification. His personal commitment, together with the practicality of his message, won numerous converts and facilitated a formal confederation. Binding the tribes together was a council of fifty chiefs, or sachems, chosen proportionately by the five nations. These hereditary leaders negotiated differences between tribes but lacked the power to interfere directly in internal tribal matters. Nor could this council coerce individual tribes to abide by its decisions. But the system brought peace to the Iroquois and enabled them to expand their influence among other native groups. As an independent force the Iroquois played a crucial role in the balance of power once the European nations began to colonize North America.

The political structure of the Iroquois League reflected the social organization of the tribes. At the core of Iroquois society was a matrilineal family system. Mothers and daughters perpetuated the kinship unit, while the sons departed at marriage to live within their wives' families. Children belonged to the mother's lineage and followed the matrilineal branch in cases of divorce. The inheritance of possessions at death passed in a similar manner from mother to daughter.

The basic political unit of the Iroquois was the "fireside," which consisted of the mother and all her children. Groups of firesides joined by blood along matrilineal lines—sisters, for example— formed groups called *ohwachiras*. At the heads of the *ohwachiras* were the oldest women, the village matriarchs. These leaders chose male delegates to represent the group at the clan and tribal councils as well as in the grand council of the League of the Iroquois. The male sachems served for life and possessed considerable power. Yet the matriarchs wielded ultimate power and could depose the male delegates if they disagreed about policy. The political process among the Iroquois thus depended upon consent rather than authority. In the final analysis, it was the community that shaped political decisions.

The unity of the Iroquois made them especially strong enemies, and the neighboring Algonquian peoples greatly feared their warriors. Believing that the confederation was destined to expand over the continent, the Iroquois often engaged in wars of conversion. Yet, although they occasionally adopted some of their captives into the group, more frequently they tortured their prisoners to test their bravery. "One must be there to see a living picture of Hell," reported one Jesuit witness.

South of the Iroquois confederacy, in what is now the southeastern United States, there existed a large number of different peoples, including the Creeks, Yamasees, Seminoles, Choctaws, and Cherokees. Based upon mixed economies of hunting and agriculture, these tribes possessed large populations, lived in settled villages, and maintained extensive trade networks with other native groups. All of them had been influenced by an earlier civilization, the Mississippian, which was characterized by gigantic earthworks, or mounds. These structures, some of them larger than the great Egyptian pyramids, were used for burial and ceremonial purposes.

The most striking of these cultures was the Natchez, a group of people numbering about four thousand that occupied at least nine villages along the Mississippi River. The Natchez were a rigidly hierarchical and authoritarian society headed by an absolute chief called the Great Sun. Believed to be a descendant of a sun god, the Great Sun enjoyed spiritual as well as secular power. The French explorers and missionaries who encountered the Natchez about three hundred years ago were deeply impressed by the power of the chief, perhaps because their own society—the France of Louis XIV—was authoritarian also.

Nevertheless, the French colonizers quickly destroyed the

Natchez, first by bringing epidemic diseases, then by killing the natives in war. In 1699 the Natchez rose for the last time, but French retaliation was brutal and thorough. All the survivors, including the Great Sun, were sold into slavery, and the eternal fire that had burned from the sacred Natchez temple was quenched forever. Only the silent artifacts, dug up periodically by archaeologists, testify to what was once a magnificent civilization.

A similar fate befell an even more powerful society, the Aztec of Mexico. No brief discussion could adequately describe the grandeur of this culture. But consider the words of Bernal Díaz del Castillo, a soldier who accompanied the Spanish conquistador Cortés on his triumphant march into Mexico. "Some of the soldiers among us," he reported, "had been in many parts of the world, in Constantinople, and all over Italy, and in Rome." But "so large a market place and so full of people, and so well regulated and arranged, they had never beheld before." And some of these soldiers "even asked whether the things we saw were not a dream."

Surprisingly, the Aztecs had arrived in Central America only five hundred years before the Spanish soldiers. Benefiting from the sophisticated agricultural tradition in the area, they built their capital city, Tenochtitlán (at the present site of Mexico City), by draining the local swamps and creating a complex system of irrigation. With an abundant food supply, their population grew quickly, and the Aztecs began expanding their influence by military conquest. The Aztecs made exacting demands upon their defeated neighbors: control of trade and markets and the payment of tribute and human bodies to be sacrificed in bloody religious ceremonies before the Aztec gods. At the time of the Spanish invasion, Tenochtitlán numbered at least sixty thousand people and the Aztec empire dominated about five million more.

Despite the severity of their rule, or perhaps because of it, the Aztecs had created a poorly integrated empire. Many conquered groups had managed to maintain some independence, and many more remained restive under Aztec administration. Such problems ultimately facilitated the Spanish conquest. But until that time, the Aztecs exploited their subjects unrelentingly, and as a result they had created a rich culture that staggered the minds of the Europeans. It was this very splendor that attracted the Spanish and doomed the Aztec empire. Aided by smallpox epidemics, imperial disintegration, and, ultimately, Aztec credulity, Cortés vanquished the native peoples within three years.

The new conquerors proved as ruthless as the Aztecs themselves, killing and enslaving thousands of people, destroying the fabulous city with its massive pyramids and temples. "The streets, squares, houses, and courts were filled with bodies," reported one spectator, "so that it was almost impossible to pass. Even Cortés was sick from the stench in his nostrils."

This mortality revealed not so much the superiority of European weapons as the vulnerability of the natives to European diseases. There are, of course, no exact statistics of mortality among the indigenous populations. But it is clear that the introduction of European microorganisms devastated the natives at an incredible rate, killing leaders as well as followers, and thoroughly disrupting and destroying the native cultures. These hidden allies followed the Europeans everywhere in the Western hemisphere, passing from body to body, until vast numbers had perished. In New England, for example, the epidemics had come with the fishermen who dried their catches on the coastal beaches. When the first European colonists arrived a decade later, they found piles of unburied skeletons as mute testimony of the catastrophe.

Lacking previous exposure to European viral strains, the Native Americans never developed natural immunities to the European infections. The Europeans were similarly vulnerable to American diseases. Soon after the contact between Americans and Spanish, the Europeans began falling victim to a mysterious and often fatal malady that modern medicine would call syphilis. It was a curious exchange, then, that took place in the Caribbean five hundred years ago.

The unique development of the Native American populations can be traced back about thirty thousand years. During the last Ice Age, when large portions of North America were covered with thick ice, the levels of the seas dropped considerably, perhaps as much as three hundred feet, because the ice incorporated large amounts of water. The enormous glaciers did not cover the earth uniformly, and the lowering of the sea level exposed land areas that previously had been submerged. Portions of Siberia, Alaska, and western Canada were, at various times, virtually free of ice and yet connected by a "land bridge" caused by the lowered sea level. Depending upon the estimates of the level of the seas, it is now believed that this land bridge extended in width for at least several hundred miles, perhaps much more. About ten thousand years ago, when the glaciers began to melt, the land bridge became inundated again and is now called the Bering Sea.

It was over this land bridge that the first human beings crossed to the American continents. Probably they were pursuing large mammals that had preceded them into an area filled with vegetation. These early humans survived by hunting, perfecting their weapons and strategies. One technique involved stampeding huge herds of bison over high cliffs to obtain food from just a few beasts. As they followed these mammals, human beings dispersed over the American continents, reaching the tip of South America at least ten thousand years ago.

At about that time, radical changes began occurring in the climate of the Western hemisphere. Temperatures rose, drying out portions of the land and with it, the thick vegetation; simultaneously, to the north, the glaciers thawed, pouring off water that formed into lakes and rivers. The most dramatic effect of these ecological changes was the rapid extinction of the large mammals that had lived off the abundant vegetation. Woolly mammoths, giant mastodons, camels, horses—to name only the most famous American mammals—quickly disappeared.

Human beings who had hunted these huge animals for food and other necessities, faced similar extinction, and no doubt many nomadic groups succumbed. Others, however, seeking alternative means of subsistence, shifted to small-game hunting, fishing, gathering, and, most significantly, agriculture. The invention of agricultural techniques brought immense changes to human life and human culture. The cultivation of land meant that groups could abandon nomadic patterns and settle in one place. The existence of a controlled food supply—usually a combination of hunting, gathering, and agriculture—also accelerated the growth of population. These changes, in turn, encouraged the diversification of society. Political, social, religious, and economic distinctions between individuals became more necessary and more evident.

These early agricultural societies did not develop at the same rate or in the same manner. Rather, human beings created cultures that seemed to them to be best integrated into the natural environment. Salmon runs in the Pacific Northwest, for example, influenced the cultural patterns of the local peoples, just as the rainfall affected the Aztec cultivators of maize. Yet this adaptation was not determined simply by geography and climate. Not all people surrounded by fish learned, like the Yurok, the mysteries of smoking and drying. Nor did the Iroquois of the woodlands develop the irrigation techniques of the Aztecs. Instead, a continuous interrelationship between human culture and the natural world took place, an interaction that varied enormously in time and in place. From the Arawak to the Yurok, from the Iroquois to the Aztec, millions of people survived and flourished on the changing surface of the continent.

Then, on an otherwise ordinary autumn day shortly after sunrise, the Arawak inhabitants of the Caribbean Islands noticed strange ships sailing on the horizon, much larger than their dugout canoes. As these ships moved closer and closer, they saw strange-looking people with light skins aboard, making odd gestures. The Arawak youths stood at the banks hesitantly, and then some of the braver men began swimming toward the mysterious boats.

These strangers offered the Arawak red-colored caps, glass beads, and other curious trifles. In exchange, the Arawak brought parrots, cotton skeins, darts, and other items. Then the strangers drew out swords, which the Arawak, in ignorance, grasped by the blades, cutting themselves. It was a symbolic act, this inadvertent drawing of blood. For the Arawak and the strangers looked at the world from opposite angles, and both were fascinated by what the other was not.

That first contact between Native Americans and Europeans was repeated with increasing frequency as other enterprising Europeans followed those first ships across the Atlantic Ocean. Whether the voyagers were Spanish, English, French, or Portuguese in origin, whether the Native Americans were Arawak, Yurok, Iroquois, Natchez, or Aztec, the initial confrontation was usually the same—two cultures looking at each other from opposite ends of the sword, each awed by the mystery of the other.

To the Native Americans, these seagoing peoples presented obvious differences in language, in dress, in color—so much so that the natives doubted that they were human beings. "They believe very firmly," wrote Christoper Columbus after his first voyage to Hispaniola, "that I, with these ships and people, came from the sky, and in this belief they everywhere received us, after they had overcome their fear. And this does not result from their being ignorant (for they are of a very keen intelligence and men who navigate all those seas, so that it is wondrous the good account they give of everything), but because they have never seen people clothed or ships like ours."

As Columbus and his crew sailed along the coast, native messengers raced ahead shouting from house to house, "Come! Come! See the people from the sky!" Other native peoples reacted in similar fashion, often to their subsequent confusion. The Aztecs of Mexico, including their emperor Moctezuma, believed that the invading Europeans were white gods destined, according to the Aztecs' religious tradition, to return and reclaim their people. For this reason, they initially welcomed Cortés into their capital; when they discovered their mistake, it was too late to repel him. The Florentine explorer Verrazzano, who sailed along the coast of North America during the sixteenth century, reported similar receptions by natives amazed at the whiteness of Europeans and their unusual technology.

In each of these cases, the Native Americans initially greeted the European visitors with warmth and friendship. "Of anything they have," Columbus declared, "if you ask them for it, they never say no." And his *Journal* abounds with examples of the natives' hospitality, of their bringing food and drink and gifts. Amerigo Vespucci, for whom America is named, also described what he considered the ultimate in generosity: "The greatest token of friendship which they show you is that they give you their wives and daughters; and when a father or a mother brings you the daughter, although she be a virgin, and you sleep with her, they esteem themselves highly honored; and in this way they practice the full extreme of hospitality." To the Native Americans, the Europeans constituted a strange form of creation, yet one that they endeavored to incorporate into their existing world-view. Though the Europeans were decidedly different from themselves, the natives were open and, from their point of view, understanding.

The Europeans were not free of misconceptions either. For if the natives mistakenly believed that the white-skinned sailors were gods, the Europeans mistakenly believed that the natives were "Indians." This misconception originated in Columbus' basic error (which he himself never realized) in thinking that in sailing westward from Europe he had reached the Indies, which were the true object of his voyage. To Columbus, it was literally inconceivable that he had found previously unknown lands. Like other Europeans of his time, he believed firmly in the completeness of human knowledge. What he saw, therefore, he incorporated into his existing world-view, and the Native Americans thereby became, to the satisfaction of most Europeans, simply Indians.

The Europeans' early attempts to describe the Native Americans provide valuable insights into the nature of European culture. Columbus' first observation mentioned that the natives possessed no visible religion, and he expressed hope that they might be "converted to our Holy Faith by love." Later, he described their physical appearance. "They all go quite naked as their mothers bore them," he observed, adding that they had coarse hair, "almost like the hair of a horse's tail," and that their skin color was neither black nor white. "They ought to be good servants and of good skill," the admiral concluded.

In another entry, Columbus described these "very handsome people": "Their hair is not kinky, but straight. . . . They themselves are not at all black, but of the color of the Canary Islanders." Again, the admiral used the previously known African as a reference point to depict the uniqueness of the Americans. Vespucci, who made four voyages to South America, observed that the natives "have no modesty. They do not practice marriage amongst themselves. . . . They can be termed neither Moors nor Jews; and they are worse than heathen; because we did not see that they offered any sacrifice, nor yet did they have a house of prayer." Of their economy, he noted, "They engage in no barter; they neither buy nor sell." Jean de Léry, an explorer of Brazil, maintained that "their gestures and countenances are so different from ours, that I confess to my difficulty in representing them in words, or even in pictures."

What is interesting about all these descriptions is the negative form the comments take; the Americans are described in terms of what they are not or do not have. Most other European descriptions of the American peoples are similar. John Winthrop, a leading colonist of Puritan New England, justified his claim to the wilderness lands by exclaiming that the natives "enclose no land, neither have they any settled habitations, nor any tame cattle." In short, to the explorers and colonists who followed in the wake of Christopher Columbus, the Native Americans symbolized what the Europeans were *not*.

The notion of a negative identity—of not being something else—forced both the Americans and the Europeans to consider exactly what they thought they themselves were. Each culture group, of course, dealt with this problem differently. But in a fundamental

way, the contact between Americans and Europeans produced psychological and cultural crises of major proportions.

For the Americans' side of the story, we are limited by the
extreme paucity of sources. As European diseases decimated the
indigenous populations, cultural traditions, like the people themselves, disappeared. Those who survived the epidemics then confronted aggressive European civilizations that sought to "uplift" the
"heathen" by destroying their cultures. Much was lost, but listen to
the somber voice of one survivor: "There was then no sickness; they
had no aching bones; they had then no high fever; they had then no
burning chest; they had then no abdominal pain; they had then no
consumption; they had then no headache"—all images of contrast,
framing what existed in the present with what once had been. "At
that time," he concludes, referring to a lost age, "the course of
humanity was orderly."

Implicit in this sense of order is a notion of cosmic harmony, of a
balance between nature and culture in which people knew how to
cure ordinary disease, or at least knew how to cope spiritually with
the mysteries of the universe. There is a sense of psychological and
cultural equilibrium—lost forever to the Native Americans after
1492.

Europeans in the age of Columbus saw themselves as Christians,
the most spiritually pure people in creation. This ethnocentric idea
found reinforcement in the ideals of the Roman Catholic Church,
which claimed to be a universal spiritual community. Yet this ideology clearly excluded such religiously different people as Muslims,
against whom Christians had waged holy wars for centuries, and
Jews, who remained outsiders throughout European society. Believing in a single unitary religion, members of the Catholic Church
viewed infidels as suitable either for conversion to the true faith or
worthy only of death or enslavement. Such religious attitudes
shaped the Europeans' relations with Africans as well as Native
Americans.

By the age of Columbus, however, even the internal strength of
the Roman Catholic Church was deteriorating. Perhaps the Black
Plague of the previous century, with its staggering mortality, had
undermined the spiritual security of European society. Perhaps the
increased ceremonialism, with its repetition of formalized rituals,
weakened the religious vitality of the people. Whatever the exact
causes (and they were doubtless many and complicated), many
Europeans commented on a feeling of despair that seemed to per-

Ref

vade the culture. For a number of reasons, some ecclesiastical, some liturgical, the Roman Catholic Church was failing to satisfy the spiritual needs of many of its members.

This psychological context provides the background for the Protestant Reformation, which began as a modest protest by the German monk Martin Luther in 1517 and soon exploded throughout Europe. Luther's basic disagreement with the Church of Rome was its emphasis upon intermediary institutions that separated the individual from God. Luther argued that individuals achieved salvation by faith alone and that certain liturgical practices were unnecessary. These ideas spread quickly throughout Europe and were adopted, often with some modifications, by other spiritual reformers. These Protestants, as they were called, did not always agree about all aspects of religion, and there were significant differences between such groups as Lutherans, Calvinists, and Anglicans. Despite this diversity, however, Protestants shared certain theological assumptions that distinguished them from traditional Catholics. The bitter opposition between these groups climaxed in the next century in several wars of religion, an aggressive hostility that also affected the course of history in America.

nationalism

One reason for the rapid spread of Protestantism and the concomitant intensity of religious rivalry was that the two processes were also linked to the development of political nationalism in Europe. The late fifteenth century witnessed the emergence of strong political dynasties in such countries as Spain, France, and England. In each of these countries, powerful monarchies began to consolidate their rule by centralizing government. The adoption of a fervent religious ideology often coincided with this process. Thus the Spanish rulers Ferdinand and Isabella, who sponsored Columbus' voyages to the Indies, cast themselves in the role of "Holy Monarchs," vigorous proponents of the expansion of the Roman Catholic religion. A century later, England's Queen Elizabeth I assumed a similar, but Protestant, position, which soon led to direct competition with Spain in both Europe and America.

polit central

The process of political centralization, characteristic of Western Europe in the fifteenth and sixteenth centuries, was also related to broad economic trends, particularly the expansion of capitalism. By the age of Columbus, European merchants were acquiring enormous profits through commerce with the Levant for spices, silks, and other luxury items. The lucrative trade, however, was monopolized by Italian merchants. It was the desire to bypass these Italian middlemen that led the monarchs of Portugal and Spain to seek an alternate route to Asia. The accumulation of capital by European merchants also led to the development of more sophisticated banking and credit systems. In England, the independent wealth of the merchants, rather than the treasures of the crown, supported the colonization of North America. The prime motivation for the merchants, of course, was profits. But in an age of keen national rivalry, the search for wealth and power and the passions of ideology were inextricably linked.

Equally characteristic of the age was an enhanced concern among intellectuals for knowledge about the natural world. As part of a more general cultural movement, Renaissance scholars exhibited great curiosity about such subjects as history, geography, and classical learning. This spirit of inquiry, no less than the desire for wealth, encouraged Europeans to fashion new navigational equipment, which, in turn, facilitated voyages of exploration to what appeared to be new lands. Information brought back by early adventurers whetted the Europeans' appetite for still more exploration, a process that led to the rapid expansion of European culture beyond its traditional boundaries.

It is easy to underestimate the importance of these broad cultural trends—the centralization of power, the accumulation of capital, the expanding Renaissance mind. Consider, however, the situation without these factors present.

About the year 1000, Norse adventurers, led by Leif Ericson, had landed on the coast of North America at a place they called Vinland. According to sketchy accounts, they attempted to establish a settlement there, but were repelled by the native populations. However dramatic their adventure, the Norse voyages had virtually no impact on European society. By the late fifteenth century, few Europeans even knew about these experiences. Yet news of Columbus' voyage of 1492 quickly flashed through Europe, exciting the imaginations of intellectuals and merchants, if not the common people; and thousands of explorers and colonists soon set sail for America. The difference in the effect of the Norse voyages and that of Columbus underscores the immense changes that occurred in Europe during the intervening centuries.

The race for empire began first in Portugal when Prince Henry the Navigator supported voyages of trade and exploration along the African coast. By the first decade of the sixteenth century, Portuguese sailors had rounded the Cape of Good Hope in southern

Africa and had established trading settlements as far east as India. These voyages brought fantastic profits to the Portuguese adventurers and demonstrated the value of overseas expansion. But Portugal lacked the population to consolidate these advances and merely established small trading posts. Soon other European nations began to challenge Portuguese supremacy.

For a time, Christopher Columbus had sold his services to the Portuguese crown, but he could not persuade his employers to support a western voyage to the Indies. The Spanish, on the other hand, greeted the proposal with greater enthusiasm. For them, Columbus' plan represented a gigantic gamble, but also an opportunity to bypass Portugal's growing control of trade. Remarkably, it worked— though not in the way that Columbus had anticipated.

Throughout his lifetime, Columbus believed that he had reached the eastern coast of Asia, somewhere near Japan. Yet neither he nor the many Spanish-speaking explorers who followed him managed to locate the fabled spices, which promised incredible wealth. Only much later did Europeans realize that Columbus had inadvertently located a previously unknown continent. But if the search for spices failed, the Spanish did find another source of wealth—the gold that belonged to the native peoples.

The Spanish reaction, as described by an Aztec witness, was perhaps predictable. When given presents of gold by the Aztec emperor, "the Spanish burst into smiles; their eyes shone with pleasure. . . . They picked up the gold and fingered it like monkeys; they seemed to be transported by joy, as if their hearts were illumined and made new." The lust for gold drove the Spanish onward. Wave upon wave of Spanish adventurers arrived in America, crushing the native peoples, taking their property for export to Europe. The Americans who survived the European diseases—and statistically they were not many—were enslaved and put to work in the mines until they too died. Then they were replaced by new slaves brought in chains from Africa.

The presence of Catholic priests mitigated the worst brutalities of the Spanish conquest. But the missionaries themselves often conducted a more subtle but no less deliberate form of European aggression. Anxious to convert the heathen to Christianity, they herded the natives into missions and forced them to surrender their traditional cultural styles. Under such pressure many natives made accommodations to European ways. But rebellion was not unknown. In 1680, for example, the Pueblos of the Southwest, led by the religious prophet Popé, rose against their conquerors. With a rare display of unity, the Pueblos drove the Spanish from their territory, but only for twelve years. Many other native peoples avoided direct conflict with the Europeans and so managed to preserve their cultures. More often, the natives made prudent compromises, integrating European patterns with their own, which usually resulted in the eradication of the traditional ways.

The early success of the Portuguese and Spanish empires reflected the stability of the home countries. France, Holland, and England entered the imperial contest later, because internal divisions diverted government attention. Without domestic tranquillity, these nations could support only sporadic voyages of exploration. In the early sixteenth century, French navigators like Cartier explored the coasts of North America, searching for the fabled "northwest passage" through the continent. Not until the following century, under the influence of Samuel de Champlain, did the French begin serious colonization of what is now eastern Canada. Similarly, Dutch interest in America awaited the formation of the Dutch East India Company in 1602.

England's claim to North America dated from the voyage of John Cabot in 1497. As was the case in France, however, severe internal problems, including the dynastic worries of Henry VII and his son, Henry VIII, drained the royal coffers and prevented serious involvement in colonization. Only late in the sixteenth century, under the reign of Elizabeth I, did England enter the race for empire. By that time, an important motivating force was England's rivalry with Spain.

English and Spanish competition arose not only from political considerations, but from ideological differences as well. When Henry VIII severed England's ties with the Church of Rome because Pope Clement VII refused to sanction Henry's divorce from Catherine of Aragon, he inadvertently opened the door to basic religious reforms. Though Henry himself remained unfriendly to Protestantism, the creation of a national Church of England soon led to the confiscation of monastic lands and the introduction of a vernacular Bible—both Protestant ideas in practice, if not in principle. After Henry's death, the Anglican Church became even more visibly Protestant. Though the short reign of Mary Tudor, infamously known to Protestants as "Bloody Mary," resulted in a temporary reversal, the ascension of Elizabeth in 1558 seemed to place England solidly in the Protestant camp.

Under Elizabeth, relations with Spain deteriorated completely. England provided clandestine support to the Dutch Protestants who had rebelled from Spanish rule, and Elizabeth countenanced English raids on Spanish shipping by such sea dogs as John Hawkins and Francis Drake, who pirated Spanish gold and carried their loot to England. Provoked by such aggression, Spain launched its grand Armada in 1588 to bring England to its knees. Instead, English forces defeated the Spanish fleet, opening the way for English expansion in America.

By that time, England already had planted a small colony on Roanoke Island, near the coast of what is now Virginia (so named in honor of the Virgin Queen). Inspired by Sir Humphrey Gilbert, one of Elizabeth's courtiers, and implemented by Sir Walter Raleigh, the Roanoke adventure proved a dismal failure, largely because the English alienated the native peoples by their cruelty. In retaliation for the loss of a silver cup, about which the natives claimed to be ignorant, the colonists destroyed a small village and ruined the growing crops. Such severe actions offended the otherwise friendly tribes and proved disastrous for the poorly supplied settlers. When the invasion of the Spanish Armada prevented the sailing of supply ships in 1588, the colonists were forced back on their own resources, and lacking both experience and the good will of the natives, they vanished without a trace.

The failure of the Roanoke colony demonstrated to the English the need for a self-sustaining settlement, free from dependence upon the native populations. Such an enterprise required extensive capital resources, far more than could be gathered by a single individual. In the future, joint-stock companies or corporations—early capitalistic institutions—would finance the expense of colonization.

More significant than these lessons, however, was the deliberate alienation of the native peoples by the first Roanoke colonists. In later years, the local tribes would still provide vital assistance to the European settlers. But after the Roanoke experience, relations between the two peoples were always tempered by mutual suspicions, if not outright hostility.

Roanoke, then, was a sobering experience for both cultures. It meant that the English would abandon colonial expansion until after the death of Elizabeth in 1603. For the natives, that would bring temporary respite. Meanwhile, the Spanish to the south and the French to the north continued their slow but steady invasion of the continent.

"Though it be not the Lord's day"

★ ★ ★ ★ ★ ★ ★ ★ ★ ★ ★ ★ ★ ★ ★ ★ ★ ★ ★

2

The Transplantation

The instruments of European expansion

Tudor England on the eve of colonization

Anglican and Puritan conflict

Jamestown: first permanent English settlement

Puritans in New England

Proprietary colonies

Organizing space and time

The colonial family

Colonial religion: the Great Awakening and
religious toleration

☆

Despite the excitement of the early voyages of exploration, it took Europeans several generations to comprehend the importance of the land masses they called America. In the century after Columbus' voyage, even the intellectuals remained curiously silent. Yet the discovery of flora and fauna unknown in Europe raised inescapable philosophical questions. Medieval Europeans had believed in the completeness of human knowledge and had assumed a unity of the human species after the initial Creation. The discovery of a new continent inhabited by new peoples challenged these orthodox beliefs.

In confronting these profound dilemmas, Renaissance Europeans reacted with typical ethnocentrism and concluded that God had designed America for them. Though they debated about the origins of the Native Americans and wondered aloud whether these people might not belong to one of the Lost Tribes of Israel, they agreed that God undoubtedly intended for them to be converted to Christianity. The Europeans also assumed that America was simply a howling wilderness awaiting the introduction of European civilization. Thus they determined to transform the New World into a New Europe.

First, they would send missionaries to America to teach the benighted natives the ways of European civilization and the religious truths of Christianity. Every colonizing adventure—whether Spanish, French, English, or Dutch—always cited the conversion of the natives as its primary justification. But the missionary impulse usually was fruitless; from the natives' viewpoint, the endeavors often created total disruption.

The second instrument of European expansion was even more grandiose, but as time would show, much more successful. Since America lacked the advantages of European society, the institutions and values of Europe could simply be transplanted into the wilderness. America would become another Europe through colonization—a process that promised not only to improve the New World but also to enrich the Old. This was a daring vision indeed, but one that offered immense returns to all involved.

The process of transplantation took many forms depending upon the national background of the European colonists. At a certain

45

pre-post-Rev

point in historical development—about 1500 for the Spanish, 1600 for the English—branches of European culture were severed from the main stems and replanted in America. That hundred-year interval, a century of immense change in England, explains why Hispanic America was so different from Anglo America. In the Spanish colonies, for example, the Roman Catholic Church wielded an enormous influence; while in British America, settled after the Protestant Reformation, the new religion shaped most social relations. Other differences in colonial America reflected the different social structures and economic values of the European nations. In this chapter, the emphasis is on the English colonies, the small remote outposts of what would later become the British Empire and, later still, the United States.

On the eve of colonization, the population of England was about four million. Despite important differences in status and wealth, the English people proudly shared a national identity and viewed themselves as a superior nation blessed with the Protestant religion and the Tudor monarchy. Such advantages had not come easily. During the sixteenth century, England had experienced fundamental changes that altered the traditional patterns of economic, social, and political life. Elizabethan England, the daring nation that launched the marauding activities of Francis Drake and the colonizing experiments of Walter Raleigh, was significantly different from the medieval society that had recognized Henry VII as its first Tudor sovereign in 1485.

Henry VII and his son Henry VIII, like the monarchs of the European continent, had consolidated royal power by destroying the influence of the feudal aristocracy. Reviving the institutions of local government, particularly the offices of sheriff, justice of the peace, and lord lieutenant, the Tudors undermined their dynastic rivals and linked the royal authority directly to the local counties. The success of the monarchy, however, depended upon the perpetuation of the royal line. It was Henry VIII's desire for a male heir that motivated his divorce from Catherine of Aragon, which, in turn, led to the creation of a national church.

The centralization process also affected economic affairs. Since the Tudors wished to make England self-sufficient, they encouraged the merchants to shift from the export of raw wool to the manufacture of finished woolen products for foreign trade. Such policies, besides filling the royal coffers, offered large profits to English merchants, who accumulated additional capital for further investment. This wealth provided the economic support for colonization in the seventeenth century.

The premium placed upon the production of woolens stimulated a major transformation of English society. As it became more profitable to raise sheep, English landowners began to enclose the common lands, thus disrupting traditional agricultural practices. The confiscation of monastic lands after Henry VIII's break from Rome accelerated this trend. Landlords and merchants benefited by the enclosure movement, but the poorer folk who customarily worked on other people's lands—renters, day laborers, artisans—found their lives profoundly changed. Forced from their lands and traditional occupations, these people traveled the countryside seeking adequate livings, and many found themselves attracted to London. The city's population tripled in this period, despite the unhealthiness of urban life. These dislocations convinced many observers that England was overpopulated. Writers like Richard Hakluyt proposed that colonies be used to absorb the surplus population and rid the nation of its "sturdy beggars."

This image reappeared frequently in English writing. "Wandering beggars and rogues that pass from place to place . . . are plagues and banes," exclaimed one frustrated minister. Such statements reveal a typical unsympathetic reaction to the social unheaval of the age. But they were motivated not by callousness so much as by a world-view that could comprehend social disorder only in moral terms. Despite generations of unsettledness, Elizabethans continued to subscribe to a value system based on the essential orderliness of the world. Thus social problems, however widespread, indicated personal weakness rather than the disintegration of the social fabric.

From William Shakespeare to the meanest journeyman who watched his plays in the Globe, English people believed in the natural order of the universe. Humanity, in this pre-Copernican age, lived at the very center of creation, drawn simultaneously upward by the celestial spirits of heaven and downward by the demons of hell. Each aspect of creation, even inanimate objects, held a specifically assigned place in the cosmic unity and formed a hierarchy reaching ultimately to the Throne of God. These ideas were not usually articulated because it was seldom necessary to do so. Rather, they represented the cosmic assumptions shared by most people, unquestioned beliefs about the nature of the universe. These notions remained functional even when they were not empirically

Chain of
Being — traditional
assumpt.

accurate. Seventeenth-century Europeans, for example, continued to view the earth as the center of the universe, despite the astronomical calculations of modern science.

The same tenacity applied to social assumptions as well, which is why Elizabethan commentators regarded the dislocated workers as "common rogues." The social values of the English, like their image of the universe, assumed that there was a natural harmony to social relations. Human groupings, like the human body, constituted a living organism, what they called a "body politic." Society was an organic community in which each part of the body performed some function necessary to the welfare of the whole. The king was the "head" of society, the workers the limbs. Another metaphor reflected familial values: the king was "father" to his subjects, ruling paternally over his children. In such terms, it was literally inconceivable for one segment of society to gain from the injury of another; any defect weakened the entire organism.

The notion of hierarchy, if not of order, reflected the nature of the Elizabethan social structure. At the apex of society stood the monarchy and nobility, followed by the wealthy gentry. These groups provided the social and political leadership of the nation. Beneath them came people who lived by their own labor—yeomen, husbandmen, journeymen, servants, and other landless groups. Wives and children assumed the social status of their husbands and fathers. Within this hierarchy, status distinctions were clearly understood, though not always respected. Marital choices, education, styles of dress often were restricted by societal expectations and occasionally by force of law. Yet England was not a rigid society. Social mobility was not infrequent, though it usually involved only a small rise or fall in status. Members of the upper classes ruled, and those of lesser status expected them to rule and deferred to their leadership. Such attitudes accepted inferiority as well as superiority—a mental framework that influenced English relations with peoples native to Africa and America.

These political and social values had their roots in the family structure of Tudor England. As in the political world, the father ruled the household, presumably in the interests of all, and the women and children were expected to obey his authority. The conventional household was nuclear in structure, consisting of parents and their children and perhaps a servant who held the status of a child. It was in these units that children learned their places in the social hierarchy. Even young children were forced to accept the parental will or face severe disciplinary measures. Such child-rearing practices reinforced the authoritarian values of English society. English children well understood (and, as adults, well remembered) the lessons of authority and the acceptable limits of autonomy and independence.

As in other agricultural societies, English life depended upon the rhythm of the seasons, the amount of rainfall, the size of the harvests, the appearance of pestilence and disease. Infant mortality rates were high, life expectancy low, starvation and malnutrition a common concern. English family patterns reflected these fragile circumstances. Children did not marry until they could afford to support a family, a practice that delayed marriage until children were in their middle or late twenties. This custom, in turn, limited the years of marital fertility. Such biological configurations, together with the probable practices of birth control (through abstinence or withdrawal), resulted in fairly small families, ranging on the average from five to seven children. These demographic patterns varied according to the wealth of a family, for more affluent people could afford to marry earlier and to feed more children.

The insecurity of life—the proximity of famine, disease, and death—reinforced the religiosity of these predominantly rural folk. In the transitory world of human affairs, they found spiritual solace in the eternal world hereafter. But under the Tudor monarchs, religious traditions were no longer so secure. The creation of the Anglican Church by Henry VIII, the Protestantism of his son, Edward VI, the reversion to Catholicism by Mary, and Elizabeth's *via media* (the middle road between Protestantism and Catholicism)—all undermined what previously had been viewed as the immutable principles of religion. Such ideological changes may not have altered the worship practices on the parish level, but they nevertheless confused and troubled the average Christian believer.

Out of this turmoil, there emerged among English Protestants a growing concern for rationality in religious affairs, an attempt to impose orderliness and logic on spiritual matters. This process led in two antithetical directions—one resulting in an articulate defense of the Church of England and the religious principles of Anglicanism, the other producing a radical reformist group that followed beliefs known as "Puritanism." Though disagreeing about many fundamentals of religion, both movements recoiled from what they called the superstitions of the medieval Catholic Church and both stressed the need to distinguish affairs of this world from those of the next.

This tendency to split reality into material and spiritual spheres, a characteristic of modern thought in general, constituted an important difference between European culture and the premodern cosmologies of the Native Americans and Africans.

Puritanism began as a protest by reformist ministers against the vestiges of Catholicism that remained in the Church of England. Carrying the logic of Protestantism to its extreme conclusion, the Puritans argued that many traditional ceremonies—wearing the surplice, for example, or bowing and kneeling during worship services —and certain ecclesiastical offices—such as the episcopacy—that were not explicitly *sanctioned* by the Bible undermined the purity of the church; they therefore demanded the elimination of these "corruptions." The Anglicans denied these criticisms, arguing that religious practices that were not explicitly *forbidden* by the Bible were permissible. The main disagreement between Anglicans and Puritans thus centered on how properly to interpret the authority of the Scriptures.

Though Puritanism originated among ministers and intellectuals, it soon spread among people in all status groups, particularly those whose lives had been most disrupted by the social and economic changes of the period. Puritan preachers stressed the importance of "godliness" in all human affairs and condemned "worldliness," the search for material wealth, which sidetracked a person from the more valuable treasures of heaven. Such ideas made sense to people forced from their traditional lands by capitalists who cared more for profits than for the welfare of individuals. To people confronting the chaos of London, the Puritan ideals of orderliness and Christian charity moderated the trauma of upheaval. Puritanism, like other evangelical movements, promised the security of heaven hereafter, if not in the present. Thus Puritanism offered its adherents an explanation of worldly confusion at the same time it provided emotional ballast to ease the worst frustrations of that dislocation. Within two generations, Puritanism was sufficiently powerful as a social force to stimulate the migration of thousands to America and to challenge the monarchy at home.

The men and women who established England's colonies in America had specific ideas about time and space. Their beliefs, usually held unconsciously, reflected a general trend in Western culture toward greater precision and rational definition. The English colonists, like other modern people, felt extremely uncomfortable about ambiguity in these matters, which is one reason why they failed utterly to appreciate the sophistication of the non-Western peoples they encountered, why they considered Africans and Native Americans mere savages and barbarians. Ironically, their own societies still manifested some of this vagueness, relics of an earlier cultural perspective. But increasingly, seventeenth-century Europeans were attempting to eliminate the mysteries of time and space and replace them with more rational constructs. Thus they viewed America as a territorial map rather than a geographic reality and saw its open space as a vast wilderness upon which to implement their ideas.

The first permanent English colony began in May 1607 when three vessels dropped anchor several miles up the James River in Virginia at a site they named Jamestown. Financed by the Virginia Company of London, a joint-stock corporation, and settled by ambitious young men employed by the company, the colony was expected to produce lucrative profits by locating gold mines and a water route through the continent to the fabulous markets of Asia. The vision of duplicating Spanish success, however, blinded the adventurers to the realities of colonization. Investors in London, misled perhaps by exaggerated promotional reports, underestimated the difficulties of settlement and provided poor leadership for their employees in Virginia.

The colonists themselves demonstrated equal ignorance. They chose a malarial swamp on which to erect their village, and then they allowed their meager supplies to dwindle while they searched for gold. Afflicted by disease and famine and divided by petty squabbles, they succumbed at an alarming rate. "God (being angry with us)," reported Captain John Smith, "plagued us with such famine and sickness that the living were scarce able to bury the dead." Only the timely intervention of the native chief Powhatan prevented the extinction of the colony. As it was, only one-third of the original settlers survived the first "starving times." New settlers and new supplies, sent periodically by the London investors, failed to alleviate the situation. Matters were made still worse by English provocation of the local tribes. Theft and violence disrupted trade with the natives and led to counterattacks by Powhatan's people. Several times the colonists were ready to abandon the settlement only to halt at the unexpected arrival of supply ships. One relief group found only sixty survivors, who "looked like anatomies, crying out, we are starved, we are starved."

If Virginia was to survive, the Virginia Company had to attract two major resources: capital and labor. Stock sales and public lotteries kept the limping enterprise solvent while the colonists pursued easy riches. Then John Rolfe, later famous for his marriage to Pocahontas, discovered another source of potential profit: an American plant called tobacco. The weed became immensely popular in Europe, and Virginians soon began exporting thousands, then hundreds of thousands, of hogsheads of tobacco a year to meet the demand. Increased exports brought greater capital investment, thus assuring the economic future of the colony.

The cultivation of tobacco still required an adequate labor force. The original planters of the colony had been employees of the Virginia Company, expecting to share enormous profits from colonization. The agony of settlement promptly shattered their dreams. Some investors also hoped to use native labor, much as the Spanish had enslaved the peoples they had conquered. But the tribes of North America successfully resisted such plans, partly because of the weakness of the English, partly because they lived in more scattered villages.

To solve the persistent labor problem, the Virginia Company began to contract with individual English laborers, known as "indentured servants," who agreed to work on company lands for a specific period (usually seven years) in exchange for passage to America and a promise of land. Though these indentured servants constituted the backbone of the Virginia labor force through most of the seventeenth century, their expectations of land and self-improvement were seldom fulfilled. For the Virginia Company also offered fifty acres (known as a "headright") to investors who would pay the transportation of workers to the colony. The policy enabled some people of modest means to acquire land, but more often the beneficiaries were wealthy merchants who could underwrite the cost of many servants. These enterprising investors thus acquired large landholdings. By their wealth they also obtained control over most of the available supplies, including food, which enabled them to exploit even the free workers. Where labor was so valuable, servants were treated as commodities to be leased, traded, or sold. Such attitudes were a logical outgrowth of organic social theory, the commonly held idea that some people were subservient to others. But in America these values also led, just as logically, to the creation of a slave caste.

"About the last of August came in a dutch man of warre that

sold us twenty Negars," reported John Rolfe nonchalantly about an event in 1619. Thus began the grim tale of black-white relations in British America. The development of slavery in America usually is explained as a result of a need for labor, because that is the way white slaveowners viewed the Africans. Given the shortage of workers and the difficulty of controlling indentured servants, the shift to black slavery appeared economically sensible.

But the profit motive alone does not explain the enslavement of one people by another. Rather, the forced migration of Africans to America and the institutionalization of slavery in all the English-speaking colonies required more than an eye for the marketplace. The vision of Africans as potential slaves had deep roots in Western culture; there were predispositions in the Western mind which, given the specific historical conditions such as a need for labor, encouraged the establishment of black slavery in the colonies.

There were, first, the visible differences—dark skin and kinky hair, for example—which distinguished the African from the European. As in dealing with the Native Americans, Renaissance Europeans attempted to incorporate these strange beings into their pre-existing cosmology. Black complexions suggested images of the curse of Ham, the swarthy son of Noah condemned for his sins. Such biblical metaphors reinforced cultural prejudices against blackness itself—black as dirty, evil, sinful, inferior. Then, as with the Native Americans, there was the question of religion. From the Christian perspective, the Africans had no religion, no spiritual relations with the true God. They were mere heathens who worshiped devils disguised as Gods. Such notions justified slavery as a missionary institution, a way of saving souls from the snares of Satan.

More subtle than these considerations was the Elizabethan preoccupation with order and organization. To the European eye, African culture lacked traditional institutions. People wore different clothing, enjoyed music and dance with strange rhythms, ate exotic foods; in short, they accepted a lifestyle that made no sense to white culture. Europeans therefore concluded that Africans were savages. Yet most of the peoples of Africa, particularly the sedentary agricultural societies of west Africa, had stable lives structured by conventional cultures. That the Europeans, trapped by their own value system, could not perceive these patterns is perhaps understandable. It seems likely that their hostility to African life also betrayed profound fears of disorder and the loss of traditional restraints—in other words, betrayed anxieties that they had about themselves. For while Europeans attempted to organize space and time more rationally, Africans, no less than Native Americans, lived within a cyclical order that appeared to the Europeans to be no order at all. Thus the African symbolized the evils of impulse and unrestraint, the antithesis of European social ideals.

These cultural prejudices also dominated relations between Virginians and the indigenous peoples, even when the colonists were totally dependent upon the generosity of the natives. Thus, after eating the food provided by Powhatan, John Smith remarked, with no trace of irony, that the settlers would have "all perished" but for the mercy of "those wild and cruel pagans"! Meanwhile, as tobacco cultivation spread through the colony and occupied more and more acreage, the natives increasingly realized the white threat to their lives. Under Powhatan's successor, Opechancanough, the natives launched a vicious attack on the English plantations in 1622, killing about one-third of the white population and forcing Virginians to retreat from their extended outposts. The attack, viewed by the English as a "massacre," brought prompt and bloody retribution, unleashing a restive racism that justified a policy of genocide. Eventually, negotiations ended the bloodletting, but sporadic warfare between whites and natives continued through the century.

While Virginians slowly expanded their settlements along the river banks that open on the Chesapeake, an even more grandiose enterprise commenced some five hundred miles to the north. Led by Puritans who were dissatisfied with conditions in England, thousands of colonists crossed the Atlantic to settle in areas around Plymouth, Massachusetts Bay, Connecticut, and Rhode Island. Unlike the planters of Virginia, the settlers of New England were motivated less by the search for profits than by ideological considerations.

By the 1620s, after two generations of protest, the Puritans had recognized the futility of reforming the Church of England according to their perfectionist ideals. Frustrated by this failure and resentful of the dislocations of their society, the Puritans condemned the sinfulness of England and warned that the Lord soon would punish the nation with His wrath. Such fears justified a search for a secure haven. "I am verily persuaded," declared John Winthrop, the leader of the Puritan exodus, that "God will bring some heavy affliction upon this land, and that speedily." But, he added optimistically, perhaps "he will provide a shelter and hiding place for us and ours." Surrounded by "wild beasts and beast-like men," the Puritans would establish a city of God in New England.

Midway across the Atlantic, Winthrop addressed his friends aboard the *Arbella*. "We are a company professing ourselves fellow members of Christ," he announced, and "we ought to account ourselves knit together by this bond of love, and live in the exercise of it." Thus commenced the great migration to America. These colonists sailed to New England, not only to escape the evils of England, but also to build an ideal community, what Winthrop called "A Model of Christian Charity," to demonstrate to the world the efficacy of true Christian principles. "We shall be as a city upon a hill," he proclaimed, a beacon of hope, a divine blueprint that all the world would imitate irresistibly.

These were grand aspirations, befitting a proud people, and they placed great responsibility upon each member of the Puritan community. For the most part the first colonists shared this commitment and put aside the petty squabbling that had impeded the early experiments in Virginia. In other societies, ownership of land or the fortuitousness of birth determined one's place in the community. But in New England the spiritual bonds of Puritanism dominated social relations and brought people together. This is not to say that there were no disagreements among the colony's leaders or between the leaders and some of their followers. But there was a determined self-conscious effort to mediate disputes according to principles of equity rather than the strict rule of law.

Though the Puritans expected the successful transplantation of the true faith to herald a new era of human history, they sought historical precedents and models for the Wilderness Zion. It was Winthrop's hope, for example, that there would be one community in New England, much like a medieval town. Soon after landing in Massachusetts, however, the settlers were forced to disperse around the Bay, where they formed several communities. Later still, the migration of additional colonists—by 1640, the numbers had swelled to twenty thousand—necessitated the formation of interior settlements to accommodate the burgeoning population. This geographic expansion, though unforeseen and unwelcome, did not defeat the Puritan mission. Instead, the Puritan leaders endeavored to control the scattered settlements through the institutions of town government. Thus the colony granted land not to individuals, but to the towns, which then subdivided the holdings among their resi-

dents. In forming towns, the inhabitants usually covenanted to uphold the Christian principles upon which the colony had been
founded. "We whose names are here unto subscribed," declared the
first settlers of Dedham, Massachusetts, "do, in the fear and reverence of our Almighty God, mutually and severally promise amongst
ourselves and each other to profess and practice one truth according to that most perfect rule, the foundation whereof is everlasting
love."

Town meetings resolved political questions, levied taxes, and appointed local officials, who, acting on behalf of the community,
supervised such business as the distribution of alms, the employment of schoolmasters, the use of common lands, and the repair of
the meetinghouse. In these small communities, residents worked
together, prayed together, and celebrated together, reinforcing the
solemn promises of their town covenants and their commitment to
Puritan ideals. Eventually this peace would be broken; people would
bicker about landholdings; the spirit of charity would be eroded by
the frictions of neighborliness. But that was in the future. For the
first generation, the town system constituted a communal approach
to basic secular problems.

Despite charitable intentions, however, some problems were not
easily resolved. Thus, when John Cotton and Thomas Hooker, two
of the most eminent ministers in New England, disagreed about
religious principles, the quarrel resulted in Hooker's migration with
most of his congregation to Connecticut, where they founded a new
community. The departure, like numerous others in the seventeenth
century, irritated the Puritan leadership. But it was one way of
maintaining the forms of social harmony despite basic religious
differences.

The geographic expansion of the Puritan settlers led them into
areas more densely populated by Native Americans, particularly the
Pequots and Narragansetts. From the English perspective, the appropriation of the natives' lands was entirely justifiable, since the
tribes did not properly subjugate the wilderness, which is to say,
they did not organize the land according to European models. The
Pequots had other ideas about the land, however, and these differences in perspective led to open warfare in 1637. Claiming that the
Pequots had murdered some English traders, the Puritans launched
a punitive expedition against these "minions of the devil." The result
was a brutal slaughter of the Pequots at Mystic, Connecticut. Male
survivors of the main attack were executed, while the women and

children were enslaved and shipped to the West Indies. Designed to strengthen the Puritan communities, the military affair had one ironic disintegrating effect: the armies located some fertile acreage around New Haven, which soon encouraged further inland migration and an additional splintering of the communal ethos.

The enslavement of the Pequot survivors had divine sanction under the right of conquest. Such principles had justified slavery throughout the Christian world and had been used to enslave Moorish prisoners during the medieval period. It was harder to apply this logic to African slavery, since no Africans had been captured in holy wars. But that did not matter to the Puritan colonists who, like other Europeans, viewed the blacks as an inferior and uncivilized, unchristian people. In 1638, perhaps in exchange for the Pequot captives, the first black slaves began arriving in New England from the West Indies. Black slavery never became deeply entrenched in New England for a number of demographic reasons, most notably the commitment of the Puritans to homogeneous communities. But their treatment of non-Europeans demonstrated the ethnocentric basis of their godly utopia.

Both Massachusetts Bay and Virginia had been organized and financed by joint-stock companies, early capitalistic institutions designed to facilitate the sharing of capital investment and risk. Another type of colonial endeavor also served as an institution of English expansion: the proprietary colony. The principle here was solidly aristocratic. Instead of chartering a corporation of merchants, the English crown granted American territory to influential courtiers to develop as they desired. Such gifts led to the colonization of Maryland by George Calvert, the first Lord Baltimore; the Carolinas by a handful of proprietors, including Lord Shaftesbury; and Pennsylvania by the Quaker William Penn. The royal favor also granted New York and New Jersey to the Duke of York, though both places already were settled by the Dutch. It took a small fleet to resolve that dilemma in 1664.

By giving away wilderness lands, the English kings found an inexpensive way to reward loyal subjects, particularly those willing to advance credit to the crown. For the proprietors, these grants represented a source of immense wealth—provided they could attract settlers to purchase or lease the tracts. Fundamental to these transactions was the assumption that the Native Americans held no valid claim to the territory and that English definitions of landownership would prevail. Thus the proprietors of Maryland and the Carolinas devised elaborate schemes to divide and subdivide land-holdings according to archaic feudal principles, a social blueprint thoroughly unsuitable to conditions in America. Even William Penn, who strived to implement his Quaker ideology by purchasing land from the natives by treaty, assumed that paper boundaries could contain a burgeoning population, that artificial conceptions of space could be imposed on a vast land mass.

Such attitudes reflected a general European search for rationality and order. The contrast between the Native American cultures and those of Europeans is nowhere made clearer. To the indigenous peoples, the universe itself was harmonious and orderly, thus pre-cluding from consciousness the idea of superimposing human con-straints on natural conditions. But the Europeans, products of another time and another place, saw the world differently. They were correct, nevertheless, in one regard: for better or worse, it was their image of the world that ultimately prevailed.

If colonization meant the transplantation of European notions of space, the institutional configurations in the colonies emphasized European ideas about time and history. Where most Native Ameri-cans lived by natural time, adjusting to seasonal rhythms, the sun, the moon, and the stars, Europeans had begun, with increasing efficiency, to divide time into convenient segments. During the medieval period, when most Europeans lived close to the soil, time-keeping was extremely inaccurate; even the most finely constructed clocks had only an hour hand to approximate the time. Then in the mid-seventeenth century, the Dutch mathematician Christian Huygens invented a pendulum clock that allowed much greater precision. English clockmakers, responding to the organizational zeal of their culture, promptly imported Huygens' techniques, added a few refinements, and began producing timepieces that were accu-rate to within five seconds a day. By the late seventeenth century, therefore, most English clocks possessed a minute hand and a sounding mechanism that struck at quarter-hours.

Such mechanical achievements demonstrated the Europeans' capacity to reduce time to human proportions. Yet, paradoxically, that technical ability was not always implemented in clock design. Human consciousness could not always reckon with technology. Despite the introduction of the pendulum, some English clocks,

particularly the popular lantern clocks used in the colonies, still had
only one hand.

A similar anomaly affected the measurement of calendar time. In
traditional societies, the beginning of the new year usually coincided
with the vernal equinox, the season of natural regeneration. Thus in
the Julian calendar, used throughout Western Europe until the sixteenth century, March constituted the first month of the year. The
Julian calendar contained several astronomical inaccuracies, however, and in 1582 Pope Gregory XIII introduced a new calendar
that, among other changes, began the new year in January. But not
until much later did the Protestant countries adopt the revised Gre-
gorian calendar; in British America, the changes were not introduced until 1752. In the interim, English colonials employed a
modified system in which dates falling between January 1 and
March 25 were represented by dual numbers; March 1, 1631, in
other words, would be written March 1, 1630/31. Such confusing
practices betrayed a transitional stage of development, a half-
modern, half-premodern conception of time. Yet by the end of the
eighteenth century, the dating system had been standardized and
resolved in the interests of clarity. At almost the same date, the
single-hand clock also became extinct.

This blurring of cosmic time and secular time emerged in a more
personal setting as well: the birthday celebration. The systematic
recording of live births did not begin in England until the reign of
Henry VIII. As in other premodern societies, particularly in areas
of widespread illiteracy, people often did not know their exact
birthdates, nor did such data apparently matter. To celebrate the
anniversary of a birth involved the imposition of human chronology
upon the sacred arrangement of festivals and holidays (literally
"holy days"). Thus birthday anniversaries, even those of children,
were seldom celebrated before the nineteenth century. Yet in the
colonial period there still could be considerable ambivalence about
secular time. "I am fifteen years old today," wrote a young female
diarist in 1675. "My mother hath bid me this day [to] put on a
fresh kirtle and wimple, though it be not the Lord's day, and my
Aunt Alice coming in did chide me and say that to pay attention to
a birthday was putting myself with the world's people [rather than
God's]." This family quarrel is extremely enlightening, suggesting a
fundamental clash of values and perceptions. Above all, it reveals
the intimate connection between time and progeny.

It was in the family that the English preoccupation with organizing space and time merged most clearly. Families, in this premodern
age, constituted basic economic units, serving to perpetuate business
relationships and the ownership of land. Since real estate was the
major economic asset, a tangible symbol of wealth and status, family patterns aimed at preserving existing holdings. The subdivision
of land among many children undermined the value of this basic
resource. That is why English men married so late and the number
of children remained so small. The desire to maintain ownership
over the generations also explains why English parents preferred
male children—offspring who would retain both the family name
and the title to the land.

In America, however, where available land was more abundant,
some of these restrictive patterns began to disappear. First-generation colonists appropriated enough land for their own use and reserved considerable undeveloped land for their children. One result
of this policy in New England was the lowering of the age at
marriage, since children could now afford to support a family
sooner. Since this extended the years of marital fertility, the number
of children born to colonial parents increased slightly, averaging
between six and eight per family. In the southern colonies, however,
the disproportionate number of male colonists created an imbalanced sex ratio that kept the marriage age high and the number of
children low. In black families, where the patterns of servitude
probably created an even more imbalanced sex ratio during the first
decades of colonization, these trends would be more pronounced.
By the eighteenth century, however, black families seemed to thrive
despite the increasing restrictions caused by the slave system.

But if second- and third-generation whites enjoyed unprecedented
opportunities to acquire land, their own children, particularly those
born after 1700, confronted a rapidly tightening situation. As more
real estate went under the plow, available acreage decreased, a small
but growing trend that forced some children to migrate to undeveloped lands in the interior or to seek nonagricultural employment. In
an ironic way, the initial generosity of American parents accelerated
family disintegration, for children could no longer expect an adequate legacy. The psychological implications of this pattern were
quite significant. Where seventeenth-century parents could control
the land supply and thus retain at least a modicum of power over
their adult children, their grandchildren often lacked the resources
to keep their own offspring dependent. Perhaps this demographic

situation explains why fourth- and fifth-generation Americans, the
people who matured around 1776, so resented the idea of political
dependence and were so strident in asserting their autonomy.

The importance of family estates reflected more than economic
considerations, for the perpetuation of landownership also satisfied
a profound emotional need for symbolic immortality, for feelings of
continuity and survival. As the modern world demystified the universe, separating human order from the cosmic, people sought immortality in secular ways, particularly through the lives of their own
children. Parents became more solicitous about the young, concerned for their nurture and education. They began to name their
children after themselves with greater frequency, a sure indication
of the desire for secular immortality. And when one child died, it
was not uncommon to call a sibling by the same name.

This shift in parental values coincided with an important biological change: people lived longer in America because the environment
was healthier. Not only did infant mortality decline, but more
grandparents lived to enjoy their children's children. The ecological
harmony of the continent eventually collapsed during the eighteenth
century as epidemic diseases became more common in the colonies.
But the presence of grandparents provided colonial children with
important psychological defenses against their own parents, serving
to moderate the traditional dislike of children and the usual cruelty
of child rearing. Perhaps these grandparents, older and closer to
death themselves, better understood the significance of genetic continuity.

The biological patterns that perpetuated the species also reinforced the sociological basis of sexual relations. Marriage served to
institutionalize sexuality—protecting the continuity of property and
genealogy. But despite our popular notions of puritanical sex, English colonials were a lusty people who appreciated physical pleasure for what it was. Their idea of legitimate sexuality, however,
was quite limited. There is considerable covert evidence of guilt
about nocturnal emissions and masturbation; sodomy and bestiality
were capital crimes. In 1642, a sixteen-year-old servant in New
England was, in the words of Governor William Bradford, "detected of buggery, and indicted for the same, with a mare, a cow,
two goats, five sheep, two calves and a turkey." For man and beasts
alike, the punishment was death. Still, as evidenced by the number
of "seven-months" children born in the eighteenth century, premarital intercourse was becoming more common, probably because

lessening economic opportunity encouraged the delay of marriage.

In describing the ideal family, conventional wisdom reiterated the values of English society and stressed the hierarchical nature of human relations. Husbands were superior to their wives, children subservient to their parents. In practice, obviously, there was considerable deviation in all respects. Among other things, divorce represented one form of redress, though accurate figures about its frequency are not available. As an instrument of social control, nevertheless, the colonial family did inculcate the demands of the wider society. As child-beating lost favor among the upper classes, for example, parents employed the sanctions of shame, of losing face, as a means of discipline. Colonial children learned to respect the demands of visible appearance, of saving face, of avoiding foolish self-exposure. Moreover, in eulogies for the dead and in manuals of etiquette, colonial commentators emphasized the advantages of suppressing emotions, of moderating passion, of maintaining a placid exterior. Such attributes coincided with a view of society that emphasized harmony and interdependence.

If the colonial family served to institutionalize secular time, there was an even more intense commitment to organizing cosmic time. Here the primary institution was the church. Where premodern cultures simply accepted the inexplicable mystery of the universe, modern Europeans attempted to rationalize the spiritual world and stressed the importance of organized religion. That colonial Americans devoted so much energy to analyzing the essential mysteries of life and death betrayed the fundamental paradox of colonial culture, the sense of living midway between the secular and the infinite.

Colonial religion generally derived from the tenets of the Protestant Reformation modified by the fierce ideological struggles of the sixteenth and seventeenth centuries. Though Anglicans and Puritans shared many religious principles, it was the differences that often mattered most to them. As conservatives, Anglicans accepted many of the historical innovations of previous centuries. But Puritans, driven by a powerful self-image of sainthood and spiritual purity, rejected religious practices that seemed to be human inventions.

Outside New England, the Anglican Church predominated in the colonies. Yet the patterns of settlement in America forced the Anglicans to modify their religious institutions, leading them unwittingly in a Puritan direction. Thus a shortage of Anglican ministers, together with the dispersal of population, placed increased burdens

on individual believers, an implicitly Puritan doctrine. Sometimes
these demands overwhelmed the laity, creating a spiritual vacuum
that then lapsed into secularism and religious indifference. Even
when Anglican ministers did appear, they lacked the institutional
support of an American episcopacy and often became mere hire-
lings of the local vestries that paid their salaries. These ecclesiastical
configurations nevertheless worked well in the southern colonies,
where the Anglican Church enjoyed numerical superiority. But
where the Church of England was weaker, especially in New England, the absence of an American episcopate troubled colonial
Anglicans immensely. Despite their fervent pleas, however, English
politics prevented the appointment of an American bishop during
the entire colonial period, a situation that placed New England
Anglicans at the mercy of an aggressive, often intolerant Puritan
leadership.

Religious institutions in colonial New England revealed the tenacity of Puritan ideals, even after the original zeal of the first generation had waned. Seeking religious perfection, the Puritans resolved
to eliminate the historical innovations that had corrupted Christianity in other places. While any baptized Christian could join the
Church of England, the Puritans generally insisted that church
membership be restricted to true saints—to those who could testify
to the spiritual presence of Christ. Potential communicants would
stand before the congregation and describe their religious experience, baring their most intimate secrets to their friends and neighbors. The ritual reinforced communal bonds, bringing people more
closely together. But some Christians could not endure such self-
exposure. When one woman in Dedham fainted twice in the course
of her examination, the church altered its policy about female
members, permitting them to testify through their husbands or in
private. Many more dared not speak at all, preferring to live outside
the ordinances of God rather than jeopardize their immortal souls
by deception.

Revealing the inner strength of Puritanism, such practices satisfied most people—but not all. The minister at Salem, for example, a
determined Christian named Roger Williams, questioned whether
any mortal could determine the spiritual purity of other people's
souls. Concerned that hypocrisy would sneak into God's churches,
he advocated a rigid separation of saints from sinners, of church
and state—a logical idea, given Puritan theories about perfectibility, but one totally impractical in a society seeking religious uni-

formity. For his troubles, Williams was banished by the Massachusetts authorities. He fled to Rhode Island in 1635 and established
another colony committed to the principles of religious toleration.
Other deviants, also frustrated by the Puritan establishment, soon
followed him there.

While Puritan theology denied that good works could bring salvation (the very idea was Catholic), the New England orthodoxy
could not allow moral standards to lapse even in affairs of this
world. Thus when Anne Hutchinson, a member of the Boston congregation, challenged the ministers' emphasis on moral behavior
over spiritual purity, the Massachusetts establishment moved to
suppress her beliefs. As in Williams' case, however, Hutchinson's
position—known as "Antinomianism"—was difficult to denounce
because it simply represented a logical extension of widely held
Puritan ideas. Such theological consistency did not protect this
woman, however; after a lengthy trial, she was expelled from the
church and banished from the colony in 1638.

The Antinomian crisis—as the affair was called—reveals more
than the ideological rigidity of Puritanism, for Anne Hutchinson
was not only a deviant; she was a woman. As in other areas of
society, Puritan women were expected to keep their place in church.
"The woman is more subject to error than a man," announced John
Cotton of Boston. "It is not permitted to a woman to speak in the
Church . . . ; but rather it is required she should ask her husband
at home." Intellectual activity, it was believed, threatened to unbal-
ance female minds, and John Winthrop readily explained the insanity of one woman by pointing to her propensity to write poetry.
Similar reasoning seemed to justify the persecution of Anne Hutchinson. Shortly after departing Massachusetts she delivered a "monstrous" birth, a sure sign of the influence of the devil. And when, in
1642, she and her children were murdered by natives in New
Netherland, the Puritans extolled the perfection of God's vengeance
—one satanic people butchering another.

Such zeal depended upon the personal commitment of individual
Puritans, an intensity difficult to sustain over time. Within one
generation of colonization, New England preachers detected a decline in religiosity and bewailed the failure of the Puritan mission.
"Look into families and other societies," urged one Connecticut
minister, "is there not too visible and general a declension; are we
not turned (and that quickly too) out of the way wherein our
fathers walked?" Though Puritan observers exaggerated the prob-

lem, hoping to stimulate a religious revival, the thrust of their comments was accurate. By the late seventeenth century, full participation in church services had declined noticeably, particularly among males, despite such compromises as the "Half-Way Covenant" which altered the standards of admission.

In Puritan terms, the major symptoms of decline were a loss of charity, a rise of "worldliness," a general drift toward secular, materialistic relationships. These changes were dramatized by sporadic accusations of witchcraft, culminating in the celebrated trials at Salem in 1692. To a people believing in angels and devils, the discovery of witchcraft was a frightening phenomenon, awakening genuine fear of eternal damnation. Yet witchcraft was a common crime in Europe, explicable through traditional cultural mechanisms. What is significant about New England witchcraft is its relationship to the loss of communal feelings. Most accusations involved neighbors with long histories of resentment and petty quarrels. Beset by anger or guilt for the failure to fulfill traditional obligations, people accused one another of collaborating with the devil to destroy the social order. In time of social crisis—the late seventeenth century, for example—such accusations could reach epidemic proportions. At Salem, about two hundred persons were charged with witchcraft, and twenty died for the crime. Once the inner hostility was purged, however, once people became reconciled to a more competitive secular society, accusations of witchcraft abruptly ceased, and the devils departed from New England forever.

The crisis in Puritanism reflected the messianic temperament of its proponents, their aggressive search for truth and the profound disillusionment at failure. Another group of radical Protestants, the Society of Friends, or "Quakers," who founded the colony of Pennsylvania, experienced a similar transformation. Believing that each human being, as a divine creation, possessed an "inner light" of grace, the Quakers launched a "Holy Experiment" to put their ideals into practice. Unlike other English Protestants, the early Quakers sought to uphold their principles in negotiating with the Delaware tribe, carefully demarking land boundaries and property rights, seeking the peaceful coexistence of two cultures.

By the mid-eighteenth century, however, the pursuit of material wealth—land speculation and the fur trade—had undermined the Quaker commitment. Treaties were broken, friendly natives killed, land stolen. The immigration of non-Quakers, especially Scotch-Irish and Germans who desired land claimed by the Delawares, hastened this process. Quaker idealism regarding Africans also vanished as Pennsylvania merchants reaped the profits of the slave trade. Yet both these trends did not go unchallenged. As in New England, important members of the Quaker community protested the loss of zeal and the surrender of values. These idealists eventually formed the antislavery vanguard in America and advocated the emancipation of human chattel. By that time, William Penn's vision of a wilderness utopia had long been abandoned.

By the fifth decade of the eighteenth century, therefore, colonial churches everywhere confronted a fundamental tension between their professed values and the behavior of their members. People continued to believe in the ideals of Christian love and social harmony even while they pursued secular concerns that destroyed those values. Similar paradoxes exist in most societies, partly because language and imagery lag behind worldly experience, partly because people do not like to acknowledge their innovating practices. Such intellectual resistance was especially true in America, since most colonials still believed in the moral superiority of the first generation of colonists, the community-builders of the seventeeth century. To betray their ancestors involved considerable guilt and anxiety. These psychological tensions produced a generalized uneasiness in the colonies, a gnawing doubt about the thrust of American culture, a dissatisfaction with the fruits of materialism.

Such unarticulated concerns combined with several immediate events—a war with France and Spain, a diphtheria epidemic, several slave insurrections—to create a tinderbox of emotions. The tinderbox exploded in 1740 with a massive religious revival known as the Great Awakening. The igniting factor was the presence of an itinerant English preacher, George Whitefield, who traveled from New England to Georgia proclaiming the gospel of Jesus Christ and winning converts for the Lord. "He speaks from a heart all aglow with love, and pours out a torrent of eloquence which is almost irresistible," declared one admiring woman in New England. People dropped their tools in their fields, mounted their horses, and raced to hear the apostle preach in crowded churches and open fields. Benjamin Franklin, with his typical concern for details, once estimated that Whitefield's voice could reach twenty-five thousand people in the open air.

Like the Puritans of the seventeenth century, proponents of the Awakening stressed the majesty of God and His promise of redemption to true believers. People could attain salvation, according to the

"New Light" preachers, only by undergoing a conversion experience by which the Lord imputed His grace to otherwise helpless sinners. Thereafter, however, once reborn, these saints joined the Elect of God, destined for life everlasting in heaven. It was a powerful transformation they described, filled with passion and spiritual ecstasy.

Consider the sermon of Jonathan Edwards, "Sinners in the Hands of an Angry God," preached at Enfield, Massachusetts, in 1741. "The God that holds you over the pit of hell, much as one holds a spider, or some loathsome insect, over a fire, abhors you," Edwards intoned; "his wrath towards you burns like fire, he looks upon you as worthy of nothing else, but to be cast into the fire." Such hellfire preaching alarmed godly Americans and aroused their latent guilt. They responded first with terror—"some sighing, some groaning, some screeching," reported an eyewitness. The brimstone, however, contrasted with the joyous visions of heaven, images of peace and tranquillity and love. The message became compelling. People reached the depths of despair, lay helpless before the Lord, and then discovered the inner energy of conversion, rising to "raptures, and transports, triumphing and singing psalms and hallelujahs." The beauty of holiness replaced the mortal world of humanity.

Evangelical preachers won considerable success throughout the colonies, appealing to people in all regions and in all classes. But they were particularly effective in reaching people in vulnerable places—areas undergoing rapid social change, communities worried about disease or impending warfare. One social group—adult white males—seemed especially responsive to the revivalists. Perhaps young men were closer to the visceral dangers of war or the spiritual crisis of materialism. Perhaps, too, they found in the evangelical religion a sense of self, what modern psychologists call "identity." During the colonial period, young men usually became "adults" not at the end of puberty, but somewhat later, when they married and formed autonomous families. This delay created a period of ambiguity about their place in society. During social crises, such people are susceptible to ideological movements that promise to alleviate their psychological doubt. In receiving the evangelical message, therefore, young men in America resolved their inner crises and found coherence both on earth and hereafter.

Not everyone, of course, welcomed the revivalist religion. Many conservatives, known derisively as "Old Lights," resented the disruption of customary practices and saw chaos, rather than grace, con-

quering the land. Their antipathy to the Awakening soon precipitated a major intellectual war with the evangelicals. These debates
between New Lights and Old had several salutary effects. When
both sides eventually realized that they could not extirpate their
opponents, it became possible to imagine a pluralistic approach to
matters of religion. Thus the idea of religious toleration quietly
slipped through the back door of American culture. Toleration, of
course, did not imply equality, and several state governments maintained an established church well into the nineteenth century. Nor
did prejudice against religious minorities simply vanish. But among
Protestants, at least, the imperatives of religious truth, the old Puritan idea that "rightly informed consciences" would inevitably agree,
gradually gave way to a more liberal attitude that allowed most
groups to flourish.

The willingness of eighteenth-century colonials to tolerate Protestant dissenters reflected the growing secularization of American society, a shift from mystical insight to rational inquiry. This transformation received institutional validity after 1776 by the formal
separation of church and state. That split, long seen as the triumph
of enlightened ideas, represented the culmination of a fundamental
and profound cultural development. Where once life and death had
been merged in a cosmic harmony, now they were separated into
discrete areas—the secular and the sacred, one governed by the
dictates of reason, the other by the passions of faith. Thus the
miracles of time and space were reduced to problems of timekeeping
and territorial boundaries. It was one way of rationalizing the
unknown.

"The sudden rise of their estates"

★ ★ ★ ★ ★ ★ ★ ★ ★ ★ ★ ★ ★ ★ ★ ★ ★ ★ ★

3
Colonial Economy
and Social Structure

New England commerce and the southern tobacco economy

Commerce and conflict in the Middle Atlantic colonies

Mercantilism and the Navigation Acts

Westward expansion vs. Native American interests

Slavery and black society

The provincial elite

Social mobility and social stratification on
the eve of revolution

The secularization of time and space in the seventeenth and eighteenth centuries—the subdivision of hours into minutes and wilderness into colonies—was largely an unconscious process. The early idea of New England *as* the wilderness (instead of *in* the wilderness), for example, and the perpetuation of old-style calendar time reflected the slow development of the modern mind, the genuine blurring of mystery and experience, of faith and reason. Such ambiguities usually remained latent and unarticulated. Yet as fundamental assumptions about life, these cosmic attitudes inevitably affected the ordinary world of human relations. It was in the visible realm of social affairs that the paradoxical vision of the universe became most manifest, most acute, and, from the perspective of colonial Americans, most alarming. As mystery drained from the cosmos and rationality replaced it, the emotional network of social obligations also dissolved, leaving a hollow inexplicable void at the core of society.

These changes came slowly and subtly. The first English colonists, like their medieval ancestors, accepted the view of society as a living organism in which social interaction occurred for the health and survival of all. That biological metaphor was extremely important, for it suggested an intimacy between the physical world and the social, between nature and humanity. Such a system presumed a hierarchy of social relations, headed by natural-born leaders—royalty and aristocracy—and supported by the faithful devotion of the ruled. Mutual love and responsibility, what Puritans called "the welfare of the commonwealth," were expected to preserve the social order. This did not always occur, of course, but such failure was explained in terms of human frailty rather than as a failure of the social structure itself.

The organic world-view represented the social assumptions of most English colonists, whether they sailed to Virginia to find gold or fled to New England to create a godly utopia, and so pervasive was it that people adhered to it even when it no longer could contain their experiences. After the American Revolution, the tension between social ideals and social realities became more apparent and led to the formulation of a different, more individualistic vision of society.

* * *

The departure from cosmic time and sacred space encouraged a pattern of economic arrangements that also moved from the communal values of the medieval world toward the individualistic capitalism of modern times. In traditional societies, the development of natural resources through human activity constituted a sacred operation by which the "mysteries" of a craft were applied to divine creation. Labor and land were therefore simultaneously spiritual and secular. But the needs of life in the colonies advanced ideas that separated the cosmic from the artificial and destroyed that intimacy. Thereafter, the land and the people who cultivated it lost their mystical functions. Instead they became objects and commodities to be bought, sold, and manipulated for purely secular interests.

Though this process occurred everywhere in colonial America, it emerged most clearly in Puritan New England, a society unusually self-conscious about its historical thrust. In his mid-ocean address to the first colonists, John Winthrop had reiterated the Puritan commitment to social hierarchy and Christian charity. Underlying that harmony was the Puritan concept of "calling," the idea that God summoned each person to a particular vocation to perform some secular task. Thus labor possessed spiritual attributes designed to reinforce communal bonds. Each calling had specific value, but no calling logically could benefit at the expense of another, for that would topple the cosmic order. Some would be wealthy, of course, and some "mean and in subjection." But private interest remained subordinate to the common good.

During the first decade of settlement, the steady flow of migrants and their property to New England assured the economic prosperity of the colony. But following the outbreak of the English civil wars in 1640, as Puritans in England became more optimistic about conditions at home, the great migration slowed to a trickle, causing a severe depression in the colonies. To bolster the economy, Puritan leaders encouraged the expansion of trade, the marketing of foodstuffs, fish, and furs in the West Indies, in England, and in Europe. Such activity, well befitting the aggressive Puritan style, eased the depression, provided a valuable outlet for secular energy, and, in time, became the bulwark of the New England economy. Trade networks, usually with kindred spirits or family members who could be trusted, soon placed New England in the mainstream of Atlantic commerce, and offered vast profits to the coastal merchants who

fitted the ships and, depending upon the harvest, modest returns to
the farmers who supplied them.

Economic prosperity eliminated many of the problems facing the
wilderness communities. But the lure of profits, in its own way,
threatened the spiritual basis of Puritan society. Workingmen in
Massachusetts Bay took advantage of the labor shortage and raised
their rates, provoking widespread criticism of their loss of charity.
Such practices contravened the Puritan commitment to the "just
price," the intrinsic value of a particular commodity. To redress
such grievances, the colony government enacted legislation to regulate wages and prices, a policy that proved difficult to enforce despite wide public approval.

People resented, above all, the large, almost usurious, profits
accumulated by mercantile investors. In 1639, Robert Keayne, the
wealthiest man in the Massachusetts Bay Colony, was fined £200
for amassing "excessive" profits and forced to make a public confession in church. Unlike some other thriving capitalists, Keayne was a
faithful Puritan. Although he apologized sincerely to his neighbors,
he maintained his innocence to the end, even drafting a fifty-page
"Apologia" in which he explained the dilemma of balancing the
fruits of his calling against the spiritual treasure of heaven.
Keayne's paradox persisted well into the eighteenth century,
plaguing other Puritan consciences by its insolubility: how to be an
assiduous Christian in this world without surrendering the keys to
the kingdom of heaven.

While commerce thrived in New England, the settlers along
Chesapeake Bay concentrated on growing tobacco for export to
England. So profitable was this product that southern planters rejected all suggestions to diversify their crops. Instead, they enlarged
their plantations to increase tobacco cultivation. Virginia planters
with wealth or political influence obtained the best land, along
rivers navigable by oceangoing ships to facilitate the export of tobacco and the importation of other goods.

These favored planters soon began acting as merchants for their
neighbors, exporting their tobacco and selling them imported commodities, a role yielding them great profits. Tobacco production
thus stimulated commercial activity despite the absence of a major
southern port. The excessive cultivation of tobacco often worked
against the planters' best interests, for overproduction brought lower
prices and intermittent depressions. Some planters responded by

deliberately destroying growing crops. More typically, however, planters compensated for declining profits by more intensive cultivation, which served only to lower prices still more.

Eventually, the tobacco growers attained greater economic stability through crop control and careful management. But throughout the colonial period, they remained dependent upon English and Scottish merchants for credit. In the mid-eighteenth century, fluctuations in tobacco prices, together with excessive borrowing, created endemic indebtedness among the Chesapeake planters. Moreover, British interests often used their political influence to protect their investments. Thus when the Virginia legislature attempted to prevent the overproduction of tobacco by curtailing the slave trade, the English Privy Council, responding to the pleas of British merchants, vetoed the law. This exemplifies one of the ways in which the colonial economy was tied to the wealth and power of the metropolis across the sea. The future tobacco industry hinged ultimately upon the development of virgin lands. As planters moved westward, fertile acreage increased in value. Investment in land thus became profitable, despite the uncertainty of tobacco production. Land no longer served merely as a geographic place on which to perform a secular function; land was a commodity, easily bought and just as easily sold. Though still an important symbol of status, land had lost its mystical qualities.

Nor was this secular attitude limited to the Chesapeake colonies. In New England, too, the growth of population, largely through natural increase, undermined the collective society envisioned by the first colonists. During the seventeenth century, New England authorities carefully regulated frontier expansion by granting townships only to settlers who promised to transplant families and "godly churches" in the wilderness. But by the next century, these restraints had vanished. No longer was land granted solely to members of a community. The colony *sold* land to speculators, some of them nonresidents, who would reap large profits when other settlers moved to the area. Land speculation quickly became widespread in New England, attracting even small investors and inflating the price of land everywhere, often beyond the means of poorer folk.

To orthodox Puritans, this search for worldly wealth symbolized the spiritual apostasy of New England. "Land! Land! hath been the idol of many in New England," complained Increase Mather, a staunch defender of the old religion, "how many men since coveted after the earth, that many hundreds, nay thousands of acres, have been engrossed by one man, and they that profess themselves Christians, have forsaken churches . . . and all for land and elbow-room enough in the world." What Mather lamented was not simply a loss of religious zeal, but a rejection of a spiritual ethos—the repudiation of a cosmic vision that viewed the earth as Creation rather than as real estate to be consumed.

The insatiable thirst for land soon led to direct conflict with Native Americans. In Virginia, tobacco planters disregarded earlier treaties and encroached on the natives' land, allowing their livestock to trample the growing crops. After repeated affronts, the Doegs and Susquehannocks retaliated with arms in 1675. The frontier settlers reacted by attacking the natives, despite the official disapproval of royal authorities. The episode revealed the racist attitudes of white society, what one rebellious colonist admitted was "our open and manifest aversion of all, not only the foreign, but the protected and darling Indians." One group of settlers even proposed "that the Indians taken [prisoner] in the late war be made slaves."

The conflict in Virginia paralleled the situation between the Wampanoags of New England and Puritan expansionists. Though Puritan missionaries labored to convert Native Americans to Christianity, they required the "barbarous heathen" to reject their traditional cultures, live in "praying villages," and adopt an English lifestyle. Their ethnocentrism allowed no tolerance for Native Americans who did not accept Christian gospel and who maintained their own spiritual beliefs. By 1675, the Wampanoags had suffered considerably. Under the leadership of their chief, Metacom (known to the English as King Philip), they set out to attack Puritan settlements, hoping to drive their oppressors into the sea. Fear spread through New England, and the Puritan militia counterattacked. But it was the exhaustion of supplies among the natives, rather than Puritan military strength, which finally brought the Puritans victory in 1676. Even in the aftermath of their victory they continued to kill Native American survivors of the conflict, or enslaved them to pay for the war. The people who viewed the land as an object to be owned could just as easily view its inhabitants as commodities to be captured and sold.

Where the Puritans cloaked their racism with the rhetoric of Christianity, the settlers of the Carolinas, many of whom previously had been slaveowners in Barbados, proved more direct and more brutal in dealing with Native Americans. The trade in deerskins was extremely profitable, and control of it legally belonged to a group of proprietors in London, who attempted to create a monopoly. But in order to develop their holdings, the proprietors had invited settlers from other colonies, especially from the West Indies. These colonists resented the proprietary regulations and determined to eliminate them by dealing directly with the natives. The Carolina traders decided to exterminate the uncooperative tribes, particularly the Westos, who continued to trade with the proprietors. Those natives who survived the warfare were promptly sold into slavery, thus establishing a commerce that became even more profitable than deerskins.

Relying upon the services of rival tribes, the Carolina merchants supported slave-raiding attacks on numerous native peoples. First the Westos, then the Apalachees, later the Tuscaroras, and later still the Yamasees—all fell victim to the aggressive traders. In 1708, the South Carolina slave census listed 1,400 Native Americans; more still had been exported to other English colonies. The native slave trade, besides enriching the Charleston merchants, also hastened the depopulation of the local tribes, a demographic catastrophe that opened additional lands for settlement. By the early eighteenth century, Carolina planters were earning comfortable profits from the cultivation of rice and indigo, both staple crops, on large plantations worked by slave labor. These planters, like the slave traders they supported, well understood the material advantages of treating human beings as items of commerce to be demystified and exploited, like the land.

These economic patterns also emerged in the "middle colonies"—New York, the Jerseys, and Pennsylvania—where English capitalism reinforced similar economic propensities in other ethnic groups. In New York, the original Dutch authorities had granted enormous tracts of land to private investors, a policy the English perpetuated after the conquest of New Netherland in 1664. Like the Dutch, English landowners did not always sell these holdings but often leased them, thus establishing a dependent class of tenant farmers. As an area rich in natural resources, New York exported furs, naval supplies, and food to other parts of the British Empire.

The fur trade, particularly the fierce competition between Albany merchants and the French in Canada, brought the English colony into close contact with the Iroquois. The strong unity of these tribes prevented the immediate destruction of their culture, and the Iroquois proved to be astute negotiators. Both England and France recognized the Iroquois' potential power and desired to placate these potential allies. After the defeat of France in 1763, however, the Iroquois lost this crucial advantage in the balance of European power and increasingly became victims of aggressive English land-owners.

Though the Dutch colonists maintained their ethnic integrity long after the advent of English power, there was no essential conflict between the two cultures, particularly in the realm of economic affairs. Such harmony contrasted markedly with the pattern in Pennsylvania, the colony that attracted the most non-English set-tlers. Founded by Quakers, Pennsylvania became a cauldron of ethnic antagonism as Scotch-Irish and Germans flocked to the col-ony. Driven to America by religious persecution and economic op-pression and attracted by promises of religious toleration and free land, these groups clamored for fertile acreage. They quickly settled the eastern counties of Pennsylvania and pressed westward and then southward into the Shenandoah Valley and the frontier portions of Virginia and the Carolinas.

The influx of these new settlers inflated the value of undeveloped land and encouraged further land speculation. Even the Quaker merchants, once known for their fair dealings with Native Ameri-cans, succumbed to the lure of wealth. Breaking treaties with the Delaware tribe, Pennsylvania officials grabbed vast tracts of western land, which quickly soared in price. Meanwhile, the growing num-bers of Europeans forced the local tribes farther westward, depriv-ing them of their traditional lands and disrupting their agriculture. Burning resentment brought the Delawares back, however—as allies of the French during the Seven Years' War. Then they attacked the frontier settlements and spread terror throughout the colony, forc-ing the pacifist Quakers of Philadelphia to take a more militant stand.

The acquisition of western lands not only profited the specula-tors, but also accelerated the expansion of commercial agriculture in Pennsylvania. Surplus crops moved eastward to Philadelphia and then in Quaker ships to the West Indies, a trade pattern that re-warded both the farmers and the merchants who exchanged their goods. Such commercial profits often were reinvested in western lands, which stimulated still more agricultural production.

The accumulation of wealth by Quaker merchants did not neces-sarily contradict their religious impulses; like the Puritans of New England, the Quakers viewed material success as a sign of divine blessing. But the pursuit of profits nevertheless undermined Quaker idealism, encouraging an individualistic attitude toward contractual relations. Nor did Quakers shun the profits of the slave trade. Even the City of Brotherly Love possessed a large slave population, employed mostly as artisans, laborers, and domestic servants. Like other Europeans, therefore, the Quakers gradually acquired the emotional detachment that characterized the modern mind.

The pattern of economic relations linking the colonial economies to the mother country was defined by a loose policy known as mercantilism. According to mercantilist principles, a nation's prosperity depended upon the creation of a self-sufficient economy, free from foreign competition. In theory, colonies were sources of raw materials and markets for the finished goods produced in the home country. Ultimately, it was the mother country that would benefit most by this arrangement, but the mercantilist theory held that the colonists too would prosper proportionately; since organic social theory assumed a natural harmony of interests, such a conclusion seemed self-evident.

The idea of a regulated economy had deep roots in European societies, and most Europeans expected government supervision of economic affairs. In the English colonies, town and county officials attempted to regulate wages and prices in the interests of the community. In imperial affairs, these attitudes led to the formulation of a series of Navigation Acts enacted by the English Parliament to regulate the flow of commerce. First passed in the mid-seventeenth century, the Navigation Acts protected English shippers from foreign competitors by requiring the use of English vessels in all colonial trade. Additional legislation enumerated specific commodities— tobacco, sugar, cotton, and indigo, for example—which could be sold only in England; eventually the list included rice, furs, lumber, iron, and naval stores as well.

This monopoly of trade was intended to assure the mother country a cheap and reliable flow of natural resources protected from foreign competition. A similar protectionist attitude led to the passage of several manufactory laws. The Hat Act of 1732, for example, protected English producers from the competition of colonial hat manufacturers, while the Iron Act permitted Americans to produce only pig and bar iron. Despite attempts to compensate colonials for the loss of foreign markets, such legislation demonstrated the primary importance of the English economy. The Navigation Acts functioned not to raise revenue, but to direct the flow of

trade. In theory, such direction protected all members of the British
Empire, regardless of their geographic habitation. The mercantile
system thus reflected the underlying assumptions of organic social
theory.

.The Navigation Acts were seldom as exploitive in the counting-
houses as they appeared on the statute books. Though the mercantile laws required the colonies to trade certain goods exclusively
with England, most colonial commerce would have sailed in that
direction anyway. Since trade networks usually depended upon loyal
agents and kin, colonial Americans probably would have formed
alliances with English merchants. English manufactures, moreover,
exceeded European goods in quality, availability, and cheapness, a
logical reason for the development of trade with America. More
specifically, the Navigation Acts encouraged a thriving shipbuilding
industry in New England, and by 1776, one-third of England's.
commerce moved in American-made ships. The mother country
also subsidized certain staples, especially indigo, thus artificially
bolstering an otherwise marginal industry.   blue dye
Colonial Americans recognized these advantages and ascribed
them to the peculiar blessings of all English people. Yet they knew,
too, that the system did not always function efficiently or wisely.
The Molasses Act of 1733, for example, which was passed through
the influence of the West India sugar lobby, established a prohibi-
tive duty on imported sugar, a rate so high as to threaten the
manufacture of rum in New England. Colonial merchants responded by ignoring the law and shipped their goods with impunity
for three decades. However, this disobedience was not always possible in other areas of the economy, and the Navigation Acts bore
heavily on tobacco and rice planters, creating sporadic depression in
both industries. Such burdens seemed particularly acute at the end
of the seventeenth century when economic grievances, combined
with other more subtle pressures, created a major social crisis in
English America.

The clumsiness of the Navigation Acts betrayed the uncertainties
of economic activity throughout the British Empire. Caught between a world-view that stressed the harmony of economic interests
and a capitalistic perspective that demanded greater rationalization,
colonial planters and merchants searched for a modicum of worldly
security without sacrificing the personal nature of economic relations. As they violated English laws, borrowed freely from their
neighbors, or scrambled for friendly legislation from their repre-

sentatives, colonial entrepreneurs demonstrated a remarkable, even poignant, capacity to be humane and understanding. Consider, then, the ambivalence of the Puritan merchant Robert Keayne: "I have not lived an idle, lazy, or dronish life," he asserted with certainty, if not with pride, but "more happy would it have been for me if I had [kept] as careful . . . an account of my sins and the debts I owe to God." Those spiritual omissions, haunting in their silence, speak plainly about the thrust of America.

The paradoxes of colonial economic development, the tension between precapitalistic and capitalistic values, emerged in social relations as well, influencing the colonial social structure and the articulation of social values. These tensions partly reflected the larger transition occurring in European culture, a subtle but continuous shift from an organic community to one characterized by individualistic relationships. Whereas medieval Europeans found their identity within specific status groups or "estates," modern societies emphasized the importance of personal uniqueness and individuality. Midway between these perspectives, seventeenth-century Europeans felt early strains of that process of historical change.

Yet it was not in London or in Paris that these trends first appeared with clarity. Rather it was in the remotest outposts of European culture, in the small, struggling settlements that perched along the Atlantic coast, where powerful symptoms of change emerged. For the transplantation of European society was a self-conscious process, a deliberate attempt to define coherently what most Europeans simply took for granted. Thus it was in America that the clash between modern and premodern grated most loudly and, considering the reverberations of that collision, most prophetically.

Virginia, the first colony to be settled, was the first to experience these changes. As Elizabethan Englishmen, the first Virginians expected aristocrats to rule the colony, a situation that prevailed under the control of the Virginia Company. But within one generation, many of the colony's leaders had either died or returned to England, leaving a void at the apex of the social structure. Into this vacuum slipped the wealthiest residents in the colony, rich landowners who had exploited the "headright" system by importing indentured servants and claiming large tracts of real estate. These self-made leaders lacked the traditional symbols of high social status that, in

England, legitimized the control of power. Thus Virginians perceived a significant difference between their social values (which linked status to power) and the existing pattern of social arrangements. Disturbing as this may have been, Virginians did not then reject their traditional values, but sought to implement them more perfectly.

After the English civil wars began in 1640, many wealthy young men migrated to Virginia to escape the crisis. In America, their social status enabled them to obtain land and power, and they gradually became important leaders of the colony. By about 1660, the transplanted elite had formed valuable political alliances, some of them as colleagues of the royal governor. Those aspiring planters who did not attain political influence were frustrated and resentful of the rule of the power-holders.

This anomalous situation, where power rested with *new* wealth, provided the background for a major social crisis in 1676 known as Bacon's Rebellion. The precipitating cause of the insurrection was the refusal of the royal governor, William Berkeley, to send soldiers against the Doegs and Susquehannocks who lived on the western fringes of the colony. Anxious to remove the local tribes from the lands, frontier settlers, under the leadership of Nathaniel Bacon, seized the initiative, first attacking the natives and then challenging the governor's authority. After a dramatic confrontation between Berkeley and Bacon, in which the rebel forced the governor to surrender his power, the sudden death of Bacon abruptly ended the uprising. Berkeley then crushed his opponents, executing twenty-three men for treason, before being recalled himself by the royal government in England.

Though ostensibly a conflict of power between the political elite in Jamestown and the county leaders on the frontier, Bacon's Rebellion also revealed profound tensions within the social order. "We appeal to the country itself," declared Bacon in a "Manifesto" written during the crisis. "Let us trace these men in authority and favor . . . ; let us observe the sudden rise of their estates [compared] with the quality in which they first entered the country or the reputation they have held here amongst wise and discerning men, and let us see whether their extractions and education have not been vile." What Bacon protested was the rise of a provincial elite lacking the traditional accouterments of power—old wealth, high social status, a "liberal" education. That these tensions coincided with the passage of the first Navigation Act and a depressed tobacco economy only emphasized the general frustration that prompted the uprising.

Bacon's Rebellion constituted a desperate challenge to a social structure based upon new wealth. His vision of social order, however, looked to the past. Bacon was not a modern man calling for autonomy and independence. Rather, he decried the loss of traditional order and coherence and summoned Virginians backward to an older social form. The defeat of Bacon and his allies by the provincial elite not only allowed these wealthy planters to preserve their power against the rebels, but, through intermarriage and business alliances, to become even more solidly entrenched in subsequent decades. By the beginning of the eighteenth century, they had consolidated their strength, once again linking wealth, and power to status and had emerged, finally, with the prestige of social leadership.

Thus colonial society saw European notions of status replaced by provincial images of success. Colonial elites never consciously rejected the traditional ideology of aristocratic leadership; if anything, they tried, like provincials elsewhere, to imitate the lifestyle and deportment of their metropolitan models. Such posturing was accepted for the real thing in all colonies, enabling the colonial elite to wield power with greater authority. A fluid social system, characterized by considerable mobility, became more rigid, more stable, and ultimately more stratified.

This changing social climate was reproduced in other English colonies. In New England, the transformation coincided with the decline of Puritanism and the emergence of a more secular society. Where first-generation Puritans expected a correlation between godliness and social leadership, their descendants, more pragmatic and more worldly, thought more about power and wealth.

In 1637, for example, the townspeople of Ipswich, Massachusetts, beseeched the younger John Winthrop to return to their community, explaining that "his abode with us hath made our abode here much more comfortable than otherwise it might have been." Such "able men" offered emotional security to people living in remote places. For similar reasons, the Puritans bestowed high social status on their ministers. During the seventeenth century, however, as New England merchants amassed enormous fortunes in the Atlantic trade, they discovered another way of looking at the world. Merchants, men with international concerns, were the first to recognize

New England's secondary place within the British Empire; Winthrop's city on a hill constituted, in reality, a mere appendage of English society. When Puritan conservatives threatened their commercial interests and stood in the way of their search for status, these merchants aligned with British politicians to break down the New England Puritan social structure. "We are some of us English gentlemen," exaggerated one Puritan scion, "and we should labor to support such families because truly we want them."

These social changes, particularly the redefinition of leadership roles, reflected a new estimation of individual worth. In Europe, change affecting all social classes occurred gradually and was characterized by the destruction of feudal obligations, the separation of workers from the land, and the rise of laissez-faire capitalism. In the colonies, however, the transformation of social relations occurred more abruptly. It did not occur without selecting a victim—not the European peasants but the African slave.

During the first decade of settlement, the tobacco planters of Virginia and Maryland relied primarily upon the labor of indentured servants, a contractual relationship that, if not always equitable, at least acknowledged the rights of both parties. White servants often received extremely cruel treatment at the hands of their masters, which suggests that African servants, about whom there is little reliable information, suffered similar cruelty.

By 1640, colonial authorities were treating some blacks, though not all, as slaves, a status that meant, in North America, lifetime hereditary servitude. This policy reflected a major departure from traditional English practice, which usually stressed the mutual obligations between masters and servants. The notion of perpetual slavery also differed radically from African traditions, in which slavery served to assimilate conquered peoples and still protected the rights of individual slaves. Such innovations strongly suggest that economic considerations alone do not explain the evolution of black slavery in America. It does suggest that there existed a deep antipathy to Africans, which encouraged their enslavement. Slavery, in turn, reinforced racist attitudes, since it placed nearly all blacks into the lowest caste.

This process attained legal recognition by the 1660s, both in the colonial legislatures and in the judicial system. In one Virginia ruling, the courts held that conversion to Christianity did not alter a slave's status, thus undermining the "heathen" argument long called upon as rationalization of the slave system. This can be seen as one demonstration of the self-conscious creation of a slave society in America. The Fundamental Constitutions of Carolina, drafted ironically by the English philosopher of liberty John Locke, also protected the institution of slavery in spite of religious conversion. Other legislation in the Chesapeake Bay colonies stripped the Africans of basic defenses, including the right to testify in court, the right to own property, and the right to legal marriage. Human beings were thereby viewed outright as chattel.

The tightening of the slave system during the late seventeenth century reflected other social developments. After 1690, the expansion of the tobacco economy increased the demand for slave labor, leading to massive importation of Africans. The increasing numbers of blacks and the growing fear of slave revolt led colonials to restrict their activities, a policy culminating in the Virginia slave code of 1705. This law significantly coincided with the emergence of an indigenous provincial elite. As the planter class consolidated its power in the aftermath of Bacon's Rebellion, it also established a clearly defined slave caste at the lowest level of society.

The institutionalization of slavery in the southern colonies mirrored the demands of a plantation economy. In New England the presence of fewer blacks made the problem appear less urgent. Slavery never became deeply entrenched there, and the black population possessed certain civil rights denied them in Virginia. Not until the last decades of the seventeenth century did Puritan legislation specifically inhibit the activity of blacks—establishing curfews, prohibiting the consumption of alcohol, limiting emancipation, and prohibiting interracial marriage and sexual relations between the races. The timing of these enactments is as important as their content, for they coincided with a period of social crisis. Confused about the drift of their society, Puritans, like the tobacco planters, responded by imposing an artificial legal order upon otherwise vaguely defined social relations.

As an institution, slavery varied according to the social conditions of each region. The Dutch West India Company had encouraged the importation of slaves to New Netherland during the seventeenth century, a policy continued by the English. As a result, New York became the largest slaveholding area north of the Chesapeake. In the urban centers of Albany and in New York City slaves constituted approximately one-fifth of the population; about one-third of the white population owned at least one slave. In the northern colonies Africans constituted a small minority of the population. They lived in close proximity to whites, often isolated from other slaves, and worked as farm hands, artisans, and domestic servants. In the southern colonies the absence of urban centers and the economics of commercial agriculture determined that most slaves worked on plantations. The typical agricultural unit remained relatively small, averaging less than thirteen slaves in Virginia and Maryland at the end of the eighteenth century; and even on the southern plantations, blacks interacted closely with whites. The greater density of a black population in the South, however, provided slaves with certain defenses against white culture. In the privacy of the slave quarters African culture could flourish more readily. In the North, where slaves lived more intimately with whites, closer supervision was more likely.

The slave population increased considerably during the eighteenth century. This demographic trend was a reflection of an equal balance of black males and females that encouraged marriage, and the general healthiness of the North American climate. Black women born in America seemed to be more fertile than native Africans living in America. The lower fertility of first-generation slaves may well have been a deliberate form of resistance to American slavery. However, the expansion of the American-born black population lessened the importance of the slave trade with Africa and the West Indies, resulting in a steady decline of the percentage of foreign-born slaves in North America. In isolated areas, native Africans probably were unknown.

Such demographic patterns affected the blacks' response to slavery, for their level of acculturation determined their relations with whites. Africans with no understanding of the English language found themselves consigned to menial work requiring strength rather than skill. Better-assimilated slaves, capable of communicating with their masters, could become trained craftsmen—carpenters, coopers, blacksmiths, or boatmen. These occupational opportunities increased their personal freedom, for they were sometimes required to perform tasks away from home. Travel offered unique opportunities for escape, and skilled artisans, more experienced than other blacks in coping with white culture, constituted the largest class of runaway slaves.

The success of the slave economy depended upon efficiently organizing the labor of the Africans. Such discipline might require physical brutality, but planters also relied upon pecuniary incentives to increase production. Recognizing the interest of the planters in efficiency, slaves frequently resisted the system by deliberately performing inefficiently. "My spinners," observed one Virginia planter, "imagining I was gone yesterday instead of their usual day's work spun but 2 ounces a piece."

Opposition to the slave system occasionally took violent forms. In 1712 a group of slaves in New York City launched a bloody assault on some white men, an uprising that was suppressed only by the presence of English soldiers. White retribution proved incredibly cruel—torture and execution of the insurrectionists—and the colonial Assembly promptly passed a new slave code severely restricting the movements of the black population. Even more desperate than this clash was an uprising of slaves in Stono, South Carolina, in 1739. There blacks captured a cache of arms and began marching toward freedom in Spanish Florida. Intercepted by the white militia, the blacks used their guns in a futile effort at escape.

Though armed rebellions occurred rarely, blacks did not passively succumb to American slavery and did not easily abandon their culture for the values of white society. The isolation of American blacks from their native roots, however, undermined the strength of African culture, producing a cultural blend that was partly African, partly English. This occurred subtly, as it involved the superimposition of European forms onto a bedrock of African beliefs. Thus the religions of west Africa emphasized the importance of a powerful conversion experience, similar to that of evangelical Christianity. Perhaps that parallel explains why American blacks proved so receptive to the preachers of the Great Awakening and came forward in great numbers to be baptized. But black perceptions of Christianity remained highly selective, drawing primarily upon aspects of Western religion that coincided with previously held feelings and ideas.

The emergence of a slave caste in colonial America was part of a general trend toward a more stratified and polarized social order. This pattern varied from area to area, depending upon the nature of economic activity, the environmental context, and the cultural predisposition of the settlers. Yet certain generalizations still may be made. All regions witnessed a remarkable expansion of population, largely the result of natural increase. In 1700, about 250,000 people inhabited British North America; by 1776, that figure had increased tenfold, approaching 2,500,000, of which about one-fifth were black slaves. The sheer growth of population accelerated the process of social differentiation, accentuating the anomalies between articulated social values and the actual working of the social system.

On the eve of the American Revolution, power, wealth, and status in all colonies rested firmly in the hands of a provincial elite. Despite their bourgeois origins in the previous century, these planters and merchants wielded great political power and modeled their lives on their image of aristocracy. They built spacious houses, employed numerous servants or slaves, and imitated the latest English fashions. For pleasure and instruction, they read English books and periodicals, founded liberal-arts colleges that instituted traditional European curricula, and followed with interest the scientific proceedings of the Royal Society of London.

Despite their apparent gentility, however, they were hardly an idle class of aristocrats. In an age of personal business relations, commerce required long hours in the countinghouse, drafting instructions to ship captains or letters of credit to other merchants. Similarly, the richest plantation owners generally maintained personal control of their operations, assigning work tasks, checking the crops, dealing with slaves. No wonder, then, that Benjamin Franklin's *Poor Richard's Almanack,* filled as it was with the aphorisms of business, became enormously popular in the colonies. And when Franklin and John Bartram founded the American Philosophical Society in Philadelphia in 1743, it was "useful knowledge" they promised to study.

Wealth required work, but it brought important social advantages as well. The European distinctions of status failed to survive the first generation of colonization. Titles like "esquire" and "mister" lost their clarity and consequently their importance. But colonials continued to acknowledge the value of status and rank, generally related to wealth. The assignment of seats in the churches, for example, reflected the prominence of each family, a visible sign of worldly standing if not of spiritual perfection. Harvard and Yale ranked students by the social position of their families rather than by standards of intellectual excellence. Indeed, higher education aimed not simply to improve the minds of young men (women were excluded from these intellectual citadels), but also to develop their characters, to inspire their natural qualities of leadership.

In this age of personality, members of the provincial elite cultivated their behavior to win the respect of others and so they were concerned about their public images. Courtesy, temperance, and

equanimity constituted basic social virtues, evidence of superior
status. Few people, of course, attained such distinction. But most
white property owners—what colonials considered "the middling
sort"—probably aspired to improve their social position and therefore accepted the stratified system. It was this hopeful attitude, rather
than any vestigial respect for aristocracy, that perpetuated the patterns of deference in colonial America.

By European standards, the American social order was considerably more fluid, allowing resourceful people to rise in wealth and
status. Certainly the career of Benjamin Franklin, the model of a
self-made man, attested to that possibility. But increasingly in the
eighteenth century, such opportunities became rare. As wealth consolidated in the hands of the elite, the disparities between the upper
and lower classes became more pronounced and stratification lines
became harder to breach. Social mobility was not entirely impossible, but the fluidity associated with frontier society no longer
existed.

The coastal regions experienced the most overcrowding, the result
of the population explosion. As available land disappeared, rural
poverty became more evident; many young men chose nonagricultural occupations, swelling the population of the nearby towns.
Such decisions might hasten economic advancement, for colonial
artisans enjoyed moderately high wages. But the urban centers also
attracted ever larger numbers of propertyless workers—day laborers, journeymen, sailors—who scratched out a livelihood or
joined the growing list of unemployables supported by public charity. Only the black population, victimized by all white groups,
seemed lower in status. For all these working people, lacking both
property and the privileges it brought, the hardening of social lines
often fostered deep class antagonism.

Such antagonism often led to armed rebellion. In areas of New
York, tenant farmers demanded the end of long-term leases; in
Pennsylvania, frontier settlers demanded a more militant policy toward the native tribes; in North Carolina, western farmers demanded a voice in government. They resorted to violence to effect
these social changes. Though indications of profound dissatisfaction, these rebellions were typically unsuccessful and failed to produce significant reforms. In the cities, violence was more spontaneous and more common, usually involving ethnic or racial rivalry.
But at times of crisis, the urban poor constituted an important
social force. Bread riots in Boston, protests against impressment

into the Royal Navy, electoral dissent in Philadelphia—all represented the systematic use of raw power to influence the political process. Such outbursts, significant as they now appear, nevertheless were exceptional events in colonial America. Most people, captivated by illusory visions of upward social mobility, remained loyal to the system and awaited their turn.

By the outbreak of the American Revolution, therefore, provincial society contained a hierarchy of relations extending from the wealthiest planters and merchants to the destitute poor who crowded the almshouses. To the European eye, such distinctions seemed natural, merely a visible manifestation of inherent class differences. For Americans, however, the organization of society concealed a fundamental change in social assumptions, a shift from the spiritual organicism of the body politic to the exploitative arrangements of modern individualism.

Though men of power, people like Thomas Jefferson and John Adams, might speak of "natural" leaders and a "natural" aristocracy, the provincial elite, unlike its European counterpart, was a leadership of wealth rather than of birth, a decidedly artificial, *un*natural standard of distinction. Thus status in America came to rest solely upon secular values, the accumulation of material riches and the concomitant acquisition of political power. Aristocratic postures, powdered wigs, and a genteel eloquence could not alter that essential truth. It was wealth, therefore, and the power it bought, not some mystical system of estates, that structured relations between individuals and thus paved the way, in the next century, for the expansion of American capitalism.

"On the side of power"

* * * * * * * * * * * * * * * * * * *

4

Politics and the American Revolution

Political values and the emergence of modern politics

Colonial political structure

The imperial wars and the Treaty of Paris

England's great war for empire and colonial protest
against taxation and other Intolerable Acts

The War for Independence: origins, military
engagements, peace settlement

Establishing state governments

The Articles of Confederation: the first
national government and the call for reform

Changes in economic and social relations in colonial America were closely intertwined with emerging patterns of political activity. As individuals became merely units of economic development, as wealth purchased prestige and status, the political process also became more secular. In a society where elite groups lacked the traditional advantages of aristocratic birth, the manipulation of politics often served as a necessary substitute. In addition, the pursuit of material rewards more often depended upon the acquisition of political power—the ability to influence executive policy or the passage of legislation. Proximity to power, in turn, reinforced other secular trends by encouraging a prudent defense of self-interest, even at the expense of other members of society.

These attitudes contrasted markedly with the values and assumptions transported to America by the first colonists. Those early settlers had embraced a cosmic vision based upon the orderliness of all human relations. As in economic and social matters, so too they believed that the political world reflected a natural harmony of interests. Power, they assumed, served the needs not of particular groups or individuals, but of the entire community. Since a conflict of interests was literally inconceivable short of treason, these assumptions justified the institutions of monarchy and aristocracy. The leadership of a few, they believed, protected the interests of the many.

By the sixteenth century, however, some of these institutional patterns had begun to change. In England, the power of the Tudor dynasty often hinged upon the cooperation of Parliament. When Henry VIII established a national church, he relied upon parliamentary statutes to legitimate his decision. Parliament still remained subservient to the throne, summoned and dissolved at the monarch's will, restricted from encroachment on the royal prerogative. Yet the Tudor monarchs realized—and this was their special genius—that Parliament could not be ignored on substantive issues. This blurring of power, so typical of the emerging modern mind, often perplexed the Stuart monarchs of the seventeenth century, resulting in strident ideological battles between king and Parliament. Yet even the English civil wars did not fully clarify the question of sovereignty. Parliamentary legislation still risked the royal veto, a power exer-

93

cised as late as the reign of Queen Anne (1702–14) and a real
threat even thereafter. Nor did the House of Commons of the
eighteenth century pretend to represent the interests of its constituents in any modern sense of political representation. Thus to the
end of the colonial era, English political values manifested the paradoxical tendencies of the larger society, a tenuous composite of
premodern organicism and modern individualism.

In America, the tensions between political values and political
practices emerged more clearly. As a people dominated by English
influences, colonial Americans attempted to reproduce English political institutions. Though geographically isolated from the seat of
British government, they remained loyal to the English constitution,
praised its unique advantages, and repeated the rhetoric of English
politicians. Yet as outposts of empire, colonial interests often conflicted with those of the mother country, thereby underscoring the
tension between organic unity and interest politics. What was deemed
necessary and proper in England was not always appropriate or
desirable in America.

The three thousand miles separating colonials from London prevented the satisfactory implementation of the English political system in America. However much colonials might voice adherence to
their English heritage, they could never reduce that distance nor
lessen the effects of that oceanic barrier. Lacking a locus of power
in America, colonials gradually realized, much to their chagrin,
that the rights of Englishmen would not always protect them from
the politics of the mother country. It was that realization, the culmination of a painful but logical process of political awakening,
that led finally to the Declaration of Independence and the creation
of a republican form of government.

Though provincial politics and imperial relations ultimately
dominated the political process in the colonies, it was the local units
of government that directly affected the lives of most people. In
New England, town meetings served as the primary unit of government, resolving disputes between neighbors, supervising economic
activities, parceling land, and electing delegates to the colony legislature. In other areas, county governments, modeled on local government institutions in England, provided the basic political services.
Among many other responsibilities, these institutions registered land
deeds, probated wills, levied taxes, supervised roads, meted out justice, and served as the basic units of political representation. Such

fundamental power, especially its proximity to daily lives and daily concerns, emphasized the local orientation of these rural people.

Implicit in this arrangement was a belief in paternalistic government. Colonials assumed that local officials best understood their needs and interests, much as the medieval lord of the manor was thought to regulate affairs for the common welfare. In England, such attitudes justified the perpetuation of political representation by "estates" of the realm. Thus landlords, even nonresidents, continued to sit in Parliament on behalf of their "constituencies"— whether or not they shared the interests of the other residents. But in the colonies, local government *followed* the dispersal of population, thus linking geographic units to particular constituencies. Representation in America was more specific than in England from the beginning of colonization, and as a result it became more secular earlier.

However, the expectation of paternal government influenced the selection of political leaders. In the New England towns, all male residents voted for town officials and usually chose men of standing to act as "selectmen" to oversee public affairs. The openness of the town meetings, unusual in an age of aristocratic rule, reflected the Puritans' desire to wield power by consensus rather than by majorities. The popular nature of town government contrasted with the workings of the county system. As in England, the county officials —justices of the peace, sheriffs, coroners, and clerks—were appointed by the central authority—usually in America by the royal governor. But in practice, the governor appointed men from a list of nominees submitted by other local officials. Thus a group of local leaders could form a self-perpetuating oligarchy that screened political candidates and assured the protection of their interests. The system was hardly democratic, but neither were the assumptions of most people living in America.

Nowhere was this paternalism clearer than in the electoral process itself. Since the units of local government provided the basis of representation in the colony legislature, elections were supervised by the county sheriffs, men firmly entrenched in the local oligarchy. At the instruction of the governor, the sheriffs in each county established a date and place for polling and publicized the election to candidates and eligible voters. In a society which recognized the preeminent importance of property, suffrage was restricted by property requirements, usually the ownership of land. The requirement for officeholding was even higher. In England, such standards severely limited the number of voters, but in America, where landownership was more common, this was not the case. Approximately 75 percent of the adult males in New England qualified to vote, and in the southern colonies the figure was somewhat lower, approaching 50 percent. Nevertheless, large groups of people were excluded from voting for other reasons. People who were considered "dependents" —women, children, servants, and slaves—did not have a sufficient stake in society and consequently were denied the vote. The system also excluded certain minority groups—Catholics, Jews, free blacks, Native Americans, non-English-speaking Europeans. These limitations partially reflected an organic world-view that presumed the establishment of homogeneous communities. Yet they also revealed an aggressive ethnocentric aspect of English culture, a sense of superiority that ultimately became established in what has been identified as the dominant WASP system.

Though political participation remained the privilege of white male Protestant property holders, even eligible voters, then as now, often neglected their duty. One reason for this apathy was that most candidates represented similar interests and articulated a similar ideology; the voters faced no significant choices. Moreover, distance from the polling place—usually the county courthouse—frequently deterred voter participation. Occasionally, a corrupt sheriff might deliberately summon the voters to a particularly remote site, hoping to influence the outcome. Finally, the very conception of politics as a paternal responsibility reinforced voter apathy.

On election day, the voters found the sheriff seated behind a long table, flanked by the justices of the county and, at the extreme ends, the rival candidates. Already the hopeful officeholders had demonstrated their gentility by providing the citizens with abundant food and drink, usually hard cider and rum punch. "Some of them drank drams in the morning," reported one observer, "and went merry to the court house." To vote, presumably. The sheriff opened the proceedings by reading the governor's writ calling for the election. Then he invited the voters to come forward. One by one, each citizen stood before the sheriff, announced his choice, and watched the clerk tally the count. The favored candidate usually rose from his seat and, with the grace befitting a gentleman, thanked the voter for his trust. Afterward, the candidates, losers as well as winners, treated the voters to more drinks and celebration, a raucus rural festival that occasionally degenerated into brawls and hell-raising. George Washington, whose consummate skill won him the abiding affection of his neighbors, understood the importance of such fare: "I hope no exception were taken to any who voted against me but that all were alike treated and all had enough," he explained to a colleague; "it is what I much desired." Then, with food in their bellies and liquor on their breaths, the voters rode homeward, confident that they had exercised their civic duties.

The electoral process underscored the personal nature of colonial politics. People voted neither for slates nor for parties, but for particular individuals. To persuade the populace of their qualifications, therefore, candidates had to demonstrate their claim to leadership. Public generosity was one such sign; the refusal to solicit votes was another. Yet candidates could not be too aloof from the people, lest they offend the voters by their pretense. There was a fine line to be drawn. Thus one unsuccessful candidate complained that he had lost the election despite the fact that he had "kissed the —— of the people"! The importance of personality became even clearer in the context of open balloting procedures. Where people cast their votes in public, it was indeed risky to challenge the existing power structure. In any case, few people ever tried. Rather, they accepted the traditional standards of political excellence—wealth, status, gentility.

The rule of the oligarchs provided a modicum of stability in local politics, despite the factional strife on the provincial level of government. In a culture that stressed the advantages of political harmony, the endemic discord that characterized provincial politics seemed inexplicably perverse. "The greatest care [should be] taken not to go into parties and separate interests," warned one conservative, but he admitted that " 'tis fondness for a party . . . that possesses, biases, and determines us on all occasions." This conflict between values and practices partly reflected a larger transformation within Western culture, the gradual loss of an older communal ethos. But in a more immediate way, the tension also revealed the peculiar nature of colonial politics. Though Englishmen on both sides of the Atlantic claimed to share a common interest, American politics ultimately depended upon the political activities of English politicians. The very idea of being colonial thus undermined the political stability of the colonies.

The dependent status of colonial politics was dramatized periodically by the arrival of a royal governor appointed by the crown. Amid much ceremonial splendor—the formal introduction of pro-

vincial leaders and the consumption of an elaborate dinner inter-
spersed with solemn toasts—the newcomer would attempt to
ascertain the balance of power in the colony. Already the governor
possessed a long list of instructions, drawn by the English Privy
Council, which he had sworn to follow to the letter. He knew that
some of these orders would imperil the interests of certain colonials
and arouse their opposition. But he hoped that these provincial
Englishmen would respect the royal prerogative and honor the
wishes of the British government.

From the colonial perspective, the arrival of a new governor
created an aura of uncertainty. Since most governors obtained their
positions through the patronage obligations of English politics, they
were usually Englishmen by birth, complete strangers to colonial
affairs. Yet they possessed considerable power in matters that
affected the lives of each inhabitant. As the personal representative
of the crown, the governor was responsible for enforcing parliamentary and colonial legislation, including the Navigation Acts, which
regulated American commerce. As commander-in-chief of the colony militia, the governor supervised military defense and contracted
with local merchants to supply the troops. With the approval of the
colonial council, the most stable branch of colonial government, the
governor bestowed grants of land, an enormously important power
in an agricultural society bolstered by heavy land investment. Besides these executive responsibilities, the governor possessed important legislative functions. He could summon or dissolve the colonial
legislature, order new elections, and recommend appointments to
the colonial council, which served as the upper house of the legislature, somewhat like the English House of Lords. He also controlled
appropriations and expenditures and could veto legislation. Finally,
the governor and his council constituted the highest judicial court in
the colony. To many colonials, these extensive powers seemed
greater than those exercised by the king in England. That is why
American politicians shuddered at the arrival of a new royal governor. It was not arbitrary power that they feared, but simply that the
person who held it was an unknown quantity.

The governor's council was a body usually consisting of twelve
men, appointed by the crown at the recommendation of the governor. As an ally of the governor, the council often served a conservative role in the legislative process, forcing the lower house to
moderate its proposals. By manipulating the council, many a governor averted the politically unpleasant task of vetoing provincial

legislation. The compliance of the council reflected not only its dependence upon the authority of the executive, but also its social composition. As the wealthiest men in the provinces, councilors cherished their influence with the royal authorities. By aligning with English interests, they themselves drew closer to the seat of English culture, to what provincials generally regarded as a more sophisticated society. These psychological advantages reinforced the more obvious material gains that came from supporting the royal authority. Since members of the council received no salaries, they often supplemented their incomes by accepting other government positions, which increased their political dependence on the governors.

Members of the colonial elite who lacked the favor of the governors but who also aspired to greater influence in provincial affairs entered the power structure through the "assemblies" (the lower house of the legislatures). With strong ties to the county oligarchs who nominated them, the members of the assemblies were elected to office through the provincial electoral process. As men of wealth and status, they too commanded the respect of their constituents. But they often remained outside the mainstream of provincial power, forced to acknowledge the political pre-eminence of the governor's inner circle. Their estrangement from royal power undermined their commitment to the imperial system and made them more willing to challenge the governor's authority.

In Massachusetts, members of the House of Representatives quarreled with the royal governor about the appropriation of salaries, using this platform as a wedge to wrest additional power at the expense of the prerogative. In Pennsylvania, a strong antiproprietary faction waged perennial warfare against the Quaker establishment, in search of a more aggressive policy against the Delawares. These pressures reinforced basic ethnic antagonisms in that colony, resulting, at the end of the colonial period, in an abortive attempt to have William Penn's colony placed under direct royal supervision. In New York, the political issues involved not only Anglo-Dutch rivalry, but also a conflict between the mercantile interests centered in New York City and the landed wealth of the Hudson Valley. In Connecticut, disputes between New Light Protestants and Old Lights spilled into the political arena, creating bitter rivalry for control of power. Questions of taxation and political representation emerged to undermine the political peace in all colonies.

This pervasive contention had important implications for the distribution of power. Where provincial politicians lacked the security
of an entrenched elite, they could ill afford to cooperate with a
governor whose presence threatened their leadership. Thus the
leaders of the assemblies gradually began to erode the power of the
prerogative by challenging some of the governors' basic privileges.
Consider the problem of spending public monies. Most royal officials conceded that the assemblies, like the English House of Commons, had the right to approve all tax legislation, for that was
considered the essence of representative government. Once such a
measure was passed, however, royal officials tried to curtail the
power of the assemblies; disbursement of funds, audits of accounts,
awards of contracts, and the establishment of salaries remained a
matter of the royal prerogative. But gradually the assemblies began
to claim those other powers. At times of crisis, for example, when a
war with France galvanized colonial energy, the assemblies might
assume the right of awarding government contracts along with the
appropriation of funds for defense. The royal governors, of course,
denied the validity of such actions. In times of calm, they might
even dissolve an assembly that made such extravagant demands. But
there were times when that was not possible, and there were governors who lacked the courage to try.

In acquiescing to legislative inroads, the colonial executives seriously weakened their future positions. It was not simply that they
lost the principles of power; they also surrendered its substance. The
appointment of a government contractor, for example, could be an
important source of patronage, a means of rewarding loyal allies or
punishing recalcitrant opponents. Without such powers, the governors lost the ability to harness votes in the legislatures. Besides
weakening their own hands and those of their successors, they also
encouraged the proliferation of political factions whose pursuit of
power often obviated cooperation with government officials.

These political configurations reflected not simply the jealousies
of an emerging provincial elite, but also the persistent problem of
dealing with imperial authority. Just as the arrival of a new royal
governor might jeopardize a decade of rapprochement, so too did
other branches of the English government intrude in colonial
affairs, creating a highly uncertain political environment. English
interference was not only frequent, but complicated. Simply listing
the various offices responsible for colonial administration illumi-

nates the bewildering maze of political relations: the Board of Trade and Plantations, a branch of the Privy Council, reviewed colonial legislation, proposed bills to Parliament, and adjudicated colonial disputes; the Secretary of State for the Southern Department issued instructions to royal officials in the colonies; the Treasury Board supervised the collection of customs duties; the Admiralty Courts regulated the enforcement of the Navigation Acts; Parliament enacted legislation affecting all members of the British Empire. Other, less official bodies were equally influential in imperial affairs—merchants, lobbyists, and political pamphleteers. For colonials, three thousand miles from England, the quagmire of offices often proved an insurmountable obstacle to political effectiveness.

This institutional structure, despite its bulk, remained very active in American affairs. Though historians have spoken often of "salutary neglect," English officials affected colonial politics in profound ways. By retaining the right to veto provincial laws, the Privy Council could supervise the American legislatures whether or not it exercised its powers. Nor were these merely theoretical constraints. The veto of legislation or, more commonly, the delays caused by the bureaucracy undermined the colonists' search for political order. Even matters of immediate concern were often suspended until the royal assent crossed the Atlantic. Moreover, in this age of personal politics, English policy often contradicted itself. What satisfied some royal authorities might offend others, a confusing pattern that was aggravated by the overlapping jurisdictions within the administrative machinery.

In economic affairs too the British supervision kept American interests subservient and insecure. A major problem within the colonial economy was the scarcity of gold and silver to serve as a medium of exchange. To alleviate this shortage, several colonial governments issued paper money as legal tender. English merchants were alarmed by this and fearing that the currency would depreciate in value they convinced Parliament to prohibit the circulation of such money. Although this decision was enforced unevenly it nevertheless posed a serious economic problem. Georgia and Maryland simply ignored the restriction, while Massachusetts searched in vain for a satisfactory alternative. The controversy revealed, not so much English tyranny, as the basic powerlessness in American society.

This sporadic intervention in colonial affairs, serious as it now appears, was dwarfed ultimately by the international repercussions of British imperialism. As loyal Englishmen, most provincials viewed the British Empire as the bastion of liberty and rallied to its defense in time of need. But such times occurred with unsettling frequency during the colonial era. Between 1689 and 1763, England engaged in four major wars with her European enemies, especially France, and each of these conflicts produced a parallel conflagration in America. The wars gave colonials an opportunity to demonstrate their martial valor, bringing such celebrated victories as the capture of the French fortress at Louisbourg in 1745. But the conflicts also reinforced a sense of powerlessness when, for reasons of diplomacy, the British ignored colonial sacrifices and negotiated away captured territory.

Colonial participation, however it was regarded in London, proved immensely valuable to Great Britain during the Great War for Empire that erupted against France in 1754. Considering its vast implications, nothing less than the control of the American continent, the war had obscure origins on the western frontier. French fur traders had moved into the Ohio River Valley and established a network of trading posts and forts, hoping to contain British expansion. Meanwhile, colonial land speculators from Virginia and fur traders from Pennsylvania also had entered the area. Gunshots were exchanged, provisions stolen. Soon the entire frontier was ablaze.

England's early military strategy proved dismally ineffective. In 1755, General Edward Braddock led the pride of the English army into an ambush set by French soldiers and their allies from Canada. Braddock's defeat—soon enshrined in American folklore to epitomize British arrogance—shocked colonials everywhere. Subsequent French victories in New York and Pennsylvania aggravated the tension, convincing some pious provincials that God was punishing the people for their sins. Perhaps it was Providence that turned the tide. At least many colonials fervently believed that William Pitt's ascension to power signified a divine blessing. Pitt determined to eliminate France from North America and began rushing men and supplies to the colonies. British troops responded with alacrity, winning victory after victory until the heroic encounter between Wolfe and Montcalm on the Plains of Abraham resulted in the conquest of Quebec in 1759. That triumph effectively sealed French resistance in Canada, though the war did not end officially until the signing of the Treaty of Paris in 1763.

News of British success bolstered colonial enthusiasm, and the coming of peace brought spontaneous jubilation from New England to Georgia. Benjamin Franklin, then living in London as a colonial agent, viewed the events optimistically and predicted unprecedented growth and prosperity in America. Such expansion, he suggested, would enrich the whole empire, because "the growth of the children tends to increase the growth of the mother." Franklin's filial metaphors, dutiful as they were in 1760, nevertheless concealed a basic problem within the imperial family. The children were growing older and more restive; the parent, stiffer and less flexible. Earlier, Franklin had warned of such dangers. "To weaken the children," he had advised, "is to weaken the whole family." By 1763, as the British patriarchs carved up the spoils of war, it was becoming evident that the colonial children were chafing under the parental restraints.

Despite the chronic instability of provincial politics—the endemic disputes between the governors and the legislatures, the interference of English politicians, the vulnerability of the colonies during wartime—colonial Americans generally believed in a political system based on natural harmony and moral order. That is why political writers such as Franklin relied so heavily upon family metaphors, and that is why most colonials, even as late as 1776, remained loyal to the English crown. Throughout the revolutionary crisis, the most commonly cited justification for political obedience was the Fifth Commandment—*Thou shalt honor thy father and mother*—which, in context, meant one's political parents.

As interest in politics became more visible, however, and destroyed even the illusion of political harmony, a new ideology also emerged to explain the intensity of political conflict. By the mid-eighteenth century, most politically conscious colonials recognized that the expansion of power in England constituted an important threat to the American political order. Yet as loyal Englishmen, they continued to venerate the institutions of British politics. The only satisfactory explanation of conflict, therefore, was that the particular individuals who wielded power in England—not the system itself—might be corrupt. This linking of power and morals revealed the paradoxical vision of the eighteenth-century mind, the blurring of organic politics and modern individualism.

These ideas emerged first in England. They were articulated by a group of political writers, known as Independent Whigs, who had been excluded from the informal arrangements of power then dominating English politics. Seeing themselves as victims of the system,

Independent Whigs bitterly resented the political machinations—the use of patronage, for example—which preserved the position of those in power. Their writings became extremely popular in America and were reprinted in numerous colonial newspapers and periodicals. For provincials, too, remained outside the political citadel and thus appreciated this denunciation of the establishment.

According to the political ideology of the Independent Whigs as well as of provincial politicians, power and liberty stood at opposite poles of the political system. In an ideal world, that polarity balanced naturally; the rich and wellborn enjoyed privileges and responsibilities denied to ordinary folk. But the growth of secular politics had weakened that natural balance, creating a more brittle tension between power and liberty. Most Englishmen still believed that the British Constitution—the peculiar blend of monarchy, House of Lords, and House of Commons—served to institutionalize those political forces and thus prevented the collapse of either pole. Within the English system, liberty and power could coexist in a tenuous balance that allowed maximum liberty to the citizens without degenerating into license and anarchy. That remained a very delicate balance, however, and it easily could be subverted by corrupt politicians.

The Independent Whigs and their American sympathizers emphasized the potential dangers of such a system. Corrupt leaders, they warned, would overthrow the Constitution, subvert the balance of power, and establish a tyranny—unless, that is, the people guarded their rights. This thesis, imbued as it was with conspiracy and distrust, won remarkable popularity among provincial Americans; the instability of provincial politics had prepared them for it. To a people already suspicious of royal governors and the power of the Privy Council, such ideas possessed a special clarity.

The conspiracy theory of politics also offered a solution to the dilemma. Where corrupt politicians exceeded the "natural" limits of power and threatened the constitutional order that protected liberty, the people had the right to rebel. It was the *unnatural* exercise of power that would provoke that awesome decision. "The people know for what end they set up and maintain their governors," declared the New England minister Jonathan Mayhew in 1750—in a sermon preached appropriately on the anniversary of the execution of Charles I!—and the people "are the proper judges [of whether] they execute their trust as they ought to do it;—when their prince exercises an equitable and paternal authority over them;

when from a prince and common father he exalts himself into a tyrant; when from subjects and children he degrades them into a class of slaves, plunders them, makes them his prey and unnaturally sports himself with their lives and fortunes." Good parents, natural parents, did not do such things.

Mayhew's position represented an extreme in colonial thinking, one that few Americans would accept without serious qualification. Yet it was based upon many widely shared assumptions. First, there was the fear of corruption. Though most people believed that the monarch, as God's anointed authority, was innocent of deliberate evil, there were suspicions that the sovereign's ministers—the members of his Privy Council—lusted after power. "The king can do no wrong" was the popular truism, but the king's advisers quite obviously could. Opposition to the royal power therefore focused not on the monarch, but on the ministers who formulated policy in his name. Thus the colonial children would remain loyal to their royal parent, even as they condemned the power of his servants.

Closely related to this idea was the provincial attitude toward English society. For most eighteenth-century Americans, England remained the center of sophisticated culture, the source of enlightenment, learning, and cultural achievement. American visitors stood awed at the magnificence of that country, literally astounded by the architecture, the gardens, the curious inventions, the historical monuments. Yet, like provincials everywhere, they also distrusted the luxury and opulence of the metropolis, believing that the facade of sophistication concealed a pervasive evil and degeneracy. These images helped explain the pattern of English politics. The king's advisers, surrounded by the corruption of the metropolis, had become tainted themselves. By contrast, American society seemed simpler, more innocent, more virtuous.

These cultural values remained amorphously defined, seldom spoken with the clarity of Mayhew's discourse. Large segments of the provincial population simply ignored, or were excluded from, political considerations. Slaves on Patrick Henry's plantation undoubtedly could not understand what the Virginia orator meant when he demanded liberty or death. Nor is it likely that white propertyless workers who labored from "sun to sun" six days a week shared with politically aware colonials the antipathy to English interference. These disenfranchised classes did not shape colonial politics; rather, they responded to decisions already taken by their political leaders. When summoned by these leaders many rallied to the banner of colonial liberty, hoping to acquire some of its benefits for themselves. But many others, already distrustful of the provincial leadership, lagged behind; they did not require an elaborate ideology to understand their best interests.

Thus several dissatisfactions influenced the colonial response to British policy in the years after 1763. The Great War for Empire, instead of resolving the difficulties of imperial administration, accentuated the problems facing Great Britain. The war itself had been very costly, precipitating a rise in taxes. The acquisition of Canada added to that financial burden, and the decision to garrison British troops in America increased still further the cost of colonialism. When English officials contemplated this unhappy situation, they noted that the American provinces had benefited greatly by the war and concluded that the colonists should share in the added taxes. Bolstering this economic consideration was a more important political concern. During the war, the colonists had violated British interests by trading with the enemy. They also had refused to provide adequate supplies and manpower for the English forces. Such resistance reflected the general inefficiency of the colonial administrative system. With the arrival of peace in 1763, British officials determined that it was time to reform. The result was a series of executive orders and legislative enactments designed to reorganize the British Empire.

The first royal order aimed at coordinating British relations with Native Americans. In the Proclamation of 1763, George III prohibited English settlement west of the Appalachian Mountains and ordered British troops to the frontier to prevent violations and to oversee the fur trade. Decisions made in England, however, were not always enforceable in the wilderness.

Alarmed by European invasions of the Ohio Valley, the interior tribes had fought on the French side in hopes of maintaining a balance of power. After the French defeat, the tribes lost this critical advantage. The new English policy further restricted their trading opportunities, forcing them to carry furs to British forts, eliminating the annual gifts of European goods, and prohibiting the trade of alcohol. In these straitened circumstances, the natives became increasingly restive. "Wherefore do you suffer the whites to dwell upon your lands?" asked the Delaware prophet Neolin. "Drive them away; wage war against them."

The message was clear and compelling. In 1763, the Ottawa

chief, Pontiac, led his people against the British and terrorized the white settlements. British reinforcements managed to quell the immediate threat, but it was mainly the absence of the French with their supplies and munitions that doomed the Ottawas' efforts. For colonials, however, the uprising demonstrated the inadequacy of British defense, despite the new policy of standing British troops in America.

English attempts to curtail western expansion proved equally unenforceable. Land speculators and colonial officials blithely ignored the territorial restrictions imposed in London and continued to occupy the Ohio Valley. The natives, bereft of outside support, resisted sporadically; more often, they sold their lands, acquiescing to the colonial invasion.

The failure of England's policy on American western lands revealed the vast distance, political no less than geographical, that separated colonial interests from those of the mother country. Even with the best intentions, the British perspective conflicted with that of provincial Americans on such issues as representation, taxation, and military necessity. These problems were compounded by a system of communications that was not only slow but also unreliable, and by a political climate in England that prevented the formulation of a consistent political course.

Consider the matter of revenue. Burdened by an enormous war debt, the English ministry determined to apportion some of the needed taxes on Englishmen who resided in America. This policy was consistent with the mercantilist view of community, especially because the colonies had benefited by the recent war. In 1764, Parliament passed the Sugar Act, which sought to prohibit illicit trade with other nations and which, unlike the earlier Navigation Acts, sought to raise revenue by enforcing the duties on sugar. The following year, Parliament enacted the Stamp Act. This law required the use of taxed stamps on certain legal documents, newspapers, and other printed matter. Significantly, both measures bypassed the provincial legislatures in levying taxes. Sandwiched between these laws was the Currency Act of 1764, which prohibited the circulation of paper money as legal tender, an enactment designed to protect British interests from having to accept depreciated money in payment for debts. Ironically, it reduced the available currency at the very time Parliament was increasing the tax burden.

From the British perspective, such legislation was eminently fair; but Americans saw things differently. Following the departure of

the French from Canada, a diplomatic act that freed the colonists
from their traditional dependence upon the British military, Americans found themselves in a severe postwar depression caused by the
overstocking of goods and the abrupt loss of sales to war con-
tractors. The decline of trade affected not only the merchants, but
also the dock workers, sailors, and day laborers they employed.
Meanwhile, southern tobacco planters, who had begun to consume
English commodities at an inflationary rate after 1750, found their
resources curtailed by British creditors. Heavily indebted, they faced
a bleak economic future. It was at this difficult juncture that colonial Americans learned of the new imperial measures.

The reaction to the legislation in the colonies unleashed a century
of political frustration and revealed an abiding fear of powerlessness. One New York merchant warned that the Currency Act would
destroy "the intercourse between the mother and her offspring."
"Why should they punish the colonies indiscriminately?" he asked
in confusion. "Parents seldom do, good ones at least, with their
children." Such unnatural behavior clearly violated normal family
relations and indicated a moral deficiency within the British government.

Convinced that the king's ministers had hatched a sordid conspiracy to destroy American liberty, colonials organized an elaborate protest against the laws. Petitions flooded to Parliament
demanding a repeal of the obnoxious legislation. Merchants boycotted English goods, hoping to use economic pressure to force a
redress of grievances. Urban workers, distressed by the disruption of
business and long resentful of such royal policies as impressment,
organized secret groups known as the Sons of Liberty—a significant
filial designation—to harass uncooperative officials and prevent the
enforcement of the new legislation. Occasionally, their activities
provoked mob violence, as when an irate crowd stormed the house
of Massachusetts Governor Thomas Hutchinson, leaving it a shambles. Such protests, destructive though they appeared, possessed an
important inner logic. They were not random mobs of drunken
workers, as alleged by royal officials. Rather, they were politically
alert groups who selected their victims with care and, in their eyes,
with justice. Nor were extralegal activities confined to the lower
classes. In 1765, nine colonial legislatures sent delegates to a Stamp
Act Congress in New York City where the leading lawyers of the
colonies drafted a "Declaration of Rights and Grievances" that
denied the legitimacy of the Parliamentary legislation.

These protests, though often motivated by suspicion, fear, and interest, also possessed an important philosophical basis that was widely articulated and loudly defended. The question focused upon the nature of the British Constitution and locus of sovereignty. Parliamentary leaders, long accustomed to conflict over the royal prerogative, insisted that sovereignty belonged solely to the English legislature, an opinion which justified imperial legislation that affected the colonies. That opinion was not shared by American colonists, who traditionally paid taxes levied by the provincial legislatures, bodies in which they enjoyed direct representation. Even the Navigation Acts, which taxed certain types of trade, served primarily to regulate commerce, not to raise revenue. Thus the passage of the new imperial legislation evoked bitter cries of taxation without representation.

British politicians argued that the colonists indeed enjoyed the full rights of Englishmen, including the right to legislative representation. They observed that Parliament, as the representative body of all the estates of the realm, already represented American interests. This notion of "virtual representation," truly a legacy of the medieval world-view, made no sense to American protestors. "The people of these colonies are not, and from their local circumstances cannot be, represented in the House of Commons in Great Britain," responded the Stamp Act Congress. This constitutional impasse, which was essentially a clash between the old organic vision of politics and a modern sense of interest, dominated all subsequent debate.

How the issue ultimately would be resolved was perceived with remarkable clarity by a lawyer from Annapolis, Maryland, named Daniel Dulany: "If the claims of the mother country and the colonies should seem on such occasion to interfere, and the point of right to be doubtful," he wrote in 1765, "it is easy to guess that the determination will be on the side of power, and the inferior will be constrained to submit." William Pitt, England's savior during the Seven Years' War, disagreed. Speaking in Parliament for the repeal of the Stamp Act, he admitted that "the force of this country can crush America to atoms. . . . But on this ground, on the Stamp Act, when so many here will think [it] a crying injustice . . . your success would be hazardous. America, if she fell, would fall like a strong man."

Such arguments, together with the economic coercion of the boycott and the persuasion of colonial agents, eventually prevailed. In

1766 Parliament repealed the Stamp Act, conceding the immediate issue, but at the same time announced in the Declaratory Act that it retained the constitutional principle of legislating for the empire. Americans generally ignored this latter enactment and celebrated "the joyful tidings." Yet their satisfaction contained a perverse irony. For the ideology of conspiracy had convinced them that corrupt politicians had plotted the destruction of American liberty. The repeal of the Stamp Act merely confirmed that fear, for Parliament certainly would not have rescinded a good law. "We always have had enemies, and we may always expect them," warned a Thanksgiving Day preacher. "We may depend upon it that they will lay new schemes, and disappointment may but whet their rage."

Americans, therefore, possessed a full ideological defense against subsequent imperial policy. In 1767 Parliament enacted the Townshend Acts, which, among other things, established new customs duties, created a new board to enforce the Navigation Acts in Vice-Admiralty Courts (which did not require jury trials), allowed the customs revenue to pay the salaries of colonial officials and thus freed them from legislative appropriations, and suspended the New York Assembly for refusing to comply with an earlier Quartering Act. In each of these provisions, Parliament reasserted its claim to sovereignty and ignored colonial protests over the right of representation.

Once again, Americans saw the work of conspiring politicians and responded with alacrity. In response to the Townshend Acts, John Dickinson published an influential tract, *Letters from a Farmer in Pennsylvania,* which argued against Parliament's right to tax the colonists even in matters of trade. Colonial merchants, hoping to pressure their English creditors, again instituted nonimportation agreements. And the Massachusetts House of Representatives, under the leadership of the resourceful Sam Adams, issued a "Circular Letter" urging all colonials to join the protest. These were firm, even strident decisions. But the statements were also carefully guarded in language and respectful in tone. "This House cannot conclude, without expressing their firm confidence in the King our common head and father," declared the Massachusetts legislature.

While English officials contemplated their next step, colonial resisters took matters into their own hands. American merchants continued to violate the Navigation Acts despite the aggressive tactics of the new customs commissioners. Then in 1768, one of John Hancock's ships—appropriately named the *Liberty*—was confis-

cated for smuggling. News of the event aroused the Boston populace and that night a mob attacked the commissioners and destroyed
public property. Outraged by the violence, British officials dis-
patched several regiments to Massachusetts. These redcoats not only
symbolized the potential of English tyranny, but also annoyed
members of the working classes who competed for odd jobs with the
otherwise idle soldiers. Tension remained taut for months, exploding periodically in minor brawls. But on the evening of March 5,
1770, the insults were particularly vicious, and the crowd especially
angry. Unnerved, British troops fired on the agitated crowd, killing
five civilians. The atrocity, known ever after in America as the
Boston Massacre, confirmed the colonists' worst fears about English
authority and the danger to American liberty.

The outburst ironically coincided with a British decision, which
had not yet reached the colonies, to repeal the offensive legislation.
England, of course, never relinquished the principle of Parliament's
sovereignty, and to make that point clear, retained a small tax on
tea. But Americans, convinced of their moral superiority over the
corrupt Europeans, concentrated more on the good news, heralded
by repeal of the Townshend Acts, and celebrated the return of
prosperity. But it was a tenuous peace at best, interrupted by political squabbles within the legislatures and by overt conflicts between
colonial smugglers and royal customs officials.

This calm, fragile though it was, might have persisted indefinitely
had politicians on both sides of the Atlantic focused on immediate
problems rather than on the ideological principles they espoused.
But amid the general atmosphere of suspicion, the issues came to a
head again when, in 1773, the English government approved the
Tea Act, a measure designed to protect the East India Company
from imminent bankruptcy. In economic terms, the legislation
benefited the colonies by lowering the price of tea. But the political
consequences were more dangerous. Besides assuming England's
right to tax the colonists, the law also created a trade monopoly that
American merchants feared might eventually be extended to other
commodities. These were theoretical matters, to be sure; but in an
age of strenuous political activity, theory was the essence of the
question. While intellectuals criticized the laws, crowds in every
port tried to prevent the unloading of the tea. In Boston, a group of
colonists, thinly disguised as Mohawks, dropped the chests into the
harbor.

News of this event outraged English opinion. Not only had the colonists defied legal authority, they also had destroyed private property. Parliamentary retribution was prompt. In a series of Coercive Acts (known in America as the Intolerable Acts) passed in 1774, Parliament closed the port of Boston pending payment for the tea; altered the government of Massachusetts by, among other things, restricting town meetings; authorized the transfer of legal cases to other colonies; and reinstituted a Quartering Act to support British troops in the colonies. To Americans, this legislation constituted a fundamental violation of the British Constitution. If Parliament could, by a mere majority, alter the structure of government, American liberty was indeed imperiled. Nor could any colony be more secure than Massachusetts. Those who believed in conspiracy politics had no trouble identifying the threat and condemned the corrupt politicians. But it was a conservative who best articulated colonial fears when he asked, with a trace of nostalgia, "if old England is not superannuated and become a child again."

Amid such despair, colonial leaders summoned a conference to discuss mutual problems, and in September 1774, delegates from every colony except Georgia convened in Philadelphia. The sessions of this First Continental Congress reflected the tensions within the wider society. Moderate leaders, alarmed by the recent crisis yet fearful of a separation from the mother country, desired to protect American interests without destroying the British Constitution and rallied to a compromise Plan of Union proposed by Joseph Galloway of Pennsylvania. The plan, based on a sharing of sovereignty between Parliament and an intercolonial council elected by the provincial legislatures, represented an important departure from earlier colonial thinking. Yet even this proposal, innovative as it was, failed to satisfy the more radical delegates, who defeated the measure by a single vote. Instead the Congress took a more militant position, declaring the Coercive Acts null and void, and addressed a "Declaration of Rights and Grievances" to the king. In this missive, they promised loyalty to the crown, but rejected Parliament's legislative supremacy. Then, in an attempt to strengthen their demands, Congress adopted the "Continental Association," which prohibited the importation and consumption of British goods. Unlike the earlier economic boycotts, compliance with the association would not be voluntary, for the Congress also recommended that "committees of safety" in each province enforce the program.

These extralegal activities hastened the polarization of political opinion in America and in England. As the Sons of Liberty harassed uncooperative citizens, popular pressure occasionally spilled over to produce mob violence. Such tactics, though economically effective, alarmed conservative members of the community. In England, parliamentary leaders looked askance at the colonists' intransigence. William Pitt and Edmund Burke, both friends of the American cause, tried to placate their colleagues, but amid rising passion and ideological commitment, it was too late. Parliament responded to the Continental Congress by ordering additional troops to Boston and restricting New England's trade. Meanwhile, the people of Massachusetts prepared for war. When British regulars marched toward Concord in April 1775 to seize a stockpile of weapons and ammunition, they were met by colonial minutemen. A brief skirmish at Lexington Green climaxed months of uncertainty and began to force political decisions that most people had preferred to avoid.

In May 1775, while other colonies were still absorbing the shocking news from Massachusetts, a Second Continental Congress opened session in Philadelphia. More radical in composition than its predecessor, the Congress nevertheless hoped to reconcile differences with the mother country. In an "Olive Branch Petition" addressed to George III, the delegates reaffirmed their loyalty to the crown and prayed for a cessation of hostilities. Yet they realized too the urgency of the situation. "We are reduced to the alternative of choosing an unconditional submission to the tyranny of irritated ministers," they explained solemnly, "or resistance by force." And they prudently appointed the Virginian George Washington to head the Continental Army in the besieged city of Boston. In June 1775, colonial soldiers and British regulars had clashed again, this time in bloody battles at Breed's Hill and Bunker Hill.

These encounters, full with human sacrifice, further polarized political passions. Once begun, the process became self-generating, almost inexorable. And then the winter of 1776 brought harsher news. Parliament, still hoping to assert its power, ordered all colonial ports closed, an act that imperiled the interests of all American inhabitants, regardless of their political persuasions. As word of this reached the colonies, Americans also learned that George III, disgusted by the apparent anarchy, had hired Hessian mercenaries to suppress the rebellion. The specter of foreign soldiers hunting English subjects terrorized the colonists, and many again thought they saw the hand of conspiracy threatening American liberty. But it was a recent English immigrant, the son of a Quaker corset-maker, who

dramatically perceived the crisis at hand. In a brief pamphlet entitled
Common Sense, Thomas Paine launched a devastating critique, not
simply of Parliament and king, but of the institution of monarchy
itself. It was not a coterie of wicked ministers who sought to destroy
America, he declared with stunning logic, but the "Royal Brute"
himself, George III. In six months, colonial readers had consumed
150,000 copies of the tract, a striking testament to the steady radi-
calization of American politics.

With the hardening of political positions, the earlier equivoca-
tions no longer sufficed. Some conservative citizens, even those who
had criticized imperial policy, now repudiated the revolution and
became outspoken supporters of the British Empire. Some, for personal and psychological reasons, discovered that they could not
choose at all. William Samuel Johnson, once a delegate to the
Stamp Act Congress, identified the source of the dilemma when he
admitted the difficulty of separating from "the parent state." The
radicals, however, suffered no such qualms. In the spring of 1776,
the Congress recommended that each colony overthrow the royal
authority and create new state governments based on republican
principles. And in June, as the crisis passed all previous bounds,
Richard Henry Lee, a delegate from Virginia, introduced a resolution declaring America independent from the British Empire. Hoping to generate large-scale support for the proposal, the Congress
appointed a committee headed by Thomas Jefferson to draft a co-
herent explanation of that momentous decision. On July 4, 1776,
two days after approving Lee's resolution, Congress adopted the
Declaration of Independence.

When other colonials affirmed their allegiance to the mother
country and their political fathers, Jefferson offered a stinging re-
buke to the king's parental authority. His was an indictment not of
Parliament and the wicked advisers, but of the king himself. "The
history of the present King of Great Britain," exclaimed the Declaration, "is a history of repeated injuries and usurpations, all having
in direct object the establishment of an absolute Tyranny over these
States."

But the Declaration of Independence did not simply rehash traditional politics. In justifying separation from England, Jefferson appealed to "self-evident" truths and the "unalienable rights" of "all
men." These were revolutionary premises. The principles of revolution, Jefferson explained, did not lurk in the intricate mysteries of
constitutional law; they were not obscure or scholarly. Rather, they

were intuitive, within the capacity of most people, and they legiti-
mated bold acts in defense of "life, liberty and the pursuit of happiness." Such "rights," of course, did not exist in American society in
1776. Abigail Adams, the wife of one of the signers of the Declaration, stated this other truth most eloquently in a letter to her husband. "I cannot say, that I think you are very generous to the
ladies," she complained with startling perception, "for, whilst you
are proclaiming peace and goodwill to men, emancipating all
nations, you insist upon retaining an absolute power over your
wives." Less articulate Americans, denied the educational advantages of Abigail Adams, might have had much more to add.

Jefferson's statement never claimed to be descriptive of social
conditions in America. Rather, he asserted the fundamental principles that justified political revolution. Governments, he declared,
derive their power "from the consent of the governed." And when
government threatens the basic rights of the people, "it is the right
of the people to alter or to abolish it." In 1776, those rights vali-
dated the destruction of monarchy and the institution of republican
forms of government. But in Jefferson's words they possessed a
universality that "in the course of human events" justified other
revolutions throughout the world. That potential power, alarming
though it may have been to the signers of the Declaration, was the
colonists' legacy to the world.

And so on July 4, 1776, it was done. The "Thirteen United States
of America" declared their independence from Great Britain. Now
they had to demonstrate the viability of their premises and the
power of their convictions. It would not be a simple matter. "And
for the support of this Declaration, with a firm reliance on the
protection of Divine Providence," Jefferson concluded, "we mutually pledge to each other our Lives, our Fortunes, and our sacred
Honor."

Ten years later, while serving as the ambassador to France, Jefferson looked back to the Spirit of '76. "If our country, when pressed
with wrongs at the point of the bayonet, had been governed by its
heads instead of its hearts," he asked, "where should we have been
now? hanging on a gallows as high as Haman's. You began to
calculate and to compare wealth and numbers: we threw up a few
pulsations of our warmest blood: we supplied enthusiasm against
wealth and numbers: we put our existence to the hazard, when the
hazard seemed against us, and we saved our country." Dramatic as

it sounded, Jefferson's reminiscence was only slightly exaggerated.

In 1776, the colonial position indeed seemed precarious. Militarily overpowered, economically underfunded, politically divided, diplomatically isolated, the colonies fought the mightiest nation in Europe. Royal officials remained thoroughly optimistic about an easy victory. Yet the British confronted numerous obstacles to success. Fighting three thousand miles from the home islands, Great Britain had to transport troops, supplies, and, most important, directives and reports. In contrast, colonial soldiers could be easily activated and conveniently dispersed. In addition to these tactical advantages, colonials benefited by their ideological resolution, what Jefferson called the "pulsations of our warmest blood." Certain of their objectives, American revolutionaries knew what they risked, while English officials vacillated between war and peace negotiations.

If the radicals acted with revolutionary zeal, many of the colonists, perhaps even a majority, remained politically neutral or friendly to the king. Like rural folk in other ages, American farmers did not always share the political passions of their leaders and preferred to live in peace. Thus many citizens simply sat out the war. Yet inactivity was not always possible, given the presence of British armies and colonial militia, and the maltreatment of the civilian population by British troops often served to politicize otherwise unaligned people.

Despite such pressure, many colonials—approximately 20 percent of the total population—openly sided with the crown. Revolutionary leaders called them "Tories" to emphasize their aristocratic origins and make the war for independence seem more like a popular uprising. But Loyalism generally involved not so much class interests as broader social configurations. Thus people belonging to minorities often remained loyal to Great Britain. In New England, they were Anglicans, victims of Congregationalist discrimination; in New York and Pennsylvania, they were ethnic minorities threatened by the encroachments of English Protestant culture. Political affiliation also reflected larger tensions within the political structure. In New York, tenant farmers opposed the Revolution because their landlords supported it. Similarly, in North Carolina, western farmers who had been alienated by the provincial establishment moved into a Loyalist position to protest the power of the entrenched elite. And in the anomalous situation where slaveowners fought for "liberty," many black slaves, when given the opportunity, supported the British.

These patterns may explain why American supporters of the Revolution proved so hostile to their political foes and treated them so harshly. Loyalists were tarred and feathered, ridden on rails, flogged, even executed. The term "lynch law" probably originated from the proceedings of one Charles Lynch, a justice of the peace in Virginia, who achieved a certain notoriety for his treatment of Tories.

In addition to the brutal treatment they received, Tories had their property snatched from them by the newly formed revolutionary governments. Many Tories were forced to seek shelter behind British lines. These actions reflected not only a tradition of social antagonism but also a strong desire among revolutionaries to achieve a united front. By the war's end, nearly one hundred thousand colonial inhabitants had gone into exile in Canada and England. Their banishment brought profound psychological alienation —"a dismal gloom," reported one unhappy exile from London.

One month after the adoption of the Declaration, General William Howe landed with twenty thousand soldiers on Long Island. Washington waited with the Continental Army at Brooklyn Heights, hoping to stall the British advance. But when the redcoats opened fire, the colonial militia broke ranks and began a frantic retreat. Washington managed to ferry his troops to Manhattan, but Howe pursued him into the city, forcing the Americans to retreat to New Jersey. Several times, Howe narrowly missed capturing the American army, but as winter set in, he returned to New York City, where he established his headquarters. Meanwhile, on Christmas Day, the Americans surprised a Hessian force at Trenton by crossing the Delaware River at night. The effort, celebrated by revolutionaries everywhere, was the only good news of the war. Throughout this first campaign, the Continental Army had displayed an alarming lack of unity and skill. But Washington inadvertently discovered the key to military success. He could trade territory falling back from position to position, almost indefinitely—as long as he had an army to move.

The British still believed that the colonial rebellion centered in New England and that the isolation of those colonies would bring peace everywhere else. In the spring of 1777, therefore, they

launched a three-pronged attack in New York. General Burgoyne
would march from Canada to Albany, while Howe would move
northward from New York City and General St. Leger would lead a
force from Lake Ontario toward the same vicinity. The three armies
were supposed to converge, rally the Loyalists, and deliver a final
blow to American hopes. On paper, a brilliant plan; but in the
wilderness, surrounded by a hostile population, it proved a colossal
error. Burgoyne began marching southward and captured Fort Ti-
conderoga. But St. Leger encountered a force led by Nicholas
Herkimer and retreated to Lake Ontario. Meanwhile, Howe, for
some mysterious reason, ignored the master plan and moved southward from New York City, defeated Washington at Brandywine, and
invaded Philadelphia just after the members of the Congress had fled
the city. Henry Clinton commanded a residual force in New York
City and moved toward Albany; but after a brief trek, he too
returned to his base. This decision left Burgoyne floundering in
upstate New York, unable to find the expected Loyalists and severely harassed by local militia. Desperate for an escape, Burgoyne
attacked at Saratoga, but was beaten back. He tried again, unsuccessfully. At last, on October 17, 1777, Burgoyne surrendered to
Horatio Gates. "The fortune of war," he declared, "has made me
your prisoner." To which Gates replied, "I shall always be ready to
testify that it has not been through any fault of your excellency."

Such niceties aside, the American victory at Saratoga had immense political importance. In France, news of the battle transformed a secretly friendly nation into an open ally. Louis XVI, still
angry at France's loss of Canada, promptly recognized the new
republic, while his foreign minister Vergennes met with the American ambassador, Benjamin Franklin, to negotiate an alliance. Word
of those conversations soon reached England, producing fears of
active French intervention. But Parliament remained as dilatory as
ever, taking several months to establish a peace commission. Eventually the British agreed to all American demands—except independence. But by then it was too late. In 1778, France had signed a
formal treaty of alliance with the new nation, a pact in which both
parties agreed to fight until England recognized American
independence.

After 1778, the main theater of war shifted to the southern
colonies, where the British still anticipated a strong Loyalist following. In 1780, the redcoats invaded Charleston, South Carolina, and
captured five thousand American soldiers, and Lord Cornwallis won

a smashing victory at Camden. But Americans, too, had their victories. An important battle was won at King's Mountain and another at Cowpens. Even the British victory at Guilford Court House in 1781 brought them heavy casualties, forcing Cornwallis to retreat to safety in Wilmington, North Carolina. Washington, meanwhile, chafed in New York, keeping a cautious eye on Clinton's movements. In midsummer of 1781, the American general learned that Cornwallis had established a position at Yorktown on a narrow peninsula that extended into the Chesapeake Bay. Washington feinted an attack on New York to keep Clinton bottled up and then raced his army to Virginia. Meanwhile, the French Admiral De Grasse had sailed from the Caribbean into the Chesapeake, sealing Cornwallis from outside assistance. Surrounded and outnumbered, Cornwallis surrendered on October 19, 1781, and seven thousand redcoats relinquished their guns to the popular tune "The World Turned Upside Down." So ended the military conflict.

It took another two years to consummate the peace negotiations, but on September 3, 1783, England accepted the Treaty of Paris, formally ending the war. The most important provision of the document was George III's recognition of American independence. Other clauses established territorial boundaries, protected American fishing rights in Canadian waters, guaranteed navigation of the Mississippi River, promised the restoration of all prewar debts, and provided that the Congress would recommend the restoration of Loyalist property confiscated during the war. The firmness of the American diplomats—Benjamin Franklin, John Jay, and John Adams—thus won Americans an almost total victory. On November 25, 1783, the last British troops sailed from New York City, and the date—called by New Yorkers "Evacuation Day"—became an annual holiday celebrated with patriotic festivity for the next half-century.

If the Treaty of Paris fulfilled the demands of the Declaration of Independence, the practical political results had emerged much earlier and with less formality. In May 1776, the Congress had urged the separate states to replace the British political system with governments based on republican principles. The disruption of the British Empire made that request academic, and each state confronted the question of political forms within the context of its own political tradition. In Pennsylvania, where radicals had seized power quickly, the new government possessed a unicameral legislature and

eliminated the office of governor entirely. The Massachusetts constitution was more conservative, creating a bicameral system and an
executive office with limited authority; yet even there, the draft
constitution was submitted to the people for approval.

Such variations, significant as they were in each state, should not
obscure an essential unity that dominated American political thinking. Until 1776, revolutionary Americans had defended the British
Constitution as the bulwark of liberty. It was the king's ministers,
they said, and later the king himself, who had perverted that delicate system. Fundamental to American thought, therefore, was the
idea of separating power within the government, reducing executive
authority, and making power directly responsible to the people.
These ideas influenced the formation of the state governments in the
period after 1776. The new state constitutions provided for legislative powers vested in bicameral legislatures (except in Pennsylvania) in which the lower houses theoretically represented the
interests of the "people" and the upper houses, or senates, protected
the interests of property. Such an arrangement endeavored to balance the power of all classes. But there was one paradoxical outcome. By reducing the power of the executive branch, the state
constitutions increased the power of the legislatures, allowing them
executive and judicial functions previously held by the colonial
governors. To protect the people from legislative tyranny, therefore,
most states also adopted a bill of rights or inserted appropriate
clauses directly into their state constitutions to guarantee civil
liberty.

The importance of the legislatures made questions of political
representation more pressing than ever before. In organizing republican governments, American politicians assumed that the legislatures represented specific constituencies and spoke for that
amorphous group they called "the people." They agreed, nevertheless, that the power of the people could easily degenerate into
anarchy and destroy the governmental balance. To reduce the likelihood of mob rule, the state constitutions restricted political participation to male property owners and often established still higher
property qualifications for officeholding. Despite occasional demands for wider democracy, the older habits of elitist politics prevailed. Consequently political representation remained with the
more affluent citizens even though there is some evidence that
members of state senates were slightly less wealthy than the councilors of the colonial period.

The conservative nature of these changes tells much about the American Revolution. Despite the revolutionary implications of the Declaration of Independence—the demands for government by consent of the governed and the assumptions about political equality—power generally remained in the hands of moderate leaders who were concerned as much with the interests of property as with the cause of liberty. Thus the American Revolution did not lead to a drastic redistribution of property. When the state governments confiscated the Loyalists' estates, they sold the property to investors to help finance the war. Similarly, another form of property—the ownership of slaves—remained inviolate despite the rhetoric of Jefferson's Declaration. Indeed, one of the allegations raised against George III was that he "excited domestic insurrections amongst us"—an oblique reference to the offer made by the royal governor of Virginia to grant freedom to any slave who deserted his master.

This institutional conservativism contrasted markedly with the intellectual revolution that underlay the Spirit of '76. The defense of political liberty soon led many Americans to question the validity of the "peculiar institution." Several northern states made provisions for the gradual emancipation of slaves, and abolitionist societies, usually inspired by Quaker idealists, emerged throughout the North. Such programs were conservatively implemented, allowing black slavery to persist well into the nineteenth century. And the pervasive racial hostility and discrimination largely went unchallenged. Yet the doctrine of natural rights provided the ideological underpinnings for further protest and additional reforms. Some slaveowners, distraught at their own paradoxical stances, simply liberated their slaves voluntarily.

In placing their faith in the state constitutions, Americans testified to their abiding distrust of centralized authority. Having successfully challenged the claims of the British Empire, they were not about to accept some other distant power. With visions of Parliament and George III prominent in their minds, they turned to the question of intercolonial union. The result was the Articles of Confederation, first adopted by the Congress in 1777, but not ratified by the states until 1781. Usually seen as a dismal failure, the Articles of Confederation revealed the political prejudices and political interests of the American people in 1776. Since the state governments remained pre-eminent, the Articles limited the power of the national government. The Congress could declare war, negotiate treaties, establish a post office, and standardize weights and measures; but it could not tax the citizens, nor could it regulate commerce—both important powers retained by the states. Within the Congress, each state possessed one vote, and nine states had to agree to all legislation; amendments required unanimous votes. Such legislative caution also reflected the fear of usurpation, for the Articles made no provision for an executive or judicial branch. It was the Congress, burdened by the bureaucratization of the Revolution, which eventually established executive committees to handle administrative matters.

The major questions facing the new government were financing the War for Independence and negotiating a treaty of peace with Great Britain. To solve the first problem, the Congress proposed an "impost" tariff, but the legislature of Rhode Island, concerned with protecting local interests, rejected the measure; a second bill stalled in the New York assembly. The new nation therefore relied primarily upon requisitions from the states (which, in this age of state supremacy, were not always forthcoming) and from foreign loans. Negotiations with Great Britain tediously continued, and in an ironic way, ultimately solved the financial problem. By acquiring the Northwest Territory in 1783, the new nation obtained a gold mine of potential resources: the vast tracts of land, still occupied by the native tribes, could be sold to American investors.

Already, western settlers and eastern land speculators had moved into the territory. Congress had approved the Land Ordinance of 1785, which divided the lands into townships and square-mile sections to be sold at public auction. Though orderly and open, the system still created parcels of land too large to be purchased by ordinary citizens, thus assuring that this profitable property would fall into the hands of affluent investors. Other congressional policies proved more liberal. The Northwest Ordinance of 1784, drafted by Thomas Jefferson, established the principle that any states formed in the western territories would enter the union on an equal basis with the original thirteen. Three years later, a second ordinance elaborated a systematic program for the admission of the states carved out of the Territory. True to the principles of republicanism, the plan incorporated popular representation and a bill of rights guaranteeing civil liberties. In an unprecedented step, the law of 1787 prohibited slavery from the region. Thus the revolutionary generation reaffirmed its commitment to the Declaration of Independence, in theory if not in practice.

Foreign interest in America did not end with the Treaty of Paris. Congress was mindful of the diplomatic developments that took place as it dealt with new western territory. Great Britain refused to relinquish its trading posts near the Great Lakes and ignored ambassador John Adams' offers to negotiate. More serious was Spain's decision to close the Mississippi River to American commerce, an act that not only jeopardized western farmers, but also undermined the economic plans of southern expansionists. When John Jay negotiated a treaty with Spain in 1786 that traded American commercial rights in the West Indies in exchange for the loss of navigation on the Mississippi, Congress split violently along sectional lines. Southern congressmen, enraged by Jay's willingness to disregard their interests, questioned the viability of the existing confederation. It was these congressmen, anxious about their vision of western expansion, who urgently summoned a constitutional convention to revise the Articles of Confederation.

Other political nationalists, most notably Robert Morris and Alexander Hamilton, also had advocated the creation of a strong national government. As allies of the southern coalition, people like Hamilton proved extremely influential in rallying popular support. Their success reflected the changing political climate of the 1780s.

Throughout the revolutionary period, problems of power and politics usually crystallized in the states. Since few people—mostly merchants and army officers—had any interstate interests, Americans generally looked to the state governments to enact necessary laws. But in many states, people began to question the wisdom and efficacy of the legislatures. In Massachusetts, western farmers led by Daniel Shays had closed the judicial courts to prevent the collection of debts. The state militia acted to suppress the uprising, but the event traumatized conservatives everywhere, evoking specters of anarchy and disorder. In other states, people complained about the inadequacy of public finance, the proliferation of inflation, and the burden of taxation.

These local concerns troubled people across all social and economic classes, heightening a sense of political impotence and feelings of political instability. As citizens grew disillusioned with the state legislatures, they began to consider reform of the national confederation as a step toward alleviating their grievances. It was from this local perspective that people rallied to the outspoken nationalists when they proposed a conference in Philadelphia in 1787 "to render the constitution of the federal government adequate to the exigencies of the Union." That convention, full of consequences unimagined by its sponsors, climaxed a century and a half of political experience and was the culmination of a generation of revolutionary protest.

"From the infancy of creation"

★ ★ ★ ★ ★ ★ ★ ★ ★ ★ ★ ★ ★ ★ ★ ★ ★ ★ ★

5

The Constitution and American Identity

Cultural nationalism after 1776

Constitution making: the Philadelphia convention, Federalists vs. Antifederalists, ratification, and political consensus

The emergence of national identity

Thomas Jefferson's legacy to America

The Declaration of Independence provided the ideological basis of the new American republic. But neither separation from the British Empire nor the subsequent War for Independence could easily transform the cultural identity of the people. Thirteen colonies with thirteen different histories and, in 1776, thirteen different futures found themselves inextricably woven in a war of liberation. Yet it was not a war of *national* liberation, as Benjamin Franklin well understood when he warned, with more than a trace of anguish, that "we must hang together, or assuredly we shall all hang separately."

Lacking a unified culture, American patriots worked to create one in the years after 1776. "Every engine should be employed to render the people of this country national," proclaimed the lexicographer Noah Webster; "and to inspire them with the pride of national character." That was a formidable task. For though "they may boast of Independence, and the freedom of their government," he observed, "yet their opinions are not sufficiently independent; an astonishing respect for the arts and literature of their parent country, and a blind imitation of its manners, are still prevalent among the Americans." Webster therefore proposed a new orthography—a "national language," an "AMERICAN TONGUE"—to strengthen the "band of national union." Such schemes, self-conscious as they were futile, revealed basic tensions at the core of the American identity.

Prior to independence, the colonies had shared one unifying theme—the culture of provincialism. Merchants in Boston, tobacco planters on the Chesapeake, and farmers in Georgia had acknowledged the intellectual pre-eminence of the English metropolis and had advocated "a blind imitation of its manners." The provincial outlook also contained an internal dialectic that proclaimed the positive advantages of nonmetropolitan, nonurban, unsophisticated culture. This perspective emphasized the blessings of simplicity, frugality, and authenticity. The virtues of plainness thus distinguished Americans from the inhabitants of Europe.

These cultural images were politically important. For if, as Jefferson announced, government derived its just powers from the consent of the governed, then the character of the citizens would

127

determine the quality of their political institutions. The revolutionary generation's optimism about the American people thus explains their dedication to a republican form of government. "I think our governments will remain virtuous for many centuries," declared Jefferson in 1787, "as long as they are chiefly agricultural; and this will be as long as there shall be vacant lands in any part of America. When they get piled upon one another in large cities, as in Europe," he warned, "they will become corrupt as in Europe."

This optimistic spirit was no less important than the frustrations of Confederate politics in influencing the delegates who journeyed to Philadelphia in the spring of 1787 "to form a more perfect Union." Jefferson, surveying the scene from his ambassadorship in France, considered them the most talented politicians in the nation—"an assembly of demigods," he exclaimed—and most Americans, even their opponents, would have agreed. From Virginia came George Washington and James Madison, from New York Alexander Hamilton, from Pennsylvania Benjamin Franklin and Robert Morris; in sum, fifty-five men averaging about forty-two years of age, most of them well born and well connected, all of them the "first characters" of the American states.

They carried with them a sophisticated political ideology and a keen understanding of American society. They determined to create a republican form of government, a political system capable of protecting the interests of property without endangering the "liberty" of the citizens. Political leaders believed, however, that republican governments were extremely fragile entities, vulnerable both to the machinations of enterprising tyrants and to the anarchic demands of the common people. It was necessary, therefore, to create a system that would balance the power of all groups. Such a government would still be susceptible to the vagaries of popular politics and public opinion, what conservatives considered the rule of the mob. But those fears were eased somewhat by the optimistic attitude toward American society. A virtuous people, it was commonly believed, could be trusted to select wise and good leaders. Only then could a republican government actually survive.

This ideological consensus, basic as it was to the framing of the Constitution, could not conceal certain fundamental cleavages among the delegates about the distribution of power. As representatives of their states, the members of the Constitutional Convention attempted to protect their constituencies on such crucial matters as

representation and taxation, liberty and property. The delegates
from the larger states preferred a system of representation based on
population and advocated a strong legislature directly responsible to
the citizens. Representatives from the smaller states desired a legislative system based on the equality of states regardless of population
or wealth. Their position hinged on the assumption that local sovereignty should not be subsumed by a national government with direct
power over the people. Despite strenuous arguments, neither side
could fully convince the other, and out of this deadlock came the
Great Compromise. Accordingly, legislative power was divided into
two houses, one—the House of Representatives—based on population, the other—the Senate—representing the states.

Closely related to the debate about legislative representation—indeed, for some delegates the essence of the issue—was the status of
slaves within the political system. Did black slaves, as human beings, deserve political representation, or did they exist merely as
property? Under the Articles of Confederation, when the Congress
discussed the possibility of levying a head tax, the delegates from
the northern states insisted that slaves should be counted as full
human beings. But the southern representatives, loyal to their investments, insisted that slaves were merely chattel; they proposed
that five slaves be counted as three whites for purposes of taxation.
In 1787, however, when the issue focused on representation, these
positions reversed. Now the southern delegates demanded equal representation for slaves, and northern spokesmen asked ingenuously
whether they might have representation for their livestock. The
question involved political power rather than ideology, and prag-
matically, it was resolved by compromise. In the Three-Fifths Compromise, therefore, five slaves equaled three free persons for
purposes of legislative representation and taxation.

Other provisions of the Constitution prevented congressional
interference in the slave trade before 1808—a convenient future
date that perpetuated the foreign slave trade. The delegates also
provided for the return of fugitive slaves in language sufficiently
vague to create serious problems for free blacks kidnapped by un-
scrupulous profiteers. As for Native Americans, they were simply
excluded from the body politic and placed in the category of "foreign nations." Meanwhile, the electoral process remained under the
scrutiny of the state legislatures, which preserved the existing
suffrage limitations. In short, the Constitution institutionalized the
political power of the white male establishment.

Their work completed, the delegates in approval signed the document (those in opposition had prudently departed from Philadelphia earlier) and transmitted it to the states for ratification. It was Benjamin Franklin, then in his eighties, who captured the sanguine temper of the final proceedings. Glancing at the president's chair, on which a rising sun had been painted, he remarked that "painters had found it difficult to distinguish in their art a rising from a setting sun." Throughout the convention, he continued, "I have . . . looked at that behind the president without being able to tell whether it was rising or setting." Now, in September, with the heat of the summer passed and the fires of debate quenched, he was more certain. "I have the happiness to know," he declared with a wink, "that it is a rising and *not* a setting sun."

Still, the new Constitution required the approval of the American public, a people suspicious of government at a distance and distrustful of politicians and power. Many citizens were satisfied with the Articles of Confederation and believed in the value of state sovereignty. Fearful that political representatives might ignore the interests of their constituents, they wished to keep government close to home. This principle appealed to people with local concerns—small farmers, state politicians, and those who believed that republican governments could survive only in small geographic regions where political representatives truly shared the interests of the inhabitants. This Antifederalist position represented a logical extension of the colonial tradition, the demand for local self-government.

Supporters of the new Constitution—people who styled themselves Federalists—argued that state governments were too susceptible to popular control, that the masses did not respect the interests of property, that liberty threatened the stability of the republics. The Federalists appealed to people with interstate interests—merchants, commercial farmers, public creditors, and urban workers whose livelihoods depended upon the prosperity of their employers. They also attracted politicians who lacked power within the existing state governments, men who hoped to supplant the entrenched political groups. As defenders of property, the Federalists saw a strong national government as a bulwark against the caprice of popular politics. Moreover, they argued against the Antifederalist allegation that republican governments could exist only in small territories. They took the position that no single group could control power in a large pluralistic nation. Thus the very size of the

United States would guarantee the twin blessings of liberty and property.

Despite the absence of majority support, the Federalists rallied their followers carefully, argued feverishly, made adroit concessions, and in the end prevailed—though by a slim margin. That they succeeded is an indication of the general apathy the American public felt to questions of national politics. More important, the entire debate underscored a basic consensus among American politicians about the nature of government and the future of American society. Nowhere was this more evident than in the rapid dissipation of opposition once the Constitution had passed the hurdles of the ratifying conventions. Though modern Americans see the Constitution as the basis for strong government, in 1789 federal powers were more potential than actual. Thus all powers not specifically granted to the national government remained in the states. Citizens continued to pay most of their taxes to the local governments and consequently remained more interested in statewide politics. Voter participation, for example, was often higher in gubernatorial elections than in presidential contests. The Constitution, in other words, had enormous implications for the future of the United States, but most Americans still regarded the national government as a remote power in their lives.

The intensive debate over the Constitution uncovered many political assumptions that would also influence subsequent American history. Foremost seemed to be a general distrust of politicians. Antifederalists feared the expansion of aristocratic influence. Federalists, on the other hand, worried about the masses, who lacked a real stake in the social order. James Madison stated the problem succinctly in the *Federalist Papers*, a series of essays written with John Jay and Alexander Hamilton, which urged the ratification of the Constitution. "In framing a government which is to be administered by men over men," Madison declared, "the great difficulty lies in this: you must first enable the government to control the governed; and in the next place oblige it to control itself."

American politicians were slowly admitting that the ideal of community no longer determined their political associations. "The political creed of an individual may almost be ascertained with certainty from his connections, or speculative prospects," complained "A Citizen" in 1786. To modern Americans, the notion of interest politics seems utterly self-evident. But for the Founding Fathers, the idea was, if not exactly new, at least profoundly discomforting. In an age that professed an essential harmony of human relations, the existence of parties and factions—of fundamental political cleavages—revealed an abiding human perversity rather than a normal pattern of political exchange.

Yet the Founding Fathers recognized too the inevitability of political discord and sought merely to institutionalize its effects. Madison admitted that "a factious spirit has tainted" the body politic, but he argued that the new government would curtail the spread of that infection. A large nation composed of numerous factions would prevent any single group from accumulating power. Politics would reduce to the art of the possible, the balance of interests, and the compromise of power. Though hostile to the specific remedy, Antifederalist writers shared Madison's analysis. "On the preservation of parties, public liberty depends," observed "A Farmer." "Wherever men are unanimous on great public questions, wherever there is but one party, freedom ceases and despotism commences."

The Constitution therefore became, for friend and foe alike, an institutional expression of interest politics. With a bicameral legislature and an independent executive, the framers of the Constitution separated power and, in theory at least, balanced it between the branches of government. Citizens-at-large elected the members of the House of Representatives, but senators, chosen by the state legislatures, belonged to a different constituency; and the President was selected by electors appointed in the states. More specifically the Constitution appealed to the citizens of the southern states by perpetuating the slave trade, promising defense "against domestic violence," and prohibiting export duties. Other provisions benefited northern interests. These included the easing of interstate commerce and the implicit promise to settle outstanding debts. For the "people," that amorphous body in whose name all had been transacted, the Constitution offered few defenses of their cherished liberty. Lacking a bill of rights, the document established an independent judiciary free from political control and permitted impeachment of civil officers for "treason, bribery, or other high crimes and misdemeanors." These institutional constraints did not impede the exercise of power; they sought only to channel its direction. By establishing the principles of national citizenship, the Constitution formed a direct link between individuals and government, based upon law. The Constitution could prevent the arbitrary use of power, but it could not—nor did the founders wish it to—create a national community of mutual obligations and responsibilities among all citizens.

Consider, for example, the clause that declared: "No title of nobility shall be granted by the United States." That phrase plainly institutionalized the egalitarian principles of Jefferson's Declaration and, in theory, assured equal rights to all citizens. But the commitment to an egalitarian ideology also altered the definition of appropriate economic and social activity. The elimination of a hereditary aristocracy simultaneously undermined the social obligations that traditionally had accompanied wealth and status.

Political theory aside, American society did not exist apart from the real people who inhabited the country, and what was observable in the states was the perpetuation of social and economic inequality. During the revolutionary era, the disparities of wealth had increased, and there had been a tightening of class lines. The post-Revolution egalitarian credo thus left the most vulnerable citizens at the mercy of their more affluent and more powerful compatriots. The idealization of the individual encouraged the emergence of a laissez-faire society, and the commerce clauses of the Constitution greatly facilitated its implementation. Patrick Henry, a fervent opponent of the Constitution, seized upon its implications in alarm. "What right had they to say, *We, the People?*" he asked bitterly. "Who authorized them to speak the language of *We, the people,* instead of *We, the states?*" But Henry, the patriarchal slaveowner, was swimming against the racing currents of individual liberty.

The political consensus that emerged after 1789 stimulated a self-conscious attempt to create a national culture. Thus the Founding Fathers soon themselves became heroes, and the Constitution itself became an object of patriotic veneration. The search for national unity also encouraged a new interpretation of American history that stressed the people's common heritage. "Providence has been pleased to give this one connected country to one united people," asserted John Jay in *The Federalist* No. 2, "a people descended from the same ancestors, speaking the same language, professing the same religion, attached to the same principles of government, very similar in their manners and customs." Such homogeneity partially reflected the aggressiveness of English culture, its ability to submerge minority groups, its tenacity of language, institutions, and values. The matter was stated somewhat differently by the French immigrant Hector St. John de Crèvecoeur in *Letters from an American Farmer* (1782) when he answered his famous question, "What, then, is the American, this new man? He is either a European or a descendant of a European; hence, that strange mixture of blood, which you will find in no other country. . . . Here individuals of all nations are melted into a new race of men." Thus emerged the image of the melting pot, the blurring of national and ethnic differences.

But what happened to the Germans in Pennsylvania and the Dutch in New York? Where were the Catholics and the Jews? What became of the people who were neither Europeans nor descendants of them? And in this "new race of men," where were the mothers and the daughters? To catalogue such omissions is not to correct the facts, for John Jay and St. Jean de Crèvecoeur certainly would have acknowledged the existence of other people. They did not necessarily intend to exclude Africans, Native Americans, unassimilated Europeans, and women from American history. But they did so just the same. Crèvecoeur's and Jay's ideas about "this new man" illuminated the implicit assumptions held by the American establishment. For the Founding Fathers, the American was a white Anglo-Saxon Protestant male. In the face of these biases, minority cultures actually did exist, and their presence could not be denied. Consequently the question "What then is the American, this new man?" brought forth a powerful corollary: what, then, is he not? Here was the basis of a profound tension within American society.

No one struggled more with that dilemma than the sage of Monticello, Thomas Jefferson. "It is impossible not to look forward to distant times," he declared from the White House, "when our rapid multiplication will expand itself . . . and cover the whole northern, if not the southern continent, with a people speaking the same language, governed in similar forms, and by similar laws; nor can we contemplate with satisfaction," he added obliquely, "either blot or mixture on that surface." This was a curious addendum indeed, one which attempted to conceal a fundamental fissure within the national identity.

Thomas Jefferson had been a most unlikely revolutionary. He was born to wealth in Virginia in 1743, educated at the College of William and Mary, admitted to the bar at the age of twenty-four, a member of the House of Burgesses at twenty-six. Blessed with a lucrative inheritance—some of it self-made by his immigrant father, some of it inherited by his mother—Jefferson owned considerable land and numerous slaves all his life. Like other members of the Virginia gentry, he enjoyed the perquisites of elite status, dabbling in the classics, studying the violin, supervising the routines of plantation life at Monticello. After his marriage in 1772, Jefferson came to view Monticello as a citadel of peace, a private island amid the storms of politics. Even when most fully occupied in his public career, Jefferson yearned for the solitude of his home.

Yet it was Thomas Jefferson, the Virginia planter, who declared that "all men are created equal." It was Thomas Jefferson, the American ambassador to France, who proclaimed that "the tree of liberty must be refreshed from time to time with the blood of patriots and tyrants" and who suggested, with great seriousness, that "a little rebellion now and then is a good thing, and as necessary in the political world as storms in the physical." And it was Thomas Jefferson, the elder statesman, who observed that "nothing . . . is unchangeable but the inherent and unalienable rights of man." Those grandiose thoughts befitted a person of Jefferson's stature and, in no small measure, they reflected the enormous confidence that a member of the WASP elite enjoyed. It is only against the bedrock of personal security that the paradoxes at the center of Jefferson's thought become clear—his simultaneous commitment to personal liberty and his ownership of slaves; his disgust by the institution of slavery and his own racial prejudice; his insistence that the earth belonged to the living and his unyielding attempt to transform the land into pockets of Jeffersonian civilization. Thomas Jefferson of Monticello—and few other Americans—could afford the luxury of those contradictions.

Jefferson's ambivalence about American society reflected not only the peculiarities of his social environment, but also his grand cosmic vision, which embraced all creation. Like the other rationalists of the eighteenth century, Jefferson philosophically divided life into tidy compartments of existence. His was an environmentalist interpretation of human activity. "Let a philosophic observer commence a journey from the savages of the Rocky Mountains, eastwardly towards our seacoast," he proposed. "These he would observe in the earliest stage of association living under no law but that of nature, subsisting and covering themselves with the flesh and skins of wild beasts. He would next find those on our frontiers in the pastoral state, raising domestic animals to supply the defects of hunting. Then succeed our own semi-barbarous citizens, the pioneers of the advance of civilization, and so on . . . until he would reach his, as yet, most improved state in our seaport towns. This, in fact, is equivalent, in time, of the progress of man from the infancy of creation to the present day."

When Thomas Jefferson voiced his egalitarian ideology, therefore, he applied it to those members of the human community he considered civilized. Yet he believed he was applying it to the world —provided, that is, that the more benighted peoples accepted what he described as the "march of civilization . . . passing over us like a cloud of light." If the red people of the western coasts discarded their animal skins, if the black people returned from slavery to Africa, if the "semi-barbarous" frontiersmen embraced the "progress of man," then the American spirit would conquer the continent without "blot or mixture."

The Jeffersonian transformation involved the imposition of rational order upon the natural wildness of the earth. Jefferson, like so many of his contemporaries, was discomforted by irregularity, by uncertainty, by inefficiency. His image of the world extolled the straight line, the rectangular order, the repetition of geometrical forms. In his architecture, for example, he celebrated the straight lines of classical antiquity, planning the capitol of Virginia in the image of the Maison Carrée, which he considered one of "the most perfect examples of cubic architecture." So influential was Thomas Jefferson, or, more accurately, so much did he understand the temper of his culture, that the geometry of classical architecture became a prototype for what later generations would call republican simplicity. Jefferson simply did not appreciate the sacred circles of premodern peoples.

The passion for order dominated Jefferson's vision of America's destiny, especially his understanding of western expansion. As his "philosophical observer" plainly saw, the settlement of virgin lands transformed the harmony of Native American society into linear expressions of Anglo-American culture. In 1784, while serving in the Congress, Jefferson drafted the first Northwest Ordinance, a blueprint for the creation of new states north of the Ohio River. In this document, Jefferson reasserted his commitment to republican politics by assuring equality to all states in the union—a liberal statement even today. He divided this territory into fourteen rectangular districts and gave them, as befitted his admiration of the classics, such names as Metropotamia, Pelisipia, and Cherronesus. Within these states, he advocated the subdivision of lands into rectangular sections and subsections. His ideas about city planning, as evidenced by his interest in the national capital, reflected a similar commitment to linear development, to intersecting grids—in other words, to artificial order.

These conceptual prejudices perhaps explain why Jefferson became a major exponent of American agrarianism and why he celebrated the virtue of the yeoman farmer. As governor of Virginia during the war for independence, he supported the abolition of entail and primogeniture, two relics of feudal landholding, both archaic reminders of the once-sacred earth. Instead of the land, Jefferson idealized the people who demystified the soil and sold their produce in the marketplace. "Those who labor in the earth," he announced, "are the chosen people of God." For this reason, President Jefferson overcame his constitutional scruples about the purchase of Louisiana. By doubling the size of the union, he obtained sufficient space for the expanding American farmer. Yet he also expressed hope that the Native Americans in Louisiana would abandon their traditional hunting ways, adopt a sedentary existence, and cede the remainder of their lands to the United States. There was no room in his individualistic vision for native communities and the seasonal cycles of tribal life. "The backward [tribes] will yield," he wrote in 1812, "and we shall be obliged to drive them, with the beasts of the forest into the Stony [Rocky] mountains."

Jefferson's commitment to geometrical order was a natural outgrowth of his preoccupation with orderliness and his compulsion for self-control. He was a man who deeply distrusted his emotions; he seemed to reduce life to long lists of statistics and compilations of household expenses. The difficulty he experienced in establishing meaningful human relationships may explain Jefferson's thirst for solitude as well as his apotheosis of the independent farmer. "Dependence," Jefferson advised, "begets subservience and venality, suffocates the germ of virtue, and prepares fit tools for the designs of ambition." American farmers, unlike the peasants of the Old World or the Native Americans of the New, lived on the land isolated from communities. For Jefferson, they personified American virtue, and he hoped that the United States would become a nation of self-reliant yeomen.

Jefferson's strident defense of independence suggested his deep-seated ambivalence about all human attachments. It was more than coincidental that the death of his mother in 1776 preceded by only a few weeks his drafting the formal separation of the colonies from the mother country. Jefferson, like other members of his culture, held idealized images of women. "Nothing is so disgusting to our sex as a want of cleanliness and delicacy in yours," he advised his daughter. "I hope therefore the moment you rise from bed, your first work will be to dress yourself in such a style as that you may be seen by any gentleman without his being able to discover a pin amiss, or by any other circumstance of neatness wanting." Women, he also believed, should be sheltered from the turmoil of an active life. "Our good ladies . . . have been too wise to wrinkle their foreheads with politics," he boasted. "They are contented to soothe and calm the minds of their husbands returning ruffled from political debate."

Jefferson's desire to exclude women from the vicissitudes of life betrayed his own fear of emotional relations and his transparent desire to conceal his feelings. All his known sexual encounters, with the exception of his (significantly) previously married wife, involved "forbidden" women—wives of other men and slaves. These patterns reveal a personality in a culture that consigned emotional involvement to the dusky recesses of consciousness. Genuine passion proved too threatening to the rationalistic controls of his modern mind.

Jefferson did not admit his love for his slave, Sally Hemings, nor did he ever publicly acknowledge their progeny. Only in his will did he provide for their freedom. Yet their very lives demonstrated his lack of self-restraint, for which he suffered massive guilt. Once unleashed, the fruits of passion might escape all bounds. "If something is not done, and soon done," he warned at the time of the Santo Domingo slave revolt, "we shall be the murderers of our own children."

That turn of phrase, besides its literal truth, spoke volumes about WASP attitudes toward nonwhite peoples. Though Jefferson genuinely despised slavery and lamented its unhappy effects on white society as well as black, he personally made few gestures toward emancipating his "people." He spoke once of freeing his slaves after he had paid his debts; but evidently it never occurred to him to reorder his economic priorities. Jefferson also grappled with the problem of racial inferiority and concluded ambiguously that it was difficult to determine if blacks were innately inferior to whites or if slavery made them so. His environmental explanation of human nature suggested the obvious evils of the "peculiar institution," but he shrank from the consequences of his logic. "As far as I can judge from the experiments which have been made," he replied to one questioner, "to give liberty to, or rather, to abandon persons whose habits have been formed in slavery is like abandoning children."

Jefferson remained more optimistic about Native Americans, whom he viewed as a higher form of humanity and potentially the equal of whites. He believed that Africans could never be integrated into American society but anticipated a time when red and white cultures would "meet and blend together, to intermix, and become one people." That amalgamation, of course, implied that the Native Americans would embrace the higher forms of civilization pouring out of the eastern states, and revealed the same patriarchal attitude applied to blacks. "Our Indians stand pretty much in the relation to the Government as do our children to us," declared a Jeffersonian official. "They are equally dependent; and need, not unfrequently, the exercise of parental authority." Jefferson himself would not have said it differently.

Through this regard of nonwhite people as children, the Jeffersonians not only justified their political hegemony, but also expressed a view central to American culture. For what is a child? "Completely selfish," stated a Jeffersonian evangelical in 1814. "His object is to gratify himself." In a culture that placed reason over feeling, logic over passion, childishness would represent the utter depravity of the human condition and would require immediate remedies. "If your children possess dispositions that lead them into sin," the missionary advised, "it surely cannot be cruel to check those dispositions, or give them a new and better direction." And so the Africans and Native Americans, ethnic minorities and women entered the Jeffersonian family, or, more precisely, waited at the doorstep. Meanwhile, "a new race of men" spread its influence, blot and mixture notwithstanding, across the continent.

Part Two

★ ★ ★ ★ ★ ★ ★ ★ ★ ★ ★ ★ ★ ★ ★ ★ ★ ★ ★ ★

NATIONAL EXPANSION:
FROM CONSTITUTION TO CIVIL WAR

"The mad career of self-indulgence"

★ ★ ★ ★ ★ ★ ★ ★ ★ ★ ★ ★ ★ ★ ★ ★ ★ ★ ★ ★

6
Social Patterns
North and South

Marriage and the family

Morality and religion

The organization of time in American life: the clock industry

Growth of factories, transportation, and industrial markets

Population growth and European immigration

Industrial values and the urban working class

Social structure in northern industrial society

Southern slavery and black culture: plantation economy and
King Cotton, black challenges to slavery

Attitudes toward women and children

Women's rights and Seneca Falls

The paradoxes, the ambivalences, the ambiguities—these were Thomas Jefferson's legacy to his country. Yet, like most of the Revolutionary generation, Jefferson remained optimistic about America, looking to the children of the Republic to assume the mantle of leadership. "If we do not think exactly alike," he assured his aged colleague John Adams, "it matters little to our country . . . we have delivered [the Republic] to our successors in life, who will be able to take care of it, and of themselves." Where the children of Europe were mired in a traditional world of adult corruption, the American child enjoyed unprecedented opportunities in the cradle of liberty. This salubrious environment assured the moral virtue of the nation's youth. "Before the establishment of the American states, nothing was known to History but the man of the old world," Jefferson remarked. Now, however, the child of America, full with the strength of the continent, promised a new history for all mankind.

Colonial parents had viewed their offspring as children of Adam, tainted from birth by Original Sin; republican parents, less inclined to theological determinism, saw the newborn babe as naturally innocent. American children, instead of requiring a "second birth" to attain salvation, represented a "new race of men" capable of perfection on earth as well as in heaven. This new attitude was part of a larger secularization within Western culture, the shift from a theological cosmos dominated by God to a more worldly order controlled by human achievement. The American child, still innocent in both spheres, symbolized the unlimited possibilities of the future.

During the colonial period, the number of live births had increased steadily until, by 1800, the average American family comprised about seven children. This reproductive explosion, unprecedented in Western history, expressed both the favorable economic circumstances in America and the relative healthfulness of the natural environment, which had reduced the rate of infant mortality. Whatever the exact causes, children were a larger part of society than ever before.

This biological pattern also illuminated a more subtle revolution in American values. In the seventeenth century, material conditions enabled couples to marry earlier and so it was possible for young

Changing attitude of love

people to obtain sexual fulfillment without defying social convention. Such intimacy created a new atmosphere for sexual relations. Young people now believed that love was the most important consideration in marital arrangements. Emotional involvement and personal attachment—not the settlement of property or the protection of family interests—became the accepted impulse for marriage.

This psychological transformation produced significant side effects. As marriage became a union of autonomous individuals, sexual relations became less risky, abstinence less vital. Even when economic conditions no longer encouraged early marriages—and in the eighteenth century this became the case—sexual passion was not denied. The result was a rise in the number of premarital conceptions, as measured by "seven- and eight-month" children. Thus human passion, once legitimized, surmounted the secular limitations of the American economy. Yet these premarital unions did not jeopardize the stability of the family. Rather than deliver "illegitimate" babies, couples chose either to abort the pregnancy—about which there is little evidence—or, more commonly, to marry. Premarital pregnancy, instead of being "unwanted," may well have hastened the formal union of loving couples.

When? dampened religious zeal

The emphasis on worldly love, of which the procreation of children was so central a part, coincided in the nineteenth century with the withdrawal of emotional energy from other aspects of creation. Thus religion, once the touchstone of human experience, became primarily a question of denominational affiliation—an ecclesiastical matter to be determined as much by the resonance of the preacher's voice as by the spiritual satisfaction wrought by the liturgy. For less pious Christians, the dampening of religious zeal seemed a decided improvement, leading to an appreciable drop in church membership throughout the nation. Equally significant, the quest for immortality took more worldly forms. Instead of seeking everlasting life in heaven, people turned to their progeny to perpetuate a visible lineage on earth. The children of America thus provided historical ballast—a secular immortality—for a society bent on improving the human condition through material advancement.

But the fires of religion were not so easily extinguished, and the moral precepts of traditional Christianity continued to dominate American thought if not action. Those standards had been adapted, however, to suit the needs of a burgeoning, individualistic society. Thus the notion of self-determination, originally stated as a political

imperative, extended in the nineteenth century to religious choices
as well, providing moral sanction for the principle of religious vol-
untarism, the right of individuals to worship as they wished. That
liberal perspective, so different from the authoritarian assumptions
of the colonial era, still limited religious freedom to orthodox Protestants. Religious minorities continued to suffer overt persecution as
well as more subtle forms of discrimination.

Those restrictions notwithstanding, the liberalizing tendencies encouraged religious heterogeneity within the American mainstream.
Equally important, the substance of American religion also moved
in a liberal direction, resulting in the articulation of more gentle
versions of Protestantism. The "rationalistic" elements within American Christianity, for example, rejected the awesome God of Calvin and emphasized God's love for humanity. As expressed by the
Unitarian minister William Ellery Channing, God exercised His
sovereignty in a rational manner, offering salvation to all people.
The doctrine dovetailed with the egalitarian political values of the
period. "We reason about the Bible," Channing remarked in a revealing metaphor, "precisely as civilians do about the Constitution."
The heavenly city, once the private domain of the Puritan saints,
now widened its gates for all who would enter.

These egalitarian assumptions, logical and calm in the Unitarian
pulpits, burst like kindling through the thickets of evangelical Protestantism. In the thinly populated regions of the West, circuit-riding
preachers, their saddlebags packed with Bibles, worked assiduously
to extend the territorial domain of the Christian religion. Their
exhortations won wide approval among the gospel-starved frontiers-
people. In 1800, a particularly powerful meeting produced a tidal
wave of evangelical fervor, known to contemporaries as the Second Great Awakening. By midcentury, the evangelical impulse had
captured most of the Mississippi Valley, establishing a spiritual
stronghold of Methodists and Baptists throughout the West. The
holy spirit then moved eastward, slipping into the coastal cities
where urban working people—the vanguard of American industrialism—answered the clarion call. According to Charles Grandison
Finney, the leading evangelist of the times, God had opened His
heart to all human beings, freely promising salvation to all people
who would open their hearts to Him. Unlike the evangelists of the
colonial period, Finney saw conversion as an act of human will, a
voluntary decision that all people could muster by transforming
their individual selfishness into communal benevolence.

This egalitarian doctrine, as with the Unitarians, suited the individualistic ethos of the period. It also provided a spiritual alternative to the materialism of the age. As industrial values spread across the nation, the evangelical religion spoke an older language of Christian charity, of community and love. In social terms, these tenets obligated Christians to work actively to perfect American institutions, to rid them of sin and corruption. Such imperatives offered moral direction to people who worried about irreligion and who suffered what Ralph Waldo Emerson once called the torment of "unbelief, the uncertainty as to what we ought to do."

Emerson's confusion, a profound bewilderment he shared with many of his contemporaries, was a symptom of this age of individualism. The destruction of the communal values of the colonial period had left Americans afloat on a sea of Self—of self-determination, of self-interest, and, to their utmost despair, of selfishness. Carrying the individualistic credo to its fullest conclusion, Americans had created a boundless society that promised immense material advantages for some people, but left others exposed to an awesome sense of spiritual emptiness. "As long as our civilization is essentially one of property, of fences, of exclusiveness," lamented Emerson, "our riches will leave us sick; there will be bitterness in our laughter, and our wine will burn in our mouth."

Such jeremiads, laden as much with fear as frustration, pointed directly to the capitalistic economy of the nineteenth century. Everywhere Americans seemed enmeshed in an obsessive pursuit of wealth. "The Americans arrived but as yesterday," observed the French visitor Alexis de Tocqueville, "and they have already changed the whole order of nature for their own advantage." That speedy transformation toppled traditional images of social order and alarmed more conservative citizens. "Do not be in a hurry to get rich," advised one cautious journalist. "Gradual gains are the only natural gains."

Nowhere was this cultural transformation more apparent than in American attitudes toward time. Rural folk traditionally guided their lives by seasonal time, enjoying periods of spontaneous leisure during most of the year (sowing and harvest times were the major exceptions). But the new economic ethic forced people to measure time more precisely. By the last decade of the eighteenth century, nearly every American-made clock possessed a third hand to measure seconds—more an indication of intellectual interests than a necessary appendage. At the same time, there appeared the first American-made watches, assuring the portable presence of this secular mentality.

The major revolution, however, came in the production of clocks. In 1800, only about one family in ten owned a clock—a statistic that reflected both the rural orientation of most Americans and the high cost of accurate timepieces. The expansion of industrial values soon altered those factors. Responding to the growing interest in good but inexpensive timepieces, a young Connecticut clockmaker named Eli Terry switched from brass gears to wooden works, developed a system of mass production based on interchangeable parts, and, by 1808, was producing thousands of clocks a year. Those innovations, similar to other advances in American manufacturing, created a boom in New England clockmaking. The Panic of 1837, a severe economic crisis, eventually wrought disaster in the wooden-works industry, but by then certain technological improvements in brass manufacturing as well as a greater sensitivity to consumer needs enabled American clockmakers to recover rapidly. By the Civil War, nearly every American home possessed an accurate timepiece made in the United States.

The development of the clock industry, besides demonstrating the growing preoccupation with temporal precision and regularity, tells much about the process of manufacturing throughout the nation during the early nineteenth century. As in other industries, clockmakers traditionally had built their clocks at home, relying upon self-employed skilled artisans to fashion the intricate parts. A clockmaker would then assemble the components—a hand-painted dial, individually wrought wheels and gears, a skillfully carved case. He would then deliver the finished product to a local purchaser, take his modest profits, and begin the process again. More successful clockmakers might employ several apprentices, develop a network of related artisans who also worked at home, and locate customers in other parts of the state; but the essential process, though larger in scope, did not differ greatly. An identical system existed for other types of manufacturing—whether the production of shoes or the publication of books.

The emergence of factories introduced important qualitative changes. First, the capital for Terry's enterprise came from two local merchants who contracted to sell the finished products. These investors, like many others in New England, realized that manufacturing promised much larger returns than commerce, an insight that would affect American investment throughout the economy. It is also significant that Terry's factory did not eliminate his less adventurous competitors. Artisan clockmakers continued to produce handmade clocks, but sold their wares to a different, perhaps more affluent, market. Nor were other skilled workers absorbed into the expanding factories; rather, the manufacturers preferred to employ the less expensive labor of unskilled workers. Quantity, not quality, provided the margin of profit.

Markets-
Popular??

Central to the expansion of American manufacturing was the existence of adequate markets to consume industrial production. In 1790, the American population numbered four million; by 1830 it approached thirteen million; by 1860 it surpassed thirty-one million—despite steadily declining birthrates! Simultaneously, the size of the nation's urban areas grew dramatically. In 1790, New York City contained thirty thousand people; thirty years later that figure had quadrupled, and by the Civil War it exceeded one million. Other cities expanded proportionately. This trend toward urbanization, though still embryonic by modern standards, created the population density necessary to consume the growing output of American manufacturing.

The immense surge of population could be traced to increasing immigration from Europe. Before 1840, the largest waves of European immigrants came from Germany, Ireland, and England. The immigrants were either artisans who had competed unsuccessfully with the new factories or farmers who had suffered the economic consequences of overproduction. Both groups, already possessing some material advantages, enjoyed even larger opportunities in the United States, despite the difficulties of migration and the problems of cultural alienation. Those without property settled in the port towns, while immigrants with capital traveled inland to purchase farms in the Midwest or to open shops in such new urban centers as Louisville, Cincinnati, and Pittsburgh.

After 1840, however, the composition of the immigrant groups changed greatly, because of the terrible famines in Ireland and, to a lesser extent, the crop failures in Germany. Now the immigrants were poorer and lacked the capital necessary to move to the interior states. They settled, instead, where they arrived, swelling the population of the port cities. There they formed an urban proletariat that labored in the factories and on the docks. With low incomes and scant opportunity, these industrial workers could afford to buy only the inexpensive products of American manufacturing.

The expansion of industrial markets depended not only upon the population growth, but also on the ability of manufacturers to reach their consumers. When, for example, Eli Terry wished to sell his earliest clocks, he arranged for local merchants to carry his wares to potential buyers. Thus emerged the Yankee peddler—half entrepreneur, half caricature—who traveled the countryside selling pots, pans, book subscriptions, farm implements, and a host of other products that included, more often than not, wooden-works clocks from Connecticut. He transported, too, a series of Yankee industrial values that the bucolic, pastoral images painted on the clockfaces could not conceal. Though traditional American farmers may have resented the Yankee credo, they bought the clocks anyway and often scraped the paint from the glass so they too could admire the new technology. Possibly they found vindication when the clocks went awry—as the wooden works often did in the steamier climates —but eventually the Yankee tinkered away those flaws.

The spread of industrial values, like the products they endorsed, followed various routes around the nation. During the early nineteenth century, most traffic moved along crude roads first cleared in colonial days or floated on flatboats down navigable rivers and streams. High freight costs encouraged the improvement of transportation facilities, and led to the construction of new roads and turnpikes financed by private investors and the state governments. The successful implementation of the steamboat in the regions east of the Mississippi River increased the volume of trade and reduced transportation costs. Both factors had an enormous impact on the expansion of industry in the East. These improvements soon were dwarfed by the proliferation of artificial canals, most notably the Erie Canal in New York. Such waterways further reduced the cost of inland transportation, boosting the prosperity of eastern producers. By linking the Midwest with the Atlantic ports, the canals also stimulated trade with Europe. Sleek-bodied clipper ships now carried western farm goods to the Old World not only with speed but with regularity, bringing greater profits to American merchants and the farmers from whom they obtained their goods.

By accelerating inland travel, the improvements in transportation hastened the settlement of the interior by enterprising farmers. These agrarians, surely the children of the Jeffersonian dream, quickly realized the advantages of mechanized agriculture and purchased, in ever larger numbers, such contrivances as McCormick's reaper, the thresher, and the steel plow. These inventions, together with the drop in freight charges, spurred American agriculture to unprecedented levels of production at the same time that the demand for food was increasing in Europe. The result was widespread prosperity for American farmers, which enabled them to consume still more manufactured goods shipped from the eastern states.

These reciprocal advantages—typical of the national economy by the eve of the Civil War—became more apparent with the introduction of the railroad in the middle decades of the century. Rail construction, though potentially very profitable, required large outlays of capital, most of which was supplied by European bankers. But the railroad companies also sold considerable stock to merchants and farmers living along the projected right-of-way. These investments, often the result of mortgaged farm property, enabled many western farmers to protect their economic connections with eastern markets. In urban areas businessmen recognized the advantages of having a nearby railroad terminus and became powerful proponents of additional building. In this manner a small town on the shores of Lake Michigan mushroomed into the thriving metropolis of Chicago.

The construction of transportation facilities—whether railroads, canals, or turnpikes—often required more capital than private business could arrange. The state governments therefore stepped into the breach, to provide loans, subsidies, and tax exemptions for public improvements. These supports culminated with the enormous grants of public land—more than a billion acres—to the western railroads. Such subsidies betrayed the nation's prime concern—the expansion of the marketplace. By the Civil War, thirty thousand miles of track had been laid and four trunk lines linked the eastern seaboard with the Midwest. It was no longer necessary for the Yankee peddler to hitch up his team in order to reach customers in that part of the nation.

The expansion of the railroads represented only one aspect of the new industrial ethic. As people like Eli Terry demonstrated the profitability of factories, investors turned increasingly to mass production. By introducing new machinery, cutting labor costs, and streamlining production, manufacturers reaped ever greater profits. Such expansion quickly developed a self-generating force. Improvements in one area of production often stimulated changes in others. The railroad, for example, created an industrial demand for lumber, iron, and coal, which in turn encouraged the mining, smelting, and timber industries. Business itself became a major consumer of the fruits of technology.

The transformation of the American economy not only raised the levels of production and consumption, but also strengthened the new industrial value system. The success of the clock industry in spreading technological time throughout the nation spoke impressively of that metamorphosis. Time had been harnessed, and its treatment had moral value. "Unfaithfulness in the keeping of an appointment is an act of clear dishonesty," maintained the distinguished pedagogue Horace Mann. "You may as well borrow a person's money as his time." That lesson, self-evident as it may be in our own times, did not come easily to nineteenth-century children, nor to their parents who labored in the factories.

The success of American industry required efficiency and regularity in production and the discipline of the working classes. "Who has not been delighted," asked Kentucky's Henry Clay, "with the clockwork movements of a large cotton factory?" Manufacturers established work schedules, set production goals, purchased time clocks, and expected their workers to perform. Less scrupulous employers allowed their clocks to run down, which was one way of jamming more minutes into the work hour. But even an honest industrial system forced employees to abandon traditional habits of work.

Farm labor might be difficult, unrewarding, and lonely, but it was not unceasing. Though farm workers occasionally labored more hours than industrial employees, agriculture also had long hours of slack, periods of undisciplined rest, freedom from externally imposed order. Even when Captain John Smith used martial law to compel the first colonists of Virginia to work more diligently, he demanded only six hours of daily labor and allowed the rest of the day to be spent "in pastime and merry exercises." The major problem of the new industrial society, therefore, was to impose some system of organization upon the workers, a task accomplished only with great difficulty. Thus factory owners established rigid labor rules, enforced by punitive fines. Workers were punished for lateness, prohibited from eating in work areas, fined for drunkenness. Such policies had to be taught to each generation of industrial laborers—first to the Yankees who left their unprofitable farms, later to the immigrants from across the seas. Indeed, Horace Mann's pedagogy, with its apotheosis of punctuality, aimed at the workers' children, hoping to inculcate industrial values into the youngest and newest Americans.

For rural people, the industrializing process created profound psychological traumas. Some simply could not, or would not, adjust to the routines of the factory. Many lost their jobs and joined an evergrowing number of unemployed workers who crowded the welfare rolls. Others drifted from job to job, discovering few opportunities for real improvement. Still more found solace in alcohol, a phenomenon that alarmed conservative members of society. Some workers, of course, thrived on industrial discipline, worked hard, and managed to attain significantly better living conditions. Statistically, however, they constituted a small minority within the industrial labor force.

The impact of industrialization upon the emotional life of American workers is more difficult to measure and to document. But the loss of the spontaneous leisure that had characterized pre-industrial society probably explains the rise of organized athletics in the nineteenth century. Baseball, which became popular just before the Civil War, required a modicum of organization and a system of rules within which individual athletes could measure their prowess. The institutionalization of physical activity also revealed a more general evisceration of the human body in industrial society. Living in secular time, people had to discipline all bodily activities—to use the Freudian trilogy, oral, anal, and genital. The need for such discipline surely had existed before the Industrial Revolution, but the factory system, with its emphasis on order and efficiency, greatly intensified it.

These psychological patterns, which accentuated the distance between individuals, had profound effects on social relations. "By our modes of life—our houses—our dress—our equipage; in short by what is strictly external to us," declared a contemporary philanthropist, "men detach themselves from their neighbors—withdraw themselves from the human family." Such psychic separation encouraged the celebration of the individual and the pursuit of self-interest. In the process, an older sense of community as "the human family" quietly vanished.

Tangible effects of this process appeared within the social structure. Industrial expansion offered broad opportunities to adventurous Americans—but only those who already held some capital could seize the initiative. Although industrial capitalists might supplant the older commercial elite, the new rich usually bore the same family names and possessed the same genealogical connections. Occasionally a John Jacob Astor—truly a self-made man—emerged to flaunt the unlimited opportunities of the new social order. But Astor, like Benjamin Franklin a century before, proved the exception to the rule of social immobility. Moreover, the *nouveaux riches,* few as they were, shared the social values of the old wealth, a tendency reinforced by frequent intermarriage between these groups.

This elite was overwhelmingly Protestant—largely members of the Episcopal, Presbyterian, and Congregational denominations. Genteel by birth and breeding, they enjoyed their wealth in huge mansions, patronized fashionable restaurants, joined exclusive social clubs, attended balls, concerts, and the theater. But when the local assessors came to evaluate their property, they were not above petty peculation—concealing their fortunes, underestimating their holdings. Such behavior contrasted with their public pretensions of noblesse oblige, but in this, too, they personified the laissez-faire values of industrial America. Of such stuff emerged the Robber Barons half a century later.

If few Americans worked their way up the social ladder into the enchanted circle, so too did few rich families decline significantly in wealth or status. Had they done so, they would have found themselves amid a fairly prosperous middle class composed of skilled artisans and independent farmers. Despite the proliferation of mechanized factories, skilled craftsmen seldom competed directly with mass-produced goods and thus enjoyed considerable security. In times of prosperity, these artisans formed trade unions that sought such middle-class goals as free public education, the abolition of child labor, and the shortening of the workday to ten hours. Believing fervently in the American dream, they neither challenged the industrial elite nor embraced the lower classes who suffered most by industrialization.

"Ours is a country," assured one Whig journalist, "where men start from an humble origin, and from small beginnings rise gradually in the world, as the reward of merit and industry, and where they can attain to the most elevated positions, or acquire a large amount of wealth, according to the pursuits they elect for themselves." That was the rhetoric of the self-made man, a self-congratulatory optimism contrived to mitigate the frustrations caused by the new social order. For the working classes, however, this optimism was largely illusory. The urban masses lived amid industrial poverty, sporadic unemployment, and limited opportunity. Often as immigrants or free blacks they suffered the additional indignities caused by WASP ethnocentrism—they were publicly attacked for their ideas and their values, and their children were compelled to learn the assimilationist lessons of the dominant culture.

Status differences, though hardly novel in American history, became further defined during the early nineteenth century. Stated simply, the rich grew richer and the poor grew poorer. The social order not only became more polarized, but also more stratified, and mobility between status groups became ever more difficult. Even in the newly settled areas of the West, early arrivals seized the best lands and the main chance, and thus became an entrenched elite. Late arrivals confronted a social hierarchy not dissimilar from that of the eastern states. But in the West, where geographical mobility was more feasible, it was common for settlers to tear down their balloon frame houses, load them in wagons, and resurrect them at some other site. Still, the notion of social mobility served more as a lesson in values than as a description of reality.

However sad the situation of industrial workers, few suffered quite so much as the black slaves who labored in the southern states. In the South the capitalist ethos, stimulated by great profits from cotton production, had led to a tightening of the slave system. Although Revolutionary leaders like Thomas Jefferson anticipated the gradual extinction of black slavery, the generations of Andrew Jackson and Abraham Lincoln confronted a flourishing labor system based on lifetime hereditary servitude. Southern apologists often claimed that plantation slaves lived better than northern industrial workers. This claim was a materialist argument, which, even if accurate, was largely irrelevant and not to the moral point.

The development and growth of textile factories in England and in the northeastern United States during the last decades of the eighteenth century created an increased demand for raw cotton. Not until 1793, however, when the Yankee Eli Whitney perfected the cotton gin, did southern planters obtain an effective means of transforming their cotton crops into rich profits. The innovation promptly revolutionized the southern economy, leading to the mass production of cotton for sale abroad. As cotton exports to Europe increased, capital flowed into the United States, largely through the hands of northern merchants who reinvested in other areas of the economy. So crucial was this exchange that shifts in cotton production affected financial commitments throughout the world, an economic phenomenon responsible for such banking crises as the Panic of 1837. It was southern cotton, therefore, that provided the resources for the economic surge of the nineteenth century.

Despite these factors, industrialization made meager inroads in the South. Many reformers urged southern capitalists to support local banks, railroads, and textile factories. But instead of becoming economically independent, the South relied upon northern business for most of its manufactured goods. In explaining that pattern, southerners often argued that plantation society was economically unprofitable but at least preserved the pre-industrial values of Jeffersonian America. Such rhetoric, full of imagery of magnolia trees and mint juleps, belied the economic basis of southern society. However garnished by the gentility of southern aristocrats, plantation agriculture remained as capitalistic and as profitable as the textile factories of New England. Southern investors avoided bank stock and heavy machinery, not because they were peculiarly anti-materialistic, but because they had found other, more profitable forms of investment—land and slaves.

On the burgeoning western frontiers of the South—in Alabama, Louisiana, Mississippi, Arkansas, and Texas—sugar cane and King Cotton brought great wealth to capitalistic planters. In the Old South, where soil erosion had weakened the land, commercial farmers turned to wheat and corn and harvested lucrative returns. Even the less affluent farmers managed to transform the loamy black belt into modest gains. Compared to the profits of industrial investment, southern planters enjoyed greater returns than their northern counterparts. And despite the complaints of southern apologists, the plantation economy still flourished on the eve of the Civil War. It was not soil depletion that drove southern farmers westward, but the economic incentive to cultivate more cotton. Those imperatives also led southern politicians to advocate the territorial expansion of the United States into Mexico, Cuba, and Central America, where, it was hoped, the plantation system would continue to thrive. No Yankee imperialist held more lofty ambitions!

The success of the plantation economy, like the northern factories, also depended upon efficient management of the labor force. Thus the expansion of cotton production thwarted the emancipationist impulses of people like Jefferson and led instead to a reinvigoration of the slave trade; over one hundred thousand blacks were brought into the United States before Congress implemented the constitutional prohibitions in 1808. Meanwhile, planters heading westward brought their slaves along, anticipating large profits from their labor, if not their market price.

These economic motives accelerated the deterioration of liberal humanitarianism that had followed the American Revolution. Though Thomas Jefferson grieved at the injustices of slavery, most of his neighbors lost interest in the egalitarian ideology, especially after they learned of the slave revolt in Santo Domingo in 1793. Seven years later, the danger came closer to home when anxious whites unearthed a slave conspiracy at Richmond, Virginia, under the leadership of a prophet named Gabriel Prosser. The slaveowners executed the conspirators, and to prevent future disturbances the southern legislatures enacted new laws further restricting the mobility of all blacks, slave and free. Those decisions revealed not only the power of the master class but also the fear running through its members.

As an economic system slavery continued to flourish, despite occasional tremors of unrest. On small farms, slaves lived and worked near their masters, close to the caprice of human emotion— sometimes for the better, sometimes not. But most blacks inhabited larger plantations, living within black communities in the slave quarters. From sunup to sundown, under the scrutiny of white overseers or black slave drivers, they operated with the efficiency of factory workers. But even the most efficient slaveowners had to accommodate the human needs of their workers or risk a disruption of labor. Escape—if only for a few days—broke the established patterns of work. So too did feigned illness, self-inflicted injury, "accidental" fires, broken tools, and deliberate ignorance. Such behavior, common as it was, reveals a pervasive discontent among black slaves, an ever-percolating rage against the plantation system, and an unceasing effort to assert human values.

Some blacks attained some independence within the slave system, learning skilled trades that enabled them to sell or lease their services in nearby towns and neighboring plantations. Such opportunities, besides bringing pecuniary gain, provided psychic release from the organized discipline of plantation labor.

It was through religion, though, that slaves most successfully evaded the routines of white culture. Meeting secretly in the woods at night, blacks exorcised the anguish of slavery through spiritual

arousal. Black music, heavy with the rhythms of Africa, reinforced
black identity, and the circular patterns of dance transcended the
linear modes of Western expression. Out of their past, this religious
experience strengthened communal bonds in the hostile present of
white America. No wonder, then, that it was a peculiar darkening of
the sun—the ultimate mystery of cosmic time—that launched Nat
Turner's vision of a slave revolt in 1831.

religion

These acts of rebellion forcefully challenged the southern image
of slavery. The first American slaveowners had viewed slavery as a
necessary expedient. The slaves' labor was essential, and they themselves would benefit from enforced assimilation into Christian society. By the age of Jefferson, however, most southerners saw slavery
as a necessary evil—one that should be gradually abolished. Such
attitudes had produced several schemes of gradual emancipation,
some of which were implemented in the northern states.

The eruption of black rebelliousness undermined the Jeffersonian
thesis that slavery was necessary. Moreover, evangelical Protestantism, with its emphasis on human perfectibility, aroused the messianic passion of radical abolitionists who demanded that slavery be
ended at once. Assaulted from within by hostile slaves and threatened from without by the evangelical abolitionists, southern slaveowners altered their defense of the "peculiar institution." Arguing
that blacks were naturally and permanently inferior to whites, and
hence natural slaves, they described slavery, not as a necessary evil,
but as a positive good. This position achieved further legitimacy
from the theory of polygenesis—the plural origins of mankind—
which proposed the permanence of racial characteristics. Given
scientific supports by such prestigious scholars as Louis Agassiz,
this theory justified the enslavement of blacks in perpetuity. Such
racist doctrines, cultivated far from the environmentalism of
Thomas Jefferson, clashed violently with the perfectionist philosophy of the evangelicals.

In portraying blacks as natural slaves, southern apologist inadvertently touched an extremely sensitive nerve at the root of American
culture. According to the proslavery polemicists, black slaves were
happy, shiftless, lazy, irresponsible, good-natured, docile, and ignorant—all qualities that were later stereotyped as "Sambo." In effect,
apologists of slavery transformed the barbaric savage from the African jungles into an innocent, carefree child. By equating slaves with
children, however, advocates of slavery actually helped to dramatize
the inherent evils of slavery. American Protestants believed that

southern defense of slavery

children were naturally innocent and vulnerable to adult corruptions. The description of the childlike slave aroused bitter outrage at slavery's corruption of innocent victims and so helped to stimulate the strident abolitionism of such evangelicals as William Lloyd Garrison.

To many social reformers, the plight of the slave seemed to parallel the precarious position of all American children. As a materialistic spirit spread across the land, steadily destroying the older communal morality, anxious observers turned to the family as the anchor of social order. Yet by the second decade of the nineteenth century, it appeared that the family was failing in that vital task. In demographic terms, the nation's birthrate began to drop until, by the Civil War, the average family comprised fewer than five children. Despite encouragement from conservatives to procreate, family size continued to shrink during subsequent decades. The American family, viewed by the Jeffersonians as the bulwark of the Republic, seemed, by the age of Lincoln, to be in a perilous decline.

This troubled vision prompted the publication of numerous manuals for improved child rearing. Written usually by Protestant ministers, these pamphlets urged American parents to stem the floodtide of corruption by instilling traditional values in the young. Parson Weems' *Life of Washington,* surely the bestseller of the age, described the first President as a paragon of virtue—the cherry tree notwithstanding—and a model for all children to imitate. The sheer volume of these publications indicated that there was widespread feeling that American children were fleeing the hearth prematurely, rushing, in the words of one anxious writer, "in the mad career of self-indulgence."

These writers viewed the family as a refuge from adult institutions. "In America," remarked Emerson, "out-of-doors all seems a market, in-doors an air-tight stove of conventionalism. Everybody who comes into the house savors of these precious habits: the men, of the market; the women of the custom." There was more than humor, then, in the popular saying that "a ship is like a lady's watch, always out of repair." While American men were busy rationalizing the marketplace, their women remained at home working by a different sense of time. "Instead of being the intelligent regulators of their own time," Catherine Beecher explained, "they are the mere sport of circumstances."

But if American children were to be spared from the shoals of materialism, who else could inculcate the customary wisdom? "The world's redeeming influence," answered a Protestant minister, "must come from a mother's lips." It was the American woman, sheltered like her children, who assumed responsibility for the nation's youth. "O that mothers could feel this responsibility as they might!" declared a New England Congregationalist. "Then would the world assume a different aspect."

Such obligations compelled American women to preserve their own chastity lest they inadvertently corrupt their innocent charges. That task was made somewhat easier by the general denial of female sexuality. According to conventional wisdom, women lacked sexual feelings—save those associated with childbearing. Even the medical profession viewed female sexuality as a disease, best treated by radical surgery. These attitudes were reinforced by the sexual exploitation of nonwhite women, a form of cultural oppression that consigned physical passion to inferior peoples and raised the white woman to a lofty pedestal of sexual anesthesia. By denying the organic flows of the human body, the desexualization of American women epitomized the white male's efforts to master the natural world.

The suppression of female sexuality undermined the woman's general sense of adulthood. "True feminine genius," declared a popular woman writer, "is ever timid, doubtful, and clingingly dependent; a perpetual childhood." This glorified image of the passive female assured the subordination of women in all aspects of life. Lacking the traditional protections associated with arranged marriages, American wives surrendered their independence, even losing the right to own property. The male establishment also denied women full political citizenship, prevented their entry into the nation's colleges (Oberlin became the first coeducational institution in 1837), and barred them from the professions. As perpetual children, women would remain untarnished by the corruptions of the adult world.

The infantilization of women closely paralleled the subordination of blacks by the male establishment. "The prejudice against color," complained the feminist Elizabeth Cady Stanton, "is no stronger than that against sex. . . . The Negro's skin and the woman's sex are both *prima facie* evidence that they were intended to be in subjection to the white Saxon man." Stanton also objected to the surrender of her maiden name in marriage. "Ask our colored brethren if there is nothing in a name," she suggested. "Why are the slaves nameless unless they take that of their master? Simply because they have no independent existence. . . . Even so with women. The custom of calling women Mrs. John This and Mrs. Tom That, and colored men Sambo and Zip Coon, is founded on the principle that white men are the lords of all."

These discriminatory patterns unleashed a strenuous movement for women's rights, climaxing in the Seneca Falls Convention of 1848. Adopting the language of Jefferson's Declaration, the feminists criticized male supremacists for denying their rights. "He has endeavored, in every way that he could," declared one particularly poignant paragraph, "to destroy her confidence in her own powers, to lessen her self-respect and to make her willing to lead a dependent and abject life." The women's rights movement brought limited reforms from the state legislatures, but obviously failed in the quest for full equality.

Nineteenth-century America remained a man's world in which women played subordinate roles as wives and mothers. "When our land is filled with pious and patriotic mothers," asserted a Protestant minister, "then will it be filled with virtuous and patriotic men. . . . A new race of men would enter upon the busy scene of life, and cruelty and crime would pass away. O mothers! . . . In a most peculiar sense God has constituted you the guardians and the controllers of the human family." That rhetoric, ironic as it was myopic, remained largely unchallenged amid the piety and patriotism of that busy male world, the great market "out-of-doors."

"This whole vast country from sea to sea"

* * * * * * * * * * * * * * * * * *

7

The Organization of Space

Western expansion and Manifest Destiny

Geographical exclusion: wars with Native Americans and
removal to reservations

Texas and the Mexican War

The colonization movement vs. abolitionism

Persecution of Mormons

Urban planning and the growth of cities: grid plans

Anti-Catholicism: nativism and the Know-Nothing party

Consequences of racial separation: urban violence

Nineteenth-century reforms: prisons, asylums, and the environment

expansion ~

reform ⇗

The reduction of time to secular proportions—the emphasis on precision, discipline, and regularity—paralleled a similar cultural attitude toward American space. Where Thomas Jefferson spoke of "distant times" when the nation would expand across the continent, his ideological descendants, less inclined to philosophical meditation, proceeded to implement the dream. During the early nineteenth century, they poured into the Mississippi Valley and beyond, passing into the territories claimed by Great Britain and Mexico and colonizing the Pacific Coast by midcentury.

The effect was typically Jeffersonian. "Every western traveller is familiar with the monotonous character of the towns resulting from the endless repetition . . . of rectangles," complained a nineteenth-century landscape architect named Horace Cleveland, "yet the custom is so universal and offers such advantages in simplifying and facilitating descriptions and transfers of real estate that any attempt at the introduction of a different system encounters at once a strong feeling of popular prejudice." The capitalistic marketplace indeed had conquered the "out-of-doors."

This peculiar transformation of the wilderness into linear acreage partly reflected the demographic composition of frontier society. Though people of all regions, classes, and ethnic groups settled in the western states, the predominant characteristic of these hardy migrants was their youth. Young Americans—the maturing children who no longer could expect an adequate inheritance of fertile land—packed their goods and headed west. This sense of declining opportunity, far more than any mystical lure of the frontier, was responsible for the exodus into virgin lands. Equally noticeable was the statistical majority of men who carried with them the individualistic credo of their mentors.

Northern farmers, escaping the worn and crowded lands of the seaboard, moved first into Vermont and the western areas of New York, then across the upper tier of the Northwest Territory, before advancing to the brink of the Great Plains. Meanwhile, southern planters left the tobacco-tired coastal areas for the rich soil of Kentucky and Tennessee, shouting ecstatic praises to this new land of milk and honey. But then they watched another generation, equally restive, march northward into the lower Northwest or southward into the black belt of the Gulf Plains where cotton and slavery thrived. By the Civil War, most of the Midwest and Deep South had been settled, and outposts of American culture stretched as far as the golden hills of California and the trading villages of the Willamette Valley in Oregon.

Often viewed as a tidal wave of expansion, this grand migration actually proceeded by fits and starts, by short jumps into adjacent territories. Consider the case of Thomas Lincoln, prototypical frontiersman and father of the sixteenth President. Born in Virginia in 1778, Tom Lincoln moved to Kentucky with his family at the age of six. He remained there long enough to marry Nancy Hanks, also a native of Virginia, and begin his own family. In 1816, seven years after the birth of his famous son, Lincoln led his family into Spencer County, Indiana. There he buried his wife, formed a second marriage with a Kentucky widow, and prospered moderately until 1830, when he decided to relocate in southern Illinois. After one year near Decatur, Illinois, Tom Lincoln moved once more, about one hundred miles southeast to Coles County. There, in 1851, he died.

That biography, romanticized though it has been by American folklore, tells much about the western experience. First, Lincoln followed a familiar route westward, settling near kin who had preceded him. When he picked his homesites, he chose land where the soil was similar to what he had left behind; as an experienced farmer, he did not suddenly abandon his well-tried agricultural habits. Also significant is the willingness with which he assumed his reputation as "a rolling stone." Like so many of his contemporaries, Lincoln easily surrendered his holdings to the best buyer, staked out new claims at the next homestead, developed his interests, and sold the titles again. For Lincoln, the land had lost its mystical qualities and existed merely as an interchangeable part, as regularized, orderly, and fragmented as the mass-produced gears that turned Eli Terry's clocks.

In approaching the land as a commodity, people like Tom Lincoln revealed not only their materialistic values, but also the practical economics of land acquisition. Though Congress always professed to sell the national domain cheaply to the nation's farmers, the division of public lands through auctions usually benefited speculators and brokers who could afford to purchase large chunks of real estate for resale to the actual settlers. Such practices did not prevent the proliferation of independent farms through the

Mississippi Valley. But it did make it easier for the first settlers to grab the best lands, consolidate their holdings, and then sell out at premium prices. Indeed, investment in real estate remained so common and, in some periods, so intense as to retard the expansion of the American economy by diverting capital from other forms of commercial and industrial enterprise. This phenomenon, though evident in all sections, appeared most clearly in the southern states, much to the chagrin of economic reformers who urged southern businessmen to diversify their investments.

Despite this pervasive materialism, the popular image of the American West continued to emphasize its antimaterialistic purpose. For Thomas Jefferson and his proselytes, the unsettled wilderness symbolized the boundless possibilities of national regeneration. Free from corrupting institutions, open to all settlers, the vast spaces represented the land of innocence, a veritable garden of Eden. There, in a timeless place of purity, the American nation would fulfill its destiny.

This apocalyptic vision, by linking geography with nationalism, placed special responsibilities on the American people. In the words of John L. O'Sullivan, archexpansionist editor of the *Democratic Review,* the United States had a "Manifest Destiny" to stretch its influence until "the whole boundless continent is ours." Central to the concept of Manifest Destiny was the belief in American superiority. Like the Founding Fathers, nineteenth-century expansionists lauded the uniqueness of republican governments and extolled the blessings of political liberty. By carrying these institutions across the continent, American expansion would broaden the foundations of liberty, extend the area of freedom, and elevate the benighted peoples who still lived under inferior forms of government. This missionary impulse reinforced a strenuous commitment to the Protestant religion. By transporting the Protestant gospel into the unmapped regions of the West, American evangelicals would protect the virgin lands from the machinations of heathen devils and the serpentine wiles of Spanish Jesuits. Republican government and the Protestant religion thereby promised to preserve the purity of the continent.

These ideological imperatives thrived on the spirit of technology. "Let us bind the republic together with a perfect system of roads and canals," declared John C. Calhoun in 1816. "Let us conquer space." American expansionists promised to carry the blessings of

industry to the less favored peoples of the interior. "Our government . . . should encourage the arts and sciences," advised a
Pennsylvania promoter in 1847, "and introduce . . . those mighty
improvements by which time and space are annihilated in our own
land." The sense of technological progress permeated the expansionist vocabulary. "The steam is up," shouted the *Boston Times*
from the very doorstep of industry, and "the young overpowering
spirit of the country will press onward." Such optimism—energetic,
boastful, and haughty—pointed to an "omnipotent spirit" they
called "Young America."

Manifest Destiny, besides symbolizing the energy of the Republic,
also illuminated a larger cultural theme: a gnawing fear of disorder
and an abiding hostility toward the irrational. In spatial terms, these
patterns encouraged the subjugation of the wilderness—the leveling
of forests, the organization of lands, the erection of towns and
villages. The dramatic alteration of the landscape—heralded and
applauded by all contemporaries—thus represented a grandiose attempt at imposing secular limitations over the natural boundlessness
of the continent.

The pace of progress encouraged gross insensitivity. "Rapacity
and spoliation cannot be features of this magnificent enterprise,"
argued a New York expansionist. "We take from no man; the reverse
rather—we give to man. . . . With the valley of the Rocky Mountains converted into pastures and sheep-folds," he maintained, "we
may with propriety turn to the world and ask, whom have we
injured?"

The answer came, with propriety, from Washakie, a Shoshone
forced from his lands by the white invasion. "The white man," he
complained, "kills our game, captures our furs, and sometimes feeds
his herds upon our meadows." "Every foot of what you proudly call
America," he protested, "not very long ago belonged to the red
man. The Great Spirit gave it to us. . . . But the white man had,
in ways we know not of, learned some things we had not learned;
among them, how to make superior tools and terrible weapons
. . . ; and there seemed no end to the hordes of men that followed
. . . from other lands beyond the sea." That forceful lament revealed another, more spiritual vision of the land—the sacred
Mother Earth—which contradicted the impulses of white America.

The mystical values of the Native Americans threatened the
orderly imagination of the whites. Other unorthodox groups seemed

equally dangerous. Roman Catholicism, for example, represented an alternative to WASP rationalism that aroused widespread fears among the Protestant majority. Sectarian religious movements, most notably the Church of Jesus Christ of Latter-Day Saints, also alarmed more traditional Protestants. In each case, the WASPs responded by establishing geographical barriers around the nonconforming groups. Hoping to avoid cultural contamination, WASP society imposed ever more rigid order upon American space—drawing territorial boundaries, creating ethnic enclaves, stipulating lines of demarcation. Though symptoms of fear, such strategies proved remarkably successful in isolating non-WASPs from the American mainstream and in insulating the dominant culture from these unwanted peoples.

The first victims of geographical exclusion were the native peoples living just west of the coastal tribes. Following the War for Independence, white encroachment on the natives' lands created endemic tension between the races. In the Northwest Territory, the presence of British agents, illegal occupants of the fur-trading posts, further complicated the situation. When American settlers began occupying the region, the local tribes attacked them and defeated a series of military expeditions sent to pacify them. Within the Washington administration, Secretary of War Henry Knox recognized the legitimacy of the natives' claims and urged the President to maintain "principles of justice." But when the natives refused to respect an earlier treaty, denying the legitimacy of the tribal delegates, the American government authorized the use of force. In 1794, General "Mad Anthony" Wayne destroyed a native coalition in the Battle of Fallen Timbers, and the following year dictated the Treaty of Greenville, which extinguished some of the natives' land claims and established a boundary line separating the two peoples.

The attempt to isolate the races failed, however, because Americans refused to respect the treaty obligations. White settlers seized tribal lands with impunity, penetrated traditional hunting grounds, and debauched the natives with alcohol. William Henry Harrison, appointed as territorial governor in 1800, aggravated these conflicts. Manipulating the rival chiefs, Harrison acquired additional lands and encouraged further white aggression. Meanwhile, the native peoples suffered immensely. "I can tell at once," Harrison reported with unusual candor, "upon looking at an Indian whom I may chance to meet, whether he belongs to a neighboring or to a more distant tribe. The latter is generally well-clothed, healthy and vigor-

ous; the former half-naked, filthy, and enfeebled by intoxication."
Despite these observations he did not change his policies.

Fearing total destruction, Native Americans grasped one last
hope. Under the leadership of the brilliant Shawnee chief, Tecumseh, and his brother, the Prophet, the tribes of the Northwest
formed an alliance promising to sell no more land to the whites.
The presence of American traders, beckoning with gifts and alcohol, often undermined this agreement. But Tecumseh remained
hopeful that a confederation could be established embracing all the
tribes of North America. On the eve of the War of 1812, which
once again embroiled the United States in a war with England, he
journeyed from tribe to tribe, even as far as the Creeks and Cherokees living along the southern frontier, to advocate a military confederation backed by British arms. Though greeted by sympathy by
some native leaders, Tecumseh's message challenged long-standing
traditions of tribal conflict. While local chiefs and tribal elders
debated his proposal, a skirmish between Harrison's soldiers and the
Shawnees at Tippecanoe in 1811 demonstrated the weakness of the
Northwest confederation. Then the outbreak of hostilities between
Great Britain and the United States intensified tribal divisions. With
only limited support from the British, Tecumseh began a desperate
war against the American forces. But his death in the Battle of the
Thames in 1813 effectively terminated Shawnee resistance. Abandoned by the defeated British at the war's end, the northwestern
tribes relinquished their remaining lands and moved reluctantly to
reservations west of the Mississippi.

Some, like the Kickapoo chief Kanakuk, protested bitterly against
being forced from their traditional lands. "My father, you call all
the redskins your children," he chided the American warriors.
"When we have children, we treat them well. . . . Take pity on
us," he begged, "and let us remain where we are." Such pleas fell on
deaf ears. And when, in 1832, Black Hawk led some Sauk and Fox
back across the Mississippi into Illinois, the American militia captured the red chief. One of the Illinois volunteers, a young man
named Abraham Lincoln, had just been discharged from service.
Otherwise, he would have heard Black Hawk sadly bid farewell to
his people. "Black Hawk is a true Indian," he said, but "he can do
no more. He is near his end. His sun is setting, and he will rise no
more. Farewell to Black Hawk." Thus silenced, the northern tribes
accepted a restive exile—until new outrages would bring them back
to the warpath.

For the southern tribes, the War of 1812 proved equally disastrous. The unwillingness of the Creeks and Cherokees to align with
Tecumseh heightened intertribal turmoil. During the war, the Cherokees supported the American army commanded by Andrew Jackson and helped defeat the Creeks in a bloody slaughter at Horse
Shoe Bend. This American victory enabled Jackson to dictate a
treaty of peace in which the Creeks surrendered most of their lands.
"They have disappeared from the face of the earth," boasted Jackson to his superiors. The way was now clear for further American
expansion into the Gulf Plains.

Those Creeks who survived the carnage found sanctuary among
the Seminoles living in Spanish Florida. The Seminoles readily accepted these refugees, just as they welcomed fugitive slaves fleeing
the plantations of Georgia. More affluent Seminoles even owned
black slaves. When American slavehunters crossed the border in
search of runaway blacks, Native Americans joined with the slaves
to resist the white invaders. The result was a series of pitched
battles, with numerous casualties on both sides. To end this violence
and to capture the runaway slaves, the Monroe administration
ordered Andrew Jackson, now the hero of New Orleans, to lead a
punitive expedition against the red and black guerrillas. Jackson
responded with typical efficiency, indiscriminately burning Seminole
villages. Many native resisters were killed, and many blacks were
seized. Even the Spanish flag provided no protection. In one famous
episode, Jackson executed two British subjects, allegedly for insti-
gating the border crisis. Though the United States government officially chastised Jackson for his actions, it used the affair to prove
the incompetence of Spanish rule in Florida. Shrewd negotiations
by Secretary of State John Quincy Adams soon enabled the United
States to acquire Florida in 1819 in exchange for assuming Spanish
"debts" to American citizens for loss of property. This same treaty,
sometimes known as the Transcontinental Treaty, acknowledged
American claims to the Pacific Northwest and thereby established
an important precedent for expansion in subsequent decades.

The conquest of the Creeks and Seminoles foreshadowed the fate
of another powerful native society, the Cherokee of Georgia. In the
early decades of the century, the Jeffersonian establishment hoped
to assimilate these people by propagating the Christian religion and
the lessons of republican government. In the words of one government agent, these twin blessings would hasten "the conversion of
the savage into the civilized man." However misguided, such lofty

goals required white Americans to practice a modicum of restraint. But the citizens of Georgia were more interested in land than in justice. They sold debilitating alcohol to the natives, bribed their leaders, disrupted traditional customs, and appropriated their lands.

These genocidal impulses alarmed the Cherokee leaders, many of them half-breeds, who hoped to thwart American aggression by hastening the process of assimilation. A brilliant man named Sequoia developed a written alphabet, proving that his people were "civilized." The Cherokees also adopted American agricultural techniques, imitated white styles of dress, and struggled to maintain their lands. Despite existing treaties with the United States, however, the government of Georgia denied the validity of Cherokee land titles and demanded their removal from the state. The Cherokees responded by drafting a formal political constitution to demonstrate their autonomy and declared themselves an independent nation, protected by the laws of treaty. Protesting this action, the governor of Georgia remarked that "treaties were expedients by which ignorant, intractable, and savage people were induced without bloodshed to yield up what civilized people had a right to possess."

President Andrew Jackson, long a foe of the southern tribes, proved equally unsympathetic. "If they now refuse to accept the liberal terms offered they can only be liable for whatever evils and difficulties may arise," he replied. "I feel conscious of having done my duty to my red children." In the Supreme Court of John Marshall, however, the Cherokees discovered a friendlier paternalism. Ruling in favor of their claims, the Chief Justice acknowledged the Cherokees as a "domestic dependent" nation. "Their relation to the United States," he held in 1832, "resembles that of a ward to his guardian."

But Marshall's juridical acuity, however presumptuous, proved no match for Georgia's intransigence or Jackson's executive authority. Fully supporting Georgia's claims, the President insisted on enforcing the Indian Removal Act of 1830. "Doubtless it will be painful to leave the graves of their fathers," Jackson told the members of Congress in 1833. "But what do they [do] more than our ancestors did or than our children are now doing? . . . Is it supposed that the wandering savage has a stronger attachment to his home than the settled, civilized Christian? Is it more afflicting to him to leave the graves of his fathers than it is to our brothers and children?" By removing the Cherokees from their homes, Jackson concluded, the United States was "not only liberal, but generous." Meanwhile, Georgia officials simply sold Cherokee land in a state lottery.

As white settlers arrived to claim their holdings, the Cherokees found themselves thrust from their homes. Many took shelter in the mountains of Tennessee. Even the more resolute lost hope when Congress refused their desperate appeals. Finally, in 1838, President Martin Van Buren ordered General Winfield Scott to evict the Cherokees from their lands. Thus began the infamous "Trail of Tears." American soldiers, wielding bayonets and swords, herded the Cherokees into stockades and then led them on a forced march to reservations west of the Mississippi. The Cherokees suffered enormously along the route, succumbing in great numbers to starvation, exposure, and disease. Probably four thousand people died during this period of internment. For the survivors, there were only the uncertain promises of future security. "Brothers!" one Cherokee had warned prior to the great upheaval, "Will not our great father come there also"?

The policy of racial separation, so brutally enforced against the Cherokees, revealed a striking paradox in American attitudes toward space. It was only by imposing rigid territorial order on non-WASP peoples that white Americans could preserve a sense of geographical mobility for themselves. "The white man," remarked a Shoshone, "who possesses this whole vast country from sea to sea, who roams over it at pleasure, and lives where he likes cannot know the cramp we feel in this little spot." For Native Americans took literally the Jeffersonian injunction that the earth belonged to the living. By white America's standards, consequently, their behavior often appeared unpredictable. By placing the native peoples on those "little spots of the earth," the American government assured itself of the orderly development of the western states.

This paradox—the institutionalization of space and the advocacy of geographic mobility—stimulated the territorial expansion of the United States during the nineteenth century. Although the acquisition of Louisiana in 1803 seemed to provide ample room for American farmers, within two decades, Americans were crossing into the Mexican province of Texas. At the same time as these settlers claimed loyalty to the Mexican government, they also preserved their American forms of culture, including, in many cases, the institution of black slavery. As the number of these unassimi-

lated people increased, the Mexican regime attempted to curtail
further immigration from the United States. Such policies were
intended to strengthen the central authority, but instead provoked a
violent rebellion, which led to the proclamation of an independent
Republic of Texas in 1836.

As Americans, the leaders of the Texas government appealed to
the United States for annexation. But the threat of war with Mexico, together with the possibility of British military intervention,
precluded such a course. Meanwhile, the Texas issue entered
American politics. Enthusiastic expansionists, many of them southerners with an eye on Texas cotton fields, urged the immediate
acquisition of the territory. Their pleas won the endorsement of
President John Tyler, a true son of Virginia, who presented a Treaty
of Annexation in 1844. But when his secretary of state, John C.
Calhoun, boasted that the scheme would guarantee the perpetuation
of slavery, many northern congressmen refused to support it, and
the treaty failed to pass in the Senate.

The Texas question intruded in the presidential campaign of
1844. The Whig candidate, Henry Clay, attempted to appease both
sides by blurring his position on annexation, and thus he satisfied no
one. His strategy especially antagonized some of his northern supporters, who switched to a third-party candidate, the abolitionist
James G. Birney running on the Liberty party ticket. This defection,
largely a symbol of northern political trends, ironically facilitated
the election of the Democratic expansionist, James K. Polk. Tyler,
the lame-duck President, treated Polk's victory as a popular man-
date and submitted a joint resolution (which required a bare majority) for the annexation of Texas. Amid much protest and invective,
Texas entered the union in 1845. "Who shall say there is not room
at the family altar for another sister like Texas," exulted the *New
York Sun,* "and in the fullness of time for many daughters from the
shores of the Pacific."

Despite such joy, these political machinations aggravated the controversy with Mexico. President Polk offered token concessions, but
the Mexicans, insulted and outraged, rejected his ambassador. The
collapse of diplomatic relations, followed by a border clash between
American and Mexican soldiers at the disputed Rio Grande boundary, intensified passions. In 1846 Polk requested Congress to declare war, claiming that Mexico had "shed American blood upon
the American soil." Though an obscure member of the House of
Representatives named Abraham Lincoln asked piously if the Presi-

dent could identify the precise spot of American soil upon which American blood had been shed—an indelicate question applauded by many other northern Whigs and abolitionists—the war measure passed with ease.

As a military affair the war with Mexico proved the superiority of American arms and strategy. Under the leadership of Zachary Taylor, one army defeated the forces of General Santa Anna and occupied Buena Vista. A second contingent led by Winfield Scott— once the nemesis of the Cherokee—marched into Mexico City. Within one year, American troops had destroyed virtually all opposition in Mexico. American soldiers under Stephen Kearney captured New Mexico, and American settlers in California rebelled against the Mexican government and established the "Bear Flag" Republic. These victories defined the terms of the peace settlement. In the Treaty of Guadalupe Hidalgo, the United States obtained California, New Mexico, and the disputed Rio Grande area for $15,000,000 and some monetary claims against Mexico.

The dramatic conquest of Mexico also concealed some subtler aspects of America's Manifest Destiny. During the course of the war, when the United States army occupied Mexico City, many expansionists began to advocate the annexation of all Mexico. Logical as the idea seemed in the light of American continentalism, it soon foundered on another, less obvious problem. John Calhoun, surely the least subtle of politicians, explained his objections: "To incorporate Mexico," he proclaimed in the Senate, "would be the very first instance . . . of incorporating an Indian race; for more than half of the Mexicans are Indians, and the other is composed chiefly of mixed tribes. I protest against such a union as that! Ours, sir, is the government of a white race." Other politicians were less blunt. But when the final boundaries were drawn, it was the Rio Grande—not some distant isthmus—that became the nation's border.

Nor was this sense of exclusiveness merely a southern concern. Early in the war, as it became apparent that the United States would defeat Mexico, a congressman from Pennsylvania named David Wilmot introduced a measure to prohibit slavery in any lands obtained from Mexico. Defeated twice in the Senate, the Wilmot Proviso nevertheless unleashed a bitter debate about the status of slavery in the territories. Efforts to limit the extension of slavery partially indicated the impact of abolitionism on American politics, but many expansionists simply opposed the presence of nonwhite people in the pure garden of America. Several northern states, for example, prohibited the entry of free blacks in the 1850s. Such legislation reflected a fear of economic competition from cheap black labor. More fundamental, however, was the deep-seated prejudice against black people. "It is certainly the wish of every patriot," asserted a leading Republican politician named Francis P. Blair, that "our union should be homogeneous in race and of our own blood." By excluding African people from the West, therefore, white America could fulfill its special destiny to cover the continent with free institutions.

One way of controlling the black population was to transport them back to Africa. The colonization movement had dated from the early decades of the century. Seen as a way of ending black slavery, the scheme also promised to resolve—or, more precisely, accepted the impossibility of resolving—America's race problem. Emancipated slaves, instead of remaining in proximity to their former masters, would be removed to some distant location. In 1817, the exclusionists formed the American Colonization Society, a philanthropic organization that advocated compensation for former slaveowners and the prompt exportation of blacks to Africa. The movement appealed particularly—and ironically—to evangelical Protestants who thought that American blacks might be suitable instruments for converting the African heathen to Christianity. After the founding of the Republic of Liberia in 1822, however, only about twelve thousand blacks returned to Africa.

The dwindling interest in colonization after 1830 was partly the effect of the growing influence of radical abolitionists who insisted that the American people could indeed resolve the problems of racism. Equally important was the bitter opposition of the free black community. "The colonizationists want us to go to Liberia if we will," complained one black; "if we won't go there we may go to hell." Such antipathy, repeated by many black leaders, effectively undermined the colonization program.

As political abolitionism became more powerful in the 1850s, however, white politicians again saw colonization as the only satisfactory alternative to race warfare. The prevalence of racial hatred also convinced some blacks that colonization would benefit their people. "We must have a nationality," argued one supporter of emigration. "I am for going anywhere, so we can be an independent people." Even during the Civil War, the idea of colonization and forced emigration seemed to be a viable alternative to the dilemmas of a biracial society. But black participation in the war effort, together with a resurgence of moral perfectionism, again suggested the possibility of racial harmony. Moreover, there remained an illusive hope among whites that the blacks might depart voluntarily to their natural abodes in the torrid zones. And the West, that magical territory settled from both the North and the South, would maintain its racial homogeneity, and its purity.

The fear of contamination by undesirables also motivated the persecution and exclusion of white cultural deviants, most notably the Church of Jesus Christ of Latter-Day Saints (Mormons). Founded by the prophet Joseph Smith and based upon the divinely inspired Book of Mormon, the Mormon Church originated in upstate New York, a region known for its religious enthusiasm. But the unique religious practices of the Mormons, including plural marriages, offended orthodox Protestants, and Smith was forced to migrate, first to Ohio and then to Jackson County, Missouri. "Our people fare very well," wrote one of their leaders in 1833, "and, when they are discreet, little or no persecution is felt." Discretion or no, the Mormon presence aroused the hostility of their "Gentile" neighbors, provoking mob violence and virtual civil war. Facing imprisonment, Smith chose emigration again and led his people to Illinois in 1839. At Nauvoo, they built a flourishing town, populated in 1845 by fifteen thousand people. But their material success aroused envy, and their religious deviation created storms of protest. The murder of Joseph Smith in prison indicated the depth of outrage, and at this crucial juncture his survivors again sought solace in the wilderness. One group, under the leadership of Brigham Young, made the grand exodus to Utah in 1846 and founded the state of Deseret. Beyond the territorial limits of the United States and isolated from hostile neighbors, the Mormons transformed the barren desert into a prosperous community.

The exclusion of the Mormons—like the isolation of the Cherokees, Mexicans, and blacks—depended upon the availability of open lands. As the American population spread across the continent, however, these possibilities diminished considerably. The Mormons soon discovered that the Treaty of Guadalupe Hidalgo brought them back into American jurisdiction, forcing them to confront anew the intolerance of the dominant culture. In 1857, President James Buchanan even sent federal troops to enforce the Constitution. Sheer distance protected the Mormons from additional interference. But before Utah would be admitted as a state later in the century, the Mormons had to eliminate such deviant policies as polygamy. In the end, the WASP majority had asserted its will.

Despite the prolonged controversy, the Mormons shared certain fundamental values with their antagonists. Nowhere was this more apparent than in their attitudes toward space. When the Mormons designed their first citadel in Missouri, they followed a geometric plan organized around twelve temples and square city blocks. In their other settlements at Nauvoo and in Utah, they also built cities noted for geometric order and regularity. Even today, Salt Lake City remains a monument to rectangular geometry; its numbered streets radiate in linear rows from Temple Square at its center.

These linear blueprints typified urban planning throughout the United States. Though Pierre L'Enfant's plan for the national capital at Washington, D.C., lacked a geographical center (as befitted a government based on the separation of powers), the architects of the city created rectangular blocks and right-angle intersections. The streets of New York followed a similar plan. In 1811, the city's planners instituted the grid pattern for the upper portion of Manhattan Island, created a system of numbered streets, and divided building lots into regular parcels of real estate. Four decades later, the planners of San Francisco repeated the rectangular patterns despite the steep hills and the natural contours of the land.

Such organizing principles contrasted markedly with the confusion of older, traditional cities. "The map is a perfect chaos," acknowledged a Boston editor in 1830, "and all directions are set at defiance by the abrupt terminations of our high-ways, and their sinuous and uncertain windings." Newer portions of the city, however, boasted a grid arrangement, which one resident characterized "as the true lines of civic beauty and convenience." These improvements provided clarity, regularity, and efficiency. But as the Boston commentator observed, in the older "hap-hazard streets . . . the fault of intricacy was more than repaid by the advantages of constant novelty."

The spatial relations of the nineteenth-century cities also revealed a deliberate attempt to isolate WASP America from nonrational, corrupting influences. Just as white American Protestants shrank from incorporating the premodern peoples of Africa and America, so too did they shun non-Protestant immigrants who symbolized medieval superstition. Only by establishing rigid defenses against what they conceived as irrationality could white Protestant Americans feel safe from the forces of cultural disintegration.

As children of the Reformation, American colonials had articulated a fervent hostility to the Roman Catholic Church, and their own children readily perpetuated that antipathy. Richard Henry Dana expressed the typical prejudice when he remarked sarcastically that "there's no danger of Catholicism spreading in New England; Yankees can't afford the time to be Catholics." Besides representing the irrationalism of the Middle Ages, Catholics also acknowledged the moral supremacy of an extranational authority—the pope at Rome. That divided loyalty convinced American Protestants of the unassimilability of Catholics. These popular prejudices, common though they were in Protestant Europe, lay dormant in America largely because the Roman Catholic population remained fairly small. As late as 1830, only about three hundred thousand people (about 3 percent of the population) subscribed to the Catholic faith. But even those small figures impelled some conservatives, particularly in New England, to advocate immigration restrictions.

Following the famines in Ireland and Germany, Catholic immigration to America soared dramatically. By 1860, about 10 percent of the population—some three million people—were Roman Catholics. Lacking specific skills, the Irish often constituted the poorest class in industrial society. In New England, their willingness to accept lower wages enabled them to replace farm girls in the textile mills; in the South, they often performed tasks considered too dangerous for the more valuable slaves. Such poverty encouraged crime and alcoholism—two symptoms that merely reinforced prevailing prejudices.

As the working-class immigrants crowded into the cities, living in squalor, which contemporaries called "slums," the upper classes began to move into less congested areas. The emergence of fashionable and economically exclusive neighborhoods in Jacksonian America—a phenomenon associated with the growing stratification and polarization of the social structure—paralleled the cultural exclusionism of the westward movement. Living in wealthy enclaves, the urban upper class thus minimized social contact with lower-class workers and immigrants. By erecting large mansions in undeveloped parts of the cities, the upper classes could preserve a sense of spaciousness even as they divided and subdivided the open tracts of land.

Such residential escapes required more wealth than most people possessed. Thus the arrival of working-class immigrants glutted the labor market, and threatened the economic position of other urban workers. As jobs became scarce and wages shrank, many lower-class WASPs vented their anger at the new immigrants, fomenting ethnic antagonism and mob violence. In the minds of working-class Protestants, economic oppression and anti-Catholicism easily blurred. In one celebrated case in 1834, a mob of Protestant workers displaced their hatred for the Irish workers onto an Ursuline convent in Boston, burned it to the ground, and spent the next three days rioting in the streets.

That violent reaction—characteristic of urban ethnic clashes in the nineteenth century—represented only one type of WASP protest. An avalanche of popular literature depicted the moral iniquities of the Catholic Church. Viewing Catholicism as a threat to traditional values, many Protestants attempted to use the public schools to assimilate the immigrants. But when the Catholics protested the introduction of Protestant Bibles in the schools during the 1840s, the issue spilled into the political arena. The tendency of immigrants to support Democratic candidates—probably because their antagonists voted Whig—merely aggravated the situation. Throughout the country, political groups supporting nativism emerged to advocate restricted immigration and tightened standards for naturalization.

The nativist movement, like the struggle over slavery in the territories, climaxed during the 1850s with the growth of the American, or "Know-Nothing," party. As the nation passed through sectional crisis and headed toward Civil War, many anxious conservatives looked hopefully for a resurgence of common ideals. The elimination of foreign influences seemed like a panacea for the nation's ills. Thus the American party, based on the principle "Americans must rule America," won great popularity in all regions. In the presidential election of 1856, ex-President Millard Fillmore gathered nearly one million votes and the Know-Nothings obtained considerable power in Congress. But as a patchwork alliance, the American party could not transcend the deepening divisiveness caused by the slavery issue. By 1860, political nativism had lost much of its appeal. It was not surprising, however, that many exclusionists then joined the Republican party and embraced a political platform based on free soil.

As anti-Catholicism resulted in urban violence, so did WASP attitudes toward free blacks. In northern no less than southern towns, black Americans were systematically excluded from white institutions, denied access to public facilities, and segregated in housing, churches, and schools. At times of economic crisis, black workers usually lost their jobs first. Even so, they frequently were attacked by white mobs for accepting lower wages.

Patterns of racial segregation in some ways may well have satisfied some cultural needs of black people. In segregated churches, black Americans could maintain their cultural identity and African heritage. Spatial segregation thus encouraged black autonomy in fact, if not in law. And in living apart from white society blacks avoided the constant scrutiny of white officials.

Hostility to racial integration in the North also provoked mob violence against outspoken abolitionists. A Boston mob once attacked William Lloyd Garrison in broad daylight, while an otherwise law-abiding crowd assaulted the abolitionist editor Elijah Lovejoy on several occasions, at last killing him in Illinois in 1837. Prominent in these mobs were northern colonizationists who wanted to resettle blacks in Africa and feared that the demise of slavery would herald racial amalgamation. Significantly, a high proportion of these rioters inhabited neighborhoods with large numbers of black residents. Such proximity, instead of easing racial tension, apparently intensified the commitment to exclusion.

The sharpest irony of racial separation, however, was the establishment of segregated burial grounds. Even the Quakers of Benjamin Franklin's Pennsylvania—Christian humanitarians who welcomed blacks in their worship services—maintained segregated burial places. This contradiction probably reflected not only a fear of racial contamination, but also a dread about death and decomposing bodies. New Englanders and urban dwellers traditionally established burial grounds around their churches. But in the absence of nearby churchyards, rural Americans had buried the dead on family farms. In both cases, the dead remained near the living; death constituted a fulfillment of life.

During the nineteenth century, as churchyards became crowded and individuals departed family lands, these burial traditions often proved inconvenient and apparently undesirable. Reflecting a modern secularism, urban Americans established public cemeteries in areas outside the existing city limits. The dead, as vivid reminders of human mortality, thus were removed from the body politic. Such policies symbolized a denial of physical decay, a denial of fundamental life processes. In a striking way, the rejection of the dead mirrored other taboos about the human body. Black people, as symbols of bodily activity—in work, dance, and sex—aroused such phobias and thus were excluded from white cemeteries. In yet another way did white Protestant society attempt to impose human order on the infinite. Even the dead threatened that rationalized order.

The institutionalization of space, of which the cemetery movement was a part, also provided an answer for the placement of other people who could not be integrated into the social order. The insane, paupers, orphans—all lacked a settled place in society. In the colonial period, these troubled individuals lived with sympathetic kin or legally appointed guardians, so that they could mix with ordinary members of the community. The usual punishments for crime were corporal punishment, banishment, or death; in noncapital cases, criminals, once punished, could re-enter society. Thus, social deviants did not lose their status as human beings. Underlying these patterns was the assumption that ultimate justice, for better or ill, would come hereafter.

During the early nineteenth century, American reformers suggested that socially deviant individuals be isolated from the remainder of society and placed in asylums where they would receive treatment leading to rehabilitation. Such reforms involved the reclassification of those offenses considered capital crimes and the imposition of rational justice. For the mentally ill, the poor, and the orphaned, houses of refuge, staffed by professionals, would provide rational guidelines for moral improvement. In short, nineteenth-century reforms attempted to exclude *all* deviants from interaction with ordinary people and, presumably, corrupting influences.

Life within the penitentiaries and asylums followed rigidly controlled rules and routines. "Everything moves by machinery," observed a visitor to one orphan asylum, "as it always must with masses of children never subdivided into families." An institutional regimen, authoritarian to the core, thus established order for these otherwise disorderly inmates. By controlling the pressures of ordinary life, the institutions promised to speed the process of rehabilitation. And if isolation freed deviants from the burdens of life, so did it liberate normal people from interaction with unwanted, irrational individuals. By segregating madness—like exiling Native Americans—the WASP majority hoped to perpetuate a society based solely upon reason and order. Though cloaked in the langauge of social reform, Americans maintained these separating

institutions long after they had failed to achieve their stated purpose.

The reforming impulses, grandiose as they now appear, were part
of an overwhelming optimism about the Americans' ability to control and reorganize the natural environment. They "treated nature
as a conquered subject, not as a mother who gave them birth,"
observed a European visitor in 1837. "They were the children of
another world, who came to burn, ransack, and destroy, and not to
preserve what they had found. They burned the forest, dug up the
bowels of the earth, diverted rivers from their course, or united
them at their pleasure; and annihilated the distances which separated the North from the South, and the East from the West."

By midcentury, however, as the conquering children poised at the
western ridges of the continent, some Americans—only a handful,
to be sure—began to question the meaning of that geographical
carnage. Amid the strident materialism of Jacksonian America, two
New Yorkers, Thomas Cole, the painter, and James Fenimore
Cooper, the novelist, contemplated gravely the destruction of
American nature, and with it, the forces of national regeneration. In
a series of magnificent paintings, Cole—known today as an exponent of the Hudson River School—grappled with the sublime power
of uncorrupted nature: the lonely rider fording a mountain stream;
minuscule characters dwarfed by forests—not a barnyard in sight,
nor an ax, nor a hoe. Meanwhile, Cooper produced the archetypal
child of nature, the uncorrupted Leatherstocking, protesting the
killing of pigeons, the death of innocence. Both Cole and Cooper,
romantics in an age of technology, feared the consequences of
American violence to nature.

If the destruction of nature was a technological problem, there
were other troubled Americans prepared to offer technological solu-
tions. George Perkins Marsh, a professional lawyer and diplomat,
paused in 1864 to write a book called *Man and Nature* in which he
pointed to "the dangers of imprudence and the necessity of caution
in all operations which . . . interfere with the spontaneous arrangements of the organic and inorganic world." Urging "the restoration
of disturbed harmonies," Marsh criticized his countrymen for ignoring the moral dimensions of human activity. "It is time," he warned,
"for some abatement in the restless love of change which character-
izes us." Amid the havoc of Civil War, Marsh's voice indeed cried
in the wilderness.

More influential than Marsh was the work of Frederick Law Olmsted, a pioneer landscape architect. As the designer of New York's Central Park in 1857, Olmsted stressed the importance of respecting the natural environment, of organizing space in accord with the contours of the land. His philosophy, like his art, revealed a fundamental contradiction in American attitudes toward space. The very idea of designing parks reflected the permanent loss of open space. In planning the landscape, therefore, Olmsted could only be imposing human rationalism upon an essentially undefinable subject. That his countrymen—as well as subsequent generations—have praised his vision merely underscores the culture's alienation from the natural world.

The notion of taming nature within the confines of urban parks epitomized the white American Protestant attempt to transform wildness into civilization. From this perspective, American expansion constituted a "mighty improvement" of a "savage wilderness." But in linking the national identity to the subjugation of space, the expansionists assumed that there always would be additional territory to seize and subdue. It required less than one century, however, before commentators like Frederick Jackson Turner undermined the confidence of that prophecy, and with it, the sense of national purpose.

"The principles of our happy government"

★ ★ ★ ★ ★ ★ ★ ★ ★ ★ ★ ★ ★ ★ ★ ★ ★ ★ ★ ★

8

Politics and Power

Founding the Republic: the paradox of political
parties and local politics

Alexander Hamilton's financial program and the beginnings of
national political parties: Republicans vs. Federalists

Foreign-policy formulations under Washington,
Jefferson, and Madison

War of 1812

Era of Good Feelings: nationalism vs. sectionalism,
the Missouri Compromise, and political reform

Andrew Jackson, president of the people: Democrats
vs. Whigs, the Bank War, nullification controversy,
and the Tariff of Abominations

Presidential election, 1856: Dred Scott Decision,
Lincoln in office, sectional crisis, secession
and the coming of civil war

"They who own the real estate of a country," observed a Civil War Republican, "control its vote." That simple aphorism underscored a dramatic transformation of American politics since the age of Thomas Jefferson. As economic and social relations became more secular, so too did political affairs. In the decades after the American Revolution, a spirit of democracy spread through the land, destroying forever the genteel traditions of the Founding Fathers; and political values simultaneously shifted from the politics of deference to a secular politics based on interest.

Such a transformation would have alarmed the Founding Fathers. Like their colonial ancestors, the founders of the Republic had assumed that an underlying harmony of political interests, an organic unity, would bind all citizens to "the general welfare." Those assumptions had justified the creation of a republican form of government. But the country's founders also understood that republics were especially vulnerable to the machinations of selfish politicians, and they advised against the formation of political factions, which served the interests of only one segment of society. Such factions, they feared, would undermine the tenuous balance of republican government and destroy the grand experiment in politics. "The spirit of party," warned President Washington in his Farewell Address, "agitates the community with ill-founded jealousies and false alarms; kindles the animosity of one part against another; foments occasionally riot and insurrection." Such advice, a lingering inheritance from the world of deference politics, allowed little room for serious disagreement about policy and power.

It was against this bedrock of belief that American politicians confronted the massive social changes unleashed by the new secular spirit. The expansion of American commerce, the migrations into western lands, and the early development of industry all challenged traditional expectations of social order. The reaction of politicians to these trends depended upon their previous vision of the good society.

Political conservatives condemned the disruptive effects of geographic and social mobility. Fearful of institutional disintegration, they opposed the westward migration and the acquisition of new territories, supported property qualifications for voting and office-

holding, and advocated a restriction of immigration and naturalization. Though professing loyalty to the principles of republicanism,
conservatives questioned the wisdom of majority rule, claiming that
the masses could not be trusted to exercise power unselfishly. The
true test of republican government, they insisted, was not its defense
of liberty, but rather its ability to protect the rights of property.
Despite this unconcealed elitism, the conservatives appealed not
only to the upper classes, but also to ordinary Americans who
respected the traditions of deference and expected their betters to
rule.

The clash between conservatism and change, muted through
most of the eighteenth century, emerged sonorously during the early
decades of self-government. In this age of local politics, however,
the central questions of power were resolved on the county and
state levels of government. Though the Constitution of 1789 provided the foundation for a strong national government, politicians
of the period understood the importance of controlling the county
courts and the state legislatures. Even the national capital, when it
was finally completed in 1800, did not offer the excitement of local
politics. Many elected representatives, fleeing what they considered
political exile, resigned their national offices to return to the true
seats of power.

These local and regional attachments accentuated the personal
nature of politics in the states. Political factions, some of them
dating from colonial days, were often able to dwarf the significance
of specific issues. In New York, for example, perhaps the most
Balkan of states, Governor George Clinton commanded the allegiance of the small-scale farmers despite the shifting ground of his
own politics. Political affiliations, moreover, often followed from
private connections, marriage alliances, and kinship—all highly personal forms of interdependence. Finally, local issues played an in-
ordinately important role in shaping political lines. The migration of
New England Yankees into western New York and the proliferation
of urban poverty in the state's metropolis explain much about the
rise and fall of political dynasties in the Empire State. In other
areas, the story, though substantially different, repeated similar
patterns.

The very complexity of early national politics tells much about
American political attitudes. That people identified more readily
with local and state candidates indicates not only an abiding provincialism, but also the absence of serious national questions. Only in

local power of politics

the area of foreign policy did political interests cross state lines, and
only then did political passions precipitate the formation of national
parties. Even then, the party system percolated downward, not into
a morass of haphazard interests, but upon a firm foundation of long-
existing factional groups. Indeed, the sophistication of local politics,
not the absence of formal party structures, demonstrates that
American citizens keenly understood the workings of power and
their best political interests.

The first national parties emerged in the only institutions of national power—the executive offices and the halls of Congress. Despite President Washington's attempt to transcend political divisions, his endorsement of specific domestic and foreign policies
provoked serious controversy. Such disagreements resulted from
differing visions of the nation's destiny and focused on the meaning
of republicanism. All the national leaders acknowledged the importance of balancing liberty and authority. But they disagreed about
where one ended and the other began. Washington's secretary of the
treasury, Alexander Hamilton, fearful of the disruptive tendencies
of popular politics, advocated a strong defense of the rights of
property. On the other side, Secretary of State Thomas Jefferson
and his friend James Madison, Speaker of the House of Representatives, stressed the importance of defending liberty from the encroachment of government. Such contending philosophies soon rup-
tured the harmony of Washington's administration.

The first skirmish opened when Hamilton presented a series of
financial reports designed to strengthen the national government.
Hamilton, a political conservative, believed that the Republic's
future depended upon the support of the economic elite, specifically
the creditors and speculators who had invested in the bonds of the
Confederation and in the securities issued by the separate states. By
rewarding the business interests, Hamilton argued, the United States
would win the loyalty of its wealthiest citizens (many of whom had
purchased the bonds at something less than face value) and forge
an alliance based on mutual interest. The restoration of American
credit also would attract foreign investment without jeopardizing
the independence of the new government. Hamilton proposed,
therefore, that the national government fund the existing debt at
face value and assume the outstanding debts of the separate states.

Both proposals encountered resistance from the southern states,
which would have benefited least. For Madison, however, the issue

involved more than economic interest. By expanding the size of the national debt, Hamilton's program would increase the power of government, creating a need for additional taxation and a larger bureaucracy. No less dangerous was Hamilton's undisguised manipulation of the principal of self-interest as a basis of political loyalties. Liberal republicans, on the other hand, believed the allegiance of the people should depend, not upon interest and coercion, but upon patriotism and love. Despite their sincere criticism, however, Hamilton's opponents agreed to compromise, and the measures passed through the Congress.

Hamilton then introduced a third proposal, the chartering of a national bank partly supported by government funds, which reopened the debate. Hamilton assumed that careful management by a central bank would provide capital for the expansion of American business and thus assure the economic stability of the new nation. Admitting that the bank would offer special advantages to the business community, Hamilton also claimed that other citizens would benefit indirectly by prosperity and improved government services. Hamilton's conservatism emerged not only in the specific proposal, but also in his willingness to expand the power of government. Critics of the bank, most notably Jefferson, argued that the measure was illegal because the Constitution made no reference to banks. Fearing the power of a strong government, Jefferson insisted that Congress could exercise only those powers specifically designated in the Constitution; all others remained in the states. To persuade Washington to sign the bank into law, however, Hamilton elaborated a broader interpretation of the Constitution, one that emphasized the "implied" powers of Congress to enact any measures for "the general welfare." True to his elitist predilections, the President endorsed the Bank of the United States.

The quarrel over Hamilton's financial program, besides illuminating basic ideological cleavages, also stimulated the beginnings of national political parties. To increase support, Hamilton worked with sympathetic members of Congress, providing executive reports and political advice. Hamilton's opponents also began to organize support in Congress and even established a friendly newspaper, the *National Gazette,* as an alternative to the more conservative organs. Despite this activity, national politics still did not significantly affect political affairs in the states. More concerned with local questions and local interests, American politicians watched the congressional

battles from a distance, lending only occasional support to measures
that affected their immediate concerns.

In retrospect, the quarrel over the financial program seems predictable and restrained. But contemporaries in both camps saw
things much differently. "Mr. Madison, cooperating with Mr. Jefferson," wrote Hamilton with undisguised venom, "is at the head of a
faction decidedly hostile to me and my administration; and actuated
by views . . . subversive of the principles of good government and
dangerous to the union, peace, and happiness of the country."
Jefferson replied that Hamilton's proposal "flowed from principles
adverse to liberty, and . . . calculated to undermine and demolish
the Republic." Such disproportionate rhetoric reflected a peculiar
republican myopia about political dissent. Believing still in a community of interests, politicians like Hamilton and Jefferson lacked
an alternative explanation of political opposition. Only some terrible
corruption could explain the refusal of reasonable men to agree
about politics. At issue was no mere economic policy. It was the
very survival of republican government. Aware of the fragility of
republics and the experimental nature of the United States, politicians raised the specter of conspiracy at the first signal of trouble.
For people who had challenged king and Parliament less than two
decades before, such vigilance seemed a small price for political
independence.

These questions of national survival soon provoked bitter disputes
about foreign policy. The French Revolution, by reiterating the
principles of the Declaration of Independence, had demonstrated
the value of preserving the United States as a symbol of liberty for
other oppressed peoples. But the Reign of Terror, which flaunted
guillotine politics and atheistic philosophy, promptly emphasized
the inherent dangers of popular government. These ideological matters came closer to home when war erupted between France and
Great Britain. President Washington hoped to steer a middle course
and issued a Proclamation of Neutrality forbidding any assistance
to either belligerent. But as the administration attempted to rise
above factions, a whirlwind of controversy shattered the republican
consensus. Since American economic interests remained closely
bound to British commerce and manufacturing, conservative
leaders, Hamilton among them, advocated a pro-English foreign
policy. Underlying this advice was a genuine admiration of British
constitutionalism. Less cautious Americans, however, inspired by

the leadership of Jefferson and Madison, saw in France a revitalization of the Spirit of '76, an antimonarchical surge that promised to extend the blessings of liberty to the Old World. These differing viewpoints did not remain contained in the chambers of government, but exploded in public debate throughout the states.

The issue crystallized when Washington endorsed the Jay Treaty, a commercial agreement between the United States and Great Britain, which attempted to resolve some of the grievances dating from the Revolution. Believing that an Anglo-American alliance would preserve the Republic from the storms of popular politics, Hamilton began to organize support for the treaty in Congress and in the states. Such activity, by appealing to broader questions of ideology and power, created a durable political coalition, known to historians as the Federalist party. Opponents of the Jay Treaty adopted a similar, though initially less effective course, harnessing votes in Congress, mobilizing factional support in the states, and, in the end, forging the basis of the Democratic-Republican party.

This maneuvering confused no one more than the party builders themselves. In an age that looked at political parties as subversive and conspiratorial, the emergence of strong coalitions aroused profound doubts. Each political group resolved that tension first by denying any evil intention and then by publicly accusing the other party of plotting to overthrow the Republic. Republicans accused Federalists of trying to erect a constitutional monarchy on the model of Great Britain; Federalists accused Republicans of trying to foment a rampant democracy. Partisan rhetoric was not the only weapon used. When the Federalist administration of Washington's successor, John Adams, encountered resistance to its anti-French diplomacy, the government attempted to eliminate the opposition party by enacting the Alien and Sedition laws of 1798. Prohibiting public criticism of the legal government, the measures justified the imprisonment of several Republican newspaper editors. Such aggressive policies drove the Republicans to seek constitutional refuge from the governments of the separate states. In a series of resolutions passed by the legislatures of Virginia and Kentucky, Jefferson and Madison argued that each state retained the right to nullify an unconstitutional act of Congress. That doctrine, though still only a statement of constitutional principles, revealed the precarious condition of the national union.

Even the election of Thomas Jefferson in 1800, heralded as a popular revolution in politics, failed to abate the fear of conspiracy.

"We are all Republicans," declared the new President hopefully, "we are all Federalists." Such wishful thinking betrayed distrust of political dissent and a realistic concern that Federalists and Republicans did not, in fact, share common principles. After Jefferson's election, the Federalists declined rapidly as a national party, largely because their elitism alienated a majority of the voters. Jefferson himself accelerated that demise by adopting some of the Federalists' programs and values. The legitimacy of the Louisiana Purchase, for example, hinged upon Jefferson's acceptance of a broad interpretation of the implied powers of the Constitution. Moreover, the Republican administration preserved Hamilton's financial structure, thus assuaging conservative fears about democratic anarchy.

Although the Federalists were defeated in national politics, they continued to play an important role at the state and local levels of government. After 1800, the party apparatus passed into the hands of a younger generation of politicians, more energetic than their predecessors, but equally conservative. Their success in state elections, particularly in New England, undermined Jefferson's search for consensus, and their persistent criticism of the administration raised new fears of conspiratorial subversion. A few Federalist extremists actually flirted with secession, imagining a northern confederacy composed of New York and New England. But most remained loyal to the Constitution, though President Jefferson was unconvinced. "Federalist monarchists," he remarked, "disapprove of the republican principles and features of our constitution and would . . . welcome any public calamity . . . which might lessen the confidence of our country in those principles and forms."

Such suspicions, however irrational, played a major role in the formulation of American foreign policy during the Jefferson and Madison administrations. The renewed warfare between England and France in 1803 soon embroiled the United States and raised old questions about the rights of neutrals, British violations of the Revolutionary settlement, and the impressment of American sailors by the Royal Navy. Though the Republican Presidents attempted to avert war, both belligerents—more concerned about their own national interests—challenged American rights with impunity. At last, in June 1812, Madison asked Congress to declare war on Great Britain—not because England was the sole aggressor, but because British attacks seemed more threatening to American independence. At stake in 1812 was not just the rights of neutral commerce nor the protection of private property. It was nothing less than the

preservation of the Republic. Despite a decade in power, the Jeffersonians still feared a monarchical conspiracy to undermine the government. "I have for a long time been convinced," declared a
Republican congressman with typical paranoia, "that there was a
party in our country, fully determined to do every thing in [its]
power, to subvert the principles of our happy government, and to
establish a monarchy on its ruins." According to such perceptions,
British aggression would embarrass the young Republic, undermine
popular confidence in government, and thus facilitate a constitutional revolution. By 1812, therefore, Republicans saw only one
alternative to an "unconditional submission" to British imperious-
ness: a declaration of war.

The war vote in Congress followed party lines and merely confirmed Republican suspicions about Federalist loyalty. Nor did the
war ever become a national crusade. Northern investors boycotted
American bonds. Federalist governors in New England restricted
the activities of their state militias. Northern newspapers scoffed at
"Mr. Madison's War" and predicted a dire defeat. Such claims,
partisan though they were, often proved disarmingly accurate. Despite years of controversy, American military forces were hopelessly
unprepared for war. The navy won a few celebrated victories, but
the British fleet soon blockaded American shipping, further injuring
foreign trade. Three invasions of Canada—all poorly planned and
badly executed—dashed the spirits of even the most sanguine expansionists. In 1814, a contingent of redcoats captured the national
capital, burned the White House, and headed toward Baltimore
before being stopped by a last-ditch defense. Meanwhile, Napoleon's
abdication meant that Britain could now turn its full attention to
the American theater of war.

Amid this despair, Federalists summoned a convention to Hartford, Connecticut, to contemplate the desperate state of the union.
Though some hinted broadly about secession, Federalist leadership
remained more moderate and instead proposed a series of constitutional amendments designed to protect the interests and values of
the conservative minority. Among their suggestions were a restriction of territorial expansion, limitations on naturalized citizenship,
and the protection of minority rights. These proposals, much more
than the stereotyped gestures of political impotence, showed the
passing of the old order, the loss not only of power, but of meaning.
The very idea of society, as Federalists understood that term, was
vanishing before their eyes and being replaced by a spirit of indi-

vidualism. One month after adjournment, that message paraded
boldly across the headlines of their newspapers. General Andrew
Jackson and a motley group of backwoods frontiersmen—symbols
all of the unwashed democracy—had stopped the British cold in the
Battle of New Orleans. News of the Treaty of Ghent, ending the
war, merely sealed the case.

In the aftermath of the war, the older ideological divisions
seemed less apparent. Republican politicians, no longer outraged by
Hamiltonian finance, resurrected a second Bank of the United
States, initiated protective tariffs, and appropriated federal funds for
public improvements. President James Monroe even ventured into
the Federalist citadel of Boston in 1817, winning a warm reception
from his erstwhile foes and inaugurating what the conservative press
hailed as a new "era of good feelings." Despite its inconclusive
battles, the War of 1812 had demonstrated the stability of the
Republic. "What is our present situation," asked the young Henry
Clay in 1816. "Respectability and character abroad—security and
confidence at home." The phantom of monarchical conspiracy had
been killed forever.

The willingness of politicians to submerge their differences on the
national level, however, did not erase older commitments to regional and local interests. Congressmen like Clay and John C. Calhoun supported policies such as the tariff because they believed
those measures would benefit their particular constituencies. When
the reverse occurred, when the fruits of commerce and industry
spread unevenly around the nation, the political leaders retreated
quickly to the support of states' rights. One early harbinger of that
reflex was the response to the Panic of 1819, a severe economic
depression. The crisis was largely the result of declining food prices
in Europe and the overextension of land investment, but it soon
revived sectional antipathy to the national bank and to the protection of manufactures. The vote on the tariff of 1824, for example,
followed sectional rather than party lines—with southern interests
slipping ominously into a minority status.

Even more visceral was the sectional reaction to the problem of
slavery. In 1819, when Missouri applied for admission to the
Union, a New York representative named James Tallmadge introduced a resolution to eliminate slavery from that territory. Though
Tallmadge couched his proposal in the language of morality, his
colleagues in Congress grappled instead with its political signifi-

cance. At stake was the political representation of the slave states —two seats in the Senate and congressional apportionment based on three-fifths of the slave population. As a question of pragmatic politics, therefore, the problem could be resolved. In the Missouri Compromise of 1820, Congress accepted Missouri as a slave state, balanced by the admission of Maine as a free state, and agreed to prohibit slavery in other parts of the Louisiana Territory north of 36°30′—a territorial boundary as precise as it was artificial.

But the politicians could not obscure the moral passion of the issue and the fragility of the settlement. "You have kindled a fire," pronounced a congressman from Georgia, "which all the waters of the ocean cannot put out, which seas of blood can only extinguish." And Thomas Jefferson, approaching the end of his days at Monticello, heard "a fire bell in the night," which he confessed, "awakened and filled me with terror."

While Thomas Jefferson worried about the future of the Union, a younger generation of politicians, more attuned to the rules of interest politics, had emerged as national leaders. John Quincy Adams, son of the second President, was born in 1767, as was his major political rival, Andrew Jackson. Henry Clay of Kentucky, chief architect of the Missouri Compromise, began his life in 1777. Daniel Webster of Massachusetts and John Calhoun of South Carolina, both powerful representatives of sectional loyalty, were born in 1782. These men were not the founders of the Republic; they were its children, nurtured in its principles almost from their first breath. Unlike their parents, products of a different, colonial culture, they had less to unlearn, less to fear.

All their lives, these children of the Revolution had heard patriotic orators proclaim the uniqueness of the United States. "Every child in America," asserted Noah Webster in 1790, "as soon as he opens his lips . . . should lisp the praise of liberty, and of those illustrious heroes and statesmen who have wrought a revolution in her favor." George Washington, now the political father, emerged as the symbol of national independence. Parson Weems' enormously popular biography celebrated Washington's patriotism, and even Thomas Jefferson paused, in the middle of his first inaugural Address, to applaud "our first and greatest revolutionary character, whose pre-eminent services had entitled him to the first place in his country's love and destined for him the fairest page in the volumes of faithful history." Such accolades, emblazoned on national holidays and repeated by printers, preachers, and politicians on every occasion, formed the sinews of the national identity.

If the American people were as virtuous as the orators announced, if the American Republic constituted a superior form of government, if all men possessed the inalienable rights of life, liberty, and the pursuit of happiness—in short, if all the patriotic polemics were to be believed, how could the citizens justify the antidemocratic legacies of the colonial heritage? When the Founding Fathers, respectful of the politics of deference, had established republican governments, they had instituted traditional limitations on suffrage, representation, and taxation. In the aftermath of the War of 1812, as younger politicians assumed the reins of leadership, these political anomalies were challenged and largely overthrown.

The impetus for political reform came not only from the rhetorical splendor of the pedagogues and patriots, but also from the activities of interest groups in state politics. As the centers of population shifted toward the west, as denominational rivalry destroyed established orthodoxies, as urbanization and industrialization polarized the social structure, the problems of representative government became more acute. By 1815, large segments of the population— religious minorities, propertyless workers, frontier settlers—were demanding the rights of republican government. Such pressures culminated in the summoning of state constitutional conventions to propose reforms of the existing political system.

As extensions of state politics, these conventions manifested the prevailing conflicts over political democracy. "It is not to be disguised that our governments are becoming downright democracies," complained the eloquent arch-conservative James Kent of New York. "The principle of universal suffrage, which is now running a triumphant career from Maine to Louisiana, is an awful power, which, like gunpowder, or the steam engine, or the press itself, may be rendered mighty in mischief as well as in blessings." Against such objections, the reformers stressed the egalitarian principles of the American Revolution. "Life was as dear to a poor man as to a rich one," observed a Boston politician, and "so was liberty." Those ideas, self-evident, but unimplemented by the Founding Fathers, encouraged political reform by their sons, and ultimately led to a significant expansion of the suffrage in most states.

These democratizing reforms, however, still perpetuated the existing prejudices of a WASP establishment. In Massachusetts, for example, the conservatives preserved the favored tax status of the

Congregational Church, despite the outraged pleas of the Baptist
minority. Even the concept of "universal suffrage," was given limitations. "The qualification of age, and of sex, remains," remarked
one delegate. "Women are excluded—minors are excluded." No less
obvious was the exclusion of the political "children"—blacks and
Native Americans. "They are a peculiar people," said an opponent
of black suffrage, "incapable . . . of exercising that privilege with
any sort of discretion, prudence, or independence. They have no
just conceptions of civil liberty." Nor did anyone defend the rights
of "the aborigines," described by this speaker as the "only rightful
proprietors of our soil—a people altogether more acute and discerning . . . [than] the African race." The New York convention simply disqualified thirty thousand free black residents. In other states,
the forces of reform often stumbled against the entrenched conservative opposition. Political democracy, tremendous in its potential, remained yet the special province of the white male elite.

The tenacity of the conservatives, besides reflecting a fear of
democracy, also revealed a lingering fear of political parties. "The
revival of party animosities in any shape, is mostly to be depre-
cated," warned Joseph Story of Massachusetts, a justice of the
United States Supreme Court. "If parties are to arise, new animosities will grow up, and stimulate new resentments." Yet the new
generation of political leaders, more convinced of the stability of the
Republic, remained indifferent to such advice. In expanding the size
of the electorate, the political reformers were expressing their confidence in majority rule. No longer suspicious of minority dissent,
neither were they seeking universal approval. The majority opinion,
legally expressed through the political process, would provide ample
support for the democratic politicians.

The expansion of the suffrage, by accepting the idea of interest
politics, encouraged the appearance of political parties. Once the
anathema of the Founding Fathers, the party apparatus became an
appropriate, perhaps even a necessary, instrument for organizing
masses of voters and articulating the will of the people. Party
loyalty, not some ideological consensus, became the bulwark of
republicanism. As party competition increased, moreover, the
people could perceive clearer distinctions between rival candidates,
producing a dramatic surge in voter participation. The old politics
of consensus soon followed the Federalist ideology into oblivion,
and a new egalitarian credo, charged with the energy of bandwagon

campaigns and stump oratory, captured the spirit of young America.

This political activity became evident after the election of Andrew Jackson in 1828. Though supported by a powerful coalition forged by the "Little Magician," Martin Van Buren, Jackson posed as the President of the people, the only national representative of all citizens. Where earlier Presidents, from Washington to the younger Adams, had earned their credentials in the executive branch of government, Jackson had emerged from the vicissitudes of state politics, a self-made frontiersman from Tennessee. As the hero of New Orleans, Jackson symbolized the natural virtue of the American people, their sense of national destiny, their commitment to the simple republic of the Founding Fathers. On Inauguration Day, the new President boldly opened the White House to the people, allowing the Washington crowd—"from the highest and most polished," reported a disgusted Justice Story, "to the most vulgar and gross in the nation"—to consume the ice cream and cake, lemonade and punch, while smashing china, trampling furniture, and causing a veritable riot, all of which merely confirmed the conservatives' worst fears about, as Story put it, "the reign of King Mob."

Jackson's image as President of the people—however exaggerated and self-serving—pointed out the major ideological cleavage of the times. Whether defending the infamous "spoils system" or supporting the state of Georgia over the Cherokee nation, Jackson identified his programs with the will of the majority and depicted his opponents as exponents of aristocracy and privilege. Besides illuminating Jackson's peculiar personality, his rhetorical style reinforced the appeal of the Democratic party. In an age of rapid economic and social change, the Jacksonian Democrats represented the older order, articulating an agrarian philosophy of frugality, simplicity, and virtue. Above all, the Jacksonians condemned the artificial contrivances of the new capitalism—paper money, chartered corporations, and banks. These economic institutions, the Jacksonians contended, had enabled a privileged aristocracy of wealth to steal the birthright of the common people. Old Hickory, as the symbol of national virtue, would restore the government to the people.

If the Jacksonians appealed to citizens who were dissatisfied with the changing social order, other Americans, more hopeful about the future of industrial capitalism, found comfort in the party of the

Whigs. Like the Jacksonians, the Whigs had made peace with the democratic credo and shared a commitment to economic individualism. Theirs was a philosophy of the self-made man, which promised the fruits of industry to all diligent citizens. In supporting such measures as protective tariffs, internal improvements, and national banking, the Whigs denied any special favoritism and instead predicted a democratization of wealth. "As commerce expands," maintained the sanguine Daniel Webster, "the effect . . . [is] to diffuse wealth and not to aid in its accumulation in a few hands." National legislation, agreed Henry Clay, would only accelerate that process. To the adventurous American, therefore, the Whigs symbolized the future prosperity of the nation.

Though the Whigs and Democrats shared a common political culture, the difference between the parties, like the opposite sides of a coin, seemed utterly irreconcilable; and the political clashes, when they came, assumed mammoth proportions. Consider the matter of the national bank. Chartered in 1816, the second Bank of the United States had provided sensible direction of the national economy by controlling the flow of credit, supervising the activities of the state banks, and offering a stable currency of banknotes for the public. Yet the Bank, as a direct agent in the economy, had offended numerous interests. State bankers often resented its cautious oversight; working people criticized the use of paper currency, which circulated at less than face value; orthodox Jeffersonians condemned the special interests implicit in a nationally chartered corporation. All this antipathy—and much more—converged in the violent psyche of Andrew Jackson.

The charter of the Bank was to expire in 1836. Nicholas Biddle, president of the Bank, remained optimistic about its approval by Congress and, at the advice of several Whig politicians, moved for a rechartering four years earlier, just before the presidential election of 1832. After considerable debate, Congress passed the Bank bill and transmitted it to the White House for endorsement. If Jackson signed the measure, he would have deserted basic political principles; if not, he risked his chances of re-election. Jackson did not hesitate. "The Bank," he exclaimed to Van Buren, "is trying to kill me, but I will kill it." Jackson's veto message, written with fury as well as power, denounced the Bank as a privileged institution, a threat to "the liberties of the people," and a violation of the Constitution. "Many of our rich men have not been content with equal protection and equal benefits," the President declared, "but have

besought us to make them richer by act of Congress." Then, raising
the theme of restoration, Jackson urged a return to "that devoted
patriotism and spirit of compromise which distinguished the sages
of the Revolution and the fathers of our Union."

With the election approaching, the veto placed the Bank issue
before that amorphous body Jackson called "the people." Now, as
before, they sustained him. After his re-election, Jackson proceeded
to dismantle the Bank, despite the outraged protests of the Whigs.
Though blamed for provoking an inflation in 1833 and a subsequent
depression in 1837, Jackson's policies were less significant than
distant changes in international finance. But for friend and foe
alike, the Bank War dramatized the problem of balancing power
and interest in the expanding Republic.

Even more significant was Jackson's confrontation with the state
of South Carolina over the question of sovereignty. During the
1820s, Congress had enacted higher tariffs to protect American
manufacturing, despite the growing opposition of southern politicians. After the enactment of the Tariff of 1828—known popularly
as the Tariff of Abominations—John Calhoun, then Jackson's vice-
presidential running mate, drafted an *Exposition and Protest* suggesting that a state government could nullify a law passed by Congress. Still loyal to the Union, however, Calhoun left his paper
unpublished and awaited a change in policy. It was not until the
passage of yet another uncompromising tariff in 1832 that the doctrine of nullification again emerged.

The new tariff prompted the state legislature of South Carolina to
call a special convention to consider an appropriate response. Judg-
ing the tariff to be unconstitutional (on the grounds that it taxed the
states unequally), the convention adopted an ordinance of nullification that declared the tariff to be "null, void, and no law, nor
binding upon this State, its officers or citizens." The convention
warned that any attempt to enforce the law would be "inconsistent
with the longer continuance of South Carolina in the Union." Such
threats failed to persuade the President. Jackson immediately requested Congress to lower the tariff. But he also issued a proclamation denying the constitutionality of nullification and summoning
the citizens of South Carolina to repudiate their leaders. "Their
object is disunion," he intoned. "Disunion by armed force is *treason*." Though prepared to authorize force against the nullifiers,
Congress agreed to a Compromise Tariff in 1833, which defused the
crisis. Repudiated by the other southern states, criticized by a large

unionist minority, the legislature of South Carolina could only retreat. With its last breath, however, the convention issued a final
protest: it nullified the now defunct Force Act, which had allowed
executive action against the state.

The bitterness of the nullification controversy—far beyond its
immediate significance—revealed a massive, spreading cleavage
within the structure of the Union. The real issue was not a tariff on
European imports, but a sense of isolation and powerlessness among
one segment of American society. As evangelical Protestantism lent
sanction to a small crusade of northern abolitionists, southern
slaveowners found themselves increasingly vilified as agents of
moral evil. No less threatening was the enemy within—the discovery of the Denmark Vesey slave conspiracy in Charleston in
1822 and the Nat Turner revolt in nearby Virginia in 1831. The
tariff debate merely emphasized the impotence of the once powerful
state of South Carolina. This feeling of loss—not unlike the sentiments of the New England Federalists of an earlier generation—enabled the nullifiers to win widespread support in their stand against
the national government.

The ultimate failure of the nullification movement, while disarm-
ing the radicals, merely hardened the ideological lines. During the
1830s, partly in response to the militant abolitionists, many southerners began to defend slavery as a positive good. Fearful of even
discussing the matter, others in the slaveowning establishment relied
upon extralegal force to suppress dissent. When abolitionist pamphlets were discovered in the mails, the southern state governments
confiscated the "incendiary" materials and persuaded Jackson's
postmaster general to uphold their position. Even on the floor of
Congress, the southerners fought abolitionist petitions, and forced
the House of Representatives to accept a "gag rule" in 1836, which
automatically tabled all antislavery petitions without discussion. The
only alternatives, Calhoun declared, were "to witness the assaults on
our character and institutions, or to engage in an endless . . . defense. Such a contest is beyond mortal endurance. We must in the
end be humbled, degraded, broken down and worn out."

If the slaveowning establishment saw an abolitionist lurking
within every Yankee peddler and schoolteacher, the strident defense
of slavery also convinced the abolitionists that there was an equally
conspiratorial "slave power" bent on subverting republican principles. This mutual suspicion—partly an accurate perception of

radical politics, partly the result of people projecting their own worst intentions onto their enemies—played an important role in the debate over territorial expansion. To northerners, the annexation of Texas, the war with Mexico, and the expansionist designs on Cuba all confirmed an "aggressive slaveocracy" seeking to extend the peculiar institution into previously uncorrupted lands. To southerners, however, the attempt to limit the expansion of slavery indicated a sectional plot—to deny the constitutional rights of property and to reduce the southern states to colonial status. Such clashing perceptions, each convincing in its own internal logic, made any compromises tenuous and unsatisfying.

Underlying the dispute was a common commitment to evangelical Protestantism and political democracy. Southerners and northerners alike accepted the moral perfectionism of the evangelical churches and strove to rise above sin. It was partly for this reason that southern churches redefined their attitude toward slavery in the 1830s—shifting from support of a necessary compromise with evil to a self-righteous vindication of a moral good. Northern Protestants, by condemning this position, created great tensions within American Christianity, leading to sectarian splits in the Methodist and Baptist churches. No less important was the southerners' insistence on the full rights of citizenship. By denouncing the legal right to own slaves in the territories, northern critics were consigning southern Americans to an inferior political status. "The prohibition," remarked Martin Van Buren, "carries with it a reproach to the slaveholding states, and . . . submission to it would degrade them." In a culture that asserted the uniqueness of its political institutions and proclaimed the special virtue of its citizens, the notions of peculiarity and sin caused deep and unhealing wounds.

If politicians focused upon pragmatic questions of power and ignored the moral issues, compromise was still possible. When, for example, David Wilmot moved to prohibit slavery from the former Mexican provinces, congressional leaders split angrily along sectional lines, creating a constitutional deadlock that threatened the Union. At issue was not simply the question of slavery, but also the problem of power, for the Senate was then divided equally into free and slave constituencies. The admission of California, certain to be a free state, would destroy that balance, forcing the South into a permanent minority status.

While radical spokesmen like William H. Seward condemned the

immorality of slavery, and slaveowners like Jefferson Davis attacked
the abolitionists, more moderate politicians, most notably Henry
Clay and Stephen Douglas, introduced a series of resolutions known
as the Compromise of 1850. California would enter the Union as a
free state, the status of New Mexico would remain temporarily
unresolved, the slave trade (but not slavery) would be abolished in
the national capital, and a fugitive slave law would protect the
rights of southern property. Reduced to a trading of interests, the
clash of sectional power could be avoided. But the Compromise
assumed that the voices of principle would agree to be silent, that
slavery and abolition were merely matters of policy.

That the Whig party could not survive the crisis only emphasized
the frailness of the peace. Unwilling to submerge their differences
about the status of slavery, northern and southern Whigs failed even
to adopt a national platform in 1852, and watched the Democratic
candidate, Franklin Pierce—equally noncommital but less offensive
to the South—sweep to victory. As the last remaining national
party, the Democrats controlled the future of the Union. Pragmatic
to the core, the Pierce administration attempted to preserve a facade
of neutrality, while appeasing southern expansionists with the Gads-
den Purchase (to facilitate the construction of a southern-Pacific
railroad) and by hinting at the acquisition of Cuba. Meanwhile, the
northern legislatures fanned the fires of sectional discord by enacting personal-liberty laws designed to impede the fugitive slave provisions of the Compromise. The publication of *Uncle Tom's Cabin* by
Harriet Beecher Stowe in 1852 further emphasized the emotional
distance between the sections. Morality was again creeping into
politics.

The issue climaxed in 1854 when Senator Stephen Douglas introduced a bill to organize the territories of Kansas and Nebraska
according to the doctrine of "popular sovereignty"—the idea that
the settlers of each territory, not the Missouri Compromise nor the
current federal Congress, should determine the future status of
slavery. To pragmatists like Douglas, the principle seemed eminently reasonable and thoroughly democratic. But it ignored the
moral imperatives of the issue and so aroused passionate protests
throughout the North. The repeal of the Missouri Compromise,
declared Abraham Lincoln, in a typical northern reaction, was
doubly wrong—"wrong in its direct effect, letting slavery into Kansas and Nebraska—and wrong in its prospective principles, allowing
it to spread to every other part of the world, where men can be

found inclined to take it." Even northern Democrats dissented loudly, and many of them deserted their party to form an alliance with former Whigs. It was here that the Republican party, the first major sectional party, had its beginnings.

Lincoln's protest revealed the central thrust of the new party— opposition to the expansion of slavery. Convinced that slaveowning interests were attempting to pervert free institutions and destroy the national mission, the Republicans determined to thwart the sectional conspiracy. To the South and to loyal Democrats, however, the Republicans seemed equally subversive. Identifying with the agrarian tradition of Jefferson and Jackson, the South saw its opponents as mad abolitionists, and agents of Yankee materialism, urban corruption, and capitalist exploitation. Moreover, once persuaded, once committed, neither side could transcend the self-generating logic of conspiracy.

Nor did the issues easily vaporize. Competing for the future of Kansas, free-soil and proslavery rivals moved into the territory and commenced an undeclared war of intimidation. "Bleeding Kansas," as the struggle was called, came closer to home when Senator Charles Sumner, a Massachusetts Republican, condemned "the Crime against Kansas" in an inflammatory speech. Preston Brooks, one of South Carolina's congressional representatives, retaliated by attacking Sumner with his cane, leaving the senator an invalid for years. To northerners, proof of southern barbarism needed no further testament.

Amid such violence, the presidential election of 1856 seemed a tame affair. Despite serious internal strains, the Democrats united behind James Buchanan, a "doughface" northerner (with southern principles), and reaffirmed the doctrine of popular sovereignty. The Republicans nominated John C. Frémont and campaigned to the slogan "Free Soil, Free Speech, and Frémont." The anti-immigration Know-Nothing party, rallying behind former President Millard Fillmore, drained support from both groups. When the vote was counted, Buchanan had obtained a narrow electoral victory of sixty votes. More significant was the strong Republican showing in the North. Frémont had carried the popular vote there and won eleven of the sixteen free states. The possibility of a sectional victory seemed closer than ever before.

What the Republicans could not manage at the ballot box in 1856, the Supreme Court delivered in 1857. In the Dred Scott

Decision, announced just three days after Buchanan's inauguration, the Court held that blacks were not citizens of the United States and that Congress—and by implication the territorial legislatures—lacked the constitutional authority to exclude slavery from the territories. Not only was popular sovereignty invalid, but so too had been the Missouri Compromise. While northerners bristled and southerners exulted, Buchanan attempted to end the crisis and admit Kansas into the Union. Despite his commitment to popular sovereignty, however, Buchanan ignored a rigged election that had produced the proslavery Lecompton Constitution. This perversion of the principles of popular sovereignty appalled even Stephen Douglas, who then broke with the administration. The next year, while campaigning against Abraham Lincoln for the Senate, Douglas repeated his opposition to the Dred Scott Decision. This assertion—known to historians as the Freeport Doctrine—together with his anti-Lecompton position doomed Douglas in the eyes of the South. He appeared no better than the blackest Republican.

As the Democrats prepared for the nominating convention of 1860, the southern wing announced that the party would have to endorse the Dred Scott ruling and reject the principles of popular sovereignty. Any other position would reinforce the fear of an abolitionist conspiracy. Already John Brown's raid on Harper's Ferry in October 1859 had sent chilling fears across the South, raising terrible visions of northern plots and domestic slave revolt. "Should the North fail to give some substantial guarantees . . . for southern institutions and constitutional rights," remarked one southern Democrat, "a revolution is inevitable."

Amid extreme tension and fear, the Democrats convened in Charleston, South Carolina—the very hub of southern radicalism—and discovered that they could not agree. When northern Democrats clung tenaciously to popular sovereignty, the southern delegates bolted the meeting, allowing a rump group to reconvene in Baltimore to nominate Douglas and popular sovereignty. The southern Democrats then proposed John C. Breckinridge of Kentucky and drafted a platform based on congressional protection of slavery in the territories. A small fragment of southern Whigs, still uneasy about a sectional alliance, supported the candidacy of John Bell and urged a return to national unity. The Republicans, hoping to draw support from the Midwest, nominated the little-known Abraham Lincoln from Illinois.

In the final poll, Lincoln captured the Presidency on a strictly sectional vote. Douglas carried only Missouri and part of the New Jersey ballot; Bell won three border states; Breckinridge swept the remainder of the South. Lincoln's election as a sectional President symbolized the South's alienation from the national government and its impotence before the will of the northern majority. "If we could have a Lord North in the Presidency," asserted a South Carolina politician in an unwitting play on words, "some rash insulting act might be perpetrated that would alarm and unite the South." The election of the Republican candidate, in itself, did just that. In southern eyes, Lincoln appeared as menacing to the South as that other Lord North, the minister of George III, had seemed to colonial revolutionaries less than a century before.

Shortly after Lincoln's election, the legislature of South Carolina summoned a special session to consider secession. On December 20, 1860, after brief debate, the convention formally repealed the state's ratification of the Constitution. Within six weeks, Mississippi, Florida, Georgia, Alabama, Louisiana, and Texas—all from the cotton South—had followed South Carolina out of the Union. In justifying these acts, the southern states denied any revolutionary intentions and instead emphasized the constitutionality of their positions. The federal union of 1789 had been based on a compact of separate states, they argued, and each state retained "reserved powers." Among these legal powers was the right to withdraw from the original compact. The Republican victory had placed the national government in the hands of avowed enemies—a party determined to scourge the South of its cherished institutions. Even the national President, supposedly after Jackson the representative of all citizens, threatened the southern way of life.

Besides arguing the constitutionality of secession, the southern states attempted to create a new confederation based on what they considered the original principles of the Founding Fathers. Though some extremists like William Yancey of Alabama and Robert Barnwell Rhett of South Carolina asserted the uniqueness of southern culture and urged their colleagues to repudiate the old republic, the leadership of secession remained with the legally elected governors, usually moderate politicians who sought to restore the original institutions and values of government. When the seven seceding states met in Montgomery, Alabama, in February 1861 to form the Confederate States of America, the delegates represented moderate interests and carefully chose two moderate politicians, Jefferson

Davis of Mississippi and Alexander Stephens of Georgia, as executive officers. The fire-eaters significantly were frozen out of the government.

The Constitution of the southern Confederacy revealed the conservative principles of its founders. Modeled after the Constitution of 1789, the document established similar branches of government, guaranteed the perpetuation of republican institutions, and protected the civil rights of its citizens. Noticeably different, however, was its defense of states' rights—the "sovereign and independent character" of each state. In a few particulars, the Constitution also attempted to alleviate specific long-standing grievances. Thus the Confederate Congress was prohibited from levying tariffs "to promote or foster any branch of industry." Similarly, in acknowledging the possibility of future territorial expansion, the Constitution guaranteed the preservation of slavery. Yet the delegates to the Montgomery convention, perhaps with an eye to British support, indicated their commitment to traditional values by denying the legality of the international slave trade. Such moderation placed the southern Confederacy safely within the mainstream of American history.

While the Deep South created the Confederate government, the national politicians sought to avert civil war. President Buchanan, the lame-duck incumbent, declared that secession was unconstitutional, but made no proposals to resolve the crisis. Representatives from the border states, most notably John J. Crittenden, sponsored compromise resolutions that would have restored the old Missouri Compromise line to the Pacific Ocean, guaranteed slavery where it already existed, and compensated slaveowners for fugitive slaves. In his inaugural address of March 4, 1861, President Lincoln reaffirmed his willingness to protect the institution of slavery in the South. He proposed, moreover, to enforce the fugitive slave law with the same dedication that he would suppress the foreign slave trade. But Lincoln remained adamant in opposing the extension of slavery, and on that single issue, symbolic as it was, the Union would founder.

By the time Lincoln presented his inaugural speech, most of the property belonging to the national government had been seized by the Confederate states. Despite his assurances that "there will be no invasion, no using of force against or among the people anywhere," however, the President specifically announced his intention "to hold, occupy, and possess" federal property. One of these enclaves was Fort Sumter, guarding the harbor of Charleston, South Carolina. Told that the garrison needed supplies and reinforcements, Lincoln hesitated to act lest he alienate pro-Union support in the South. But to surrender the fort would be equally damaging to the authority of government. The President chose a middle alternative—he would send only supplies to the besieged soldiers and he would announce his decision in public.

The burden now shifted to Jefferson Davis. Outmaneuvered by the President, he chose to attack this vestige of federal authority. On April 12, 1861, the shore batteries opened fire on Fort Sumter, sounding the first shot of the war. Three days later, Lincoln called for seventy-five thousand volunteers to end the rebellion in South Carolina. Two days thereafter, the state of Virginia, watching nervously, voted for secession and renounced the Union. So too did Arkansas, Tennessee, and North Carolina. The Civil War had begun.

"The home of one national family"

★ ★ ★ ★ ★ ★ ★ ★ ★ ★ ★ ★ ★ ★ ★ ★ ★ ★ ★ ★

9

The Civil War and
American Identity

The war and its aftermath: strategies, battles,
death immersion, Emancipation Proclamation

The weakness of the Confederacy and the triumph of the
nationalist attitude

The Lincoln Presidency and republican destiny: biracial
society, Native Americans, social values, and family relations

Lincoln, symbol of unity and death

Whatever the constitutional principles in question at its inception, whatever the ideological passion or the political realism of its instigators, the Civil War soon symbolized but one thing to all its participants; it was, in the words of Charles Francis Adams, Jr., "the Carnival of Death." President Lincoln had expected a short war and had called for three-month volunteers. "Lincoln may bring his 75,000 troops against us," responded Alexander H. Stephens, vice-president of the Confederacy. "We fight for our homes, our fathers and mothers, our wives, brothers, sisters, sons, and daughters! . . . We can call out a million of peoples if need be, and when they are cut down we can call another, and still another, until the last man of the South finds a bloody grave."

In July 1861, with high optimism, the Union army marched toward Bull Run, a twisting shallow creek just south of Washington, D.C. There, on the banks of the stream, the bluecoats met stiff resistance from the southern defenses. The raw Union troops hastily withdrew, broke ranks, and raced back to the safety of Washington. The First Battle of Bull Run had caused 3,000 casualties, North and South. Thus began what Walt Whitman called "the red business." In 1862 the carnage increased. In April, 23,000 soldiers fell near Shiloh Church in Mississippi. Two months later, in the Seven Days' Battles, 16,000 Yankees and 20,000 Rebels joined the casualty lists. The next month, a second meeting at Bull Run produced 25,000 victims. At Antietam, the following month, 21,000 more were killed or wounded. In December, the Battle of Fredericksburg left 15,000 additional casualties. The next year, small country crossroads like Vicksburg and Gettysburg, Chancellorsville and Brandy Station, carved their names indelibly on the national landscape. By the time Grant grabbed Lee's hand at the Court House of Appomattox in April 1865, 618,000 American men had died, and hundreds of thousands more had been scarred and maimed.

The survivors, civilian no less than military, bore invisible scars forever. "War is horrid beyond the conception of man," wrote Colonel Robert Ingersoll in 1862. "It is enough to break the heart to go through the hospitals. Old gray-haired veterans with lips whitening under the kiss of death—hundreds of mere boys with thoughts of home—of sister and brother meeting the dark angel alone, nothing but pain, misery, neglect, and death around you, everywhere nothing but death—to think of the ones far away expecting the dead to return—hoping for one more embrace—listening for footsteps that never will be heard on earth—for voices that have grown still and forever." Those mothers and fathers, widows and sweethearts, siblings and children—each carried what Abraham Lincoln once called "a living history" of war and death.

The trauma of the war struck to the core of national consciousness. For Whitman, the human slaughter opened yawning chasms of pain and shock, powerful images of tragedy. "These thousands, and tens and twenties of thousands of American young men," wrote the Wound Dresser from a Union hospital, "badly wounded, all sorts of wounds, operated on, pallid with diarrhea, languishing, dying with fever, pneumonia, &c open a new world . . . giving closer insights, new things, exploring deeper mines than any yet, showing our humanity, . . . tried by terrible fearfulest tests, probed deepest, the living soul's, the body's tragedies, bursting the petty bonds of art." Most casualties never lived to reach those haunted hospitals, seeping their lives on the stone walls that failed to shelter them, in the fresh air of the countryside, in civilian barns and sitting rooms, sometimes on passenger trains behind the lines. These were public deaths, witnessed by ordinary farmers and workers, etched in thousands of memories.

"The cannon will not suffer any other sound to be heard for miles and for years around it," noted Ralph Waldo Emerson in the season of Spotsylvania (25,000 casualties). "Our chronology has lost all [the] old distinctions in one date—*before the War, and since.*" Ever after, the American people returned to those battles and fields, memorizing tortured strategies and mad charges, erecting marble monuments, studying Mathew Brady's photographs of twisted limbs and rotting flesh, and gawking at the empty panorama. "We are met on a great battlefield of that war," they have learned to repeat. "We have come to dedicate a portion of that field as a final resting place for those who here gave their lives. . . . But in a larger sense we cannot dedicate, we cannot consecrate, we cannot hallow this ground." The stark pathos of those words, repeated interminably because they could not be assuaged, thus entered the national vocabulary, where patriotic sentimentality finally could dull the reality and create a mythological sense of peace and rest.

* * *

The staggering mortality of the Civil War, far greater than any American war before or since, reflected a perverse inability of the military leaders to comprehend the implications of technological warfare. Experienced, if at all, in the Mexican War, a conflict characterized by dashing strategic sweeps and technological obsolescence, the Civil War generals and their political leaders remained committed to grand climactic battles that would destroy the enemy at once. In traditional warfare, such victories had come from bold frontal assaults, wave upon wave of charging soldiers overwhelming an embattled adversary. In an age of slow-loading inaccurate weapons, such bravery produced celebrated heroes and casualties remained relatively low.

The introduction of new rifled weapons, however, and the invention of expanding minié bullets revolutionized warfare. Where the old smooth-bored muskets encouraged bold rushes and close fighting, guns like the Springfield rifle could annihilate an advancing infantry from across the fields. Though only a few frontal assaults succeeded during the entire Civil War, the military planners continued to order hordes of soldiers against the defensive emplacements. "Move in quick time until within a hundred yards of the fort," sounded one typical order, "then, double-quick and charge!" Meanwhile, at the top of the hill waited the enemy's artillery, pouring fire onto the upcharging troops. That casualty figures soared, therefore, is not surprising. "An assault," declared one Union soldier, "means—a slaughter-pen, a charnel-house, and an army of weeping mothers and sisters at home. It is inevitable." Agreed a Confederate officer, "It was not war—it was murder."

No less deadly than the minié bullets were the ravages of camp disease. The conglomeration of rural troops, previously untouched by childhood contagions, encouraged epidemics of the mumps and measles, which often debilitated whole regiments. Survivors of these infections faced intermittent warfare with such killers as typhoid, dysentery, malaria, and diarrhea. Though hardly as glorious as a cavalry charge, the diseases vanquished many a battalion, killing, by the war's end, twice as many soldiers as died in combat. Moreover, in the prisoner-of-war camps, in the notorious Libby and the putrid Andersonville, ravaging disease, compounded by starvation and scurvy, worked its toll, claiming some 8,500 lives in one four-month period during the blazing summer of 1864. This incredible human waste, inadvertent though it was, intensified feelings of national sacrifice and nourished a collective sense of guilt, which in its turn demanded retribution.

It was this terrible unremitting loss that transformed the war to save the Union into, in Lincoln's words, "a people's contest" that embraced the entire society. In his first war message to Congress, delivered three months after the firing on Fort Sumter, Lincoln had reiterated his limited commitment to preserve the Union as it existed in 1861. The issue, he declared on July 4, was "whether a constitutional republic, or a democracy—a government of the people, by the same people—can, or cannot maintain its territorial integrity, against its own domestic foes." As an experiment in government, he remarked in the metaphors of Jefferson, the United States had "to demonstrate to the world, that those who can fairly carry an election, can also suppress a rebellion—that ballots are the rightful, and peaceful, successor of bullets; and that when ballots have fairly, and constitutionally, decided, there can be no successful appeal, back to bullets. . . . Such," he proclaimed, "will be a great lesson of peace."

As the casualty figures mounted and the Union army seemed incapable of achieving a decisive victory, dissatisfaction with the war spread through the North. In the election of 1862, Democratic candidates, many of them outspoken critics of the administration, gained considerable strength, capturing the legislatures of Illinois and Indiana. Only the intervention of the Union army—which arrested some Democratic candidates—enabled the Republicans to remain in power in the border states of Missouri, Kentucky, and Maryland. Secret peace societies—known pejoratively as Copperheads—sprang up throughout the North, and in one celebrated case, Lincoln approved the arrest and subsequent banishment to the South of a leading Ohio Democrat named Clement L. Vallandigham. Such violations of civil rights illuminated the changing direction of the war.

While the Democrats condemned Lincoln for waging an unconstitutional war against political self-determination, more radical Republicans chafed at the President's restraint. When General John C. Frémont, once the Republican candidate for the Presidency, ordered the emancipation of all slaves owned by Missouri rebels, Lincoln, fearing that the border states might be provoked to desert the Union, countermanded the order. A similar proclamation by

General David Hunter produced an identical presidential response. Those decisions reflected Lincoln's pre-eminent interest in preserving the Union. By 1862, however, the inadequacy of the military effort, together with Republican threats to form a more radical third party, impelled Lincoln to move in a bold direction.

"My paramount object in this struggle is to save the Union," Lincoln announced in 1862. "If I could save the Union without freeing *any* slave I would do it, and if I could save it by freeing *all* the slaves I would do it; and if I could save it by freeing some and leaving others alone I would also do that." By the autumn of 1862, the time to act had come. Following the Union victory at Antietam, Lincoln issued a preliminary proclamation announcing his intention to free all the slaves in the areas of rebellion on January 1, 1863. This policy, he argued, by attacking the core of southern society, would expedite a military victory. "Without slavery the rebellion could never have existed," he maintained; "without slavery it could not continue." Still defined in constitutional terms, the preliminary proclamation invited the southern states to restore the Union, offering something less than forced emancipation in return for peace. Lincoln also reaffirmed his willingness to compensate former slave-owners for the loss of their chattel.

The final Emancipation Proclamation, true to the preliminary proposal, affected slavery only in the Confederate territories. It did not touch slavery in the loyal border states. Nor did it apply even in federally controlled areas of the South, such as New Orleans. As Secretary of State William Seward remarked, "We show our sympathy with slavery by emancipating slaves where we cannot reach them, and holding them in bondage where we can set them free." In his first Inaugural Address, Lincoln had indicated his willingness to accept a Thirteenth Amendment that would have guaranteed slavery in the southern states. Now, to sanction his wartime Proclamation, he urged a different Thirteenth Amendment: to eliminate slavery in the Confederate states. A Republican Congress, more radical than the President, went beyond this request and endorsed an amendment prohibiting slavery throughout the United States. Ratified in December 1865, eight months after Lincoln's death, it represented a fundamental alteration of the Constitution of 1789.

Presented as an emergency measure, the Emancipation Proclamation served as the basis for an important change in military policy. From the outbreak of hostilities, radical Republicans and free blacks had urged the President to field an army of black soldiers. "Every consideration of justice, humanity and sound policy confirms the wisdom of calling upon black men . . . to take up arms in behalf of their country," asserted the ex-slave Frederick Douglass. "We are ready and would go, counting ourselves happy in being permitted to serve and suffer for the cause of freedom and free institutions." But arming black troops (in a cultural system that viewed blacks as inferior and unreliable) and sanctioning their use of violence against whites alarmed northern conservatives. When a small group of black volunteers began drilling privately in New York City, for example, the chief of police ordered them to disband. Even in the Emancipation Proclamation, Lincoln warned the freed slaves "to abstain from all violence, unless in necessary self-defense."

That same document nevertheless welcomed the induction of black men "to garrison forts, positions, stations, and . . . to man vessels of all sorts." The decision to use black soldiers, like emancipation itself, constituted an unalterable transformation of the war effort. Though military commanders remained suspicious about black troops, doubting their ability to endure combat conditions, black regiments promised to shorten the war and thus save white lives. Despite their enthusiasm and proven valor in the field, however, black troops remained distrusted and unwelcome allies who received the worst details and the riskiest assignments. In the navy, the black volunteer could attain no higher rating than "boy," and his pay, through most of the war, remained lower than a white serviceman's. Still, the enlistment of black soldiers and, more important, their prowess with arms provided a powerful argument to accept black citizenship in the years after emancipation.

The departure of a black regiment from New York City in March 1864 epitomized the transformation. During the summer of the previous year, a predominantly Irish mob had protested federal conscription laws by attacking the black population. For four days, the mob had control of the streets, looting, burning, and lynching indiscriminately. Only the arrival of seasoned Union troops, pulled from the reserves at Gettysburg, had restored order to the city. Less than a year later, the *New York Times* reported the farewell parade of black soldiers "everywhere saluted with waving handkerchiefs, with descending flowers, and with the acclamations . . . of countless beholders." "It is only by such occasions," the *Times* declared, "that we can at all realize the prodigious revolution which the

public mind everywhere is experiencing. Such developments are in-
fallible tokens of a new epoch."

If the use of black soldiers sealed the North's commitment to
total war, so too did it galvanize southern opposition. During the
secession crisis, southern radicals had warned that the election of
Lincoln would jeopardize the institution of slavery and threaten the
southern way of life. The Emancipation Proclamation confirmed
those dreadful predictions, leading Jefferson Davis to denounce the
policy as the "most execrable measure recorded in the history of
guilty man." By touching on the most profound southern anxieties
about racial control, the arming of black men removed the possibility of early compromise. Whatever their political disagreements
about secession, white southerners recoiled instantly from the specter of Yankee abolitionism and rallied gallantly to the banner of
white supremacy.

However optimistic southerners were in 1861 or desperate by
1865, they simply could not match the industrial superiority of the
more populous North. Equally debilitating for the Confederacy was
the lack of a national commitment. Most southerners had supported
secession as a constitutional right of the separate states. They also
shared a desire to perpetuate southern slavery. Yet southern citizens
generally lacked any symbolic loyalty to the Confederate government. Such prominent politicians as Governor Joseph E. Brown of
Georgia objected to the centralization of power in the Confederacy
and refused to cooperate with such policies as conscription and the
use of local militia beyond state lines. Nor did Jefferson Davis, as
the creature of a states' rights tradition, possess informal party
connections with the citizens-at-large. Where Lincoln could expect
the support of loyal Republicans, Davis had to operate within the
narrow, often provincial, contours of state politics. In the absence
of a national culture, defenders of states' rights like Governor
Brown and General Robert E. Lee commanded far deeper allegiance—and, in the aftermath of the war, far greater respect—than
the Confederate officials of Richmond.

The doctrine of national loyalty, so vigorously denied within the
southern Confederacy, emerged in the North as a central tenet of
Union ideology. In rejecting the constitutionality of secession, the
North also repudiated the argument that the southern states were
merely exercising the right of political self-determination. Pointing

out the contradiction between a slave society and one committed to free institutions, northern polemicists denied the contemporary relevance of the Jeffersonian doctrine. By challenging the free elections of 1860, by disregarding the southern Unionists, by perpetuating slavery, the Confederacy violated the basic principles of majority rule and so proved the falseness of southern constitutionalism. In the North, loyalty to the established government assumed a new importance and, because of the massive spilling of blood, attained intense emotional validity.

One result of this shift was a dramatic rewriting of Revolutionary War history. "Little allowance has hitherto been made for those who steadily adhered to the cause of the Crown during the War of the Revolution," remarked a northern historian in 1865. "The Loyalists . . . have been rudely assailed by American historians. . . . The time has come for a more dispassionate consideration of their actions. The events of the last four years . . . must teach us to entertain a higher respect for the men who did not at once join in the cause of independence, violate their oath of allegiance, and disown submission to the long-established government." The Spirit of '76, once considered the beacon for popular revolution, was being examined in an entirely different light. Indeed, when the Paris Communards returned to the barricades in 1870, they earned few plaudits from the once-kindred revolutionaries in America.

Tied to this emphasis upon political loyalty was a new commitment to the concept of nationalism. While a young politician in Illinois, Lincoln had advocated a "political religion of the nation." As the Revolutionary generation had supported the Declaration of Independence, he declared, "so to the support of the Constitution and Laws, let every American pledge his life, his property, and his sacred honor." This attachment to the Constitution, common as it was throughout the nation, dominated the secession crisis, each section arguing the constitutionality and, consequently, the legitimacy of its position. So venerable had this tradition become that the last amendment to that fundamental law had been ratified in 1804. As the Civil War became a total war, however, the need for constitutional change became clear. Three amendments passed between 1865 and 1870 bestowed the rights of citizenship upon the former slave population. Not until 1913, when different political pressures again demanded reform, would another series of amendments be approved.

The willingness to tinker with the Constitution after 1865 reflected a new attitude toward the national government. Until the Civil War, American politicians agreed that certain "domestic" institutions— like slavery and suffrage—fell within the domain of the state governments. The secession of the southern states, considered illegal by the North, forced the national government to intervene in those previously exclusive spheres. The national government now claimed the right—and the victory of the North confirmed the right—to directly coerce individual citizens. Moreover, the notion of "reconstruction," despite its plethora of meanings, always assumed that the national government—Congress or the President—would determine the political structure of the southern states. The conquering North, committed to national unity, would direct the future thrust of American history.

It was Abraham Lincoln, more than any other American, who grappled with the new problems of national identity. "The only thing like passion or infatuation in the man," Walt Whitman remarked about the sixteenth President, "was the passion for the Union of these states." As the chief executive of the United States, its wartime commander-in-chief, Lincoln assumed, reluctantly at first, and then with greater intensity and purpose, the burdens of reforging the nation. "That portion of the earth's surface which is owned and inhabited by the people of the United States," he declared in a message to Congress in 1862, "is well adapted to be the home of one national family; and it is not well adapted for two, or more. Its vast extent, and its variety of climate and productions, are of advantage . . . for one people, whatever they might have been in former ages. Steam, telegraphs, and intelligence, have brought these, to be an advantageous combination, for one united people."

At the core of his passion for the Union was Lincoln's sense of historical destiny, his belief in a national mission. Even as a boy, he confessed in 1861, he had seen "something more than common" in the Spirit of '76. "I am exceedingly anxious that that thing which they struggled for; that something even more than National Independence; that something that held out a great promise to all the people of the world to all time to come . . . shall be perpetuated," and he hoped that he personally might be "an humble instrument" for the "almost chosen people" of God "for perpetuating the object of that great struggle." "We cannot escape history," he repeated in another address. "We shall nobly save, or meanly lose, the last best, hope of earth."

The vision of providential destiny, not unlike the grand optimism of the Revolutionary War patriots, seemed to explain, even justify, the terrible calamity of Civil War. "Our fathers brought forth on this continent," he intoned at Gettysburg, "a new nation, conceived in liberty, and dedicated to the proposition that all men are created equal." Now, however, the Civil War was "testing" the viability, the validity, the future of that experiment. Lincoln returned to the theme of cosmic destiny in his second Inaugural Address. Both the North and the South, he explained, "read the same Bible, and pray to the same God; and each invokes His aid against the other." Perhaps, then, the "Living God" had brought "this mighty scourge of war" to purge the nation for its sins. As the armies of Ulysses Grant hammered viciously at the soldiers around Lee, Lincoln asked seriously whether "every drop of blood drawn with the lash should be repaid by another drawn with the sword."

Though phrased in the same providential language, Lincoln's sense of American destiny had changed radically during the course of the war. When, in 1862, he had spoken of "one national family" composed of "one united people," he was expressing his commitment to a white society. Just as Thomas Jefferson envisioned American expansion without "blot or mixture," so too did Lincoln expect the black population to leave the United States. Lincoln's hopes for emancipation were linked to colonization—the departure of all blacks—free as well as slave—to some other, presumably more congenial, environment.

In articulating his devotion to a white America, Lincoln never qualified his hostility to the institution of slavery. Unlike Jefferson, who viewed slavery as a necessary evil, Lincoln considered black servitude "the greatest wrong inflicted on any people." Though he had been willing to accept southern slavery to preserve the Union in 1861, he clearly viewed that proposition as socially unnecessary but politically expedient. "One section of our country believes slavery is *right*," he asserted in his first inaugural speech, "while the other believes it is *wrong*." Lincoln's decision to press for emancipation, however hesitant, required no major ideological conversion, no psychological metamorphosis. The changing war merely pushed him in that direction.

Although Lincoln reversed his position on southern slavery, he remained ambivalent about the problem of race. "I am not, nor ever have been in favor of bringing about in any way the social and political equality of the white and black races," he had asserted in his debates with Stephen Douglas in 1858. "There must be the position of superior and inferior," he assured a cheering audience, "and I . . . am in favor of having the superior position assigned to the white race." As President, Lincoln repeated these sentiments to a delegation of free blacks, hoping to convince them to support colonization. "On this broad continent," he assured the committee, "not a single man of your race is made the equal of a single man of ours. . . . I cannot alter it if I would. It is a fact, about which we all think and feel alike, I and you." In this spirit, "it is better for us both," he concluded, "to be separated."

Despite strong opposition within the black community, some black separatists, led by Henry Highland Garnett, welcomed the opportunity to escape American racism and emigrated to Haiti. Others, with financial support from the federal government, settled in Panama and in the Caribbean islands. Both experiments proved unmitigated failures, which forced Lincoln to re-evaluate his ideas. Meanwhile, black soldiers had demonstrated their value to the Union cause, thus proving their readiness for political citizenship. By 1864, Lincoln himself was redefining his image of the "national family." In a private letter to the governor of the reconstructed state of Louisiana, Lincoln suggested that certain blacks—"the very intelligent, and especially those who have fought gallantly in our ranks"—be granted the vote. "They would probably help," he remarked, "in some trying time to come, to keep the jewel of liberty within the family of freedom."

Lincoln's attitudes toward Native Americans reflected similar racial assumptions. As a young man in Illinois, he had volunteered for service in the Black Hawk War, but his only distinction was in protecting a friendly native from a lynching. The written language, he asserted in 1859, "distinguished us from savages. Take it from us, and the Bible, all history, all science, all government, all commerce, and nearly all social intercourse go with it." During the Civil War, Lincoln declined the services of Native American soldiers just as he had declined those of blacks; eventually, to a limited extent, he reversed that policy. Lincoln's view of the native tribes emerged more clearly in 1862 when the Sioux of Minnesota, angry at the invasion of white settlers, rose in arms. "Attend to the Indians," Lincoln telegraphed the territorial governor. Yet when Minnesota settlers ordered the execution of 303 Sioux, Lincoln intervened, commuting the sentences of "those guilty only of participation in battles." Lincoln's cautious policy indicated his desire to minimize racial violence but also assured the dominance of white society.

If Lincoln's racial attitudes reflected his frontier heritage, those same experiences also conditioned his image of white society. "I am a living witness," he told an Ohio regiment at the White House, "that any one of your children may look to come here as my father's child has." Though not the first President to boast about his humble origins, Lincoln fervently believed in the promise of American capitalism. "On the side of the Union," he declared in his first war message to Congress, "it is a struggle for maintaining in the world, that form . . . of government, whose leading object is, to elevate the condition of men—to lift artificial weights from all shoulders—to clear the paths of laudable pursuit for all—to afford all, an unfettered start, and a fair chance, in the race of life." Here was a commitment to free labor as the basis of a free society.

As a Whig politician and later as a Republican, Lincoln reiterated the values of American capitalism. "That some should be rich," he told a working-class group in New York, "shows that others may become rich, and hence is just encouragement to industry and enterprise. Let not him who is houseless pull down the house of another but let him labor diligently and build one for himself." This doctrine of the self-made man, personified in his own life, underlay Lincoln's opposition to the economics of slavery. In the same sense, however, it implied that a capitalist economy would bring material rewards to all segments of society. Certainly that was the thrust of his own administration in supporting transcontinental railroads, tariffs, centralized banking, and the Homestead Act. But as a child of the frontier, Lincoln did not perceive the social implications of such policies—the growing disparities of wealth, the emergence of massive corporations, the reckless appropriation of natural resources and the national domain.

Lincoln showed himself considerably more sensitive to the plight of European immigrants who flocked to America in the decades before the Civil War. Though his rhetoric betrayed occasional slurs at Irish workers Lincoln explicitly repudiated the anti-Catholic violence of the 1840s. Moreover, while supporting some restrictions on naturalization, he criticized the exclusionism of the Know-Nothing party. "As a nation, we began by declaring that *'all men are created equal,'"* he wrote privately in 1858. "We now practically read it 'all men are created equal, *except negroes.'* When the Know-Nothings get control, it will read 'all men are created equal, except negroes, *and foreigners, and catholics.'* When it comes to this," he concluded, "I should prefer emigrating to some country where they make no pretense of loving liberty." For this child of Anglo-Saxon parents, the land of self-made opportunity remained open to all white settlers.

It was in the bosom of his family that all Lincoln's dreams and emotions converged. As a boy, the death of his mother, Nancy Sparrow Hanks, had created a profound sense of loss, and ever after he remained suspicious about human dependence. His relations with his father were equally ambivalent, perhaps because he blamed his father for his mother's death. Though Tom Lincoln summoned his only child to his deathbed in 1851, Lincoln avoided the visit and sent benign homilies instead. "Tell him to remember to call upon . . . our great, and good, and merciful Maker," the absent son advised; "who will not turn away from him in any extremity." Then, inadvertently punning on one of his mother's maiden names, Lincoln reminded his father that God "notes the fall of a sparrow . . . and He will not forget the dying man, who puts his trust in Him." "If we could meet now," added the son in a revealing statement of his alienation, "it is doubtful whether it would not be more painful than pleasant."

Lincoln's ambivalence about the family of his birth influenced his attitudes toward other personal alliances. In marriage, he chose—reluctantly—a more polished, more sophisticated woman named Mary Todd, whom he frequently referred to as "Mother." Seemingly satisfied by the union, Lincoln's public statements about marriage focused on the anomalies of such bonds. In explaining his antipathy to miscegenation, for example, he asked why "because I do not want a negro woman for a slave I must necessarily want her for a wife," a remark which brought yelling cheers and laughter from his Illinois audience. "I am now in my fiftieth year," he continued, "and I certainly never had had a black woman for either a slave or a wife." Such disclaimers, typical of the fine art of stump oratory, pointed to Lincoln's—and his culture's—sensitivity to the blurring of racial and sexual roles.

Lincoln's description of the secession controversy revealed a parallel ambivalence about the larger question of Separation and

Union. Speaking about "the lovers of the Union" who criticized the use of force against the South, Lincoln remarked that "in their view, the Union, as a family relation, would not be anything like a regular marriage at all, but only as a sort of free-love arrangement,— [laughter]—to be maintained on what that sect calls passionate attraction. [Continued laughter.]" "A husband and wife may be divorced," he stated at another time; "but different parts of our country cannot do this." Lincoln's passion for the Union, therefore, satisfied not only political needs, but emotional ones as well. It was this commitment to the Union that shaped his entire wartime policy —from the resistance to secession to the arming of black troops and to his generous offers of reunification after the peace. Ideology and emotions, in Lincoln's life, came easily together.

Most dramatically, Lincoln personified the death immersion of the country. As the war leader, he carried the awful burden of sending young soldiers to their deaths, a responsibility that weighed heavily on his conscience and evoked the genuine compassion for which he became justly famous. In his celebrated letter to Mrs. Bixby of Boston, whose sons had died for the Republic, the President revealed his own powerful grief for "the loved and lost." And he mourned profoundly the loss of his own son, Willie, to malaria. The sense of judgment hovered in his mind as he composed his second Inaugural Address, still quoted today for its rejection of malice, its espousal of charity, its fervent plea "to bind up the nation's wounds; to care for him who shall have borne the battle, and for his widow, and his orphan."

Five weeks later, on April 9, 1865, the war was over. "We must be more cheerful," Lincoln remarked to his wife on the evening of the fourteenth. "Between the war and the loss of our darling Willie —we have both been very miserable." And then as the President sat watching *Our American Cousin* at Ford's Theatre in Washington, John Wilkes Booth fired a single shot from a small derringer pistol. Lincoln died in a boardinghouse the next morning.

Millions mourned his death and lined the streets to watch his coffin on its solemn journey across the country to his final resting place in Springfield, Illinois. In the outpouring of grief, the nation purged four years of collective guilt, four years of death. And Lincoln's words, like the war itself, became part of the national mythology, metaphors to be repeated ritualistically, not for their meaning alone, but for their magical powers of cure, the last catharsis of death.

Part Three

★ ★

AN INTERNATIONAL FRONTIER OPENS
AS THE WESTERN FRONTIER CLOSES

"The nation's hoop is broken"

★ ★ ★ ★ ★ ★ ★ ★ ★ ★ ★ ★ ★ ★ ★ ★ ★ ★ ★ ★

10
The Collapse of
Nineteenth-Century Culture

Debacle in the West for Native Americans:
reservations and the Dawes Act, disaster at Wounded Knee

Spiritual crisis and other threats to white Protestant
values and religious manifest destiny: divorce, fear of
sex and death, changing role of women

Social activism: the Purity Crusade

The Teddy Roosevelt ideal

Socializing adolescents and dependent children for class roles

Blacks: citizens only in the eyes of the law

As Civil War broke out in 1861, almost three hundred thousand Native Americans were living west of the Mississippi. The most powerful tribes were the Sioux (Dakota) in Minnesota and the Dakotas; Cheyenne, Arapahos, and Comanches lived on the plains of Kansas, Nebraska, Colorado; in the Southwest was the home of the Apache and Navaho; the Utes and the Nez Perces inhabited the Rocky Mountain areas of Utah and Idaho. The one hundred thousand Native Americans in California were divided into many small and peaceful tribes until white Americans began to move westward and settle on the Pacific Coast in the 1840s and 1850s.

Early in the war, Union troops, under General James Carleton, marched east from California into Arizona and New Mexico to block Confederate forces. Afterward General Carleton prepared to clear the Southwest of its Native American population to make way for white settlement. "There is to be no council held with the Indians," he ordered, "nor any talks. The men are to be slain whenever and wherever they can be found." Many of the Apache retreated into Mexico. But the Navaho were not so easily moved; they had an agricultural settlement based on orchards and herding. As a result they suffered starvation as their trees and animals were destroyed by the white army. Even then, some of the surviving Navaho fled into the mountains rather than move to a distant reservation. As one of the rebel chiefs, Manuelito, declared, "My God and my mother live in the West, and I will not leave them. It is a tradition of my people that we must never cross the three rivers—the Grande, the San Juan, the Colorado. Nor could I leave the Chuska Mountains. I was born there. I shall remain." Finally, in 1868, the United States government permitted the Navaho to return to the most desolate and barren part of their former territory. Only the Navaho, alone among the tribes of the 1860s, could preserve their sense of place, of being in harmony with the sacred center of their universe. "We came back and the Americans gave us a little stock and we thanked them for that. When we saw the top of the mountain, we wondered if it was our mountain, and we felt like talking to the ground, we loved it so, and some of the old men and women cried with joy when they reached their homes."

The sudden and dramatic disruption of the Southwest and Pacific

Coast tribes in the middle of the nineteenth century was comparable to the experience of the East Coast tribes when they suffered the initial shock of the invasion of English settlers in the early seventeenth century. In Minnesota, however, at the northern end of the white man's frontier, another kind of tragedy awaited the Native Americans in the 1860s. The Santee, a Sioux tribe living in the eastern part of the state, knew that Native Americans in Ohio, Indiana, Illinois, and Wisconsin had made treaties with the white man and surrendered much of their territory in exchange for a guarantee that they would have perpetual title to a small portion of their land. Then as the white man continued his westward advance, the treaties had been broken, all the land had been taken, and tribal survivors had been moved westward.

A chief of the Santee, Little Crow, had participated in the signing of treaties that ceded much of Minnesota to the whites. His tribe was supposed to retain a strip of land along the Minnesota River and to receive annual payments from the national government. In 1862, he was sixty years old. He had been to Washington and had seen the vast numbers and the strength of the white men. He knew that his tribe could not outfight them and so he tried to make the transition to the white man's way of life. He joined a church, established a farm, built a square house.

But soon young warriors came to his house to ask him to lead them in battle against the whites. The annuity from the government had not come, and their people were starving. When they had asked the white traders for supplies, they had been told to eat grass or their own dung. Now they wanted to fight and take the supplies for their hungry women and children.

When Little Crow told them they could not win such a war the young warriors declared that he was old and a coward. Afterward, Little Crow's son remembered that his father replied, "You are full of the white man's devil water. You are like dogs in the Hot Moon when they run mad and snap at their own shadows. We are only little herds of buffalo left scattered; the great herds that once covered the prairies are no more. See!—the white men are like locusts, when they fly the whole sky is a snowstorm. You may kill one-two-ten; yes, as many as the leaves in the forest yonder, and their brothers will not miss them." But then, he continued, "Ta-oya-te-duta [Little Crow] is not a coward; he will die with you."

All along the Minnesota River, the Sioux attacked forts and settlements. But in six weeks, American troops had defeated the

Santee. The entire tribe was gathered as prisoners. Little Crow was shot and killed when he tried to escape. Three hundred and three tribesmen were sentenced to death. Lincoln ordered that only thirty-nine were to be killed. On December 26, 1862, thirty-eight were hanged in the largest legal execution in American history. Those who survived were informed that their treaty was no longer valid; they no longer had land in Minnesota and would be sent into permanent exile on a reservation in the Dakota Territory.

A young Teton Sioux, Tatanka Yotanka, Sitting Bull, who visited these cousins, came to the conclusion that there could be no repetition of the tragedy of Little Crow. Native Americans could not compromise with the whites. To negotiate was to accept a slow, ignominious death. If death came in war, it would be quick and dignified.

In the summer of 1865, General Patrick E. Connor marched into the Great Plains to deal with the Sioux and Cheyenne. For the next two years, Arapaho, Cheyenne, and Sioux, under the leadership of Red Cloud, defeated the soldiers. Finally, in 1868, the United States government abandoned the forts it had built in this territory and signed a peace treaty with Red Cloud, recognizing the tribes' right to this land.

In Washington, however, some were determined that this would be the last treaty to be made with the Plains tribes. "The idea that a handful of wild, half-naked, thieving, plundering, murdering savages," declared a government official, "should be dignified with the sovereign attributes of nations, enter into solemn treaties, and claim a country five hundred miles wide by one thousand miles long as theirs in fee simple, because they hunted buffalo and antelope over it, might do for beautiful reading in Cooper's novels or Longfellow's *Hiawatha,* but is unsuited to the intelligence and justice of this age, or the natural rights of mankind."

Abandoning the idea of further direct military conflict with the tribes, the government strategiests conceived of a plan to destroy the buffalo upon which the Native Americans depended for their existence. "Let them kill, skin, and sell until the buffalo is exterminated," General Philip Sheridan stated, "as it is the only way to bring about lasting peace and allow civilization to advance." In 1870, fifteen million buffalo remained on the plains. Within a decade, systematic slaughter by white troops and hunters had purged them from the landscape.

By 1874, the government felt strong enough to send Colonel

George Armstrong Custer on a military expedition to explore the Black Hills, the sacred center of the area guaranteed to the Sioux in the Treaty of 1868 for "as long as the grass should grow and the rivers flow." But gold had been discovered in the Black Hills, and the national government wanted possession of the territory and the removal of the tribes. The chiefs were ordered to sell the land and move into restricted reservations to the east, where they would be forced to adopt white customs. For Sitting Bull, the answer was clear: "If the Great Spirit had desired me to be a white man, he would have made me so in the first place. It is not necessary for eagles to be crows. Now we are poor but we are free. No white man controls our footsteps. If we must die, we die defending our rights." And the young war chief, Crazy Horse, agreed: "A man does not sell the land on which the people walk."

When the bluecoats marched into the territory, one column under Custer's leadership was annihilated in the summer of 1876 at the battle of the Little Big Horn by Sioux and Cheyenne warriors. But now the soldiers came like the snowstorm of locusts that Little Crow had feared. When Crazy Horse fled to the mountains, there was little game to sustain his people. During the winter and spring of 1877 most of his people surrendered. Crazy Horse wandered along until September when he was captured. Brought to Fort Robinson he was met by a bluecoat who thrust a bayonet into the chief's abdomen. Sitting Bull fled with another band into Canada, and when General Alfred Terry crossed the border to persuade him to return to the reservation, Sitting Bull insulted the general by having a woman, The-One-Who-Speaks-Once, speak at the council. "I wanted to raise my children over there," she declared, "you did not give me any time. I came over to this country to raise my children and have a little peace. That is all I have to say to you. I want you to go back where you came from."

But the Canadian government put pressure on Sitting Bull to return. Canadians, too, made it clear that there was no room on their plains for native hunters, and that the buffalo must give way to farms and wheat and fences and cattle. When Sitting Bull returned to the United States in 1881, he was taken prisoner. Later when he was allowed to return to his people on the Standing Rock Reservation, he opposed the government's attempt to reduce the size of the reservation. When the other tribal leaders told him that he must not anger the white man, Sitting Bull at last declared, "I am here to apologize for my bad conduct, and to take back what I said. I will take it back because I consider I have made your hearts bad."

He listened silently to Senator John Logan, member of a Senate commission, who instructed him in his new identity as a dependent child: "You have no following, no power, no control, and no right to any control. You are on an Indian reservation merely at the sufferance of the government. You are fed by the government, clothed by the government, and all you have and are today is because of the government. I merely say these things to you to notify you that you cannot insult the people of the United States of America or its committees. The government feeds and clothes and educates your children now, and desires to teach you to become farmers, and to civilize you, and make you as white men."

In confining the natives to the reservations, white Americans were merely extending their definition of social deviance. They believed that the Plains tribes had to be segregated because they could not accept the dominant values and laws of white society. The army restricted them to the reservation, and the Indian agents fed and clothed them just as prison officials provided for criminal convicts. The reservation differed from the prison in that Native Americans were able to remain together as families. Government officials warned of the dangers of such intimacy. "As long as Indians live in villages," advised one agent, "they will retain many of their old and injurious habits. Frequent feasts, heathen ceremonies and dances, constant visiting—these will continue. I trust that before another year is ended, they will generally be located upon individual land or farms. From that date will begin their real and permanent progress." Not until 1887, however, did Congress pass the Dawes Act. It allotted 160 acres of land to the head of each Indian family. The common reservation land of the tribe would be distributed into pieces of private property. The surplus reservation land was to be sold by the government to white settlers.

Helpless to resist this assault on their cultural values, many Native Americans, among them the Sioux tribe, were ready at the end of the 1880s to make a pilgrimage to hear the good news from a messiah, Wovoka, who had appeared in the Paiute tribe. Here, they believed, was a returned Christ. The white men had killed Christ and rejected his message, but now he had returned as a red man. "I have sent for you and am glad to see you," declared the red Christ. "My children, I want you to listen to all I have to say to you. I will teach you how to dance a dance, and I want you to dance it." He prophesied that the next year would see the coming of a new soil that would spread over the entire earth, burying all the white men and their evil. The Indians dancing the Ghost Dance would be lifted into the air while the new soil spread. When they came down to the new surface, it would be covered with deep grass and endless herds of buffalo, antelope, and wild horses.

Kicking Bear and Short Bull, two Sioux who had traveled on the white man's iron horse into the Shining Mountains to learn the Ghost Dance, returned to teach their people this dance of salvation. Indian agents, however, did not believe that this strange religious enthusiasm, which reached so many and such different tribal groups across thousands of miles, was based on the red Christ's words, "You must not hurt anybody or do harm to anyone. You must not fight. Do right always." In 1890, officials in Washington ordered the arrest of potential war leaders, and Sioux who served the white men as an Indian police force came to arrest Sitting Bull in his cabin, where Sergeant Red Tomahawk shot him through the head.

Sitting Bull's frightened Hunkpapa Sioux fled their reservation to the camp of Minnecanjou Sioux under the leadership of Big Foot. Fearing further violence, Big Foot led them out on the plains, where they were captured on December 28 by four troops of cavalry and forced to camp at Wounded Knee Creek. The next day, Colonel Forsyth of Custer's Seventh Regiment ordered a search for weapons. A shot was fired when the soldiers handled a deaf warrior, Black Coyote, roughly. Cannon placed on a ridge were fired into the tepees. The Indians ran, pursued by soldiers. For some, the race with death lasted two miles. In the end, 300 of the original band of 350 had fallen in their tracks and then frozen into grotesque shapes along the grisly gauntlet.

A young survivor named Black Elk caught the drama of 1890 when he reminisced a half-century later as an old man. "I did not know then how much was ended," he confessed. "When I look back now from this high hill of my old age, I can still see the butchered women and children lying heaped and scattered all along the crooked gulch as plain as when I saw them with eyes still young. And I can see that something else died there in the bloody mud, and was buried in the blizzard. A people's dream died there. It was a beautiful dream. The nation's hoop is broken and scattered. There is no center any longer, and the sacred tree is dead."

Black Elk's historical vision seemed correct. In 1889, the United

States government broke the agreements it had made to the Five Civilized Tribes of the Southeast when it had forced them to move to the Oklahoma Territory, promised as a refuge for the Indians forever. Here these tribes had transplanted their sophisticated patterns of agriculture, government, and education, only to meet white men poised at the boundary of Oklahoma waiting to rush into what they considered to be vacant land. Once more the Cherokees, Creeks, Seminoles, Chickasaws, and Choctaws would experience the tragedy of displacement, as would the Cheyenne, Arapahos, and Kickapoo. Their communal land would be fragmented into private allotments so that they, like their new white neighbors, would live by the system of private property.

But the irony of Black Elk's perception of the events at Wounded Knee in 1890 was that perhaps more of the Anglo-American dream died there than that of the Native Americans. After 1890, it would truly be said of the white Americans, "There is no center any longer." The mythology that had sustained the Englishmen who had come to America was a reversal of the one that had sustained their medieval ancestors. For medieval Europeans, as for Native Americans, place was sacred and individuals were fulfilled spiritually by being buried with their ancestors. Modern secularized society, however, promised fulfillment to those who left the traditional places and moved into new spaces. As a symbol, America offered sanctuary from the disharmony and the evils of the Old World.

At the Columbian Exposition in Chicago in 1893 to celebrate four centuries of white progress on the continent, those gathered there listened in dismay to the young historian Frederick Jackson Turner proclaim the impending demise of national values in a paper titled "The Significance of the Frontier in American History." The signs of declension, Turner declared, were to be found in the census statistics of 1890, which indicated the end of the American frontier. "This brief statement," he explained, "marks the closing of a great historic movement. Up to our own day, American history has been in a large degree the history of the colonization of the Great West. The existence of an area of free land, its continuous recession, and the advance of American settlement westward, explain American development.

For Turner, the uniqueness of America came from breaking the links with the Old World conception of place. "American democracy was born of no theorist's dream. It came stark and strong and full of life out of the American forest and it gained new strength each time it touched a new frontier." American nature was a space in which Europeans were allowed to reject the cultural identity of the Old World and could be reborn as free individuals. "Into this vast, shaggy continent of ours poured the first feeble tide of European settlement. European men, institutions, and ideas were lodged in the American wilderness, and this great American West took them to her bosom, taught them a new way of looking upon the destiny of the common man, trained them in adaptation to the conditions of the New World. And ever as society on her eastern border grew to resemble the Old World in its social forms, ever, as it began to lose faith in the ideal of democracy, she opened new provinces, and dowered new democracies in her most distant domains."

For Native Americans, the mythological sources of rejuvenation came from the natural cycles of birth, death, and rebirth. As Turner expressed the national mythology, however, cultural renewal depended upon movement through space. As long as Americans moved west, they would remain young. The tragedy of 1890 for Turner was that "the free lands are gone. The material forces that gave vitality to Western democracy are passing away." It was inevitable that America would cease to be a New World and would regress into Old World conditions. When people ceased to be mobile in space, as in the East, then they began to live in the corrupt cultural conditions of Europe. Once the western lands, the last space, had been filled, there would be no new frontiers to revitalize American democracy. "Never again can such an opportunity come to the sons of men. It was unique." He concluded, therefore, that "the familiar facts of the massing of population in the cities and the contemporaneous increase of urban power, of the massing of capital and production in fewer and vastly greater industrial units, especially attest the revolution." The United States was destined to establish industrial conglomerates based on an urban concentration of people.

White Americans in 1890 wanted the Native American to become a Jeffersonian yeoman so that he could enjoy Anglo-Saxon liberty and democracy. But in 1890, there was no space for this yeoman, red or white, no future for the Jeffersonian dream. Looking to the East from Wounded Knee one saw the population of cities almost double every decade. Even the number of cities multiplied, moving steadily westward: Pittsburgh, Cleveland, Cincinnati,

Detroit, Chicago, St. Louis, Milwaukee, St. Paul, and Minneapolis.

Such urban growth increasingly depended upon immigration from Europe, including millions of Catholics and Jews. In 1862, as Yankees in Minnesota cleared the Sioux from the land, the center of St. Paul, ironically, was filling with Irish Catholics.

In 1865, the white American majority identified the nation with Protestant, especially evangelical Protestant, values. It had been easy to relate this kind of religious emphasis to the autonomous spiritual life of the individual and to the assumed economic autonomy of the homestead. It was easy to fear the loss of this autonomy in the city. For these Protestants, the index of the health of their Christian nation was the observance of the Sabbath. The nation was healthy if its people observed the day in sober worship with no concessions to work or play. By this standard, Protestant leaders already had found signs of great decadence by 1877. As one churchman wrote, "Owing to the demoralization consequent on the late Civil War, and the laxity of all moral restraint growing inevitably from such social disturbances; owing to the introduction and acceptance of trans-Atlantic theories and practices; owing to the mixed character of our great population, representing too many divergent types of thought, Sabbath desecration has assumed alarming proportions and summons the Churches of Christ to a new and vigorous campaign for its repression."

The virtues of evangelical Protestantism and its relationship to American nationalism were expressed in popular public-school textbooks. Warren's *Common School Geography,* for example, stated that "Christian nations are made powerful, and much more advanced in knowledge than any others. Their power also is continually increasing. There is little doubt that, in the course of a few generations, the Christian religion will be spread over the greater part of the earth."

For Christian, of course, read Protestant, and by the 1880s, this sense of religious manifest destiny was ironically threatened in the very heart of the American citadel by the waves of Catholic immigrants who challenged Protestant domination of the public schools. A Methodist bishop charged that "the combined and persistent efforts made by the bishops and priests of the Romish Church [threaten] to destroy our system of common schools. It becomes us cordially to unite with all intelligent Christians and all true patriots to cherish the free institutions bequeathed to us by our Protestant forbearers."

Josiah Strong, one of the great evangelical theologians, wrote *Our Country* in 1884 to warn that "the city" represented the "seven perils" facing the nation. The first six were Romanism, Mormonism, intemperance, socialism, wealth, and immigration, and they all blended into the seventh peril, the city. The city was the base for the alien army that had invaded America, "an army twice as vast as the estimated numbers of Goths and Vandals that swept over Southern Europe and overwhelmed Rome."

Everywhere one looked in late-nineteenth-century America, one sensed the failure of space, of the geographical frontier, to provide an environment for individual liberty and equality. One indication was the formation in 1884 of the Zion's Watch Tower Society by Charles Tazl Russell. This group, which was to grow to major proportions in the twentieth century as the Jehovah's Witnesses, expressed the first doubts by lower-middle-class Protestants about the necessary relationship between the American political state and Christian values. Russell rejected the orthodox Protestantism of his youth after concluding that an established elite was in control and manipulating American society. He believed that their satanic conspiracy worked through "the religious, commercial, and political combine." As corrupt as any European nation, he predicted that this American establishment would be destroyed in 1914 by the armies of God. Only those who refused to be loyal citizens of the evil nation, only those who became Russell's followers, would be safe from this Armageddon and would inherit the purged and purified earth.

Another major spokesman of disenchantment was Mark Twain. As early as his 1868 book, *The Gilded Age,* written with Charles Warner, Twain expressed his horror at the political corruption that followed the Civil War. In *Life on the Mississippi,* he tried to reaffirm his faith that the fantastic economic growth, which seemed related to political corruption, was really a progressive force, lifting the American South out of European decadence. "The signs are that the next twenty years will bring some noteworthy changes in the valley, in the direction of increased population and wealth and in the intellectual advancement and the liberalizing of opinion which go naturally with these." One finds, he concluded, "all the enlivening signs of the presence of active, energetic, intelligent, prosperous, practical nineteenth-century people which don't dream; they work."

But by the end of the book, Twain emphasized that this dedication to work did not bring independence to the individual; rather, it trapped him in the social system. Twain stated that he loved the profession of river pilot "far better than any I have followed since and I took a measureless pride in it. The reason is plain; a pilot in those days, was the only unfettered and entirely independent human being that lived on the earth. In truth, every man and woman and child has a master, and worries and frets in servitude; but in the day I write of, the Mississippi pilot had none." At the time Twain wrote, however, the pilot was no longer free; he was forced to work from the charts that outlined the artificial channels imposed on the river by the Corps of Engineers.

In books his readers interpreted as humorous tales for children, Twain came to question whether American nature had ever expressed a redemptive purity that contrasted with the corruption of European society. Tom Sawyer found terror and death in the cave, which on the surface seemed to promise a sanctuary for children from the corruption of adult society. He also found gold there, an element that initiated him directly into that adult society.

Twain's bitterness toward nature became more intense in *Huckleberry Finn*. It was not enough that the yeomen along the shore of the Mississippi, the Grangerfords and the Shepherdsons, were homicidal maniacs ready to slaughter children as well as women and men. But the river itself, which promised peace for Huck, as the cave had for Tom, was also the messenger of terror and death. Promising to carry him and the runaway slave Jim to freedom, the river instead carried them into the darkness and hopelessness of the Louisiana swamps.

When Twain turned his sights to the man-made technological world in *The Connecticut Yankee,* his vision remained as bleak as that of his contemporary, Henry Adams. The direct descendant of two presidents, Henry Adams was sensitive to the political corruption of the 1860s and 1870s. Like Twain, he felt trapped by the forces of urban industrial society. Both men shared the idea that this new energy would destroy rather than liberate the individual and that by 1890 they were approaching the end. "I am living," Twain wrote, "in the noonday glory of the Great Civilization, a witness of its gracious and beautiful youth, witness of its middle-time of giant power, sordid splendor and men ambitious, and witness also of its declining vigor and the first stages of its hopeless retreat before the resistless forces which itself had created and which were to destroy it." His final vision of the future was a holocaust created by an engineer-dictator who destroys America with an ultimate weapon.

American nature for L. Frank Baum, creator of the Oz stories, had failed to provide independence for the yeomen or a refuge for the fantasies of children. Baum intended to write fairy tales for children that would have happy endings, unlike the European stories filled with sex and death. His Oz stories ultimately became the fairy tales for twentieth-century American culture. Baum placed his orphan-hero Dorothy on a farm in Kansas. But she would never grow up to become a self-made success, able to compete in a world of constant conflict. Instead, she would fly away to Oz, where she would join the ruler of that magical space, Ozma. Dorothy and Ozma never age. They remain presexual adolescents forever, and they protect every inhabitant of Oz, young or old, male or female, from any threat.

Nineteenth-century Americans had repressed the experience of sex and death in order to sustain their belief in continual linear expansion. Oz had neither sex nor death, neither secular time nor cyclical time. It came to symbolize the nineteenth-century home, a point in space without time.

The separation of innocent children from corrupt elders depended upon the separation of the home from public life. Family life in the modern world was a private affair, and the wife and mother shielded her innocent children from the corruption of outsiders. Raised in the innocence of the home and taught to fear the public life of their fathers, children would not be attracted to the ways of those male elders when they reached the point where they must leave home. If the East and Europe represented the place of fathers, then young adults could move on, if only imaginatively, to the American West, where the purity of geographic space could be substituted for the purity of the space of the home.

But the disappearance of the frontier would have its effects on the idea of the innocence of the home and the corruption of life outside it. Almost at the same time that the 1890 census indicated the end of a frontier for white men, another government bureau reported that divorce had become a national problem. The growing divorce rate was only one indication that middle-class women were beginning to break the social convention that confined them to the privacy of the home. Increasing numbers of young women attended colleges, choosing to become teachers, librarians, and social workers. In many cases, the members of this working minority remained unmarried and lived a celibate life, and enjoyed the friendship of other women. Well-to-do married women and women who worked joined clubs by the thousands. Their numbers grew to the hundreds of thousands in the decade before World War I.

The confinement of the middle-class woman to the privacy of the home had served not only to produce children who would want to reject the tradition of their fathers but also to segregate sexuality. In a time when regularity and predictability were prized, the unpredictability of sexual desire (and by implication all biological and cyclical time), was very threatening. The symbolic asexual American woman served to neutralize sexual desire and these "irrational" biological rhythms in the interest of protecting the rational male world of political, economic, and intellectual life.

This fear of female sexuality is documented in the writings of many doctors in the last decades of the nineteenth century. According to medical advice, young men needed energy to compete successfully in the marketplace, and they needed to be taught by their mothers not to waste that energy through masturbation. Each adolescent possessed a limited amount of energy to use in his struggle for success in adulthood. In his penis, however, each boy had a potential "worm hole" from which that energy might escape. The advice to the young man was not to masturbate, not to frequent prostitutes, and to marry as quickly as possible a woman like his mother. He would choose his wife for her qualities of thrift and prudence. An article in the Boston *Medical and Surgical Journal* concluded that this kind of wife would not tempt him to "spend" his energies too frequently in his marriage bed because "sturdy manhood loses its energy and bends under the too frequent expenditure of this important secretion."

Faced with the possibility of greater sexual unpredictability as women began to reject their identity as sexless mothers, medical practitioners moved to reduce the threat of sexuality through the strategies of rational science. One device was measurement. "I do not know that anyone has thought of measuring the quality of semen, ejected in the act of copulation," wrote Dr. J. Marian Sims. "I was induced on several occasions to remove semen with a syringe and to measure it subsequently, and I found that ordinarily there was about a drachm and ten minims."

For the medical profession, "woman was what she is in health, in character, in her charms, alike of body, mind, of soul because of her womb alone." Dr. Augustus Gardner warned that there was among this "other sex a widespread uneasiness, a discontentment with woman's lot, impatient of its burdens, rebellious against its sufferings, with an undefined hope of emancipation, propagating theories, weak, foolish, and criminal." When a physician wrote that the "well-being of society demands that means shall be adopted to separate its good elements from the bad," he had in mind, among other things, clitoridectomy. The medical profession also began the practice of removing women's ovaries. After the operation, one doctor claimed, women became "treatable, orderly, industrious, and cleanly." Dr. Sims described his invention of the speculum for the observation of the womb in the same terms that English and American explorers were using to describe their conquest of the mysteries of Africa, the dark continent. He was able to see, he wrote, "everything as no man had ever seen before. I felt like an explorer in medicine who first views a new and important territory." Controlling the beginning of the life cycle, American doctors by World War I had largely persuaded middle-class women that they could give birth to their children only in hospitals. Midwives were deplored as vestiges of the dark ages. Women needed the guidance and control of male physicians when they gave birth.

The cultural mythology of an unlimited American geographic frontier, expressed by the historian Turner, was that the nation would remain young and vital as long as it was in motion. When the frontier was gone, Turner had stated, the New World would become like the Old World. The nation would age. Death followed aging.

If the country had a new fear of death, its reaction, as with sex, was to control it. The medical profession gained more prestige as people increasingly viewed doctors as salvation figures who could conquer death. While waiting for the conquest, however, Americans created a new profession, that of the mortician. At the end of the nineteenth century, the middle class would be buried in caskets, not coffins. Caskets are made of metal, and unlike coffins, give no suggestion of the outline of the human body. Human bodies were embalmed, and cosmetics were employed to restore to them the appearance of health and vitality. The cemeteries of the well-to-do became more elaborately landscaped; they were spacious and park-like. The gravestones became more monumental, often modeled after the Egyptian obelisk, a symbol of eternity. All these developments suggested that the departed had passed away, not died. The embalmed body, encased in metal, could not become part of the earth's cycles. Instead, the parklike cemetery suggested that American space was not part of that nature which operates according to the cycles of the seasons. Moreover, according to the books of etiquette of 1890, death was a family embarrassment. "When a death occurs in the house, all matters should be at once placed in charge of a relative or a friend of the family. The family itself should be kept away from everyone as much as possible, and none of the sad details left to them. They should not be seen until the day of the funeral. Front windows should be shut, blinds and shades pulled down. It is not customary for any except the nearest relatives to go to the cemetery. Ladies of the family do not accompany the remains to the cemetery. As to periods of mourning, Ward McAllister advocates short mourning even for the nearest relatives."

The middle-class women who were coming out of the privacy and cleanliness of their own homes into public life were no longer shielded from the activities that were part of the male-dominated world. From the Civil War to World War I, many feminist leaders advocated the elimination of the male double standard, which allowed men to have sexual relationships with prostitutes, and elimination of prostitution.

In 1865, many cities with large numbers of prostitutes had a Gentlemen's Guide to Houses of Prostitution. A movement to legalize prostitution gained in popularity by 1870, which prompted Susan B. Anthony and Elizabeth Cady Stanton, leaders of the women's suffrage movement, to oppose it. They were joined by Dr. Elizabeth Blackwell, the leader of the small group of women in the medical profession, and her sister, Antoinette Brown Blackwell, the first woman ordained as a Protestant minister. The Reverend Ms. Blackwell expressed her horror at the dirty cities, and she rejoiced at the Boston fire of 1871 because "the crooked city will now be compelled to straighten her paths. Will it be New York's turn next to be purified so by fire?" And Frances Willard led the effort of the Woman's Christian Temperance Union (WCTU) to remove the corrupting power of alcohol from the city.

Operating with the slogan "No sex in politics and no sex in industry," women created numerous organizations to make the city safe for the feminine principle in public life. The American Committee for the Prevention of Legalizing Prostitution in the 1870s was followed by the Social Purity Alliance of the 1880s. In the next decade, the National League of Working Women's Clubs and the National Consumer League both helped working women to resist the temptation of the city. By the first decade of the twentieth century, they were fighting immorality through the League for the Protection of the Family and a National Vigilance Society. These Protestant-dominated groups began to forge some links with the Catholic hierarchy in establishing their purity crusade. Archbishop Ireland gave support to Prohibition, and Cardinal Gibbons served with President Charles W. Eliot of Harvard on a National Vigilance Committee. This pressure climaxed when the United States Congress passed the Mann Act in 1910, making interstate traffic in white female slaves a federal crime.

The combination of Protestant and Catholic pressure succeeded in these decades in persuading the states to pass legislation prohibiting abortion. Until after the Civil War, the states continued to accept the common-law tradition that permitted abortion during the first months of pregnancy.

Another area in which the middle class attempted to legislate morality related to drugs. Experts today believe that addiction was eight to ten times more common in 1870 than it was in 1970. Addiction was concentrated among the middle-aged and middle class, especially women. Drugstores dispensed morphine and heroin without prescription to anyone with the money to buy them. States began to prohibit drug sales as they did sales of liquor before there was national legislation. Then Congress passed the Harrison Narcotic Act in 1914, which forbade the sale of drugs except through prescriptions for legitimate reasons. As arrests jumped from 888 in 1918 to 3,477 in 1920, many cities created clinics to aid addicts during withdrawal. But as the numbers of those arrested shifted from the middle class and middle-aged to the young and the poor, especially blacks, the clinics were abandoned.

Undercurrents of anti-Semitism ran through much of the purity crusade. The great New England historians George Bancroft, Francis Parkman, John Motley, and William Prescott had written at the time of the Civil War that world progress would take place through the mechanism of competition and that the white Anglo-Saxon Protestants would emerge as the survivors on the field of racial battle. This meant, in their vision, that not only would the Native Americans and Afro-Americans disappear by the end of the nineteenth century, but also that the weaker and less energetic Mediterranean and Eastern Europeans, Catholics, and Jews, who had lacked the forcefulness to pioneer in colonial America, also eventually would die out. As David Levin has pointed out in his book *History as Romantic Art,* these historians ascribed feminine characteristics to Catholics and Jews. Like women, they depended on stealth, craft, and conspiracy to defeat their enemies. But ultimately these wily ways by which the French, Spaniards, and Portuguese had won initial power in the New World were overcome by the honest, straightforward battle tactics of the Anglo-Saxons (WASPs).

A considerable number of German Jews, however, had immigrated at midcentury and subsequently had prospered. Their way of life in Germany had imbued them with modern secular attitudes of progress. Many German-American Jews had reached the highest levels of education and wealth by the 1880s. Many were converting to Unitarianism and Congregationalism. In a generation, these German Jews had closed much of the social distance between themselves and the two-centuries-older eastern aristocracy.

Appalled by the vitality of the German Jews, many young white Protestants in eastern colleges fantasized that one of their ancestors had been Jewish. A Boston blueblood, Barrett Wendell, wrote, "The racial agony in which we are being strangled by invading aliens, who shall inherit the spirit of us, grows heavier with me, as the end of me—and of ours—comes nearer." Henry Adams also identified his sense of decadence with Jewish vitality: "I don't want to go home. Washington is repulsive. If I were growing rich, it might be a consideration, but as far as I know, I am relatively a good deal poorer than I was five years ago. The Jews have fixed the cards all round."

It is little wonder that so many of the fears and fantasies of white slavery, the seduction of pure country girls into a life of prostitution in the city, centered around the "absolute fact that corrupt Jews are now the backbone of the loathsome traffic." George Kibbe Turner declared in the United States Immigration Report of 1911 that "there are large numbers of Jews scattered throughout the United States who seduce and keep girls."

A major response to Jewish competition was segregation. Tuxedo Park, established in New York in 1886, was the first suburb deliberately restricted to WASPs. New boarding schools like Groton were founded, and enrollments at the older ones, Exeter, St. Paul's, and Andover, increased as children of the elite were being withdrawn from the public schools. The most socially prestigious Ivy League colleges were also rigidly restricted, because as one alumnus said, "If the Jews once get in, they would ruin Princeton as they have

Columbia and Penn." The white Protestant businessmen did not socialize with Jewish businessmen in their city clubs; in the suburbs, they established restricted country clubs. As the great banker J. P. Morgan said, "You can do business with anyone, but only sail with a gentleman."

The wives of the threatened elite founded the Daughters of the American Revolution. The DAR, by carefully keeping family genealogies, could determine whether a wealthy, well-educated Congregationalist had ancestors who had come over on the *Mayflower* or who merely had fled from Europe in the nineteenth century.

For these women the final model for pure Americans was that of citizenship. Loyalty to the nation would overcome vice and moral confusion. The Mothers' Congress, which became the national Parent-Teachers Association, began a successful lobbying effort to have an American flag placed in every classroom. Young truants were redeemed by having them march and sing songs like "Down with the pauper; down with the scamp; up with the Freeman; up with the wise; up with the thrifty; one to the prize; we love our land and we should die; to keep Old Glory in the sky."

For the most part the Protestant elite did not sink into apathy like Henry Adams, but decided to act vigorously. It adopted as its model Theodore Roosevelt. Roosevelt's vision was of a renewed masculine society of soldiers and engineers, men of action, not civilization. "Woe to our nation," he wrote, "if we let matters drift."

Roosevelt tied the nation's spiritual and moral crisis directly to the end of the Indian Wars. "The most ultimately righteous of all wars is a war with savages," he declared, "the fierce settler who drives the savage from the land lays all civilized mankind under a debt to him." As Roosevelt recounted American history, the nation had been vital and disciplined from 1600 to the 1880s because of the constant warfare against the Indians. "The qualities needed to make a good soldier," he remarked, "are the qualities needed to make a good citizen." When Americans were no longer at war they had lost that martial élan. Roosevelt discovered pacifism among young men, and even worse, the rejection of motherhood by young women. Roosevelt snorted, "A race is worthless and contemptible if its men cease to be willing to fight hard and if its women cease to breed freely. Voluntary sterility among married men and women, even more than physical cowardice, is the capital sin of civilization."

Roosevelt self-consciously withdrew from the "effete" East into the western wilderness to prepare himself to become a national savior. An American hero had the strength of nature and the strength of military discipline. When Roosevelt led his Rough Riders into battle in Cuba in 1898, it was clear that he shared his interpretation of the hero with much of his culture. Many journalists described him in exactly the terms Roosevelt applied to himself.

"Here in the West for years," one newspaper reported, "he lived a life of vigor and activity, developing those lungs that had suffered somewhat in living in cities, and wakened as well the resourcefulness in danger, that self-reliance and the power which his future career was to require." "Young Roosevelt," a journalist declared, "was born with an iron indomitable will. His career is another illustration of the truth that that which a man wills to become, that he is sure to become."

Roosevelt and many like him believed that the revitalization of the nation would come from the youth who expressed a natural wildness and fighting spirit and could be encouraged to channel this energy in efficient, military forms. This new category of youth was adolescence, the years between fourteen and eighteen. The American psychologist G. Stanley Hall, who first described this new stage of life in *Adolescence*, published in 1904, proudly declared that "semi-criminality is normal for healthy boys."

It was in the private boarding schools of the upper middle class that the social patterns of adolescence emerged. Earlier in the century, young people of these years were often identified with radicalism. Freed from parental control, they might experiment with political ideology, with art, with sexuality, or with the world of work. But in the later nineteenth century these children were more apt to be confined within the institutional control of the school, acting *in loco parentis*. Like the armed forces, the school was a total institution. Young men of similar backgrounds lived and studied together, separated from the larger society. They experienced a regimented day, waking, eating, studying, playing, and sleeping at sharply defined times under the rigid discipline of their schoolmasters. Their play was organized, uniformed, competitive team sports. They were taught that to be a man, one must develop physical prowess and the will for power. They were taught to avoid the ways of women, which were those of weakness, emotion, and unreliability. They were taught that they would become men and marry good women. To deserve the love of this virtuous wife, they were to be law-abiding churchgoers. But from their peers they learned the double standard. They were taught to anticipate adult life when they could drink, gamble, and have brief, violent, sexual relationships with prostitutes. Most who tried to live as adults while they were still adolescents were punished by school authorities. But they knew that they had the secret admiration of their superiors, who accepted the double standard that young men will be young men.

Upon initiation into this society of militant boys, first as freshmen in boarding school and then again as freshmen in college, the newcomer had to accept hazing from the upper classmen. This rite of passage supposedly tested the courage and discipline of the young man to be a soldier. Another traditional ritual, though of a higher status, was physical combat with one's peers. At the end of their first year, the freshmen at Princeton University, for instance, had won the right to fight with the sophomores in a ritual battle in which the classes attacked each other with bamboo canes. They also had won the right to throw away the hats that symbolized their position as initiates. The following fall, they would join in the hazing of new freshmen and compel them to wear the identifying hats. These customs spread to most colleges, even those that enrolled only high-school graduates.

The private schools where this military code first emerged had a strong relationship to the Protestant Episcopal Church. Much of the nineteenth-century aristocracy was Episcopalian. American churchmen borrowed enthusiastically from English spokesmen for a muscular Christianity, often quoting with approval Charles Kingsley's comment that "God made man in His image, not in an imaginatory Virgin Mary's image."

Sports reflected the militant spirit. One of the pre–Civil War games of the upper class had been popularized as baseball and was played and watched by the lower middle class. A later development, football, was a game that would prove the manhood of its adolescents. Unlike baseball, football was characterized by intense group discipline. The team had to move as a perfectly synchronized unit in complete obedience to the leadership of the quarterback. The territory to be conquered was clearly marked off in ten-yard segments. If the team, given a set number of plays, successfully took that segment, it was rewarded with the opportunity to try to take the next segment. The offensive team could march to the whole length of the field, winning all the territory from the defensive team.

Modern space, clearly defined and measured, had become the

context for a sport. And football also included the modern sense of time. Unlike baseball, football, was played under the discipline of the clock. One no longer had an indefinite period in which to win or lose. As the clock ran down, stress increased as the opportunity to win decreased minute by minute.

Playing without helmets at first and without adequate padding, Ivy League players suffered many deaths as well as serious injuries, including the loss of eyes. Theodore Roosevelt, as President, defended the game against those who wanted to prohibit it because of its excessive violence. As a visiting French military officer put it, "Le football is a veritable little war, with its necessary discipline and its way of getting participants used to danger and to blows."

The violence of football could not spread to baseball, but its emphasis on statistics did. Increasingly baseball players were evaluated by their batting and fielding averages; the pitchers, not only by the numbers of their victories and losses, but by their earned-run averages. Baseball managers were evaluated by their ability to impose discipline. The umpires became more important as the figures responsible for imposing absolute adherence to the rules of play.

By the beginning of the twentieth century, it was clear that culture leaders were using sports as social models. At the end of World War I, the Black Sox scandal echoed the massive corruption in politics that had come to light. There was decisive action to restore the purity of baseball through the establishment of a commissioner who was given "czarlike" powers of regulation and punishment of management and players. Sportswriters, who had become important newsstaffers with regular columns, cooperated by limiting their coverage to the players' activities on the field. No discussion of the private lives of the players was allowed to destroy the public image of these "created" national heroes.

If the private schools were mobilizing the adolescents of the elite to provide aggressive leadership for the conquest of new frontiers for the nation, it was assumed by Theodore Roosevelt and his generation that the public schools would mobilize working-class adolescents to become the soldiers who would follow the commissioned officers of the elite. Between 1890 and 1914, the high school was added to the public school system. Compulsory attendance laws were passed, forcing the young people to remain dependent children through high school.

It was hoped that the high school would "Americanize" the children of the new immigrants. In citizenship classes, they would learn to revere the national leadership. For similar reasons, organizations such as the Boy Scouts were created to mobilize the energy of working-class children. Marching and singing in uniform, revitalized by contact with nature, taught loyalty to God and the nation, a Scout expressed his experience when he said, "The Scout movement teaches you to be good citizens, and not to know anything about politics."

Theodore Roosevelt's friend Owen Wister provided a cowboy hero for these militant adolescent boys in his novel *The Virginian*. Living alone in nature, the cowboy hero, although over twenty-one, served as a model for boys because he did not engage in adult activities, especially sex. When confronted with a villain, the adolescent had been taught that the naturalness of youth could always defeat a man corrupted by convention. In this confrontation, the cowboy, the hero of adolescence, always enjoyed total victory.

As this Purity Crusade against prostitution, drug addiction, and alcohol consumption was defining new groups of criminals, the invention of "adolescence" created another criminal class—delinquents. Many lower-class young people refused to accept the status of dependent adolescents and give up their independence as responsible persons who could choose their own patterns of work and sexuality. A whole group of middle-class male and female "child-savers" appeared between 1890 and 1914 who would operate as "disinterested" altruists to segregate "sick" young people from their "infected" environment. As the great progressive sociologist Charles H. Cooley wrote, "When an individual actually enters upon a criminal career, let us try to catch him at a tender age, and subject him to rational social discipline."

Since the delinquents were defined as dependent children, they had no civil rights of due process when they were arrested. Sent to reformatories, without trial, they had no definite sentences because they were being redeemed, not punished. They could earn their way back to a normal adolescent life by showing that they had learned the values of "sobriety, thrift, industry, prudence." They also were encouraged to acquire "realistic" ambitions befitting their social station. For these lower-class young people, as for the children of the Native Americans, wrote Cooley, "the organized and ordered discipline of reform schools can make respectable citizens out of a class of children who are quite unmanageable and even anti-social in their own homes."

The purity crusaders had reached the conclusion that the children of Catholics, Jews, and Native Americans could be Americanized through the institutions of the school and the reformatory. The children of the white Protestant elite could provide energetic leadership for these groups of docile followers. But as distinctions between good and clean citizens and evil and dirty criminals were more dramatically drawn, Afro-Americans were considered permanently a part of the deviant group. The consensus of cultural leaders in 1890 was in agreement with the anthropological position of Joseph Le Conte that "modern ethnologists have thoroughly established the fact that in all essential qualities the Negro race seems to be totally incapable of development."

This "child race" had received total guidance from whites during the period of slavery. The Civil War and Reconstruction, however, had transformed black men into citizens with the right of geographic mobility. Most blacks had remained in the South as sharecroppers, but they were not under the direct economic control of white leadership. The explosive growth of black churches after 1865 also gave the Afro-Americans a vast new experience of independent social life. Even an incomplete public-school system represented a revolutionary change from the systematic denial of education under slavery. The emergence after the Civil War in the South, where 90 percent of the blacks still lived, of a small number of black political leaders, businessmen, teachers, lawyers, and doctors threatened white attitudes toward the Negro. "There is absolutely no place in this land for the arrogant, aggressive, school-spoilt Afro American who wants to live without manual labor," Tom Watson, the white Populist leader in Georgia, affirmed. "Yes Sir! We know Sambo, and we like him first rate, in his place. And he must stay there, too." But it seemed impossible to restore blacks to their pre–Civil War dependence.

The cultural conventions of white society defined every independent black man as a potential rapist. For Mississippi political leader James K. Vardaman no black man had "congress with the opposite sex, having in mind the making of a child," but "copulate[s] solely for the gratification of the passion—for the erotic pleasure it affords him." Southern politicians like Ben Tillman of South Carolina and writers like Thomas Dixon of North Carolina created in the 1890s the foundation of an anti-Negro crusade, comparable in some ways to Adolf Hitler's war against the Jews in Germany in the 1930s. Whites from different classes were asked to forget their economic differences and unite to preserve their racial purity.

In his novel *The Leopard's Spots,* Dixon endeavored to convert white readers from their perception of the black as "Sambo." He dramatized the end of plantation servility and predicted the reversion of free blacks into animal aggressiveness. His novels reiterated the warnings of the political speeches of Tillman and Watson that the independent black men had regressed "back, back into barbarism, voodooism, human sacrifice."

What was needed, according to Dixon and many southern political leaders, was a militant uprising of white society to destroy black independence as their fathers had crushed the threat of black autonomy during Reconstruction. This crusading prejudice produced rigid forms of social segregation between 1890 and 1910. Blacks had often been banned from public areas in the South during the 1870s and 1880s, but on occasion they had been accepted. Soon state laws were passed officially separating whites from blacks in every conceivable area of public life—trains and streetcars, stations, theaters, and restaurants. Southern cities passed laws limiting blacks to specific residential blocks. Whites were forbidden the use of black houses of prostitution; laws were even passed forbidding the races to play checkers together, and textbooks to be used in white and black schools could not be stored in the same warehouse.

White southerners who had permitted male "Sambos" to serve their food and female "Sambos" to suckle their young were suddenly obsessed by the idea that blacks were carriers of dirt and disease. Under slavery, Tom Watson insisted, the Negro had "practiced continence and was but slightly contaminated by venereal disease." Now, however, blacks were "rotten with it and the constant deterioration is glaringly evident."

More than any other region, the white South committed itself to Prohibition between 1890 and 1920. For southern leaders like the Reverend Edward Gardner Murphy, Prohibition was "the deliberate determination of the stronger race to forego its own personal liberty for the protection of the weaker race." When President Theodore Roosevelt created a national Country Life Commission in 1908 to study ways to preserve the health of rural America, he received a major recommendation that "the saloon must be banished from all country districts. The evil is especially damning in the South because it seriously complicates the race problem." Alcohol could easily turn "Sambo" into the "devil."

But if Dixon was right, even Prohibition could not keep blacks from becoming devils. More drastic measures were necessary. While some antiblack spokesmen advocated the deportation of blacks, other northern leaders listened to more extreme proposals, such as "to emasculate the entire Negro race and thus prevent any further danger from them, and the horrors of their crossing continually with the Anglo-Saxon stock." And Congressman James Griggs of Georgia had entered into the *Congressional Record* on April 17, 1908, a vision of the ultimate solution: "The utter extermination of a race of people is inexpressibly sad, yet if its existence endangers the welfare of mankind, it is fitting that it should be swept away."

When Woodrow Wilson, a son of the South, became President in 1912, his administration, dominated by southerners in Congress and in his Cabinet, moved to apply the standards of social segregation won by the anti-Negro crusade to the federal civil service. Investigating committees, under the direction of the postmaster general and the secretary of the treasury, found evidence of the threat of black sexuality and black disease to white government workers. White women, Secretary William McAdoo found, were "forced unnecessarily to sit at desks with colored women." Affidavits were collected from white women "that the same toilet is used by both whites and blacks, and some of said blacks have been diseased, evidence thereof being very apparent; that one Negro woman had been for years afflicted with a private disease, and for dread of using the toilet after her, some of the white girls are compelled to suffer physically and mentally."

President Wilson agreed with his Cabinet members that segregation in toilet and eating facilities should be instituted and black men limited to such menial jobs that they would not be in contact with white women. When he was confronted by black leaders who protested the establishment of Jim Crow segregation in the federal civil service, Wilson replied, "Segregation is not humiliating but a benefit, and ought to be so regarded by you gentlemen."

Afro-American leaders well understood white willingness to use violence as a means to gain their end. R. R. Wright, Jr., a leading black social worker and social philosopher who was editor of the *Christian Recorder*, reacted to the fact that, from 1890 to 1917, a black man or woman had been lynched on the average of one every two days. "We are lynched," he cried out, "we are hanged, riddled with bullets, and burned. Excursions are run to have the daughters and sons of 'respectable leading citizens' witness the barbecuing of a nigger."

Who were these white men and women? For Wright, they called themselves Christians but were the antichrist. Like so many black ministers who had emerged as the leaders of the freedmen during Reconstruction, Wright used Christian theology to understand and criticize white society. For him, "the Anglo Saxon and the Teuton had failed." Forsaking Christian humility, "the Anglo-Saxon race is the greatest fighting race that has yet appeared on the stage of history." Forsaking Christian charity and spirituality, the Anglo-Saxons had become the most selfish and materialistic of peoples. Only blacks, therefore, could make America a Christian nation and redeem whites. Wright's friend Reverdy C. Ransam, editor of the *African Methodist Episcopal Church Review,* argued that the innate poetry and spirituality of blacks made them natural Christians. "The Negroes are a kind-hearted people." Because of their influence, "the heart of America has been softened with more kindness, a sweeter spirit has filled its life and a stronger wave of emotion has swept the whole range of its philanthropy and religion."

In 1917, most Afro-American leaders had more hope than the Native Americans had had in 1890. Christ was black, but he could find a place for whites who would be redeemed from their sinfulness by black spirituality. All whites would not have to perish as Wovoka had prophesied.

"The day of combination is here to stay"

★ ★ ★ ★ ★ ★ ★ ★ ★ ★ ★ ★ ★ ★ ★ ★ ★ ★ ★ ★

11
The New
Industrial Economy

Railroads transform regional trade to a national economy

The modern corporation

Growth of organized labor

Expansion and mechanization of agriculture

Growth of the metropolis and the urban labor force

The black ghetto: treadmill of poverty and underemployment

On May 10, 1876, the tolling of the bell in Independence Hall sounded the beginning of the nation's centennial celebration. All the church bells in Philadelphia shared in the joyful expression of gratitude for the century of progress that had carried the American people so far and so fast from the simple republic of the Founding Fathers. The city of Philadelphia, whose growth had not been so rapid as that of New York, hoped to recover its momentum by holding the Centennial Fair in its magnificent Fairmount Park—three thousand beautiful acres at the fork of the Schuylkill and Wissahicken rivers. The theme of progress was so strong that the state used no colonial models for the buildings that were erected. Nor was there any hint of the eighteenth century within the huge main buildings. In the central exhibition hall, the gigantic Corliss machine, thirty feet high and weighing seven hundred tons, released fourteen-hundred-horsepower units of energy to provide power for all the fair's exhibits. This engine symbolized the spirit of the Centennial, a celebration that did not look backward to the past, but focused instead upon a future of unlimited power and energy.

Thousands of citizens came each day to stand in awe of the Corliss engine and its ability to regulate its speed automatically, to respond instantly to moments of low and high demand for its energy. It represented a steady and uninterrupted flow of power. New automatic and self-regulating turnstiles allowed a constant flow of people into the grounds. Special streetcar and railroad lines, the first capable of moving twelve thousand passengers an hour, the second, twenty-four thousand an hour, transported the spectators from the central city to the fair. Within the centennial grounds, people traveled on a narrow-gauge railroad, which circled the fair. The United States of America in 1876 was presented as a river of progress, flowing downhill, away from its small and distant origins, growing constantly in size and gathering speed and momentum as it moved inexorably and majestically into an unknown but assuredly splendid future.

It was the explosion of railroad building during and immediately after the Civil War which had provided the foundation for the mood of progress at the Centennial. Thirty thousand miles of track had been flung down just in the years from 1866 to 1873. Suddenly, railroads stretched from the Atlantic to the Pacific. Rivers of steel flowing from east to west, from north to south, had created a national economy by 1876.

In the 1860s, the major industries had been regional, servicing an agricultural society. They processed the farmers' crops and provided the farmers with tools, clothing, and other supplies. The raw materials were furnished locally, and the finished goods were sold within their separate regions. But the fantastic growth of the railroads provided a huge market for industrial producers. Iron, steel, coal, and lumber were in direct demand for the railroads. These industries in turn made it possible for regional specialization to be linked to the national economy. The forests of Michigan, Wisconsin, and Minnesota, of Washington, Oregon, and California, could provide lumber for the whole nation. Minerals from the mines of the Rocky Mountains could easily be brought east. So could cattle from Texas and the northern plains and wheat from Minnesota and hogs from Illinois. Factories in Boston, New York, Pittsburgh, Cleveland, Detroit, and Chicago could supply markets in the far reaches of the South and West.

To hold together a railroad network spread across the country required a new form of organization—the corporation. Railroad companies became the first major private bureaucracies. It took a hierarchical structure comparable to an army to mobilize and utilize efficiently the energies of the tens of thousands of men employed by the railroads. The corporation thus patterned itself on the Union army, the first major public bureaucracy. The company was composed of several major divisions. Under the leadership of a general staff, the heads of the corporate divisions, like the military generals, possessed considerable autonomy. These private divisions were broken down into smaller units comparable to regiments, battalions, companies, and platoons. Each had its own leadership linked in a chain of command up to the president of the company and his staff, the chief company officers and the board of directors.

This first modern private company made a fetish of Time. The railroads ran by timetables. All railroad employees had their railroad watches synchronized to keep the company schedules. The railroad's large-scale, professionalized, bureaucratized management established the model for other burgeoning industries. The captains of industry who were creating companies to produce for the national market—men like Gustavus Swift in meats, Charles Pillsbury in grain, Henry Havemeyer in sugar, Frederick Weyerhauser in lumber, John D. Rockefeller in oil, Andrew Carnegie in steel, James Duke in tobacco—all divided their business into autonomous departments of marketing, processing, purchasing, and accounting, and they all delegated great authority to the heads of these divisions.

The vision of the 1876 Centennial—the idea of a productive national economy, smoothly and efficiently integrating the physical power of the machine with the social power of a machinelike institution, the corporation—served to inspire men like John D. Rockefeller. By 1870 Rockefeller had rejected the idea of a nation of free and equal producers, of a marketplace of small and autonomous competitors. He envisioned an America in which a few gigantic corporations dominated production. He saw a marketplace of huge, integrated companies, cooperating to avoid competition. The virtue of this new form of production, for Rockefeller, was its efficiency. The movement to consolidate small companies into large companies, he wrote, "was the origin of the whole system of modern economic administration. It has revolutionized the way of doing business all over the world. The time was ripe for it. It had to come, though all we saw at the moment was the need to save ourselves from wasteful conditions. The day of combination is here to stay. Individualism has gone, never to return."

To achieve consolidation in oil, Rockefeller went to war against his competitors. He built pipelines to force railroads to give him rebates if they were to carry his products. With rebates, he could undersell his rivals. Then he set out to eliminate competition: they could sell out to him at his price; they could become his agents; or they could be destroyed. The Panic of 1873 facilitated his effort to buy out or ruin rival companies. Ohio was the scene of his first takeovers, where Rockefeller had begun his refining business. Refiners in New York and Pennsylvania were his next target. By 1880, the superior size and organization of his militant company made it possible for him to control 90 percent of oil refining in the nation. The victory, he said, came because "we had taken steps of progress that our rivals could not take. They had not the means to build pipe lines, bulk ships, tank wagons; they couldn't have their agents all over the country; couldn't manufacture their own acid, bungs, wicks, lamps, do their own cooperage—so many other things; it ramified indefinitely. They couldn't have their own purchasing agents as we did, taking advantage of large buying."

Small businessmen approached the state and national governments for help in fighting the new corporate giants. But William

Vanderbilt, testifying before a congressional committee in 1879, warned politicians that they could not control them. "Yes, they are very shrewd men," he insisted. "I don't believe that by any legislative enactment or anything else, through any of the states or all of the states, you can keep such men down. You can't do it! They will be on top all the time."

Many of the small businessmen threatened by the Robber Barons saw the problem in a limited way. They did not see the larger, more profound revolution that would place the corporations in control of the economy by 1900. Hence they did not organize political opposition to stop the trend of monopolization in the key areas of industrial production.

The first economic groups to grasp the full implications of the corporate revolution were the workers in the craft unions. Organized labor had expanded dramatically immediately before and during the Civil War. Union leaders usually regarded owners of small factories with ten to twenty workers as fellow producers and considered small industry no threat to the open economy. But by 1869, the organizers of the National Labor Union were aware of the danger to their independence if they became industrial soldiers dominated by a rigid hierarchy of managers. William Sylvis, the president of this new group, saw monopoly, inequality, and plutocracy as the major trends of the day. "So long as we continue to work for wages," he declared, "so long will we be subjected to small pay, poverty, and all of the evils of which we complain." His answer then was cooperation. The workers must form producers' and consumers' cooperatives. They could preserve political and social democracy only if they engaged in economic democracy.

The National Labor Union grew rapidly until 1873, when a depression and widespread unemployment made it easy for employers to ruin them. There was a constant influx of unskilled labor from Europe and from rural America, and advancing technology enabled employers to use unskilled workers to replace the skilled workers who were most likely to belong to unions. Workers despaired at the destruction of their unions and sometimes formed underground organizations, one of which was the "Molly Maguires" in the coal mines. Irish miners used guerrilla tactics against their employers, but their organization was infiltrated by company spies. A young Irish immigrant, James McParlan, a Pinkerton detective, became an official of the Molly Maguires and informed on his fellows. On his testimony, ten were hanged.

Railroad workers throughout the country rebelled against pay cuts in 1877. They rioted in Baltimore, Altoona, Reading, Scranton, Buffalo, Toledo, Louisville, Chicago, St. Louis, and San Francisco. Everywhere the authorities summoned government troops to end the riots. In Reading, for example, eleven were killed in the streets; in Pittsburgh, twenty more were shot down.

When prosperity returned in the 1880s and full employment gave the workers more bargaining power, there was a dramatic resurgence of union efforts. Two or three hundred thousand workers had joined the National Labor Union. Now almost a million joined the Knights of Labor. The new organization's president, Terence V. Powderly, announced that its aim was "to make each man his own employer." All productive Americans were invited to join the Knights; only parasites, professional gamblers, stockbrokers, prostitutes, lawyers, bankers, and liquor dealers were barred.

By 1890, however, the position of the worker had not much improved. Factories were growing larger. The majority of industrial workers seemed to be passive wage-earners. Twenty years of labor agitation had failed to create a viable cooperative alternative to the corporation. Though some workers considered violent revolution as the only way to overthrow the corporation, the establishment proved equally effective in the use of force. In 1886, as thousands of workers in Chicago went on strike for shorter hours, some of the union radicals began to act. On May 3, a bomb exploded in Haymarket Square during a confrontation between police and strikers. The police arrested eight known anarchists, of whom seven were condemned to death, although there was no evidence to link them with the bomb.

In 1893, a major economic crisis again encouraged employers to slash salaries and reduce the power of the unions. When the Pullman Company in Chicago reduced wages, it did not lower the rents it charged in its model town. A strike by the angry Pullman workers expanded rapidly into a major walkout of railroad employees headed by Eugene V. Debs. President Cleveland then sent federal troops into Chicago, and the army killed more than thirty people in a confrontation.

Debs and other strike leaders had been sent to prison for "conspiracy" against the government, and it was then that Debs converted to socialism. He could no longer believe in the restoration of a pre–Civil War America run by free and equal capitalist producers. But neither could he accept those socialists who called for a violent overthrow of the establishment. Instead Debs believed that the increasing monopolization of the economy by a few large corporations was acceptable because such centralization would facilitate a peaceful revolution of the economy when socialism had been voted into power by the American people. Debs helped to found the Socialist party, which was based on the belief that political democracy could reform the social and economic patterns.

Samuel Gompers agreed with Debs that there could be no violent overthrow of the new corporate order and no restoration of an older and more socially and economically democratic America. As a member of the cigar-makers' union, Gompers would emerge to lead the American Federation of Labor (AFL). Speaking in 1888, he urged workers to acknowledge the corporate revolution and accept their place within that structure. "The fact is being fast forced upon the consciousness of the wage-workers of this continent that they are a distinct and practically permanent class of modern society," he declared, "and, consequently, they have distinct and permanent common interests." Like the socialist Debs, Gompers believed that the growth of the large corporation was inevitable. "We are convinced," Gompers continued, "that the State is not capable of preventing the legitimate development or natural concentration of industry."

The future, as Gompers and other leaders of the AFL predicted, was one in which the business leaders would permanently control the means of production. The sole interest of these corporate officers was to increase the profits of their organizations. The interest of the workers, the enlisted men, was simply to organize in unions and bargain for a share of the profits. As Adolph Strasser, another AFL leader, explained, "We have no ultimate end. We are going on from day to day. We are fighting for immediate objectives."

In launching the AFL, Gompers and Strasser were seeking to free the craft unions from the anticorporate ideology that had characterized organized labor under the Knights of Labor. Where the Knights appealed to all industrial and farm laborers, the AFL comprised a loose federation of craft unions, the unions of the skilled workers. In effect, these elite workers had abandoned any hope for the unionization of the masses of unskilled industrial workers. The failure to generate unity within the total labor force was recognized by union leaders. They were also aware of the union's inability to solve the problem of white racism. The refusal of white workers to consider unity with black workers did not go unnoticed. "It is useless to deny the fact that there is a great amount of race prejudice still existing among white workers," Gompers declared, "and it is well to keep this fact in mind. It is useless to be simply trying to ram our heads through stone walls."

AFL leaders were similarly pessimistic about reducing friction between white Protestant workers and the newer Catholic and Jewish immigrants. Indeed, there was little unity among Catholics—Irish, German, Slavic, and Italian. In the cities, immigrant workers from the industrial cities of northern Italy were easily unionized, but the immigrant workers from rural areas in southern Italy and Sicily were bewildered and confused by their first contact with industrialism in America.

Corporate leaders well understood and exploited the ethnic groups within the labor force. They deliberately worked to deepen resentments between them by using blacks as strikebreakers against whites or by using one white ethnic group against another. Explaining why he was hiring Swedes, an employment agent for a Chicago meat-packing plant stated, "Well you see, it is only for this week. Last week we employed Slovaks. We change about among the different nationalities and languages. It prevents them from getting together. We have the thing systematized. We have a luncheon each week of the employment managers of the large firms of the Chicago districts. There we discuss our problems and exchange information." Even more brutal was the assessment of the captain of industry Jay Gould: "I can hire one half of the working class to kill the other half."

Some business leaders, represented by the National Association of Manufacturers (NAM), wanted to eliminate the AFL, just as the Knights of Labor and the National Labor Union had been destroyed earlier. Others, however, argued that the AFL should be encouraged because of its apolitical attitudes, its refusal to engage in fundamental social and economic criticism. For millionaires like Senator Mark Hanna of Ohio and August Belmont of New York, a safe labor movement was preferable to the radicalism that seemed to be surrounding Debs' Socialist party. These corporate leaders founded the National Civic Federation in 1900 with Hanna as president and Gompers as vice-president to demonstrate the common interests of management and labor within the capitalist system. President Theodore Roosevelt shared this position and supported conservative labor leader John Mitchell, the president of the United

Mine Workers, against the coal-mine owners. Roosevelt was particularly angry at coal executive George Baer, because he would not make a distinction between conservative and radical union activity. Writing to Mark Hanna, Roosevelt declared, "From every consideration of public policy and of good morals, they should make some slight concessions." Ultimately, Roosevelt forced arbitration on Baer.

As the number of large corporations jumped from twelve in 1893 to 318 in 1904, controlling 5,288 manufacturing plants, the AFL increased its membership from 265,000 to 1,700,000. Accepting cooption by the corporation seemed to guarantee the survival of a limited union movement.

Meanwhile the corporations were free to mobilize the unskilled and nonunionized workers as they pleased. The International Harvester Corporation taught its Polish workers enough English to carry out their tasks. The major thrust of the lesson was to develop a sense of discipline and time.

> I hear the whistle, I must hurry.
> I hear the five minute whistle,
> It is time to go into the shop.
> I take my check from the gate board
> and hang it on the department board.
> I change my clothes and get ready to work,
> The starting whistle blows,
> I eat my lunch.
> It is forbidden to eat until then,
> The whistle blows at five minutes of starting time.
> I get ready to work.
> I work until the whistle blows to quit.
> I leave my place nice and clean.
> I put all my clothes in the locker.
> I must go home.

Hatred of this new discipline of the clock was expressed in poems like this written by an immigrant worker, Morris Rosenfeld:

> The clock in the workshop—it rests not a moment;
> It points on, and ticks on; eternity time;
> Someone told me the clock had a meaning;
> In pointing and ticking had reason and rhyme.
> At times, when I listen, I hear the clock plainly;

The reason of old—the old meaning—is gone;
The maddening pendulum urges me forward to labor and still
    labor on.
The tick of the clock is the boss in his anger,
The face of the clock has the eyes of the foe;
The clock—I shudder—Dost hear how it draws me?
It calls me "machine" and it cries to me "sew."

A much more elaborate popular literature was produced to educate the large white Protestant population coming to the city from
the farm in the late nineteenth century. Manuals that taught young
rustics how to succeed in the city stressed the importance of time.
"Holding punctuality among the major virtues, the good worker is
ever true to the appointed hour and as he goes and comes, men set
their watches by him, as though he were a clock—face of the sun
and moved by solar machinery."

Spiritual and economic success were linked in this literature.
"Those who will their salvation and diligently cultivate industry,
frugality, sobriety, perseverance, punctuality, loyalty, obedience will
find the reward of success." Success for the young man from the
farm was defined as finding a secure place in the corporate army.
Respect, even fear of authority, was inculcated. "Your employer,
like God, knows the ways of the just and unjust. There are no
secrets before God, or your employer. He knows who shirks, who
watches the clock, who clips a few minutes, who is a little late and a
little early to leave. He records your sins and good works in the
book of judgment and on the day of reckoning knows who deserves
poverty and who deserves wealth."

In the immensely popular dime novels of Horatio Alger, there is
the same moral lesson of loyalty and obedience. His young orphan
heroes come to the city from the country looking for a protective
father figure. In his series of Ragged Dick stories, Dick dreams that
"some rich man would adopt me, and give me plenty to eat, and
drink and wear, without my havin' to look so sharp after it." Dick
also expresses his limited ambition when he says, "I'd like to be an
office boy, and learn business, and grow up 'spectable.' " Alger's
heroes succeed because they are morally correct and they have the
good luck to find someone who rewards their virtue.

Between 1880 and 1900, a self-consciously Catholic literature developed very rapidly which preached similar advice to young

Catholics. In those years, the Irish and the German Catholics were being joined by new millions of Italian and Slavic Catholic immigrants. The Catholic minority was growing large enough for ecclesiastical and lay leaders to begin advocating a movement for Catholic power. Decisions were made to build a national Catholic school system that would parallel the public school system run by Protestants. Such separation, it was hoped, would preserve the church identity of young Catholics. Yet Catholics themselves continued to disagree about the nature of that identity. The Irish prelates, who dominated the hierarchy of the American church, persuaded the Church at Rome to crush the movement of German Catholics who desired to preserve the variety of European languages in the parochial schools. Under the influence of the Irish, Catholic schools, like the Protestant-dominated public schools, would teach in English. Catholic power would find expression only in the English language.

Between 1880 and 1900, magazines like the *Catholic Reading Circle Review* and *Catholic World* were founded "to get Catholics to read Catholic literature." In addition to the pressures of the schools to remind young Catholics to remain within prescribed cultural boundaries, the Young Men's Catholic Association was founded as a symbolic alternative to the Protestant Young Men's Christian Association (YMCA), the Catholic summer school as an alternative to the Protestant Chautauqua, and a guild of Catholic authors as an alternative to the national literature dominated by Protestants. Catholic self-consciousness as a separate community was strong enough by the end of the nineteenth century to provide a market for "A Game of Quotations from American Catholic Authors," "The Pictorial Game of American Catholic Authors," and *A Catholic Speller*. By 1900, a hundred American Catholic authors were being identified by adult magazines such as *Ave Maria* and *The Messenger of the Sacred Heart* and children's magazines such as *Our Boys' and Girls' Own*. The central message of these novelists, as expressed by the most popular, Maurice Egan, in such novels as *The Vocation of Edward Conway* and *The Success of Patrick Desmond,* was the necessity of pride in the Catholic heritage and the right of Catholics to claim a full and equal share of the American experience.

One great danger to Catholicism was a marriage to a non-Catholic. Many plots elaborated by Catholic writers involved the temptation to form such a marriage and a last-minute rejection of the temptation, often through the help of a supportive priest. The other great temptation examined by the novelists was that of worldly ambition. The virtues of hard work, sobriety, cleanliness, and propriety as taught by nuns in the parochial schools were emphasized. But ambition should never allow personal greed to separate the Catholic from his membership in the Catholic community. Other novels dealt with the Catholic tempted by conversion to Protestantism in order to increase the likelihood of achieving material wealth. Often, at the last moment, with the help of a priest, the Catholic reaffirms his belief and rejects temptation. Modest, not exceptional, success was the norm preached in the Catholic literature and schools. And it was Catholics, the readers of these novels, who later constituted the majority of the membership of the AFL trade unions. These were the ethnic workers who heeded Gompers' advice to accept the leadership of the mainstream elite who dominated the corporations.

Many farmers did not share the industrial workers' fears of the corporation. Although the large railroad companies symbolized the mobilization of labor in rigid, hierarchical, bureaucratic patterns, for the farmers it still symbolized the possibility of fulfilling the agrarian dream of Thomas Jefferson. The rapid westward expansion of the railroads ironically provided the economic conditions for the expansion of the number of farms from about 2,000,000 in 1860 to almost 6,000,000 in 1900 and a comparable increase in the land under cultivation from about 150,000,000 acres to almost 400,000,000. Without the extension of the railroads, hundreds of thousands of white settlers could not have taken advantage of the Homestead Act of 1862, which entitled them to a 160-acre farm. The railroads also had been given millions of acres by the national, state, and county governments to encourage their push into the West. The railroads subsequently sold these lands at prices ranging from two dollars to ten dollars an acre.

Recognizing the profitability of settling the West, the railroads also joined with the midwestern and western state governments in sending agents to the East and to Europe to encourage immigration. As Governor Alexander Ramsey of Minnesota declared, "Give us the capital of more men and we will vivify and infuse the breath of life into the dead capital of millions of acres now growing only prairie flowers. Immigration will multiply capital, diffuse wealth, sell our town lots and increase activity in every pursuit and business."

This boom psychology and the almost religious idealism of

achieving yeoman independence inspired hundreds of thousands of settlers to fling themselves into the space of the newly conquered Indian territory. But the idealism that drove them west was not enjoyed in the lives they led there. One wife described a typical day as "done my housework, then made fried cakes, squash pies, baked wheat bread and corn bread, cut out a night dress and partly made it," and then "am very tired." On the edge of white settlement, without family or friends or medical help, women bore many babies and then watched a high percentage of them die. Again a wife recorded the experience of sitting up with a sick child. "At half past five this A.M., he died after much suffering." Then she added, "made his pants Aunty sent him and buried him about sun down. All well with him."

This final farmers' frontier was characterized by a total commitment to technological progress. "The Minneosta farmers do not go out there in the old ways in which their fathers had," reported the New England writer Mary Dodge, "for the very good reason they have neither ways nor fathers. They make experiments. Indeed, their farming itself is an experiment." And one could see the twentieth-century future of corporation farming on the incredibly flat land of the Red River Valley between Minnesota and North Dakota, where men like Oliver Dalrymple put together farms of thirty thousand acres. There, commanding twenty-five reapers moving through the wheat fields, "a superintendent on a superb horse, like a brigadier directing his forces, rides along the line, accompanied by his staff of two on horseback. They are fully armed and equipped, not with swords but with wrenches, hammers, chisels. An army of 'shockers' follow the reapers, setting up the bundles to ripen before threshing."

The rapid mechanization of agriculture made it possible for fewer farmers to feed more people. But the irony for this agricultural community was that the farmers, because they depended on the natural cycle of the growing season, could not equal the linear productive output of the urban factories. Although the farmers could use machines to accelerate planting and harvesting and eliminate much of the manual labor in these critical periods, the machinery sat idle after the planting. The farmer, unlike the industrial producer, had to wait for the cyclical maturing of his crops and remained dependent, to a large degree, on the amount of sunshine and rain needed by those crops. Again, after the harvest, the machinery was not used during the fall and winter as the farmer awaited the return of spring and the new planting season. The machines in the factories, of course, could run every day of the week, every week of the year, even day and night if necessary. But the farmers did not pay less for the machines or the energy they used than did industrialists.

By 1900, the value of industrial products surpassed those of agriculture for the first time. It was possible for 5,000,000 factory workers to produce goods worth $11,500,000, while 11,000,000 farm workers produced goods worth $8,500,000,000.

As fewer men and more machines produced greater amounts of goods, prices fell. Farmers, however, were not producing as efficiently as industrial workers, although the prices of their agricultural products were set by industry. Even by 1890, many farmers found that they simply could not compete; they could not pay off mortgages because their costs were not diminishing as they did for industry. In the following years, even into the 1930s, an ever increasing number of farmers lost their farms and became tenants on the land; others moved into the cities after the loss of their farms; still others survived by acquiring more machinery and increasing the size of the farm, and sent their daughters and sons into the cities. In 1860, 6,000,000 people lived in the cities; in 1910, it was 45,000,-000, almost half the national population. At least 11,000,000 of the city dwellers in 1910 had come from rural America; almost another 20,000,000 were immigrants, European peasants, driven from the land by the same processes of industrial efficiency operating in the Old World.

The demographic explosion of urban America was directly related to the new forms of technology. Until the middle of the nineteenth century, the size of American cities remained limited by the absence of mass transportation. Most people walked to work or climbed aboard horse-drawn vehicles capable of carrying only a few passengers. In these walking cities, no more extended than the time it could take the poor to walk to and from work, the rich and powerful lived in the urban center, where their important commercial and banking activities were concentrated. But with the development of trains and streetcars the rich were encouraged to move to the outskirts of the city and commute to their downtown business. The use of coal, and later electricity, for industrial power made it possible to concentrate factories in the central cities. Formerly, manufacturing had been dispersed in factory towns spread along

rivers that supplied water power to run the machines. New technology provided water for these expanding cities, and new technology
created sewage systems to handle the wastes of several million
people as well as the wastes that came from the huge new factories.
Nonelected specialists came to control water, sewage, transportation, and the other services—gas, electricity, and the telephone—
that made life in the gigantic metropolis possible.

Spatial specialization, even fragmentation, came to characterize
this new streetcar metropolis. In the smaller, pre–Civil War cities,
rich and poor lived side by side. Stores, offices, small-scale industry,
residences, and schools existed in the same neighborhoods. In the
early twentieth-century cities, not only did the rich flee the downtown area to live in suburbs, but even the rapidly growing middle
class and white- and blue-collar workers moved away from the
urban center to establish modest neighborhoods apart from the
inner-city poor.

At the very center of the downtown areas proliferated skyscrapers, serviced by elevators. Commercial and banking activities
were concentrated there. The executives came into this center every
day from the suburbs, and their white-collar workers arrived from
the edges of the city. Here also were concentrated the professional
men, lawyers, and doctors. The suburbs and the more modest lower-
middle-class neighborhoods became specialized as places for family
life dramatically separated from the work place or the place of
professional services. Major department stores and theaters became
part of the downtown landscape. The wives of businessmen, doctors, and lawyers traveled along their husbands' commuting route to
the center of the city for their shopping and entertainment.
Grouped around this specialized downtown area was a ring of housing for the poorest city dwellers. Unable financially to construct
their own dwellings, they subdivided housing abandoned by the
wealthy and the middle class.

Chicago, which expanded from 300,000 in 1870 to 3,000,000 in
1920, is a classic example of the pattern of residential rings that
characterized metropolitan development during that half-century.
Around the area of residential poverty that surrounded downtown
Chicago was a ring of blue-collar and lower-middle-class residences.
Here there were some small single-family cottages, but most lived in
flats and apartments. In the middle-class suburbs were numerous
single-family homes. Running through these rings were corridors of
commercial and industrial activity that radiated from the downtown

center into the farmland, like the railroads that came into the central city from every direction.

For the millions who surged into Chicago by World War I, the major concern was economic and social survival. Protestants, Irish, German, and Italian Catholics, a variety of Slavic groups, and blacks settled in separate neighborhoods and maintained their ethnic identity. Most aspects of life were experienced on the job and in the neighborhoods. Work took place in factories or offices; there was no interest or ability to see the economy of the city as a whole. There was no connection between ethnic social identity and economic class interest. Poor blacks, Catholics, and Jews in the innermost ring of poverty did not associate with one another politically to put pressure on city leaders to provide housing or jobs or medical care. Nor did blue-collar lower-middle-class white Protestants and the various Catholic groups and Jews see their common interests.

Only the mainstream Protestant elite, who dominated the city's economic life from downtown offices, seemed to look out from their skyscrapers and see the city as a whole. But even for them, the whole might be seen as a series of autonomous parts. Working their way to the top of the corporation, they had been specialists in one of the company's departments. They were trained to see the functioning of only their department. In a stable, corporate world where each department was fulfilling its corporate responsibility, an overview might not be necessary. Their political and economic control of the city did not include social planning.

To all appearances community leaders believed that all economic and social problems would be solved by continued expansion. If the city grew new rings as it responded to economic growth, then the inner-city poor could move outward—into the ring formerly filled with the blue-collar lower middle class who would also move outward into the middle-class sector. The same hopes apparently were held in regard to employment, education, and social services. Expansion, not planning, was supposed to solve the urban problems of 1914.

The social and economic evidence of 1914, however, did not support this belief in the inevitable benefits of economic expansion. The black ghettos of Chicago and every other American city in 1914 showed no signs of moving their inhabitants onto the corporate escalator.

In 1890, there were fifteen thousand blacks in Chicago, where 80 percent of the population was foreign-born or had foreign-born parents. By 1915, blacks numbered fifty thousand as more and more left a South that seemed to offer few economic opportunities and much social and political oppression. At the end of the Civil War, blacks had hoped that the plantations would be broken up and the land distributed to the former slaves. "The way we can best take care of ourselves is to have land and till it by our own labor," declared a black leader, and he insisted that "no such thing as a free democratic society can exist in any country where all lands are owned by one class of men and cultivated by another." But only a few radical Republican leaders, like Thaddeus Stevens, agreed with the blacks that "the whole fabric of southern society must be changed." Stevens asked, "How can republican institutions, free schools, free churches, free social intercourse exist in a mingled community of nabobs and serfs?" But most radical Republican leaders shared so strongly the racial prejudice against blacks that they would not confiscate the property of the southern white planters.

Most of the former black slaves saw no alternative but to continue to work for the white man, on the white man's land for the white man's profit. The new pattern of southern agriculture was sharecropping. Because of a shortage of capital to pay wages and because blacks preferred the autonomy they could have as sharecroppers, the planters divided their land into a series of small farms worked by separate black families. A share of their crop was returned to the planter to pay their rent. In practice, however, the system of credit and indebtedness came to be dominated by storekeepers located at country crossroads.

Northern bankers loaned money to southern bankers, who loaned it to storekeepers, who used it to buy supplies of food, clothing, tools, and seeds, which they sold to the sharecroppers on credit. Under the burden of high interest rates, only a small percentage of black farmers could save enough money to buy their farms from the white owners. For the children of these sharecroppers, white as well as black, there was very little future in farming. And many blacks and whites began the trek to the city.

Most migrants headed for the opportunity of a northern city. Stripped of its huge capital investment in slaves, the white South had little capital to invest in industrialization. Some northern and European capital entered the region to finance the expansion of railroads, tobacco factories in North Carolina, cotton mills in South

Carolina, steel mills in Birmingham, Alabama, and lumbering in Mississippi and Louisiana. But this investment was so small in comparison to that in the North and the Midwest that industrialization and urbanization in the South fell far below national growth patterns.

There were few employment opportunities for blacks in the southern cities. Slaves and free blacks had been artisans and craftsmen in these cities before 1865. But between Emancipation and 1900, they were driven systematically from those jobs by hostile whites. This created an ironic situation for black educational leaders like Booker T. Washington. Born in slavery, Washington had received an education at Hampton Institute in Virginia. Hampton was one of a number of schools begun by the American Missionary Association. This group, dominated by New England Congregationalists, like other northern white church groups was concerned with giving blacks the opportunity of formal education that had been denied them under slavery. Southern state governments, under radical Republican leadership, had created public schools in that region for the first time. This system included provisions for segregated black schools. Since these institutions did not include high schools, secondary or college education had to be provided by northern or southern philanthropy.

Northern white philanthropists visualized black education producing more efficient agricultural and industrial workers and consequently financed colleges for the training of black teachers to staff the primary schools. Booker T. Washington, who had left Hampton to help build Tuskegee Institute in Alabama, asked for funds from Carnegie and Rockefeller and other northern philanthropists to teach young blacks the virtues of thrift, punctuality, cleanliness, sobriety, and hard work. Blacks, he insisted, would use any gifts responsibly because they were "the most patient, faithful, law-abiding, and unresentful people that the world has seen." Education would not make them wish for social or political equality, he continued, because "in all things that are purely social we can be as separate as the fingers, yet one as the hand in all matters essential to mutual progress."

Washington had been persuaded by his white New England teachers that everyone could become a self-made man in America. He was certain that if black people worked hard in agriculture and industry and in small business, they could climb the ladder of economic success. But blacks were prevented from making progress in those occupations by the prejudice of white southerners in 1900. And when they moved into northern cities, they encountered the same prejudice. Skilled black artisans, barbers, waiters, and caterers were deprived of jobs that subsequently went to white immigrants.

White immigrants were often able to apply their European work experience to their jobs in America. Skilled workers from England and Germany and Russian urban Jews frequently found well-paying jobs in industry. Irish, Italian, and Polish peasants, among others, with nothing but agricultural experience, found jobs as unskilled labor. But on the average, these unskilled, uneducated whites were given better jobs than northern blacks, who had generations of urban experience, possessed more occupational skills, and had acquired more formal education.

For the unskilled, uneducated, rural blacks who entered northern cities in larger numbers in 1900, there was almost no hope of advancement on an occupational ladder. In Boston, for example, a second generation of Irish-Americans increased their number of white-collar workers to 24 percent, doubling the 12 percent of the first generation. In contrast, black immigrants in Boston increased their number of white-collar workers only from 7 percent to 9 percent as the descendants of the first generation came of age.

Most ethnic neighborhoods in the early twentieth century were no more than 60 percent occupied by a dominant immigrant group such as Irish or Italian or Jewish. But blacks, who had been scattered throughout northern cities in 1880, were soon pushed into ghettos that became 90 percent or more homogeneous after 1900. Although most black men were confined to low-paying jobs as day laborers and most black women confined to domestic service, these poor people paid higher rents than their white neighbors because they were forced to find housing within the restricted boundaries of the ghetto. In Chicago in 1910, an apartment for working-class whites was "seven room, $25," but a "seven room for colored people, $37.50."

Within these developing black ghettos in every major northern city, there was a revolution in leadership. In Chicago, for example, the black community leaders of 1900 were doctors, dentists, and newspaper men who were hopeful for integration. Within a decade, however, they had been replaced by self-made businessmen like Oscar DePriest, who made a fortune in real estate. Formerly from Alabama, DePriest and a few other black businessmen acquired wealth from the people of the ghetto and thus had an interest in preserving it. "I believe that the interest of my people lies with the wealth of the nation," declared a black leader in Chicago, "and with the class of white people who control it."

But when Chicago's black population doubled during World War I, a result of a decline in white immigration, and the great migration of five hundred thousand blacks into northern cities that served to fill the labor shortage caused by the war, the obsequious attitude of these black leaders toward the white establishment did not protect them from savage white criticism. As the black ghetto pushed into Irish and Polish working-class neighborhoods on its western edge and into a middle-class white Protestant neighborhood on the south, street conflicts occurred. White "athletic clubs" physically attacked blacks on the streets and white "neighborhood improvement" societies even bombed black homes. Rigid racial segregation was established in city parks and beaches, restaurants, hotels, theaters, and stores. By the spring of 1919, bombings were taking place every day, and finally a major race riot exploded in July. Comparable riots had taken place in other cities that had experienced large black migrations.

From 1890 to 1917, Anglo-Americans had been reassuring themselves that the industrial and urban frontiers could replace the vanished geographic frontier. It was more than ironic, therefore, as white Americans expressed their hope to control the vast colored populations of the world through the industrialization and urbanization of every continent, that they seemed unable to control the black population within their own national boundary. "Black man, stay South," thundered the *Chicago Tribune* in 1918. Blacks, wrote the newspaper, couldn't fit into the northern way of life because they didn't have the white work ethic. "Mo' rain, mo' rest, mo' niggers sleep in de nest"—this, said the *Tribune,* was black philosophy; "today's the day, not tomorrow with them." And the *Chicago Tribune* offered financial aid to any blacks who would agree to return to the South.

"Nation is a word of unity and power"

★ ★ ★ ★ ★ ★ ★ ★ ★ ★ ★ ★ ★ ★ ★ ★ ★ ★ ★

12
Politics in the Late Nineteenth Century

Reconstruction

Democratic party and the "new South"

The new industrial elite and the politics of corruption

Populism: the People's party allies with Democrats

Harnessing racial resentment against blacks:
disenfranchisement, legalized segregation, and
the Ku Klux Klan

Women in politics and women's suffrage

Regulation of power in Washington

"Pride is abolished, America. The monster is dead," rejoiced the New England Transcendentalist Cyrus Bartol in 1861. "The war is purging away our idolatry. This is the first truly religious war ever waged." Most northern intellectuals agreed that the Civil War was eradicating the evil of slavery from the South and simultaneously eliminating the evil of having tolerated slavery from the North. It was not enough, therefore, for these northerners to view the war as a "conflict between liberty and slavery, civilization and barbarism, between Christianity and anti-Christ." They also had to seek divine punishment of their own region. "Monstrous has been the nation's crime," declared William Ellery Channing, "total let the repentence be, and costly the sacrifice of atonement."

Northern writers were prepared, then, in April 1865 to interpret the murder of Lincoln as the final expression of a Christlike sacrifice of all the Union soldiers who had died to atone for the nation's sin in accepting slavery. Now the sin was gone. For Ralph Waldo Emerson and his friends, "Best of all, whatever else comes, emancipation has come—whether the slaves are free or not—we ourselves are free."

When, however, Emerson wrote during the war that "the magnificent sweep of purification grows more and more impressive to me," he was forgetting the problems of the freedmen and the Confederate leaders. White majorities in most northern states, during the war, where only 5 percent of the blacks lived, continued to deny voting rights and other symbols of citizenship to blacks. In their prejudiced eyes, and, of course, in the eyes of most southern whites, Afro-Americans were so intellectually inferior, so morally irresponsible, so spiritually unclean that they could not share citizenship with the intellectually and spiritually superior white race.

Nor did northerners think well of the white Confederate leadership. If blacks were seen as an alien race, planter aristocrats of the South were defined as an alien class. In the decades before the Civil War, northerners had described this aristocracy as a living vestige of the medieval past. It was said that these feudal lords defied the rationality of capitalism by holding blacks in peasantry and defied middle-class morality by sexually exploiting their female slaves.

Radical Republicans had disagreed with Lincoln throughout the war about the strength and danger of the planter aristocracy. Economically, radical Republicans represented the rapidly developing industrial capitalists of the Northeast and Midwest. They were strongly committed to creating a uniform and standardized national marketplace for their products. They had been frustrated by southern opposition to their legislative program in the 1850s and feared that southerners returning to Congress would join with northern Democrats to dismantle the favorable economic legislation, particularly the tariff, passed during the war.

Persuaded by the myth of a feudal South, radical Republicans had objected violently to Lincoln's plan for a lenient reconstruction which would permit the continuity of Confederate leadership in the southern states after the war. With Lincoln's death, congressional radicals were in a position to seize control of reconstruction from the new President, Andrew Johnson, a Tennessee Democrat, who had been made Lincoln's running mate in 1864 to symbolize the nonpartisan and national nature of the war effort.

Radical Republicans not only could outmaneuver this stranger to their party, but also could use Lincoln's death, ironically, to discredit the continuation of Lincoln's policies. The assassination of the President, declared the radicals, demonstrated that the planters were still in conspiratorial rebellion. "Now is the critical time," asserted Wendell Phillips, "the rebellion has not ceased, it has only changed its weapons. Once it fought; now it intrigues." The *New York Tribune* argued that "the hands of the rebel are again red with loyal blood."

Although only a few radical Republicans, Thaddeus Stevens and Charles Sumner among them, advocated the revolutionary idea of citizenship for free blacks, they were able to persuade other radicals and even some conservative Republicans to endorse their position by arguing that black citizenship was necessary if the planter aristocracy was to be destroyed.

Southern whites, organizing their state government under the Lincoln-Johnson Plan of Reconstruction, passed "Black Codes" which held the freedmen on the plantations where they had worked as slaves. From the perspective of the radical Republicans, the freedmen under such restraints were still a peasantry. There could be no disestablishment of the South's feudal aristocracy until blacks obtained the right to leave the plantations. Not until blacks could travel freely could they be free workers, able to respond to the rational demands of the marketplace. This reasoning led many Republicans to support the idea of black citizenship.

As the congressional elections of 1866 approached, northern Democrats often endorsed southern political leaders who, in the words of South Carolina's B. F. Perry, insisted that the states should have a "white man's government intended for white men only." For many northern Democrats, such as Representative James Brooks of New York, a leader of congressional opponents of radical reconstruction, blacks were a "repugnant race." And Francis Blair, Democratic vice-presidential candidate in 1868, warned that "unless Negroes submit to the intelligent-guidance of the powerful white race, their fate will be that of the Indians, they will be exterminated." President Johnson identified himself with these Democrats when he warned the voters that "of all the dangers which our nation has yet encountered, none are equal to those which must result from the success of the effort now [being made] to Africanize the half of our country."

Despite the strength of the southern Democrats, the Republican majority in Congress simply refused to seat any representatives from the southern states. The radical Republicans also won smashing victories over the northern Democrats by waving the "bloody shirt." Remember, said Robert Ingersoll, "every man that shot Union soldiers was a Democrat. The man that assassinated Abraham Lincoln was a Democrat. Soldiers, every scar you have got on your heroic bodies was given you by a Democrat."

The radical Republicans by early 1867 had a large enough majority to override any veto by President Johnson. First, they passed a Freedmen's Bureau Act and Civil Rights Act. Next, on March 2, 1867, they voted a Reconstruction Act that dismantled the southern state governments and divided the states into five military districts, each under the control of an army general. The army assumed responsibility for registering white and black voters. Confederate leaders were disfranchised and constitutional conventions were called to draft new state constitutions. The conventions were ordered by the army to accept the Fourteenth Amendment, which created national citizenship for all males. Acceptance was a necessary prerequisite for the states to avoid military occupation and re-enter the Union.

Congressional Republicans moved to consolidate their control of the national government by reducing the size of the Supreme Court and by intimidating the remaining justices. They also impeached

President Johnson and came within one vote of convicting him in the Senate. This assumption of power by the legislative branch, unprecedented in American history, depended upon the support of the northern constituency. Most northern labor leaders identified their interests with those of the industrialists; they largely supported the disintegration of the nonproductive economic and social systems of the South. Similarly, the officer corps of the army chose to support Congress rather than the President.

Through the use of the army, the Freedmen's Bureau, and the Union League, organized by the Republican party throughout the southern states, seven hundred thousand blacks were registered to vote. Because many white southerners chose to stand with their disfranchised Confederate leaders and refused to register, only six hundred thousand whites were eligible to vote. The northern Republican party had effectively taken political control of the southern states.

In 1868, the Republicans elected the war hero General Ulysses Grant to the Presidency. A majority of northern and southern white voters cast their ballots for the Democratic candidate in 1868. It was only the ability of the Republicans to deliver the electoral votes of the southern states, based on black majorities, that elected Grant. Northern Republicans moved to consolidate this new power base by enacting the Fifteenth Amendment, which stated that the right to vote "shall not be denied, on account of race, color, or previous condition of servitude."

It was whites, of course, who dominated the national Republican party, and it was whites who dominated the state Republican parties in the South. White army officers, white civilians from the North who went South as carpetbaggers, and southern whites, scalawags, who collaborated with these northerners, provided the top political leadership in every southern state. No black was a governor during Reconstruction. Blacks were never a majority in any state senate. Only in South Carolina, where 65 percent of the population was black, were blacks elected a majority in the lower house. Only two blacks, Hiram R. Revels and Blanche K. Bruce, served in the United States Senate, and both were from Mississippi, which was also more than 50 percent black.

Most of these black politicians were content, at first, to follow the white leadership. They agreed with P. B. S. Pinchback, a black leader of Louisiana, that "it is false, it is a wholesale falsehood to say that we wish to force ourselves upon white people." They accepted the social segregation imposed on them by the northern carpetbaggers and southern scalawags. "There is an antagonism which we all have against the Negro race," said B. H. True, a New York carpetbagger in Georgia, "that I cannot get rid of; I do not believe any white man can." These white Republicans initiated legislation that prohibited intermarriage between the races and created a system of segregated public schools.

Both the carpetbaggers and the scalawags had more respect for the disfranchised white leadership of the South than for their black constituents, and they sympathized with the desire of these whites to regain their individual status as first-class citizens and to have their states return to a normal relationship with the Union. Pardons from the President and Congress began to restore that individual citizenship. Normal relationships with the Union would be established when outside military and political control ended, and the southern states could choose, as the northern states did, their own leadership.

The majority of white southerners, therefore, hoped to re-enter the Union in 1869; they were not struggling to retain a regional way of life. Their representatives and senators wept on the floor of Congress when they were permitted once more to participate in the nation of their southern fathers, of Washington and Jefferson and Madison and Monroe and Jackson and Polk. But in 1869, they perceived their inferior status because other states were free of military rule and other states did not have to share political power with blacks.

There would be no black congressmen from the North until the election of Oscar DePriest in 1928, no black senator until the election of Edward Brooke in 1966, and few local officials or mayors until the 1970s. For white southerners, however, the black majorities in many counties throughout the region posed a real threat; blacks could claim the right to share leadership. And in states like South Carolina, Mississippi, and Louisiana, where black majorities existed, the trend was for blacks increasingly to claim that right. Unlike the situation in the North after acceptance of the Fourteenth and Fifteenth Amendments, southern blacks, with the rights of geographic mobility and the vote, were not going to quietly accept second-class citizenship and docilely follow white leadership. They would compete with whites for political, economic, or social leadership.

As the hysteria of the Civil War receded, however, northern Republicans were willing to listen to reports from army officers and carpetbaggers that indicated that they had wrongly perceived the anticapitalist nature of southern leadership. They recalled that southern Whigs once had supported a national banking system, internal improvements, and even, in some cases, a high tariff which protected manufacturers from competition with more efficient English industry. They were informed that many southern Democrats believed that, with the collapse of the plantation economy, their future lay with Yankee forms of industrial and financial capitalism. Seventy-five percent of the high-ranking Confederate officers had become executives in northern-owned corporations, banks, and railroads, which had emerged in the South.

In the election of 1876, therefore, the Republican party reversed its strategy. It would appeal to the traditional elites of the South, many of whom were former Whigs, asking them to join with their natural allies, the social and economic elites who dominated the Republican party in the northern states. To this end, President Rutherford B. Hayes, on taking office in March 1877, appointed a Democrat, Senator David Key from Tennessee, as his postmaster general. It was hoped that Key would distribute patronage to attract former southern Whigs into the Republican party.

By 1876, however, this strategy was no longer viable. In every southern state, former Whigs had joined the Democratic party to end the military occupation, to re-establish the political rights of the ex-Confederate leaders, and to deprive blacks of first-class citizenship. The Democratic party had become the respectable party in the South because it served as the vehicle upon which white southerners hoped to escape from what they considered second-class status in the nation. No regional leadership developed in the South because each state was struggling to regain a normal relationship with the Union. Radical Reconstruction ended as early as 1869 in Virginia and Tennessee, and by 1871 in Georgia and North Carolina. Only South Carolina, Florida and Louisiana still contained Union troops in 1876.

Much of the control of the Democratic party in the South had slipped into the hands of former Whigs, despite the fact that the majority of white voters were small farmers who opposed the economic policies of the national Republican party. Most white voters, unlike these leaders, disapproved of Republican policies on banking, tariffs, and railroads.

Democratic party leaders in the South in 1876, whether former Whigs or old-line Democrats, were committed to building a "new

South," an urban-industrial South. Thus they approved those Republican policies that they believed would help the economic development of their region. But since the Republican party was anathema to the average white southern voter for both emotional and economic reasons, they saw no opportunity of achieving those policies by joining the Republican party. They had a better chance of obtaining their political goals at the helm of Democratic leadership. If Democrats with Republican principles were elected to Congress, then "Republican" legislation could be passed that would be favorable to the industrial leaders of both regions.

It is not surprising, therefore, that these southern Democrats chose to solve a constitutional crisis in 1876–77 by helping to elect a Republican, Rutherford B. Hayes, to the Presidency. Since neither Hayes nor the Democratic candidate, Samuel Tilden, had received a majority of the popular or electoral vote in 1876, the election had to be decided in Congress; this decision depended upon which electoral votes Congress would accept from South Carolina, Florida, and Louisiana, the last states occupied by Union soldiers. Southern Democrats in Congress had the power, if they aligned with northern Democrats, to keep a President from being named by March 4, 1877. But they voted with northern Republicans for the Republican candidate, thrusting Hayes into the Presidency.

At the centennial year of 1876, the Republicans retained the Presidency they had held since 1860, but they failed to turn the majority of the nation's white voters away from the Democratic party. Republicans had not persuaded the people that a centralized society was better than the Democrats' vision of the nation as a decentralized country of semi-autonomous regions where the most important political activity occurred at the state and local level. During the next twenty years, the Republicans lost the Presidency twice, in 1884 and 1892, and at no time during these decades were they ever in a position to control both houses of Congress. Not until 1896 could they begin to fulfill the political vision of Senator Charles Sumner. "Nation is a word of unity and power," he had declared in 1866, "it brings to mind intelligent masses enjoying the advantage of organization."

Instead of growing in strength in the 1870s and 1880s as the party that had hitched its wagon to the star of an urban-industrial future, Republicans seemed on the verge of being destroyed as a viable political organization by the new social and economic forces.

Defeated in its southern strategy, the Republican party appeared to be undermined by the northern industrialists it was trying to befriend. Impatient with the failure of the Republican party to provide leadership at the national and local level, the new industrial leaders resorted to massive bribery at all levels of government to buy the legislation they believed was necessary to their new economic order. "If you have to pay money to have the right thing done," the railroad magnate Collis P. Huntington stated, "it is only just and fair to do it." And the Central Pacific Railroad budgeted $500,000 annually for bribes in the decade from 1875 to 1885.

Pre–Civil War businessmen and the intellectuals they supported were appalled by the corruption of the new industrial elite. The mainstream aristocracy had always associated corruption with the Democratic party, the organization that had appealed to the immigrants in the northern cities. They expected Boss Tweed of New York City to say that "this population is too hopelessly split up into races and factions to govern it under universal suffrage, except by the bribery of patronage or corruption." But they still recoiled from the open cynicism of Republican leaders like Roscoe Conkling and James G. Blaine.

These "mugwump" gentlemen, disgusted by political corruption, bolted the Republican party in 1872 and again in 1884. But by the late 1880s, many of the sons of this merchant aristocracy were ready to join the Republican party to try to impose political, social, and economic order on the cities, the states, and ultimately the nation. Theodore Roosevelt was one such child of inherited wealth who became contemptuous of his father's effete generation. "It is also unfortunately true," wrote Roosevelt, "that the general tendency among people of culture has been to neglect and even to look down upon the rougher and manlier virtues, so that an advanced state of intellectual development is too often associated with a certain effeminacy of character." Roosevelt intended to throw himself into the fight against the corruption of city politics, state politics, and finally national politics, sure that he and other strong-willed reformers could bring order out of chaos.

It was in the cities that the reformers, known to contemporaries as Progressives, began work in the 1880s and 1890s, and it was there that the new corporations had their headquarters. It began to occur to the reformers that the corporate model—so useful in creating economic order—might be used to create political order.

In numerous industrial cities corrupt political bosses operating through personal bureaucracies were in control of local governments. Through patronage they surrounded themselves with local supporters in the police, fire, and sanitation departments. They supplied contracts for the construction of public buildings. In one celebrated case, an estimate of $250,000 for a courthouse in New York City reached a cost overrun of $14,000,000. These politicos also juggled tax assessments for major companies as well as for residential property owners; they influenced banks which held city deposits; they provided tips to real-estate men about future public building or park construction; they found government jobs for doctors and lawyers beginning their careers; they protected gamblers and prostitutes from police and judges.

The political bosses could exist only as long as they were able to deliver the vote at the precinct and ward levels of government. Many of the inner-city poor, mostly new immigrants, identified themselves with America by supporting the political machine. Scorned and rejected by the mainstream elite, they received psychic warmth and political favors from these politicians. But the staying power of the political boss depended upon his ability to touch the lives of the poor with something tangible, such as public jobs, coal and food in a family emergency, legal aid, or an occasional outing to an amusement park. Many municipal bosses gained popularity by supporting the Old World holidays and festivities, which white Anglo-American Protestants hoped would be left behind in Europe.

All of these activities contradicted the business leaders' sense of orderly space and predictable time. They wanted efficient transportation and adequate fire and police protection for their property. They perceived the bosses as inefficient, especially in the distribution of jobs to poorly educated immigrants who had no professional qualifications. To challenge the bosses, business leaders began to push for the elimination of a large city council elected from the wards. A small council elected from the city at large, they felt, would bring talented, honest men to city hall. The reformers advocated a stronger mayor, or a city manager, and a visible bureaucracy of civil servants chosen rigorously for their professional qualifications. The city would be run by a mayor, and like the president of a corporation he would be surrounded by able department heads.

A crucial urban reform for the new industrial elite was to take control of the public schools away from the ethnic neighborhoods. Just as the city should be considered a corporation and run as one, so should the schools. If the purpose of the schools was "the training of recruits for our leading mechanical industries, high privates who can adequately meet unexpected situations and an industrial rank and file who shall rise to the possibilities of the less skilled type of work," then the schools must be made efficient. Education, said an industrialist spokesman, is a "problem of economy: it seeks to determine in what manner the working unit of the school plant may be made to return the largest dividend upon the material investment of time, energy, and money." Created out of the need to teach efficiency, insisted upon by business leaders, was the "platoon" system, which taught students to march in an orderly fashion from room to room at the end of each class period.

One effort reformers made to gain control of the schools was to replace the large school boards elected from the neighborhood wards with smaller boards chosen in city-wide elections. The large school boards had been dominated by lower-middle-class and middle-class members. The new smaller boards were dominated by upper-class and upper-middle-class members.

The presidential election of 1896 marked the climax of a successful effort by the new industrial elite, in alliance with the old mercantile aristocracy, to gain political power in the cities. For the first time, a Republican presidential candidate, William McKinley, won almost every large northern city. The Republicans had lost the Presidency to the Democrats in 1884 and 1892, and had won it in 1888 in the electoral college without a popular majority. But they had gained a strong national majority in 1896, which they continued to hold until 1932.

The year 1896 was a pivotal political year because ideological lines had been drawn so clearly between the Democratic and Republican parties. Those who still believed in the agricultural frontier aligned with Democrats and voted for William J. Bryan, the "boy orator of the Platte." Those who had interests in the urban-industrial frontier stood with the Republicans and McKinley. Since the colonial Americans had so completely identified America with the frontier, the political rhetoric of 1896 revolved around the question of who was American and who was not. This debate had deep roots in the political economy of the nation.

When southern cotton farmers and wheat farmers of the Plains, hurt by declining prices in the 1880s, became conscious of the explosive development of the corporations, they began to seek gov-

ernment assistance, first from state governments and then from the
federal government. They viewed the corporation as a threat to the
freely operating marketplace of equal producers. To restore equal
competition, they called for the creation of government commissions to regulate the corporate economy. Finding the Democratic
party unresponsive to their concerns in 1890, many of these farmers
formed a third party, the People's party, or Populists. Its platform
of 1892 warned that the disruption of the Jeffersonian marketplace
was causing the appearance of "two great classes—tramps and
millionaires," and the nation was "rapidly degenerating into European conditions." Conservative in their Jeffersonian outlook, the
Populists declared, "we seek to restore the government of the Republic to the hands of 'the plain people' with which it originated.
We assert our purpose to be identical with the purpose of the
National Constitution."

For the Populists, the only functional Americans were productive
farmers and workers. They denied that the corporations were legitimate producers and insisted that the economy basically represented
a conspiracy of bankers. One of their proposed reforms, therefore,
was to remove the national currency from the hands of private
bankers and place it under the control of the federal government.
For the Populists, this reform would not only destroy the alien
conspiracy, but also encourage a policy of currency inflation. If the
government added silver to gold as the monetary basis for determin-
ing the amount of paper currency in circulation, the resulting inflation would raise the prices of the farmers' crops.

During the severe economic depression of 1893, however, the
Democratic President, Grover Cleveland, refused to compromise his
laissez-faire principles. Amid the massive suffering, Cleveland wrote
to his bankers, "You know rich investors like me have to keep an
account of income in these days. I find I am developing quite a
strong desire to make money and I think this is a good time to
indulge in that propensity." Younger Democrats, among them William Jennings Bryan, foresaw disaster for their party in 1896 if
Republicans identified it with the depression. To defeat Republicans
in that election Democrats would need to attract the Populist vote.
One basis for such a coalition was the issue of silver coinage, an
inflationary measure supported by Populists and rural Democrats.

At the 1896 nominating convention, the young rebel Democrats
captured control from the Cleveland forces and named Bryan. In
his famous "Cross of Gold" acceptance speech, Bryan touched the

nerve center of rural America. Identifying with a Jeffersonian nation that had patiently suffered a series of wrongs from the urban financiers, Bryan evoked the scene of the innocent agrarian producers standing to fight because they had been driven mercilessly against the wall. "We have petitioned," Bryan cried, "and our petitions have been scorned; we have entreated, and our entreaties have been disregarded; we have begged, and they have mocked when our calamity came. We beg no longer; we entreat no more; we petition no more. We defy them!"

Bryan denounced the financiers for failing to see their dependence on the farmers, for failing to see "that if you legislate to make the masses prosperous, their prosperity will find its way up through every class which rests upon them," for failing to see that "their cities rest upon our broad and fertile prairies." Bryan warned, "Burn down your cities and leave our farms, and your cities will spring up again as if by magic; but destroy our farms and the grass will grow in the streets of every city in the country."

The Republicans responded by stressing the need for an industrial frontier to provide jobs. Only the Republicans, they claimed, could provide the economic growth that would end the depression. Beyond the practical economics, however, the Republicans pointed to the moral issues. As they saw it America stood for the rationality of the free marketplace. Since the Democrats had joined the Populists in calling for government intervention, which would destroy the free marketplace, Bryan and the Democrats must be un-American. "The Jacobins are in full control at Chicago. No large political movement in America has ever before spawned such hideous and repulsve vipers," wrote the *Philadelphia Press*. "This riotous platform rests upon the four cornerstones of organized repudiation, deliberate confiscation, chartered communism, and enthroned anarchy." The Democratic platform, added the *New York Tribune*, "was the hysterical declaration of a reckless and lawless crusade of sectional animosity and class antagonism. No wild-eyed and rattle-brained horde of the red flag ever proclaimed a fiercer defiance of law, precedent, order, and government."

With both parties claiming a conspiracy and both promising to purge the nation of evil, black Americans once again became powerful symbols of malevolence. In Virginia and North Carolina, during the 1880s and 1890s, black voters had formed alliances with low-income whites and challenged the power-holders in the state Democratic parties. In response the politicians created a mythic history of the Reconstruction era that effectively destroyed the interracial alliances. They described Reconstruction as a record of massive and hideous rape, murder, and arson by blacks against whites. They suggested that white men join together in the Democratic party to expel the blacks from politics, to restore order, to preserve white racial purity. They warned whites not to place economic self-interest over matters of racial unity. It was only because the white community had splintered into a variety of economic groups, they observed, that blacks returned to politics, where they now threatened a repetition of the horror of Reconstruction.

After creating this atmosphere of racial hysteria, marked by a rapid rise in the rate of lynching, white politicians called for state constitutional conventions, first in Mississippi in 1890, to disfranchise blacks despite the provisions of the Fifteenth Amendment. Black leaders had warned in 1870 that the amendment could not protect their political rights without a system of national voter registration. Twenty years later, southern state conventions proposed poll taxes and literacy tests, which applied to both races. A higher proportion of blacks, who had come out of slavery without property or literacy, were disfranchised than whites. But local white southern registrars used the literacy test to disqualify even literate blacks.

The Supreme Court did not respond to reports from the southern state conventions of the disfranchisement of blacks. The Court also turned a deaf ear to southern representatives and senators who boasted on the floor of the Congress that "niggers" had been driven from politics in their states. The Court quietly accepted the spread of "Jim Crow" laws that legalized segregation in public areas, taking the position that separate but equal facilities did not violate the rights of citizens under the Fourteenth Amendment. Black leaders had argued in 1867 that only federal control of education could guarantee equal facilities. The Supreme Court, however, did nothing to prevent southern states from spending disproportionate sums (at a ratio of ten to one) for white schools.

Low-income southern whites had struggled until 1896 to maintain coalitions with black voters. In Georgia, Tom Watson, a leader of the Populists, attempted such an alliance. "You are kept apart that you may be separately fleeced from your earnings. You are made to hate each other because upon that hatred is rested the keystone of the arch of financial despotism which enslaves you both," he declared to white and black farmers. "You are deceived

and blinded that you may not see how the race antagonism perpetu-
ates a monetary system which beggars both."

Against Watson's advice, most Populist leaders had thrown their
support to Bryan in 1896. He warned that the fusion of Populists
with Democrats in the southern states would allow the "new South"
elites to consolidate their political power. Bitterly disappointed,
Watson withdrew from politics for a time.

Partially absorbed by the Democratic party in 1896, Populism
collapsed as a viable political movement and a one-party system
dominated by the Democrats became the pattern in the southern
states. Primaries, established in these one-party states, became the
only effective elections, and blacks were barred on racial grounds
from participating in these primaries; thus they were doubly disfranchised. The Supreme Court ruled that political parties, as private organizations, could engage in overt racial discrimination.

In all the cotton states, from South Carolina to Texas, politicians
emerged to rally popular support and harness the racial resentments
of lower-class and lower-middle-class whites. Tom Watson, who
turned violently antiblack after his political defeat, and Theodore
Bilbo of Mississippi, and Ben Tillman of South Carolina were only
a few of the demagogues who kept the anti-Negro crusade alive
after 1900. They also attacked the Catholic immigrants in the
northern cities. "The Roman Catholic Hierarchy," warned Watson,
in a publication called *Watson's Jeffersonian Magazine,* "is the
deadliest menace to our Liberties and our Civilization," because of
"the sinister portent of Negro priests." He also engaged in violent
anti-Semitism. He called for the lynching of Leo Frank, a Jewish
factory superintendent accused of murdering an employee; Frank
was guilty, Watson wrote, because of his physical appearance:
"those bulging satyr eyes, the protruding fearfully sensual lips; and
also the animal jaw." He was guilty because as a Jew he had a
"ravenous appetite for the forbidden fruit—a lustful eagerness enhanced by the racial novelty of the girl of the uncircumcised." He
must be lynched, Watson wrote, because the courts were corrupted
by the "gigantic conspiracy of Big Money. Frank belonged to the
Jewish aristocracy, and it was determined by the rich Jews that no
aristocrat of their race should die for the death of a working-class
Gentile." After Frank was lynched by an unmasked and unpun-
ished crowd, Watson called for the re-creation of the Ku Klux
Klan. During Reconstruction, scattered groups of whites throughout
the South had called themselves the Knights of the Ku Klux Klan.

But these local klans had not been able to create a widespread organization with centralized leadership. In Georgia in 1915, a co-hesive and interlocking Klan was established that would become a national organization as strong in much of the Midwest as it was in the South. It was dedicated to carrying the antiblack crusade to the North and to placing the same kinds of restraints on Catholics and Jews.

Many white middle-class women first became involved in politics when they participated in the abolitionist movement before the Civil War. As they worked to free blacks from slavery and to raise the status of black men to full citizenship, they thought that the revolu-tion to increase political participation would reach out to include women. They were bitterly disappointed when white men ignored women during the passage of the Fourteenth and Fifteenth Amend-ments. Until the 1890s, however, feminist leaders continued to argue that women enjoyed the same universal natural rights as white and black men and had the right to full citizenship, including the vote.

But the merger of the two most important women's organizations, the National Woman Suffrage Association and the American Woman Suffrage Association, to form the National American Woman Suffrage Association (NAWSA) in 1890 marked a major change in the arguments used to gain the vote. The new generation of leaders represented by Carrie Chapman Catt, which replaced the generation represented by Susan B. Anthony, was prepared to link suffrage for WASP women with the Purity Crusade. The energy of middle-class women in NAWSA was blended with the energy of the Women's Christian Temperence Union (WCTU).

Abandoning the philosophy of universal human rights, the major arguments of NAWSA stressed that the vote for women would largely be used by the middle class. These Anglo-Saxon women, crusading for purity, would help their hubsands preserve the virtues of the Republic from the threat of unqualified and biologically inferior blacks and Latin and Slavic Europeans. By claiming to share the biological superiority of their men, the middle-class women were trying to disprove one of the major arguments used against them—that they were biologically incapable of rational decisions.

Opponents of the suffrage movement argued that women, like certain male minorities, were too intellectually and morally inferior to be responsible citizens. "There are millions of men in the world for whom despotism is a necessity, and it is this class who immigrate to us every day, who are undermining our institutions," declared a male conservative in the periodical *Remonstrance*, and "if woman suffrage is to be allowed we double not only the numerical force of the threatening majority, but its moral—or immoral influence."

The suffragist leader, Carrie Chapman Catt, now agreed with the male conservatives that "this government is menaced with great danger. That danger lies in the slums of the cities, and the ignorant foreign vote." But then she offered the woman's vote against the foreign and black vote. "There is but one way to avert the danger," she warned; "cut off the vote of the slums and give it to women." Middle-class men, she continued, must recognize "the usefulness of woman suffrage as a counterbalance to the foreign vote, and as a means of legally preserving white supremacy in the South."

Western states had begun to grant the vote to women in the 1890s at the same time that southern states were disenfranchising blacks. Gradually, the former trend reached the eastern states. By 1914, a group of younger, more militant women led by Alice Paul formed the Woman's party to lobby in Washington for a constitutional amendment. The outcome of this activity was the addition of the Eighteenth and Nineteenth Amendments to the Constitution in 1920. The former amendment established national Prohibition and the latter, woman's suffrage. Both were acceptable to the new industrial elites in their effort to establish order throughout the country.

The destruction of the saloon had been of great importance to the corporate leaders in their efforts to control the city. As the urban population exploded, so did the number of saloons. By 1900, in most cities there was one saloon for every two hundred city dwellers. Beer consumption had jumped from three gallons per capita per year in 1850 to thirty gallons per capita in 1912. Brewers usually financed the saloons, paying the rent and license fee and providing the fixtures and the beer.

The saloons were meeting places for the male working class and centers of immigrant culture. The saloon provided a public toilet, a check-cashing service, and a free or cheap lunch. In an emergency, a customer could spend the night sleeping on the floor. Labor unions and political ward clubs usually met in saloons. Employers often came to saloons to find temporary or permanent labor. Most importantly, however, the saloons were centers where immigrant cultures were preserved and a sense of working-class solidarity was strengthened. Here laborers came to find release from the hated routine of the factory clock; here they came to engage in uninhibited self-expression, free from the discipline of the job; here they could forget about the future.

With Prohibition the saloon was supposed to disappear, and with it the ethnic spirit that had flourished there. Many hoped it would dissipate the working-class consciousness that the saloon-goers had shared. And finally it was hoped Prohibition would undermine union organization and the ward clubs of the urban bosses.

As the Republicans became the majority party in much of the North by 1896 and as Democrats, with Republican principles, consolidated their control in the South, there was an increase in the ability of the parties to achieve discipline in the Congress. The party caucus, through the control of committee assignment, became more efficient in guiding key legislation to final enactment.

This regularization of power made the interrelationships of economics and politics less chaotic and more predictable than it had been in the 1870s and 1880s. Lobbyists established themselves as a central part of the political life in Washington. They were able to deal with congressional leaders whose influence lasted from session to session. Reaching a new level of professionalization, lobbyists provided research and speech-writing services for congressmen, as well as other forms of economic support. The industry leaders were also moved to further political action to curtail the erratic power of the urban bosses. They were able to bring to an end the practice of printing and distributing ballots through political parties, by introducing the secret ballot.

When William McKinley was re-elected in 1900, however, it would have been difficult to predict that the interests of industry would so completely have their hands on the throttle of political power in 1920. Many southern and western farmers bitterly resented Republican leadership as the new century began. Although significant numbers of industrial workers had supported the McKinley administration, many others were so hostile to the new corporate economy that they were ready to join the Socialist party, which gained rapidly in strength between 1900 and 1912. There were deep divisions within the Republican party itself. Many businessmen, especially those with small businesses, were critical of the desire of the industrial leaders to limit competition in the marketplace; nor did they sympathize with the thrust of the McKinley administration to make the United States a major world power, involved in a struggle to expand overseas markets.

Thus the United States entered the new century filled with deep social, economic, and political divisions. On September 6, 1901, President McKinley was assassinated by an anarchist. The task of creating unity out of disunity now fell on the shoulders of the vice-president, Theodore Roosevelt.

"I will not cry peace"

★ ★ ★ ★ ★ ★ ★ ★ ★ ★ ★ ★ ★ ★ ★ ★ ★ ★ ★ ★

13

The End of Isolation,
1898–1920

President Theodore Roosevelt's two terms

President Woodrow Wilson: the man in office

Exploiting foreign markets

America's Open Door policy

War in Europe, 1914, and American neutrality

The United States enters World War I

Newspapers made Theodore Roosevelt a hero during the brief Spanish-American War of 1898. He served as a lieutenant colonel with a volunteer cavalry regiment popularly known as the Rough Riders because some of its members were cowboys. Reporters wildly exaggerated the military significance of the charge at San Juan Hill. "Nothing in the lucid pages of Thucydides, nor in the terse commentaries of Caesar, nothing can surpass the story" of this battle, one wrote; "probably never before in the history of a country has so remarkable a thing happened." Republican leaders had chosen Roosevelt to be their vice-presidential candidate in 1900 because of his wartime fame. In 1901, the assassination of McKinley brought him to the Presidency. At forty-three, he was the youngest President in American history, and the press immediately identified his youth and vigor with the few years he had spent in the West.

Newspaper editors and their readers seemed to want a hero who could heal the symbolic and sectional divisions of the country. These divisions were pointed up in the presidential elections of 1896 and 1900, when McKinley was seen as the representative of a United States of America East and Bryan as the representative of an America West. Roosevelt was both an easterner and a westerner. He was a city dweller who spoke passionately of the values of rural life. "No nation has ever achieved permanent greatness," he declared, "unless this greatness was based on the well-being of the great farmer class, the men who live on the soil." Many farmers believed that Roosevelt would take up Bryan's battle against the encroachment of the large corporations, and they identified him with Andrew Jackson as a defender of western farmers against eastern exploitation. "The devouring dragon of the Jacksonian age was the Biddle Bank," wrote a western newspaper. "General Jackson destroyed it as Mr. Roosevelt has destroyed the evil trusts."

City dwellers in the 1890s had begun to echo the farmers' demands for governmental commissions to control the large corporations. Small businessmen and large numbers of middle-class professionals, who were seeing themselves as "consumers," hoped that government commissions would protect them from exploitation by big business. Like the farmers, they rallied around Roosevelt, hoping that he would revive the political strength of their interest groups.

Roosevelt came to the Presidency angry at what he saw as the irresponsibility of many big businessmen. "The folly of the very rich men; their greed and arrogance," he warned, "have tended to produce a very unhealthy condition of excitement and irritation in the popular mind, which shows itself in the great increase in the socialistic propaganda." He wanted businessmen to be socially responsible and to take a paternalistic attitude toward labor, farmers, and consumers. "Our aim is not to do away with corporations," he declared. "These big aggregations are an inevitable development of modern industrialism. We draw the line against misconduct, not wealth." During his two administrations, Roosevelt continued to stand as the unstable center of conflicting interests.

Farmers, small businessmen, professionals, women, and consumers in general saw themselves participating in a democratic upsurge that they called "progressivism." They distrusted legislatures and courts, which they believed were under the control of special and selfish interests. Calling themselves "the people," they argued that only the executive represented all the people and that executive leadership was therefore the best instrument for the democratic expression of the will of the people. This "progressive" movement lobbied for the direct expression of democracy in the initiative, referendum, and the recall of judges. It built up pressure for the adoption in 1913 of the Sixteenth and Seventeenth Amendments to the Constitution, which established the income tax and the election of United States senators by the voters rather than by the state legislatures. It called for more government by disinterested experts and less by professional politicians.

Leaders of the industrial elite, George Perkins of U.S. Steel among others, had also come to see such changes as advantageous to the large corporation. A strong executive, surrounded by a bureaucracy of nonelected experts, could provide a climate of political stability that the corporations needed for their long-range economic planning. It would be more effective than dealing with legislators and judges who represented a multiplicity of conflicting and short-range local interests. Big businessmen agreed with Roosevelt when he declared, "I am afraid all modern legislative bodies tend to show their incapacity to meet the new and complex needs of the times." Thus they supported the development of regulatory commissions. The "progressives" believed they had won a victory over the large

corporations when they persuaded Congress to pass a Meat Inspection Act and a Pure Food and Drug Act in 1906. But government
inspection did not lower prices and increase competition as the
"progressives" expected; instead it drove small entrepreneurs out of
business because they could not afford to meet the new standards
and thus solidified the control of the market by a few large meat
packers and drug companies.

Nowhere was this pattern clearer than in the area of conservation. Roosevelt added dramatically to the forest land under national
control. He placed his friend Gifford Pinchot in charge of the use
of these national resources. Trained in scientific forestry in Germany, Pinchot declared that "the object of our forest policy is not
to preserve the forests because they are refuges for the wild creatures of the wilderness." Efficiency, Pinchot said, is the primary
purpose of conservation, "a conscious and purposeful entering into
control over nature," and "the millennium will have been reached
when humanity shall have learned to eliminate all useless waste."
Again it was the large national economic interests that supported
this policy of conservation and it was local small lumbermen and
ranchers who were opposed.

In spite of Roosevelt's great personal popularity, neither the "progressives" nor the industrial leaders were satisfied with the legislative
accomplishments of his two terms. William Howard Taft, experienced as an administrator, inherited this discontent when he won
the Presidency in 1908 as the Republican candidate. Taft had none
of Roosevelt's charisma, and he did not sympathize with the demands of either the "progressives" or the industrial elite. Instead he
aligned himself with ths believers in the traditional competitive
marketplace. "Progressive" Republicans began to look to Senator
Robert LaFollette of Wisconsin to challenge Taft in 1912, while the
political leaders sympathetic to big business, such as George Perkins and the magazine publisher Frank Munsey, persuaded Roosevelt to head a third party. They argued that this Progressive party,
under Roosevelt's leadership, could complete the transition of the
nation from the irrationality of a competitive marketplace to the
rationality of a marketplace controlled by the large corporations
acting through governmental agencies.

The Socialist party reached its greatest strength in this election of
1912. Roosevelt as a Progressive won more votes than Taft. But
with the Republicans split, it was the Democratic candidate, Woodrow Wilson, who won the Presidency. And much to Roosevelt's

chagrin, it was in Wilson's administrations that the legislative hopes of both the "progressives" and the new industrial elite were to be fulfilled.

Roosevelt considered Wilson an ineffectual academic, unable to provide political leadership. And, indeed, Wilson's biography up to 1910 seemed to justify such contempt. He had been born in Virginia just before the Civil War. His father was a Presbyterian minister loyal to the Confederate cause. During his youth Wilson seemed to be a very obedient son. He seemed overawed by his father. "If I had my father's face and figure," he declared as an adolescent, "it wouldn't make any difference what I said." He was unable to learn to read until he was eleven, perhaps because he feared he could not live up to his father's expectations. He was disappointed that he felt no calling for the ministry and trained to be a lawyer. But he was unable to compete effectively enough to establish a legal practice in Atlanta, Georgia. He retreated to Johns Hopkins University to take a Ph.D. in history and political science and sought the security of college teaching.

But Wilson did not see this choice as a retreat from the real world. This new university was one of the first to make the transition from a nineteenth-century college to the twentieth-century university. The key to this transition was a change from the status of amateur to that of professional for both students and faculty. The seminar and the Ph.D. degree had been imported from Germany to establish the professional college teacher. The seminar provided the methodological skills so that doctoral candidates could achieve scholarly objective and professional neutrality. Perhaps Wilson, with a Ph.D. in political science, could think of himself as a secular priest in control of a more powerful and relevant set of universal truths than those possessed by his father.

College teaching and then politics seemed to offer Wilson the opportunity to manipulate people without becoming close to them. "I have a sense of power in dealing with people collectively which I do not feel in dealing with them singly," he admitted. "Plenty of people offer me their friendship; but, partly, because I am reserved and shy, and partly because I am factitious and have a narrow uncatholic taste in my friends, I reject the offer in almost every case."

Wilson's scholarly concern was with power. His successful book *Congressional Government* expressed his envy of the parliamentary system. The English Prime Minister, he argued, had much more power than the American President because he was not frustrated by a system of checks and balances. And Wilson saw his scholarly career as temporary. "My feeling has been that such literary talents as I have are secondary to my equipment for other things," he declared, and "that my power to write was meant to be a handmaiden to my power to speak and to organize action."

Wilson deplored the fact that his first teaching post was at Bryn Mawr, a women's college. Teaching women politics, he declared was "about as appropriate and profitable as would be lecturing to stone-masons on the evolution of fashion in dress." Lacking intellectual capacity, women made good wives, where "their life must supplement man's life." Wilson needed the support of a traditional wife, and remarried quickly after the death of his first wife.

He was glad to leave Bryn Mawr to teach at Wesleyan and then Princeton. "I have for a long time been hungry for a class of men," he rejoiced. Hungry also for power, Wilson soon accepted the presidency of Princeton with the stipulation that he have total power to hire and fire the faculty. It was his ambition to remake the college along the lines of Johns Hopkins and produce national leaders who were scholarly experts. The alumni, however, defeated his efforts to minimize social life while maximizing scholarship. He was especially disappointed by their refusal to make the graduate school a central part of the campus.

He was ready, therefore, to leave university life when he was asked by Democratic party bosses in New Jersey to be their candidate for the governorship in 1910. Wilson's speeches as a college president had attracted the attention of wealthy and conservative eastern Democrats. He had been critical of Bryan and agrarian reform, and he had been critical of organized labor. In the histories of the United States which he had written, Wilson called for the preservation of leadership by those Americans who were descended from the "English race" against the threat to "English character" posed by new immigrants, "men of the lowest class from the south of Italy and men of the meaner sort out of Hungary and Poland."

Upon election as governor, Wilson immediately repudiated the party bosses. He supported the passage of legislation to strengthen regulatory commissions; he backed "progressive" demands for the initiative and referendum and showed concern for the consumer. Hoping for the Democratic presidential nomination in 1912, Wilson saw himself in a position to surpass Theodore Roosevelt as a national leader.

Identified himself with the East, Wilson courted Bryan, retracting his earlier criticism, and won a symbolic relationship with the West. But Wilson's great advantage over Roosevelt was his identification with the South. His birthplace, the South, Wilson declared, was "the only place in the country, the only place in the world, where nothing has to be explained to me." This first southerner elected to the Presidency since before the Civil War praised the region of his youth. There was, he said, "nothing to apologize for in the past of the South—absolutely nothing to apologize for." This, for Wilson, included slavery, which "had done more for the Negro in two hundred and fifty years than African freedom had done since the building of the pyramids."

Wilson was part of a whole generation of young southern intellectuals who had come North to be educated and who hoped that the South could be integrated into the patterns of northern urban and industrial life. When Wilson and the Democrats captured the Presidency and Congress in 1912, southerners became the leaders of Congress as well as important members of Wilson's Cabinet.

Wilson's goal was to change the complexion of the Democratic party so that it would more successfully synthesize "progressivism" and the interests of the new industrial elite than Roosevelt had in remaking the Republican party. He pleased southern and western farmers and northern consumers by lowering the tariff. He supported a Federal Farm Loan Act and a Warehouse Act that fulfilled a demand for government storage of crops made by the Populists in 1890. He showed paternalistic concern for labor by supporting the Adamson Act, which established an eight-hour day for railroad workers. In his "New Freedom" speeches, like Roosevelt in his "Square Deal" speeches, Wilson promised to protect the average American against the giant corporations. "What this country needs above everything else is a body of laws which will look after the men on the make," Wilson had orated. "The only way to enrich America is to make it possible for any man who has got the brains to get into the game."

But like Roosevelt, he agreed that the corporation was "indispensable to modern business enterprise." "Nobody," he declared, "can fail to see that modern business is going to be done by corporations. The old time of individual competition is gone by." More than Roosevelt, he was able to achieve the legislation which met the "progressive" demand for government commissions to regulate the corporations and the demand of the corporations for government commissions to regulate the economy. He had moved vigorously to provide personal leadership to mobilize the new Democratic majority in Congress.

The Federal Trade Commission (FTC) and the Federal Reserve Board were the two great legislative accomplishments of his administrations. The "progressives" who believed in the possiblity of nonpolitical experts running the FTC expected it to make the corporations responsible to consumers. But those members of the industrial elite who staffed the Commission considered the purpose of the FTC to be to overcome irrational competition and encourage rational corporate planning. Edward Hurley, the head of the FTC, hoped "we can recommend to Congress some legislation that will allow them [coal companies] to come here and fix prices."

This was also the case with the Federal Reserve System. The "progressives" saw it as taking economic power out of the hands of private bankers and putting it in the hands of experts representing the people. But, in practice, the system encouraged the large national banks and discouraged the small state banks and thus solidified the pre-eminence of the great New York financial institutions.

"Our industries have expanded to such a point that they will burst their jackets if they cannot find a free outlet to the markets of the world," Wilson told the Democratic Convention in 1912. "Our domestic markets no longer suffice. We need foreign markets." A fellow student of Frederick Jackson Turner at Johns Hopkins, Wilson agreed that the closing of the agricultural frontier had caused a national crisis. He also agreed with Turner in the 1890s that overseas expansion could provide a new frontier. Again it was Wilson rather than Roosevelt who most strongly expressed the industrial elite's desire to develop an overseas frontier.

This concern for a new frontier had become a dominant theme in Congress by 1890. "A policy of isloation did well enough when we were an embryo nation, but today things are different," declared Senator Orville H. Platt in 1893. "We are the most advanced and powerful people on earth, and regard to our future welfare demands an abandonment of the doctrine of isolation." He concluded, "It is to the ocean that our children must look, as they once looked to the boundless West."

A dramatic change took place, therefore, during the 1890s in the conduct of foreign affairs. Presidents and their foreign-policy advisers began to assume that America was a world power, that vital American economic, political, and military interests existed overseas. They stressed the need for a more systematic foreign policy, one that would include a sense of continuity with the past. A new Republican or Democratic administration should perpetuate the policies of its predecessor. Those at the head of government assumed a sense of interrelatedness in world affairs: the success of American policy in the Far East would be linked to its success in Central America or any other place on the globe. It was expected that the executive branch could and should initiate policy and then generate public and congressional support for it. Policy makers in the world, then, needed an appreciation of the instruments of foreign affairs, and recognized the need for a large and skillful diplomatic corps and a large and powerful navy.

The only question that faced the political elite in the 1890s was the nature of the new empire. Some, like Captain A. T. Mahan, the great theoretician of the new Naval War College, called for annexing overseas colonies "as outlets for the home products and as a nursery of commerce and shipping." Others, like Carl Schurz, agreed that "we cannot have too many markets." But he asked whether overseas markets could be obtained "only by annexing to the United States the countries in which they are situated."

Although the United States did annex the Hawaiian and Philippine Islands at the conclusion of the Spanish-American War in 1898, the proponents of the "Open Door" empire won the larger debate. "Had we no interests in China," stated a report of the United States Senate, "the possession of the Philippines would be meaningless." Confident in the superiority of the American economy, the most rapidly growing in the world, foreign-policy leaders believed that American interests could penetrate to every area of the globe without the use of military power. "Open Door" notes were sent to Japan and all the European nations that had economic interests in China stating that the United States wanted to preserve the territorial integrity of China and opposed further colonization by Europeans.

England supported the American "Open Door" policy in China at the same time that the British government supported American domination in Central America. Forced to concentrate its naval forces against the rapidly developing German fleet, England withdrew from the Caribbean and canceled plans for a canal connecting the Atlantic and Pacific. President Roosevelt quickly walked into the power vacuum and encouraged a revolution in the Colombian province of Panama.

Roosevelt also declared a corollary to the Monroe Doctrine, that the United States would oversee the internal affairs of all Caribbean and Central American republics and intervene when necessary to keep those affairs stable. The preservation of this internal stability would remove any cause or excuse for European intervention in these areas. Having served notice of American hegemony there, Roosevelt saw to the building of the Panama Canal, which would be controlled militarily by the United States.

Roosevelt delighted in foreign affairs, where he did not have to work artfully with Congress and the public to get legislation enacted. "The biggest matters, such as the Portsmouth Peace, the acquisition of Panama, and sending the fleet around the world," he affirmed, "I managed without consultation with anyone; for when a matter is of capital importance, it is well to have it handled by one man only." Woodrow Wilson agreed with Roosevelt. "The initiative in foreign affairs, which the President possesses without any restriction whatever, is virtually the power to control them absolutely." The "progressive" commitment to a strong executive was finding its greatest fulfillment in foreign policy.

Roosevelt, Taft, and Wilson periodically sent marines into Central American and Caribbean republics to stabilize the local political situations and protect American investments. Military governments in Cuba and the Philippines after the Spanish-American War gave American leaders confidence that they could bring rational order to the rest of the world. General Leonard Wood proudly declared that "for the first time, probably in its history, Havana has an honest and efficient government, clean of bribery and speculation." An American reporter praised "the establishment, in a little over three years, in a Latin military colony, in one of the most unhealthy countries of the world, of a republic modeled closely upon the lines of our own great Anglo-Saxon republic."

Thus, for the new corporate and political elites, their success in organizing rational space in American cities, in controlling the millions of European peasants who had come to these cities, in educating these masses in the efficient ways of industry, according to the discipline of linear time, could be repeated throughout the entire world. "America's duty toward the people living in barbarism is to see that they are freed from their chains and we can free them only by destroying barbarism itself," declared Theodore Roosevelt. "Peace cannot be had until the civilized nations have expanded in some shape over the barbarous nations." It is not surprising then that Wilson was willing to intervene in the affairs of even such a major nation as Mexico. "I am going to teach the South American republics to elect good men," he affirmed.

American intellectuals, after 1890, had been engaged in a dramatic reversal of their attitudes toward Germany. From 1810 to 1890, Germany had been perceived as the most modern European nation, and Americans had gone there to be educated into the most progressive intellectual currents. But the early-twentieth-century image of Germany, firmly established by 1914, was of the most reactionary European nation, stubbornly preserving the medieval and barbaric past. England had replaced Germany as the most admired country. Wilson had shared in this change of attitude. His writings were full of praise for things English, while they described German culture as "essentially selfish and lacking in spirituality."

When war came to Europe in August 1914, Wilson strongly emphasized the necessity of American neutrality. He felt that this world war might create a situation where America would have "the infinite privilege of fulfilling her destiny and saving the world." England and France, however, in their conflict with the German and Austro-Hungarian empires were considered too compromised and corrupted by their own empires to be completely worthy of having the United States fight on their side. Wilson's vision of the world that would emerge from this conflict was one in which all empires were dissolved and the major nations imitated the pattern of the United States by pursuing a course of "Open Door" economic expansion which flowed across national boundaries.

If the United States entered the war on the side of England and France only to help them defend their empires, then the United States would have lost its soul in this imperial civil war, and "the spirit of ruthless brutality," Wilson warned, "will enter into the very fiber of our national life, infecting Congress, the courts, the policeman on the beat, the man on the street." If America did not Americanize Europe, then Europe would Europeanize America, and the nation would be locked into a cycle of European civil wars.

By November 1916, however, when he was re-elected on the slogan "He kept us out of war," Wilson feared that he had become trapped in a web of circumstances beyond his control. He and his advisers had refused to take a strong stand against England when its navy violated international law. But Wilson had issued ever stronger warnings to Germany to halt its submarine warfare, also contrary to international law. Finally, in the summer of 1916, an American ultimatum forced the curtailment of German submarine activity. The nightmarish fear that descended upon Wilson was that a German decision to recommence submarine warfare would challenge American national honor and ultimately force the country to enter the European civil war. Desperately, he tried to persuade England and France and Germany to sit down and negotiate a peace settlement. But in January 1917, German leaders decided to take the calculated risk that the restoration of unrestricted submarine activity would defeat the Allies before America could mobilize its military forces.

The great power of the Presidency in foreign affairs had made it possible for Wilson to place the United States on the verge of war without the knowledge of the average voter. These voters had re-elected Wilson because they believed he would preserve peace. The strong peace movement among women had rallied for Wilson. Many German-Americans and Irish-Americans who hated English imperialism also backed Wilson. A number of midwestern WASP "progressives," who feared the power of eastern corporations to influence foreign policy, saw the Republican party in 1916 as pro-English and prowar and supported Wilson.

Wilson shared the view of WASP leaders who had made the foreign-policy revolution in the 1890s that Germany was the chief threat to the American policy of worldwide free trade dominated by the American economy. Both the United States and Germany surpassed England in industrial production and population in the 1890s. But German leaders chose to try to expand overseas through an empire of colonies modeled after that of England. From 1895 to 1917, American naval and military leaders planned for possible war against Germany. And German leaders expected war against the United States during these years.

In February 1917, all of Wilson's advisers urged him to ask for a declaration of war. Bryan, his first secretary of state, had resigned when Wilson's eastern friends had persuaded him to bend neutrality and allow the New York bankers to make huge loans to England and France. By March 1917, these loans totaled more than $2 billion, whereas only $20 million had been loaned to Germany.

Wilson would not retreat from the right of Americans and American ships to sail into the war zone. This was the revolutionary principle of free trade to which the WASP elite was committed. Wilson asked Congress to pass legislation to arm American merchant ships. When his request was blocked by such midwestern progressive Republicans as Senator Robert LaFollette of Wisconsin and George Norris of Nebraska, Wilson armed the ships by executive order. They sailed to England and were fired on by German submarines, and they fired back. By March 1917, Wilson had involved the United States in a shooting war with Germany.

Germany made it easier for Wilson to overcome congressional opposition to the war by urging Mexico to join in a war against the United States and regain the territories it had lost in 1846. These Zimmermann Notes fell into American hands, and Wilson used them to prove the aggressiveness of the German feudal aristocracy. But when Wilson went to Congress with a war message in April, deep doubts still haunted him. "My message today was a message of death for our young men," he lamented to a friend; "how strange it seemed to applaud that."

Once the decision was made, Wilson seemed to be trying to persaude himself that it really was a crusade. "Valor withholds itself from all small implications and entanglements and waits for the great opportunity when the sword will flash as if it carried the light of heaven upon its blade," he cried out. "When men take up arms to set other men free, there is something sacred and holy in the warfare." "I will not cry peace," Wilson affirmed, "as long as there is sin and wrong in the world." Wilson still hoped, at the end of the war, that England and France would divest themselves of their empires and accept the American "Open Door" policy. Then with the end of the German and the Austro-Hungarian empires, American entry into the war would have ushered in a new era in which the entire world would become a rational space for free trade among all nations.

Wilson fiercely repressed all criticism of the war, especially by the Socialists. "This is no time either for divided counsels, or for divided leadership," he warned. "Unity of command is as necessary now in civil action as it is upon the field of battle." But as American armies tipped the balance and forced German surrender in November 1918, Wilson was faced with an overwhelming Republican victory in the congressional elections. The many Americans who opposed the war could, at least, express their unhappiness by voting for Republicans.

Just as he refused to acknowledge that England and France had not divested themselves of their imperial ambitions, he refused to admit that he was not supported by a unified national consensus on the meaning of the war and the shape of the peace. He sailed to Europe, thinking that he had it in his own power to lead the world into a new era. "I am the only person of high authority amongst all the peoples of the world who is at liberty to speak and hold nothing back," he declared. "I am speaking for the silent mass of mankind who have as yet had no place or opportunity to speak."

In Paris, however, he was forced to compromise with the imperial ambitions of England, France, Italy, and Japan. But when he came home to ask for the ratification of the peace treaty and for American membership in a League of Nations, which would guarantee the political patterns established by the treaty, he refused to listen to criticism of the treaty and the structure of the League.

Republicans demanded compromise and revision before they would support the treaty. But Wilson ordered Democratic congressional leaders to reject all compromises. In the hope of persuading the people that they must accept his treaty as the guarantee that American participation in the war had changed world history, he went on a speaking tour of the nation. Addressing the veterans in the crowds, Wilson cried out, "Boys, I told you before you went across the seas that this was a war against war, and I did my best to fulfill the promise, but I am obliged to come to you in mortification and shame and say I have not been able to fulfill the promise. You are betrayed. You fought for something you did not get."

Wilson drove himself hard on this trip; he inflicted such physical punishment on himself as he spoke several times a day, day after day, that it seemed that he was seeking martyrdom. Suddenly, he collapsed, incapacitated by a stroke. He spent the last year of his Presidency in silence and semidarkness. Meanwhile, in 1920 the voters went to the polls and elected Warren Harding, who promised a return to "normalcy."

America had refused to sign the Treaty of Versailles or join the League of Nations. Wilson's dream of world order, of a world liberated from traditional imperialism by the United States, lay silent and impotent within him. Probably the most painful thing for this invalid, however, must have been the knowledge that the self-destruction of the European civil war had made it possible for Bolshevism to capture control of Russia. For in 1920, the Soviet Union had pledged to shape a future that would eradicate imperialism—an imperialism, according to Nikolai Lenin, which dominated the policies of the United States as well as the Western European nations.

Part Four

★ ★ ★ ★ ★ ★ ★ ★ ★ ★ ★ ★ ★ ★ ★ ★ ★ ★ ★ ★

THE CLOSING OF FRONTIERS
AT HOME AND ABROAD,
1920–76

"We are entering a new era"

★ ★ ★ ★ ★ ★ ★ ★ ★ ★ ★ ★ ★ ★ ★ ★ ★ ★ ★ ★

14

Prosperity and Depression, 1920–40

Postwar disillusionment: failure of the Purity Crusade, the jazz era, and the "lost generation"

Explosion of black culture and black pride

Postwar corporate boom

Herbert Hoover: at the helm of a consumer economy

Stock-market disaster: facing the depression

Roosevelt's emergency measures

"The stage is set, the destiny is disclosed. It has come about by no plan of our conceiving, but by the hand of God who led us into the war. We cannot turn back. America shall in truth show the way." With these words, Woodrow Wilson had exhorted his fellow Americans to bring the Purity Crusade to a climax and finally to purge evil and darkness from the entire world. Now, in 1919, he continued to urge Americans to fulfill that mission which gave a "halo" to the "gun over the mantelpiece" and "the sword" that had been used in the holy war. For Wilson, this was a time when the world had embraced American soldiers "as crusaders, and their transcendent achievement has made all the world believe in America as it believes in no other nation organized in the modern world." In what appeared to Protestant leaders as the moment of their greatest triumph, their spokesman, Tyler Dennett, boasted that Protestant "religious organizations took on a new importance in the eyes of the government after the war began." The national government, its armies, and the Protestant churches, Dennett declared, had become one as "the churches offered direct and open channels for communicating with the people, for stimulating patriotism, and for education in war aims."

During 1919 and 1920, the Protestant churches planned to fulfill Wilson's exhortations through an Interchurch World Movement that would fill every nation of the world with Protestant missionaries. "Our business is to establish a civilization that is Christian in spirit and in passion," Dennett proclaimed, "in Borneo as much as in Boston."

Barely two years later, these words sounded hollow. Students, who earlier had rushed to volunteer for missionary duty, decided to stay home. Episcopalians, Presbyterians, Congregationalists, Northern Methodists, and Baptists appeared disillusioned and confused as they entered the 1920s. Suddenly, they were faced with a world that refused to be redeemed and a great financial drive to mobilize resources for the missionary effort failed. Demoralized, they suffered another shattering experience when their own respectable middle-class church people refused to uphold the Eighteenth Amendment and keep America free from the influence of alcohol.

In the larger cities nightclubs sold bootleg liquor and featured jazz entertainment as the Purity Crusade, which had gained momentum in the decades before 1920, seemed entirely forgotten. "It struck me funny how the top and bottom crusts in society were always getting together during the Prohibition era," wrote the jazz musician Milton Mezzrow. "In this swanky club which was run by the notorious Purple Gang, Detroit's bluebloods used to congregate—the Grosse Point mob on the slumming kick, rubbing elbows with Louis the Wop's mob."

The Purity Crusade had been fighting against a loosening of morality not only at the lowest socio-economic class, but also among the middle class. The divorce rate of the middle class had increased steadily from 1890 to 1920; it would double in the 1920s. Other symptoms of decline alarmed conservatives. The urban middle class had stopped chaperoning its daughters after 1900, and there was a tremendous decline in the pattern of premarital virginity by 1920. It was clear that by 1910 a new code of permissiveness was being elaborated by the young. Soon unchaperoned, sexual intimacy became acceptable within the context of an affectionate relationship that might result in marriage.

This sexual revolution was accompanied by a significant decline in the birthrate. In 1914, Margaret Sanger brought the growing interest in contraception into the open with the publication of her magazine *The Woman Rebel*. Dedicated, she wrote, to the liberation of "women enslaved by the machine, by wage slavery, by bourgeois morality, by customs, laws, and superstitions," *The Woman Rebel* advocated "the prevention of conception" by imparting adequate knowledge to its middle-class readers. Sanger violated the law by starting birth-control clinics for lower-class women. "Mothers! Can you afford a large family? Do you want more children? If not, why do you have them? Do not kill, do not take life, but prevent," read the signs for her clinic. "Safe harmless information can be obtained of trained nurses." By 1921, her efforts were achieving respectability in the American Birth Control League, supported financially by younger wealthy women.

Just as the conservative middle class could not stop its younger members from participating in a sexual revolution, neither could it stop these young people from listening and dancing to rather sensual music. African rhythms, which had survived in the black community, began to influence white popular music in the 1890s. Ragtime was an Afro-American music in which the piano captured some of the patterns of the African drum. As the audience for this music grew, the lyrics of songs began to change; they became much more explicitly sexual. Sheet music sold widely, and conservative defenders of morality were horrified by the dance crazes that swept through cities in the years immediately before World War I.

In the 1920s, blues and jazz, which had succeeded ragtime as the major Afro-American influences on popular music, seemed even more sensual and consequently more threatening. "Jazz is rhythm without soul," declared Walter Damrosch, a leader of the musical establishment, and John Philip Sousa agreed that jazz "employs primitive rhythms which excite the baser human instincts." Dr. E. Elliot Rawlings, a spokesman for the medical profession, added that "jazz music causes drunkenness. Reason and reflection are lost and the actions of the persons are directed by the stronger animal passions."

Not only did "those moaning saxophones and the rest of the instruments with their broken, jerky rhythm make a purely sensual appeal," stated Fenton Bott, head of the National Association of Masters of Dancing, but the lyrics written in "the Negro brothels of the South" were "an offense against womanly purity, the very fountainhead of our family and civil life." Many newspapers and magazines agreed to try to halt the spreading influence of jazz through a conspiracy of silence, only reporting that it was a dying fad. When this proved ineffective, the General Federation of Women's Clubs tried to have the music repressed. By 1929, many cities, including New York, Philadelphia, Cleveland, Detroit, and Kansas City, had regulations prohibiting jazz from public dance halls.

The attempt to prohibit jazz only increased its appeal to the young, who were in self-conscious rebellion against their parents and were searching for other ways of experiencing the rhythm of life.

As the American geographic frontier closed in the 1890s, the symphonic music of Western Europe and the United States began to show signs of stress. Charles Ives in America and Arnold Schoenberg in Europe introduced dissonance and atonality into their symphonies. The music critic Leonard Meyer has argued in his book *Music, the Arts, and Ideas* that patterns of Western music that had prevailed since the Renaissance had begun a process of disintegration that would continue until, by the mid-twentieth century, it was clear that there was an entirely new musical world. Another music critic, Henry Pleasants, in his book *Serious Music and All That Jazz,* argued that Afro-American music had replaced the symphonic tradition in Western Europe as well as in the United States.

The survival and increasing success of this premodern music from 1890 to 1920 was contrary to the expectations of the WASP intellectuals, who were certain that the modern sense of space and time would conquer all premodern expressions of space and time. Charles Beard had replaced Frederick Jackson Turner as the most influential historian between 1900 and 1914 because Beard promised in his book of 1901, *The Industrial Revolution,* that industrialism was a frontier force that destroyed all irrational historical cultures and liberated the individual to live in rational space and make progress along the line of linear time. There was an explosion of such optimism among social scientists during the "progressive" era. The economist Thorstein Veblen reinforced Beard by declaring that "machine discipline acts to disintegrate the institutional heritage of all degrees of antiquity" and that "the mechanically trained classes, trained to matter-of-fact habits of thought, show a notable lack of spontaneity in the construction of new myths or conventions as well as in the reconstruction of the old." John Dewey, the greatest educational philosopher of progressivism, saw the school as speeding the process of industrial liberation. The purpose of the school, Dewey declared, "is to see to it that each individual gets an opportunity to escape from the limitation of the social group in which he was born."

Veblen in his book *Imperial Germany and the Industrial Revolution* (1915), and Dewey in his book *German Philosophy and Politics* (1916), had presented the argument that the German people were living in the modern industrial world but their rulers were still part of medieval culture. American entry into the war would hasten the logic of industrialism by purging this feudal aristocracy. Agreeing with Veblen and Dewey, Charles Beard enthusiastically backed the American war effort, which was to liberate all people to live within the rationality of industrial space and time. "The years, 1917–1918," said Beard, "as surely as the age of the American and French Revolutions, will mark the opening of a new epoch."

Many northern Protestants had abandoned biblical fundamentalism in the 1880s and 1890s to accept the idea of evolution. These "liberal" Protestants identified evolution with progress, and they took their definition of progress from these social scientists. The great liberal Protestant theologian Walter Rauschenbusch used this concept of the industrial frontier to prophesy the final triumph of

Protestantism in freeing people from the ceremonies and traditions of the Dark Ages. In his books *Christianity and the Social Crisis* and *Christianity and the Social Order,* written just before World War I, Rauschenbusch reaffirmed the optimism of the academic prophets: "We are standing at the turning of the ways. We are actors in a great historical drama. It rests upon us to decide if a new era is to dawn in the transformation of the world into the kingdom of God, or if Western Civilization is to descend into the graveyard of dead civilization."

For the poets and novelists of the 1920s, the "lost generation," born between 1890 and 1900 and reared within the prophecy of the industrial frontier, World War I was even more shattering than it was for their teachers. Bitterly disillusioned, academics like Beard, Dewey, and Veblen abandoned internationalism for isolation. They abandoned hope that the entire world could be brought into industrial rationality, but they continued to hope that this could be the future of the United States.

But a young F. Scott Fitzgerald in his 1925 novel, *The Great Gatsby,* rejected such a hope. His hero, James Gatz, leaves the closing agricultural frontier of North Dakota. Reversing the mythic pattern by which Europeans coming west across the Atlantic were washed clean of their old culture and were reborn with a new identity, Gatz comes east and gets a new identity crossing Lake Superior. Now a self-made man, Jay Gatsby will work in the industrial frontier of New York City.

In contrast to the "green breast" of the geographic frontier first seen by the Dutch sailors of Henrik Hudson, Fitzgerald presented Gatsby with a "valley of ashes." In this frontier of ugliness and decadence, Fitzgerald gives Gatsby the heroic task of overcoming biological time. To fulfill his quest, he must restore Daisy, a girl whom he loved before he went to the war, to her original virginity. He must persuade her of the unreality of her marriage to another man while he was away and of the unreality of her motherhood. But instead of a rational and predictable world, Gatsby is caught up by circumstance; an automobile accident sets a chain of events in motion in which a man kills Gatsby because he mistakenly believes Gatsby was the driver of the car that killed his wife.

Earlier, in the 1890s, Frank Norris in his novels *Vandover and the Brute* and *McTeague* had expressed his fear of the sexuality of women. In *Sister Carrie,* Theodore Dreiser had described the superior power of a woman to survive the new urban environment. And in his autobiographical novel of 1912, *The Genius,* he had explicitly talked of his fears of the strength of female biology.

For the young Ernest Hemingway, who had been physically wounded in Italy during the war, the psychic wound was worse. In contrast to the industrial frontier's promise of progressive linear time, the war had forced him to confront death, the possibility of the cyclical nature of time, the cycle of birth inevitably followed by death. And woman, for Hemingway, was the symbol of this cycle.

The opening scene of his first collection of short stories, *In Our Time,* was of refugee women giving birth, how the women "screamed every night at midnight," but "the worst were the women with dead babies. You couldn't get the women to give up their dead babies." Alternating with stories of the war were stories of Hemingway's childhood in northern Michigan. Here again the boy goes with his doctor father to witness the birth of a baby in an Indian camp. During the painful Caesarean delivery, the Indian father kills himself. In Hemingway's novel *Farewell to Arms,* when the hero, Frederick Henry, deserts the insanity of the war and takes refuge in Switzerland with Catherine, the nurse he has loved, they live happily through the winter. But spring brings the birth and death of the child and Catherine.

For John Dos Passos, the insanity of the armies continued into the insanity of the corporations of the 1920s. Young Americans had believed that armies could operate rationally and bring liberation. They had believed much the same about corporations. "Men seemed to have shrunk in stature before the vastness of the mechanical contrivances they had invented—men had become antlike," wrote Dos Passos in his novel *Three Soldiers.* But it was Dos Passos' massive *USA* that best expressed the "lost generation's" horror of organization. Divided into three books, which themselves included twelve stories, Dos Passos added to the sense of fragmentation by including short newsreels, historical biographies, and statements by an introspective observer in the Camera Eye. His book had the qualities of the immensely popular silent movies—it was flat and two-dimensional; its movement did not flow but broke into jerky episodes; it went faster and then slower; it became bright and then faded; it had humor and terror.

Dos Passos in the 1920s was back with Mark Twain in the 1880s. Having lost faith in the urban-industrial frontier of his Progressive fathers, he, like Huck Finn, had no space to flee to escape these fathers. In *USA* he wrote, "The transcontinental passenger thinks contracts, profits, vacation trips, mighty continent between Atlantic and Pacific, power, wires humming, dollars, cities jammed, hills empty, the Indian trail leading into the wagon road, the macadam pike, the concrete skyway, transcontinental planes, history, the billion dollar speed up. And in the bumpy air over the desert ranges toward Las Vegas sickens and vomits into the carton container the steak and mushrooms he ate in New York."

The son of this corrupt father stands as a solitary vagabond on a highway beneath the plane. Trying to hitch a ride, he is a dropout who "went to school, books said opportunity, ads promised speed, own your own home, shine bigger than your neighbor, the radio crooner whispered, girls, ghosts of platinum girls coaxed from the screen, millions in winnings were chalked upon the board, in the offices, pay checks for hands willing to work; the cleared desk of an executive with three telephones on it—he waits with swimming head, needs knot his belly, idle hands numb, beside the speeding traffic."

Young white musicians saw in jazz a symbolic alternative to the bureaucratic prison of their fathers. Jazz had a structure that offered an opportunity to improvise. Eddie Condon, who taught himself to play jazz by ear, reported his father's reaction: "You are terrible and you can't read music." Condon's reply to his father was, "What's that got to do with being a musician?" For Hoagy Carmichael, jazz was a way out of chaos into a new world of meaning. He smoked marijuana and listened to jazz. He described what it felt like: "My body got light. Every note Louis [Armstrong] hit was perfection. I ran to the piano. They swang into 'Royal Garden Blues.' I had never heard the tune before but somehow I knew every note. I couldn't miss. I was floating in a strong deep-blue whirlpool of jazz. It wasn't the marijuana. It was the music. The music took me and had me and it made me right."

For the first time in American history, whites seemed to express an appreciation for black culture. Whites perceived in the body of black music and culture vitality, honesty, and spontaneity. In a world where traditional idealism had vanished, where traditional religion seemed bankrupt, perhaps black primitivism, outside of white culture, offered a new spiritual meaning, a new salvation. Like most premodern cultures, black culture was present-minded, with little concern for the future. The past and the future were contained in the present. For the "lost generation," with its faith in progress shattered, the present had become all-important, and whites sensed, without being able to analyze it, the present-mindedness of black music.

Music had been a significant part of the black oral tradition. This music with its sensual rhythms was a communal expression that was spontaneous and improvisational. Leadership in the musical performance could emerge spontaneously in a situation where there was no division between artist and audience, no division between the caller and the responder. In this sense, Afro-American musical influence grew stronger; it had an effect on the composed and restrained patterns of ragtime; on the immediacy of the blues, where the human voice spoke in song; and on the improvisation of jazz, where the musician conversed with his listeners through his instrument. To participate in the music was to live more fully. For Charlie Parker, the great black jazz musician, "Music is your own experience. If you don't live it, it won't come out of your horn." Music that expressed an immediate experience of sorrow and joy, of disharmony or harmony with the universe, was religious music. Unlike most white religion, it presented worship as a pleasurable activity and a release from tension. Even the white musician Paul Whiteman, who presented an extremely restrained, prettified, and commercialized jazz to white audiences, sensed some of this meaning. "Jazz is at once a revolt and a release," he said, and added, "This cheerfulness of despair is deep in America. That is the thing expressed by that wail, that longing, that pain behind all the surface clamor and rhythm and energy of jazz."

Black creativity exploded in the 1920s as talented blacks from across the country came into New York to participate in the Harlem Renaissance. Young poets, novelists, playwrights, composers flowered in an environment of black pride established by an older generation of intellectuals who were editing militant periodicals— *The Messenger, The Crusader, Challenge Magazine, The Crisis.* The two generations agreed on the militancy expressed by the young poet Claude McKay:*

> If we must die—let it not be like hogs
> Hunted and penned in an inglorious spot,
> While around us bark the mad and hungry dogs,

* Claude McKay, "If We Must Die," *Selected Poems of Claude McKay* (New York: Bookman Associated, 1953), p. 36.

> Making their mock at our accursed lot . . .
> Like men we'll face the murderous, cowardly pack,
> Pressed to the wall, dying, but fighting back!

But they disagreed on the form of the militancy. The young did not want to continue to offer themselves to whites as Christlike salvation figures; nor did they want to move in the direction of economic radicalism as the sociologist and historian W. E. B. DuBois was advocating. Indeed, their confusion about the issues of sexuality and spirituality seemed to relate them more to the white intellectuals of their generation than to the older generation of blacks who affirmed so strongly their commitment to black Christianity and to Victorian sexual morality.

The uncertainty of black poets and novelists further separated them from their white patrons, who provided financial support for their art. Whites wanted certainty from blacks, the certainty of an uncomplicated biological primitivism. "Unfortunately, I did not feel the rhythms of the primitive surging through me," complained the poet Langston Hughes, "and so I could not live and write as though I did. I was Chicago and Kansas City and Broadway and Harlem. And I was not what she wanted me to be."

Established black leaders—DuBois, Benjamin Brawley, Kelly Miller, Charles W. Chestnutt—did not understand the tortured soul-searching of Jean Toomer's novel *Cane,* or Nella Larsen's novel *Quicksand.* And Countee Cullen lamented in his poem, "Yet I Do Marvel."*

> I doubt not God is good, well-meaning, kind,
>
> . . .
>
> Yet do I marvel at this curious thing:
> To make a poet black, and bid him sing!

A few black poets, however, among them Langston Hughes and Sterling Brown, rejected the image of the biological primitive and began to define their sense of a black cultural tradition. The black establishment had nothing but contempt for blues and jazz in the 1920s. Accepting the white definition of art as something created by an exceptional artist, they dismissed popular music as worthless. But Hughes argued that black poets should look to the blues for inspiration. "To these the Negro artist can give his racial individuality, his heritage of rhythm and warmth, and his incongruous humor

* Countee Cullen, in *On These I Stand* (New York: Harper & Row, 1947).

that so often, as in the Blues, becomes ironic laughter mixed with tears." And he added that the black writer must reject the implicit motivation "I want to be white." Only the black masses, Hughes argued, were free from that aspiration; only they kept alive a separate black culture. Sterling Brown, a professor of English at the black school Howard University, was prevented from bringing jazz on campus, but his poems reminded the respectable black middle class of the reality of existence for most black people in America:

> O Ma Rainey,
> Li'l an' low,
> Sing us 'bout de hard luck
> Roun' our do':
> Sing us 'bout de lonesome road
> We mus' go. . . .*

The newly arrived black masses in the northern cities also responded to a call for black pride from Marcus Garvey, who founded the Universal Negro Improvement Association in 1914. The UNIA spread from New York to many other cities. Garvey's message was that black is beautiful; he told lower-income blacks that they should rejoice in being blacker than the colored aristocrats like DuBois. "Sometimes we hear he is a Frenchman and another time he is Dutch and when it is convenient, he is a Negro. Now I have no Dutch, I have no French, I have no Anglo Saxon to imitate: I have but the ancient glories of Ethiopia to imitate." The black, he insisted, must develop "a distinct racial type of civilization of his own and work out his salvation in his motherland, Africa." For Garvey, there was no hope for blacks in white America. Whites were devils who could not be redeemed. Ultimately, blacks would have to return to Africa to escape contamination from white evil. In the meantime, blacks should support each other by dealing only with black businesses. The UNIA organized groceries, laundries, restaurants, a printing plant, a hotel, and the Black Star Steamship Line. The United States government convicted Garvey of mail fraud and deported him in 1926 as an undesirable alien (he was a native of the West Indies). Both the black-pride movement and Garvey's efforts collapsed with the coming of the Great Depression. Last hired, and first fired, blacks struggled for physical survival through the economic catastrophe of the 1930s.

* Sterling Brown, "Ma Rainey," in B. A. Botkin, ed., *Folk-Say: A Regional Miscellany, 1930* (Norman: University of Oklahoma Press, 1930), p. 277.

* * *

"We are entering a new era," declared Henry Ford in 1920. "Our new thinking and new doing are bringing us a new world, and a new heaven, and a new earth, for which prophets have been looking from time immemorial." Business and political leaders, unlike artists, intellectuals, and religious leaders of the 1920s, did not feel a sense of postwar disillusionment. "Our country," declared Herbert Hoover, "has entered upon an entirely new era." President Warren Harding agreed that "at the moment, we are on the threshold of a new era."

Economic and political leaders at the outset of the new decade believed that progressivism had finally realized a fully rational and scientific economy and society. The evangelistic efforts of Frederick W. Taylor, the efficiency expert, to spread the gospel of scientific management had been institutionalized in a Taylor Society in 1911. And in 1914, Henry Ford had successfully installed a moving assembly line in his Highland Park plant outside Detroit which reduced the time needed to assemble a car from twelve hours to ninety-three minutes. Ford was as certain as Taylor that the souls of workers were saved by forcing them to accept the discipline of the assembly line. "The natural thing to do is work," Ford argued. "Human ills flow largely from attempting to escape the natural course. The day's work is a great thing—a very great thing! Work is our sanity, our self-respect, our salvation." For Taylor and Ford, people tried to escape from the naturalness of work through the unnaturalness of their imaginations. But the application of Taylor's time and motion studies to the workday allowed the worker no free time for daydreaming. The well-organized factory kept the employee busy every moment, and Ford rejoiced that "the net result is the reduction of the necessity for thought on the part of the worker and the reduction of his movements to a minimum." The assembly line ran constantly by the logic of linear time. "The most beautiful things in the world are those from which all excess has been eliminated," Ford exhorted. "We must cut out useless parts and simplify necessary ones."

By 1914, the fictional heroes of such popular magazines as the *Saturday Evening Post*, which reached the new urban-industrial middle class, operated in harmony with the visions of Taylor and Ford. In the 1890s, at a time when this class was trying to bring order out of chaos, fictional heroes had Napoleonic characteristics. But the need for a man of will and militant action, the need for a

Theodore Roosevelt, evidently had passed by 1914. It appeared that order already had been imposed on chaos, and sustaining that order demanded administrative heroes. "You might readily think of him as a machine of a man, with no waste words or motion, who was organizing a machine of men." This was the ideal hero presented in the middle-class magazines of 1914. And World War I, unlike the Spanish-American War, had no military hero like Theodore Roosevelt. Instead, it was an administrator of food supplies, Herbert Hoover, who fulfilled the desire of the urban middle class for a hero "who could take over existing organizations and run them with a minimum of human friction and a maximum of practical results." In an article in the *Saturday Evening Post* Hoover was said to have given the country "clean, efficient action." He was "always there with the goods." He always "could put things through." He established a "methodical system" at "incredibly low cost."

A national Chamber of Commerce, organized in 1912, had responded to war in Europe by asking for military preparedness. Between 1914 and 1917, business leaders argued that such preparedness depended upon a mobilized economy which "will make individual manufacturers and businessmen and the government share equally in responsibility for the safety of the nation." These leaders persuaded Woodrow Wilson to recognize their Industrial Preparedness Committee. "Twentieth-century warfare," declared the automobile executive Howard E. Coffin, "demands that the blood of the soldier must be mingled with from three to five parts of the sweat of the man in the factories, mills, mines, and fields of the nation in arms." When the war came, this organization of business, political, and military leaders first became the national Defense Advisory Commission and then the War Industries Board (WIB).

Run by Bernard Baruch, a Wall Street investor, the WIB planned and regulated much of the national economy. It avoided price competition as it placed contracts with large corporations without competitive bidding. The government also created a Food Administration, headed by Herbert Hoover, a Fuel Administration, and a Railroad Administration. In addition to a Shipping Board and a War Trade Board, the government established a National War Labor Board which rewarded loyal union leaders by encouraging the eight-hour day and higher wages. The Committee on Public Information mobilized college professors in its scholarship division to write propaganda for the war effort. Many of the most eminent historians helped to shape an image of Germany as a monstrous nation as they encouraged their students to enlist. For one of them, Guy Stanton Ford, "In the vicious guttural language of Kultur, the degree A.B. means Bachelor of Atrocities."

The federal government had encouraged patriotic organizations to scrutinize the teaching of American history in high schools and colleges. It also urged individuals to spy on their neighbors. After the Russian Revolution came under the control of Bolsheviks who concluded peace negotiations with Germany, the government encouraged people to identify Germany and Communist Russia as common enemies. It also identified the American Socialist party with these enemy nations. Eugene Debs, Rose Pastor Stokes, and many other Socialist leaders were imprisoned for opposing American participation in the war.

This wartime crusade for conformity had carried over into 1919. In the national capital, the *Washington Post* reported that "the crowd burst into cheering and hand clapping" when an irate citizen shot a critic of a patriotic pageant. In Indiana, a jury took two minutes to acquit a citizen for killing a man who had said, "To hell with the United States." In Connecticut, a salesman for a clothing store was sentenced to prison for calling Lenin "one of the brainiest" men in the world. "If I had my way with those ornery wild-eyed socialists," declared Billy Sunday, the nation's most powerful evangelist, "I would stand them up before a firing squad." Senator McKellar of Tennessee advocated the establishment of a penal colony on Guam for political prisoners. And Attorney General A. Mitchell Palmer set in motion widespread raids, breaking into private homes and union meeting halls without warrants to arrest thousands of suspected radicals. The accused were held without bail, denied lawyers, and often beaten after being chained and marched through the streets. Most of those arrested were ultimately released. But in Massachusetts two anarchists, Nicola Sacco and Bartolomeo Vanzetti, were convicted of murder, more for their radicalism than from the evidence. Judge Thayer, who presided, declared that he wanted to get "those anarchist bastards." Palmer helped to deport radicals, arguing that "we must purify the sources of America's population and keep it pure." He declared "I am myself an American and I love to preach my doctrine before 100 percent Americans, because my platform is undiluted Americanism." He established a special antiradical division, headed by young J. Edgar Hoover, within the Department of Justice. The New York State legislature expelled its five Socialist members despite the legal status of the Socialist party.

When AFL unions, which had grown to a membership of five million in 1920, reacted to the dramatic inflation of 1918 and 1919 by engaging in a wave of strikes, corporate leaders fought back by labeling AFL unions as radical, "connected with Russian Bolshevism, aided by Hun money." Skilled workers decided to make the first effort to unionize the steel companies since the disastrous defeat of labor in 1890. Continuing to reject the idea of an industry-wide union, they organized in twenty-four separate groups, each associated with the AFL. After the strikers had lost $100,000,000 in wages and twenty lives to the troops guarding the plants, their effort collapsed.

As the Socialist party disintegrated in the years after World War I and gradually diminished as a political force, the AFL lost its appeal to business as a safe alternative to socialism. The AFL then became the sole rival of business, and corporate leadership moved to limit its power. Between 1920 and 1930, membership in the AFL slipped from five million to less than three. Thousands of spies were hired to infiltrate labor groups and to identify leaders who not only were fired but also were blacklisted across the country. The National Association of Manufacturers, supported by the Kiwanis and Rotary Clubs and most of the newspapers and magazines, mobilized a movement for its "American Plan" that would replace "union shops" with "open shops." Business groups urged businessmen who had accepted unionization to break up the unions in their plants. In this way, whole communities, among them San Francisco, which had significant unionization, were transformed into "open shop" cities. Many workers were forced to sign "yellow dog" contracts in which they promised that they would not join a union, contracts that were enforced in the courts. Both the federal and state courts were overwhelmingly anti-union throughout the decade, issuing injunctions that made strikes and picketing almost impossible.

Many of the larger corporations established company unions as part of an effort to create a sense of team loyalty. Personnel managers listened to the grievances of workers and helped them organize recreational groups. The personnel manager was a product of the business schools of the decade, which were dedicated to scientific management. Between 1919 and 1924, 117 colleges added courses in business administration, and the pioneering schools, such as Harvard, were increasing their programs at the graduate level and engaged in massive building programs.

Within the political context of this corporate growth and con-

fidence, the Republican party at its convention in 1920 could afford
to choose an obvious nonleader, Warren G. Harding, for its presidential candidate. Harding and the other Republican Presidents of
the 1920s—Calvin Coolidge and Herbert Hoover—symbolized the
confidence of the corporate leaders that direct political power was
no longer necessary to protect the marketplace from its domestic or
international enemies. With the Republicans able to deliver 61 percent of the vote for Harding in 1920, the only challenge to the
political domination of the corporation came from within the Republican party itself. Senators like LaFollette of Wisconsin, Norris
of Nebraska, Borah of Idaho, and Johnson of California cooperated
in the establishment of a "farm bloc" that was critical of "monopoly" capitalism while calling for government support of farmers
caught in a deteriorating economic situation. This "farm bloc" convinced Congress to pass the McNary-Haugen plan by which the government would buy surplus farm crops to sell, if need be, at a loss
on world markets. But Coolidge successfully vetoed this legislation
in 1927 and 1928.

Secretary of State Charles Evans Hughes and Secretary of Commerce Herbert Hoover, who shaped foreign policy in the Harding
administration, were determined to carry on Wilson's plans for
America's world leadership. Hoover had disagreed with Wilson on
the need for American participation in the League of Nations because he feared that political commitments made within the structure of the League might introduce irrational and unpredictable
elements into the world marketplace. But Hughes and Hoover, like
Wilson, wanted to contain radicalism and to stabilize the world by
expanding the American economy into foreign markets. They believed this expansion would preserve the political order of the rest of
the world and at the same time benefit the American economy
because "the vast increase in the surpluses of manufactured goods
must find a market outside the United States."

These Republican leaders moved vigorously to use American influence to stabilize Europe and Asia. To restore the economic health
of the Western European nations and contain Communism, they
advocated the restoration of the German economy. They encouraged American bankers to make large loans to Germany and pressured England and France to reduce the reparations they were
demanding from Germany. In addition to the Dawes Plan of 1924
and the Young Plan of 1929 designed to accomplish these economic
goals, American foreign-policy makers urged the Western European

nations to guarantee their mutual borders in the Locarno Pact of 1925. The treaty significantly left the borders of Eastern Europe without guarantees in the hope that the Soviet Union might be reduced in size.

Hughes and Hoover called for a meeting of the major Asian powers in Washington, D.C. At the Washington Conference of 1921, the United States, Japan, England, and France agreed to guarantee the political status quo in East Asia, to allow China to be developed under the philosophy of the Open Door, and to stop an arms race by limiting the size of each nation's navy. But the hope of the corporate leaders for a new era in foreign policy was as short-lived as their hope would be for a new era in the domestic economy.

The significant new magazine of the 1920s was *System,* dedicated to helping business accept rational leadership. "New conditions have called a new type of man to lead the new kind of business organization," declared Walter Gifford, the president of AT&T. "These men must take a long view ahead because the company is going to be in business long after they are dead." The new statesman of industry was to be the kind of leader "who has greater reverence for scientific method than for the traditions of his class." Herbert Hoover was seen as that kind of statesman of industry. Elected President in 1928, it was believed that he would bring the rationality of the business world to the irrational world of politics.

Hoover, the son of an Iowa blacksmith, had become a multimillionaire by 1914, developing his talents first as a mining engineer in Africa, Asia, and Europe and then as a shrewd investor and administrator of his international business interests. As secretary of commerce under Harding and Coolidge, Hoover worked energetically to persuade the large corporations to cooperate in trade associations. The three or four companies that dominated each of the areas of major production such as autos, steel, and rubber could plan their futures methodically if they would agree to share the market, fix wages, and set prices. This rational planning fit the concept of linear time. With such coordination, Hoover was certain that the nation had forever left business cycles behind. Within the framework of the corporation, the assembly line would streamline production and distribute an unceasing flow of goods for American consumers.

In 1928, as Hoover prepared to succeed Coolidge as President, both were ecstatic about the dramatic increase of productivity during the first eight years of the decade. Cars, refrigerators, telephones, and radios had become a part of the lives of most Americans. All limits on human experience seemed to have been broken by the productive capacity of the assembly line. "The man who builds a factory builds a temple, and the man who works there worships there," exulted Coolidge. "We have seen the people of America create a new heaven and a new earth." And for Hoover, "The almost unbelievable magic of industry during the truly incredible decade just past has been so continuously amazing as to lead the mere inexpert bystander to be ready for almost anything in the field of material achievement."

When Hoover took the oath as President in March 1929, he was proud and confident. "We are a happy people—the statistics prove it. We have more cars, more bathtubs, oil furnaces, silk stockings, bank accounts than any other people on earth." Then in October 1929 the stock market crashed. Unemployment was two million in 1928, three million in 1929, four million in 1930, seven million in 1931, twelve million in 1932, and fifteen million in 1933. Industrial production dropped by 50 percent, and national income fell from $82 billion to $40 billion during these four terrible years.

Hoover saw no major weaknesses in the American economy. He knew that corporate profits had increased at least 60 percent in the 1920s as industrial production increased 40 percent. He knew that the national government had been able to reduce its debt from $24 billion to $16 billion between 1920 and 1930. With surpluses flowing into the national treasury, he had supported legislation in 1926 that reduced income, estate, and gift taxes for the rich. He had been concerned that farm income had dropped from $22 billion in 1919 to $8 billion in 1928 and would drop to $3 billion by 1933. Hoover hoped to solve the problem by having farmers join associations that would enable them to control prices and production in the way that large corporations did through their trade associations. What proved easy for corporate producers of cars and steel proved impossible for the hundreds of thousands of farmers who produced cotton or wheat or corn. They kept competing with one another, trying to produce more, and continued to drive the price of their crops down. Six million rural Americans were forced off the land in the 1920s by this economic downslide and by a new breakthrough in farm mechanization caused by the introduction of the gasoline-powered tractor. These unskilled workers migrated into cities, where there was little demand for their labor.

Even though most immigration was cut off by legislation in 1921 and 1924 and the birthrate continued to decline, unemployment persisted throughout the 1920s. With only a 10 percent increase in average wages for the decade, most city dwellers could not afford new housing, and there was significant unemployment in the construction industry. Meanwhile, the dynamic rate of growth in radios, refrigerators, and cars had leveled off by 1928.

Increasingly, the new consumer economy had depended upon advertising to create demand for the products of the assembly line and for credit to make it possible for low income people to indulge these cultivated desires. In 1914, $250 million was spent on advertising in magazines. This figure doubled by 1919 and reached $3 billion by 1929. The mass magazines—*Saturday Evening Post, Collier's, Ladies' Home Journal, Woman's Home Companion*—no longer considered their readers, as had the nineteenth-century magazines, to be patrons of literature or citizens to be enlightened. Rather they approached their readers as a great market of consumers. By 1929, these consumers had incurred $5 billion of time-payment debt. But it was the upper classes, profiting the most from the prosperity of the 1920s, that went furthest into debt. They gambled on the unlimited nature of the stock market. The average of industrial stocks in 1924 was 106; by 1927, it rose to 245. Banks and insurance companies increased their loans to people investing in the market from $1 billion in 1924 to $9 billion in 1929. By the summer of 1929, the market had reached 449, driven up by the frenzy of investment. Then in October, the crash came, and the market continued to plummet until it reached a low of 28 in 1932.

Hoover believed that the weakness of the European economy had pulled down the economy of the United States in 1929. He revealed a basic contradiction in his outlook by stressing the soundness of an independent American economy but also emphasizing the need for American business to expand overseas if it was to remain healthy. The United States had been a debtor nation in 1914, having borrowed money from Europe to develop its industrial potential. By 1920, however, this position was reversed, and European nations owed the United States $10 billion. Until the stock-market crash in 1929, American bankers continued to lend money in Europe, especially Germany, keeping the European economy, which had been badly weakened by World War I, from collapsing. American bankers also moved to replace European investment in Latin America and Asia, and the world owed American investors more than $20 billion by 1929. This web of economic interdependence was badly shaken by the crash that began in America in 1929.

Hoover refused to break the tradition that relief was a local and state responsibility. American business leaders were aware in 1914 that England and Germany, the major European industrial nations, had implemented certain social services: unemployment compensation, medical insurance, and pensions for the retired. As an alternative to these social-welfare policies, businessmen had decided to hold yearly Community Chest drives in their towns and cities to provide private charity for the poor, the ill, and the elderly. But with unemployment approaching 40 percent in most of the major cities, private charities proved utterly inadequate. So, too, did the efforts of the city and state governments.

As people literally starved, they resorted to city garbage. Scenes like this one reported in a Chicago newspaper became commonplace: "Around the truck which was unloading garbage and other refuse, were about thirty-five men, women, and children. As soon as the truck pulled away from the pile, all of them started digging with sticks, some with their hands, grabbing bits of food and vegetables." A survey in New York City in 1932 reported that 20 percent of the children were suffering from malnutrition. When Russia asked Americans to apply for six thousand skilled jobs in 1931, it received a hundred thousand applications.

Hoover feared that federal relief would corrupt the American character. People would no longer feel the spiritual pressure to become self-made successes; they would lose their ambition. In America, Hoover declared, "It is as if we set a race. We, through free and universal education, provide the training of the runners; we give to them an equal start; we provide in the government the umpire of fairness in the race. The winner is he who shows the greatest ability, and the greatest character." But by 1931, Hoover was asking Congress to create the Reconstruction Finance Corporation. The purpose of the RFC was to loan money to private corporations to keep them from collapsing. Otherwise, the corporate failures might ruin the banks and the mortgage and life-insurance companies that had loaned them money and undermine the entire capitalist system. The fear that forced Hoover to request the RFC was immense. To bring politics into the marketplace was to profane the sacred. And yet Hoover felt that he must be the first American President to use the artificial power of the federal government to try to control a business cycle.

Soon after he took office in 1929, Hoover faced another major threat to his ideal of a rational marketplace. Imperial Japan, heedless of American plans, moved troops into the northern Chinese province of Manchuria. But in 1931 Hoover refused to use military power to check this Japanese expansion. An important reason for his refusal to compromise his principles in the foreign-policy crisis was the fear of the Soviet Union. Hoover, like other American business leaders, had been terrified by the success of the Bolshevik revolution. The United States had managed to contain the revolution within Russian borders, keeping it from spreading in Germany and destroying it where it had gained a foothold in countries like Hungary. Hoover had decided during the 1920s that World War I had been a civil war in which the European capitalist nations had destroyed one another. This anarchy and self-destruction by the supposedly reasonable middle classes had allowed Russia to fall into Communist hands. What would happen if another such civil war, comparable to World War I, broke out among the capitalist nations? Would such conflict provide an environment for another rapid spread of Communist influence? Hoover feared such an outcome.

Hoover, the Republican, feared and distrusted the Democrat Franklin D. Roosevelt, who replaced him in March 1933. The difference between Hoover and Roosevelt was as deep and emotional as the difference between fundamentalist and liberal Protestants. Hoover was the fundamentalist capitalist and Roosevelt, the liberal. Roosevelt was willing to use political power in the marketplace without the sense of reluctance or agonized conscience that Hoover had felt. "The country needs and demands bold, persistent experimentation," Roosevelt had declared. "It is common sense to take a method and try it. If it fails, admit it frankly, and try another. But above all, try something." "I experimented with gold and that was a flop," Roosevelt laughed. "Why shouldn't I experiment a little with silver?"

Born to an old, established family, Franklin Roosevelt had not rebelled against its model of the relaxed gentleman as had Theodore Roosevelt. Satisfied with mediocre academic achievement at Harvard, he had participated fully in the social life of the college. When he became active in politics during the "progressive" years, his reform philosophy was close to the paternalism of English conservatives. He was so sure of his place in the social and economic order, and in the strength of that order, that he could contemplate the government of his class providing organized charity for the poor and dependent masses.

Roosevelt and his advisers had revealed no dramatic or radical plans to deal with the Great Depression during the 1932 campaign. Instead, his speeches criticized Hoover's experiments as irresponsible. Hoover had raised the national debt from $16 billion to $19 billion, and Roosevelt said, "Let us have the courage to stop borrowing to meet continuing deficits." Hoover had asked farmers to reduce their crops and livestock, and Roosevelt said that it is a "cruel joke" to advise "farmers to allow 20 percent of their wheat lands to lie idle, to plow up every third row of cotton, and shoot every tenth dairy cow."

When Roosevelt took office, he had received advice from the conservative farm organizations, representing the larger farmers, to go beyond Hoover's call for voluntary restrictions and have the federal government set limits on production. He responded by supporting the Agricultural Adjustment Act (AAA) of 1933, which ordered the slaughter of six million pigs and the plowing under of ten million acres of cotton. Corporate leaders also came to Roosevelt to plead for direct government backing of the trade associations. He responded with the National Industrial Recovery Act of 1933. Based on the precedent of the War Industries Board of World War I, NIRA legalized the trade-association agreements on production and prices. Section 7(a) of the law recognized the right of labor to bargain collectively. But most union growth in 1933 and 1934 came in the form of company unions.

Even before the quick passage of these acts by a Congress that did not examine or debate them, Roosevelt had used his executive power to close the national banks temporarily during his first day in office. He moved dramatically to use the power of the national government to sustain the property structure of the nation. From an average failure of 100 banks a year in the 1920s, the rate of collapse had reached the catastrophic figure of 4,004 in 1933. By his quick actions from March to June 1933, Roosevelt had stopped the disintegration of the property structure of the nation and the economic status quo in banking, industry, and agriculture had successfully been sustained.

Roosevelt also checked social and economic disintegration by releasing federal funds to the states for relief of the unemployed and the starving. The Federal Emergency Relief Administration (FERA), therefore, was a radical means to maintain stability and lessen the rebellious discontent of the unemployed. So too was the Civilian Conservation Corps (CCC), which took many jobless young men out of the cities, gave them uniforms and military discipline, and put them into work camps. An important experiment in regional planning was established with the Tennessee Valley Authority (TVA), which developed the rural area along the Tennessee River and its tributaries by building dams, fertilizer factories, and electrical generating plants.

Further stabilization of the economy came from the Home Owners' Loan Corporation. The HOLC loaned billions to homeowners to enable them to pay their mortgages, and the Roosevelt administration was much more willing to use Hoover's Reconstruction Finance Corporation. Under the New Deal, the RFC loaned $10 billion to the railroads, as well as to many large and small businesses.

All these activities, for Roosevelt, were emergency measures, with the exception of the NIRA. Once economic disintegration had been halted, he expected to stop deficit spending. But he believed that the political and legal marriage of the national government and corporations was a permanent necessity that reflected the end of American economic expansion. "Our last frontier has long since been reached," Roosevelt declared. "The day of the great promoter or the financial titan, to whom we granted anything if only they would build or develop, is over."

By 1934, Roosevelt was under heavy attack from Huey Long, a senator from Louisiana, for his lack of concern for the poor of America. Long demanded justice for those people, not relief. His twenty-seven thousand Share-Our-Wealth clubs spread across the entire country, reaching seven million people. Long demanded a minimum wage for all workers and pensions for retired people to be financed by a heavy tax on the rich.

The average age of the population had begun to increase dramatically as the birthrate declined and the immigration of young people from Europe ended. Americans therefore became aware of the elderly for the first time during the depression. Francis Townsend, a sixty-seven-year-old doctor from California, organized a national movement of older people. Townsend called for a pension of two hundred dollars a month for every person over sixty. The money was to be raised by a national sales tax.

It was a series of spontaneous strikes across the country in 1934, however, that forced Roosevelt and his advisers to consider the need for legislation to provide some permanent security for workers and the elderly. In 1932, Congress, no longer in awe of the demoralized corporate leaders, passed the Norris-LaGuardia Act, which largely protected labor's use of boycotts, strikes, and picketing from court injunctions. It also outlawed the "yellow dog" contracts. Workers had hoped that the replacement of the antilabor Republicans (in control from 1920 to 1932) by the Democrats meant a supportive administration. Finally they decided to take matters in their own hands when Roosevelt seemed interested only in stabilizing the status quo.

For the first time since the Civil War, workers demonstrated enough solidarity in city after city to enable them to match the violence used against them by the establishment. In Minneapolis, truck drivers, struggling to unionize, mobilized support from twenty thousand workers to defend themselves successfully against the police and management vigilantes who attempted to break their strike.

These militant strikers were condemned by the AFL leadership. The older labor leaders did not recognize that with the end of massive European immigration in 1914, something like an American labor force was being created as the result of a common industrial experience shared by a generation of workers. Rebellious AFL leaders such as John L. Lewis of the United Mine Workers, Sidney Hillman of the Amalgamated Clothing Workers, and David Dubinsky of the International Ladies Garment Workers, however, visualized the possibility of industrial unions and created the Committee for Industrial Organization to encourage such unionization within the AFL. Met with hostility by top AFL leadership, they withdrew to begin a new labor movement, the Congress of Industrial Organizations (CIO). The CIO rapidly gained two million members as the newfound sense of worker solidarity exploded in massive illegal sit-down strikes where the workers occupied automobile and steel plants. "It was like we was soldiers, holding the fort," one striker remembered. "It was like war. The guys with me became my buddies." No longer able to count on federal troops or even the police as they had before 1929, corporations like General Motors and Ford spent a million dollars a year for spies and a private police force to fight the strikers. But worker discipline gradually defeated the automobile and steel companies and established CIO unions throughout these industries.

In his message to Congress in 1935, Roosevelt declared that "we have not weeded out the overprivileged and we have not effectively lifted up the underprivileged." He was thus willing to accept the Wagner Labor Relations Act, which established a National Labor Relations Board. The NLRB conducted elections to determine whether workers wanted to unionize. Later Congress passed a Fair Labor Standards Act, which established a forty-hour workweek and a minimum wage of fifty cents an hour. A Wealth Tax Act in 1935 increased the income tax for upper-income groups and also established higher inheritance and gift taxes. A Social Security Act was also passed in 1935. Old-age pensions were to be provided in the future when workers reached sixty-five. They were to be payments into a government fund from their wages matched by payments from their employers. Large numbers of workers, however, were not included within social security in 1935. The law also provided funds to the states to pay unemployment compensation. Finally, federal funds went to the states to support the children of dependent mothers. Roosevelt also increased the use of federal funds to provide jobs for the unemployed in the Works Progress Administration (WPA).

"I am fighting Communism, Huey Longism, Coughlinism, Townsendism," Roosevelt declared. "I want to save our system, the Capitalist system." Unlike Hoover, however, he was flexible in the means he used to sustain the existing property patterns in the country. To head off radicalism, he was willing, in an emergency, to engage in deficit spending to keep unemployment under control. But when the economy began to make a modest recovery in 1936, he cut back on WPA expenditures. This cut in government expenditures produced a sharp recession in 1937, and unemployment again doubled, from five to ten million. So Roosevelt, the pragmatist, again increased WPA expenditures. Not until his 1940 budget message to Congress did Roosevelt speak of the possibility of permanent governmental manipulation of the economy to sustain prosperity.

"The end of American history"

* *

15

War, Economic Prosperity, and Consensus, 1936–60

Re-election of FDR

Japan and Germany threaten American neutrality

War is declared

War economy means economic prosperity

FDR on social issues

Truman completes FDR's fourth term

Cold war with the Soviet Union: Marshall Plan and NATO

The collapse of Nationalist China

Korean conflict

Eisenhower, the Red scare, and the arms race

The end of American innocence

"Foreign markets must be regained if America's producers are to rebuild a full and enduring domestic prosperity for our people," Roosevelt declared in 1935. "There is no other way if we would avoid painful economic dislocations, social readjustments, and unemployment."

Roosevelt had been confused about the place of the United States in world affairs between 1933 and 1935. He had rejected Hoover's thesis that the depression was caused by international circumstances. He refused to cooperate with the London Economic Conference, which had tried to stabilize world currencies in 1933. By 1935, however, Roosevelt and his advisers were sure that foreign trade was essential to American prosperity, and he was ready to use political and military power to protect that trade from the increasing threats of Japan and Germany to expand their commercial interests in Asia and Europe.

Roosevelt's intentions were frustrated, however, by a rising tide of neutralist sentiment within the United States. The diminished prestige of the corporations caused by the depression made it possible for the "farm bloc" senators to strengthen their critique of a foreign policy based upon corporate expansion. Senator Gerald P. Nye of North Dakota began an investigation into the profits of munitions makers in World War I. The public outrage that followed the revelations of his committee resulted in the passage of Neutrality Acts in 1935, 1936, and 1937, which were designed to keep the American economy from being integrated into that of warring nations, as had happened between 1914 and 1917.

The "farm bloc" senators had the support of many of the Protestant ministers and university professors who had been enthusiastic about American participation in World War I. During the 1920s and 1930s most historians, led by Charles Beard, became "revisionists" in their interpretation of the causes of World War I. We had assumed, Beard wrote, that the war was a battle between democracy and feudalism. But an analysis of the newly opened official archives of Russia, Germany, and Austria revealed, Beard continued, that the war had been caused by capitalist ambitions in each country. American bankers and munitions makers, through their clever use of propaganda, were the most responsible for the entry of the United States into this capitalist civil war. Now in the 1920s and 1930s, the same forces were again at work. "If the last World War grew mainly out of commercial rivalry," Beard declared, "and if we now see signs of a more intense rivalry than ever, supported by all the powerful agencies of government, what then shall we say of the future?" His answer and that of many other intellectuals, among them John Dewey, was isolation.

After he had won re-election, Roosevelt began a campaign to reverse this trend to neutrality. He made a major speech at Chicago in 1937 warning of the dangers of Japanese "aggression" as well as that of Germany and Italy. Adolf Hitler had come to power in Germany in 1933. Part of his plan to end economic and social chaos was to defy the Treaty of Versailles and the League of Nations and rearm Germany. He also planned to bolster the economy by using national political power to expand German export markets. Italy, under the leadership of Benito Mussolini, also was attempting to overcome economic problems through overseas expansion.

With Japan challenging the Open Door policy of the United States in China and Germany making similar challenges to the American policy in Europe, the Roosevelt administration felt even more threatened by the attempts of these nations to establish markets in Latin America, an area that American economic leaders had considered a special preserve of the United States since 1900. "We're just going to wake up and find that Italy, Germany, and Japan have taken over Mexico," warned Henry Morgenthau, the secretary of the treasury.

Roosevelt failed to rally public opinion to his position in 1937, but he did persuade Congress to enlarge the navy in 1938. Not until 1939, as Europe approached the outbreak of World War II, could Roosevelt persuade Congress to modify the Neutrality Acts and end the embargo on the sale of arms. In the spring of 1940, his campaign for greater political and military involvement against Japan, Germany, and Italy led to the passage of a huge $18 billion appropriation for military preparedness, and in September 1940, Congress passed the first peacetime conscription act. Roosevelt, who had been transferring government armaments to private interests so they could be sold to England, acted directly by issuing an executive agreement in which he made a gift of fifty destroyers to England in return for the right to establish American military bases on several British possessions.

As the election of 1940 approached, however, public-opinion polls continued to indicate that the overwhelming majority of Americans wanted to keep out of the war in Europe. Roosevelt, who had arranged to have the Democratic Convention draft him to run for an unprecedented third term, promised in his campaign speeches that "I have said this before, but I shall say it again and again and again. Your boys are not going to be sent into any foreign wars."

Wendell Willkie, the Republican candidate, approved Roosevelt's foreign policy. His nomination represented a victory for those Republicans who agreed with Roosevelt that political and military power must be used to defend the international marketplace. Within the Republican party, there was a tendency for corporate leaders from the East to support Willkie's philosophy of "One World," while business interests from the Midwest tended to align with the America First Committee, which was opposed to military intervention. These "isolationists," headed by Senator Robert Taft of Ohio, supported Hoover's contention that "it is fairly certain that capitalism cannot survive American participation in this war."

After his victory in 1940, Roosevelt moved rapidly to integrate the United States with the war effort of England, now standing alone against Nazi Germany. He persuaded Congress to pass a Lend-Lease Act in early 1941, making it possible for the government to give England all the arms and supplies it needed. Roosevelt and his military advisers entered into secret conferences with English leaders on the overall strategy of the war effort against Germany and Japan. These talks were based on the assumption that the United States soon would enter the war. The agreement was to defeat Germany first and then turn to Japan. Through the summer and fall of 1941, Roosevelt ordered the navy to attack German submarines that interfered with supply ships bound for England as far as Iceland, where bases had been taken over by the United States. In October 1941, Roosevelt announced to the American people on radio that "America has been attacked by German rattlesnakes of the sea" and "the shooting has started."

The undeclared war in the North Atlantic became a declared war when the Japanese armed forces attacked the American fleet at Pearl Harbor, Hawaii, on December 7, 1941. Throughout the previous year, Roosevelt and Secretary of State Cordell Hull had refused to sell crucial resources, especially oil and steel, to the Japanese. This embargo had created a political crisis in Japan between those who desired further Japanese expansion short of war with the

United States and those who insisted that war was inevitable. Now the war party demanded an immediate war to gain the economic supplies denied to Japan by America. They argued that a delay would weaken the Japanese resource base and so began to prepare for an attack on the United States. Meanwhile, the peace party was given a last chance to negotiate the reopening of trade with the United States. American intelligence had cracked the Japanese secret codes and knew of these plans. Roosevelt and Hull understood the consequences that would follow from their refusal to negotiate, but somehow the commanders at Pearl Harbor were not adequately prepared. On December 8, Roosevelt asked Congress to recognize that a state of war existed with Japan. In the Senate, the vote was 82 to 0; in the House, 388 to 1. Germany and Italy, bound to Japan by treaties, now declared war against the United States. The formal declaration of war had come, even though public-opinion polls in 1945 indicated that 80 percent of Americans still believed that President Roosevelt had violated his campaign pledge of 1940 to keep America out of war.

The outbreak of World War II, however, enabled Roosevelt to forge a new alliance with corporate leaders. In 1939, anticipating war and calling on his experience with the "industrial-military complex" of 1917, Roosevelt appointed a War Resources Board headed by Edward Stettinius of U.S. Steel. And after American entry into World War II, Roosevelt was able to fulfill his dream of a planned economy dominated by large private corporations operating without price competition. He was able once again to duplicate the experience of World War I with a War Production Board, a Food Administration, an Office of Economic Stabilization, a War Manpower Commission, and an Office of Price Administration. This planning went further, however, than that of World War I and included rationing. As in World War I, the planned economy was run by corporate leaders—William Knudsen and Charles Wilson of General Motors, Ralph Budd of the Great Northern Railroad, William Jeffer of the Union Pacific, and Donald Nelson of Sears, Roebuck as well as Stettinius from U.S. Steel.

The government promised that there was to be no antitrust activity to hinder cooperation and coordination among the giant corporations. Nor need they concern themselves with competition, since government contracts were given on a cost-plus basis in which the government agreed to pay the corporations any unexpected manufacturing expenses and financed the conversion of factories to war production.

Business leaders had bitterly attacked Roosevelt for doubling the national debt from $19 to $43 billion to help the poor and the unemployed. During the war, he found that they were willing to accept unlimited deficit spending for national defense. Between 1940 and 1945, $200 billion was added to the national debt. Industrial production doubled by 1942 and increased dramatically again by 1945. More industrial plants were built than during the years from 1929 to 1941. Full employment was reached for the first time in the twentieth century. Workers' income increased 50 percent while corporate profits doubled.

When the war ended in 1945, the country had never been so prosperous. But a pattern had been set that would lead to severe economic problems by 1975. Between 1945 and 1970, the federal government spent $1,000 billion, 60 percent of its total budget, on defense spending. The development of a cold war with Communist Russia and China at the end of the 1940s provided a convenient rationale for massive government spending that was acceptable to business, organized labor, and the average voter. Large corporations, in making an alliance with the Roosevelt New Deal during World War II, had accepted the administration's inclusion of organized labor within the establishment. Union strength, which had risen from three million in 1933 to ten million in 1941, increased to fifteen million by 1945. As membership increased another two million by 1950, labor leaders gave their blessing to the cold war and the large-scale government spending that accompanied it.

The bulk of this government spending passed to the largest corporations, where unions had most strongly established themselves. As Charles Wilson of General Motors said during the war, "This defense business is big business. Small plants can't make tanks, airplanes, or other complex armaments." After the war, Wilson as a member of President Eisenhower's Cabinet further clarified the relationship: "What's good for General Motors is good for the country."

Roosevelt's success in leading the United States into a war against the wishes of the majority of voters depended upon his popularity in the area of domestic politics. From 1933 to 1940, Roosevelt had given groups outside the male WASP establishment a new sense of participation in national life. Women, Catholics, blacks, lower-middle-class white southerners, academic intellectuals, and artists, who could not obtain a place in the business leadership of the 1920s were mobilized by Roosevelt in the Democratic party of the 1930s to support his New Deal programs. Roosevelt tried to give them the same sense of their necessary and invaluable participation in the war effort of 1941–45.

The Republicans had been the majority party from 1896 to 1932. The ability of the Democrats to replace them reflected the steep Republican losses in the big cities. Jews together with Catholics outnumbered the Protestant populations in most northern cities by 1900, but it took them a generation to develop a sense of American politics and to establish institutions of political solidarity. By 1924, Catholic political power was strong enough to make Alfred E. Smith, an Irish Catholic from New York City, a serious contender for the presidential nomination of the Democratic party. Smith was defeated in 1924 by the resistance of the southern Democrats, desperately committed to the preservation of WASP political leadership. But in 1928 Smith carried the Democratic Convention. His candidacy led large numbers of white southerners, especially in the border states, to bolt from the party and vote for Hoover. In the midst of the smashing Republican national victory, however, there was a dramatic shift of voting in northern cities, which went for Smith by a slim margin. Many Catholics voted for the first time in a national election. Four years later, when these cities provided huge majorities for Roosevelt, the upper-middle-class white Protestant elite had lost its ability to monopolize the leadership of urban industrial America.

It was the increasing political strength of the Catholics which helped encourage Roosevelt to support labor unions and social security between 1933 and 1935. In 1919, the Catholic Bishops Program for Social Reconstruction had called for minimum-wage laws and for unemployment, health, and old-age insurance. The bishops also advocated public housing for the poor. During his campaign of 1932, Roosevelt often had quoted from the Encyclical of Pope Pius XI, which denounced the "immense power and despotic economic dictatorship consolidated in the hands of the few."

Father John A. Ryan, a leading theoretician of welfare capitalism, had appeared before Congress in 1931 asking the federal government to accept responsibility for the relief of the poor and unemployed. Cardinal O'Connell of Boston, Cardinal Mundelein of Chicago, and Cardinal Dougherty of Philadelphia denounced

Hoover's commitment to a "socially irresponsible capitalism" in 1932, as did many archbishops and bishops. For them, "the Roosevelt plan of social reconstruction is the Catholic plan." They interpreted Roosevelt's attempt to minimize competition in the NIRA as the legislation of the corporate social philosophy of European Catholic thought. However, they did criticize the NIRA between 1933 and 1935 for not doing enough to make labor a major participant in the industrial process. Father Ryan and other priests, who took appointed positions in the Roosevelt administration, continued to lobby for greater support for labor as well as for social security. They were delighted when Senator Robert Wagner, a Catholic from New York, provided the leadership to pass legislation that encouraged the expansion of labor unions. And when the Social Security Act was passed in 1935, Father Ryan rejoiced that it "brings the United States up to date with Europe on the question of social insurance."

As President, Roosevelt responded to the growing political importance of Roman Catholics and Jews. He dramatically increased the proportion of Catholics appointed to federal offices and placed two Catholics, James Farley and Thomas Walsh, in his Cabinet. He also increased the percentage of Jews in government service. Both the Jews and the Catholics had brought an outlook of social responsibility with them when they began arriving in large numbers in the 1880s and 1890s. As a consequence they were more willing to support the unionization of labor and to advocate that labor play a leadership role in national politics.

During the "progressive" era between 1890 and 1917, many Protestant women were openly advocating social-welfare legislation. Florence Kelley, a leader of the National Consumers League, and Jane Addams, a leader in the settlement house movement, had called for minimum-wage and maximum-hour laws for women workers and subsequently had concluded that men needed the same kinds of protection. Women activists also endorsed programs for health, old-age, and unemployment insurance as well as public housing. Although their political aspirations were blocked in the 1920s, the concept of social welfare gained support as the number of professional social-work schools increased from fifteen to forty. When Roosevelt broke precedent in 1933 and brought the federal government into relief and welfare, he relied upon the experience of professional social workers. He appointed Frances Perkins, the first woman Cabinet member, as secretary of labor. He also called upon another professional social worker, Harry Hopkins, to be a major administrator of relief programs.

Roosevelt did not take any liberal positions on black issues until 1935. Early in his administration, he informed Walter White, the head of the National Association for the Advancement of Colored People (NAACP), that he would not support an antilynching bill because he needed southern votes for his legislative program. But northern blacks had shifted their allegiance from the Republican to the Democratic party by 1936. Although discriminated against in most government agencies, they still benefited from many New Deal programs. Blacks were appointed to important positions in the federal government for the first time in American history under Roosevelt's administration: Robert C. Weaver and William Hastie in the Department of the Interior, E. K. Jones in the Department of Commerce, Laurence Oxley in the Department of Labor, Ira DeA. Reid in the Social Security Administration, Mary Bethune in the National Youth Administration. The President's wife, Eleanor Roosevelt, visualized a new politics in 1936 in which women, blacks, and organized labor would play a dynamic role to end all discrimination against these minorities. The President, however, took no public stand on discrimination against blacks until they threatened a massive march on the national capital in 1941 to protest the failure of the government to integrate blacks into war industries. Under this pressure, Roosevelt created a committee on Fair Employment Practices to require corporations doing government work to hire black workers. He did nothing, however, to end segregation in the armed forces.

Roosevelt recruited college professors to come to Washington to serve as specialists in his administration; a few, the "brain trust," became his advisers and speech writers. Under the WPA, federal funds were channeled to support playwrights, novelists, painters, and unemployed academics. Some responded in their writings by reinforcing Roosevelt's attempt to equate his administration with that of Abraham Lincoln. Roosevelt saw himself, like Lincoln, as a leader in a time of great national crisis. Roosevelt, like Lincoln, was ready to mobilize the whole nation in order to preserve it. "Compare this panic-stricken policy of delay," Roosevelt had declared in a campaign speech of 1932 directed against Hoover, "with that devised to meet the emergency of war fifteen years ago. We met specific situations with considered, relevant measures of constructive value. There were the War Industries Board, the Food and Fuel Administration, the War Trade Board, many others." To meet the economic crisis of the Great Depression, he called for "a whole nation mobilized for war, economic, industrial, social, and military resources gathered into a vast unit."

Roosevelt had hailed "the principle of national government service by every man and woman" as early as 1917. "We may rejoice," he had written, "that the day of the man and woman who merely expect to receive things from the government is disappearing. The day will soon be at hand when the Army and Navy of this great republic will be looked on by its citizens as a normal part of their own government." Campaigning in 1936, Roosevelt continued to evoke a sense of crisis: "Three and a half years ago, we declared war on the depression. You and I know today that that war is being won." For Roosevelt, it was unthinkable that he should ever relinquish his position as commander-in-chief of this war. "I accept the commission you have tended me. I am enlisted for the duration of the war."

In an article in the *American Historical Review* of October 1973, "The New Deal, National Socialism, and the Great Depression," the historian John A. Garraty has pointed out that of the four great Western industrial nations, the United States and Germany experienced greater economic hardships than England and France. But in 1940, both the United States and Germany had escaped psychological depression in a way that England and France had not. Roosevelt and Hitler, unlike the English and French leaders, had the magic of charisma. They were able, through the power of their personalities and the genius with which they used radio, to persuade their followers that their countries were winning the war against the economic depression. Roosevelt, like Hitler, inspired people with the joy of victory. It was this power of personality joined with the power of the role of commander-in-chief that made it possible for Roosevelt to demand and be given a third and fourth term as President. The cult of personality was so strong by 1944 that Roosevelt's personal physicians were afraid to reveal to national leaders that the President was dying even as he called for his re-election because his leadership was indispensable in the wartime crisis.

Soon after 1941, Roosevelt and his advisers had decided that the United States should help create a viable international organization to replace the League of Nations. The United Nations expressed Roosevelt's commitment to the permanent use of power in international relations. Besides a General Assembly, there was to be a Security Council in which the major powers, the United States, England, France, China, and Soviet Russia, were to have permanent seats. Each member of the Security Council was able to veto any decision reached by the General Assembly, in which all nations were to be represented.

The structure of the UN reflected America's new image of world power. When Germany attacked Russia in June 1941, American and English leaders decided that it was necessary to treat the Soviet Union as an ally. German military power was so awesome in 1941 that it was almost impossible for Roosevelt and Winston Churchill, the English prime minister, to visualize victory over Hitler without the Russian front. Lend-Lease aid, therefore, had been extended to the Soviet Union. Both Roosevelt and Churchill feared, however, the expansion of Russian Communism and supported right-wing underground groups in France, Italy, and Greece. And when Russian troops began to push the Germans back, it became imperative for American and English strategy to land troops in France and drive into Germany to keep most of that country out of Communist hands.

Roosevelt died before Germany surrendered with the Russians occupying most of Eastern Europe. The new President, Harry Truman, soon learned that scientists had perfected an atomic bomb. Truman ordered its use against the Japanese city of Hiroshima on August 6, 1945. When he heard that the bomb had worked and obliterated most of the city and its population, he rejoiced that "this is the greatest thing in history." Persuaded that he must face the Russians "with an iron fist and strong language," Truman was certain that the United States held sufficient power to contain communism and would not have to share control of Japan with the Soviets. For Truman, the United States stood alone as the leader of the world. "The atomic bomb is too dangerous to be let loose in a lawless world," he declared. "We must constitute ourselves trustees of this new force."

Confronting the Russians with diplomatic toughness, the American government attempted to force the Soviets to open the Communist world to the free penetration of American capital. Government leaders agreed with corporate executives that continued prosperity depended on the expansion of overseas trade. "Private enterprise in the United States," declared Secretary of Commerce Henry A. Wallace, "can survive only if it expands and grows." The country could not possibly maintain full production and full employment, said labor leaders, unless it had available a world pool of free and prosperous consumers. And the president of the American Farm Bureau Federation argued that surpluses "will wreck our economy unless we can find sufficient outlets in foreign markets to help sustain the volume of production."

Joseph Stalin, the Soviet leader, refused to bend under this pressure and rejected American overtures. Frustrated by his intransigence, American leaders prepared for a "cold war" with Russia. The Truman administration persuaded Congress to provide billions of dollars to rebuild the economies of the Western European nations, including West Germany. This "Marshall Plan" was followed by the establishment of the North Atlantic Treaty Organization (NATO). For the first time in American history, the United States was formally committed to go to war if any of a large number of allies were involved in war. And when the English no longer had the economic strength to sustain a military presence in Greece to repress communism there, the President announced his "Truman Doctrine" and moved American troops into Greece and Turkey to further build a wall of military containment around Russia.

It was the hope of American policy makers that if Communist Russia were contained within this ring of military alliances, internal disorders would erupt and bring about the overthrow of the Communist system. It was with surprise and horror, therefore, that American policy makers witnessed the collapse of Nationalist China under pressure from Chinese Communists in 1949. With Japan under total American control in 1945 and with a friendly China, Truman and his advisers had felt that Russian Communism could not expand into Asia. They were aware that there was a strong group of Chinese Communists in northern and western China, and they had poured financial and military aid into the Nationalist regime of Chiang Kai-shek. But they were not prepared for the dramatic Nationalist collapsed and Chiang's flight to the large island of Formosa (Taiwan).

American foreign-policy makers thought the American public would not support a major war on the Asian mainland and so they did not send troops to sustain Chiang. At the beginning of 1950, officials in Washington declared that the Republic of South Korea remained outside the American defensive perimeter in Asia. Korea, a peninsula jutting out of the Chinese land mass, had been occupied by Japan since the end of the nineteenth century. At the end of World War II, it had been divided in two areas, the northern region dominated by Russia, the southern by the United States. But when North Korea attacked South Korea on June 25, 1950, Truman instantly committed the American armed forces stationed in Japan to defend the Republic of South Korea. "I felt certain that if South Korea was allowed to fall," Truman informed Americans, "communist leaders would be emboldened to override nations closer to our shores." Congress supported Truman's "police action" by tripling the defense budget and instituting peacetime conscription on a permanent basis, measures which Truman had advocated for several years.

The United States had dominated the United Nations since 1945 because of its influence in Latin America, Western Europe, and the former British Empire. In 1950, the Russian delegates to the Security Council were absent in a protest against American control. The United States therefore managed to get the United Nations to take responsibility for the police action against North Korea. General Douglas MacArthur, who had directed the American occupation of Japan, was placed in command of the United Nations forces. MacArthur still hoped that Chiang Kai-shek's government could be restored in China. When he drove North Korean troops out of South Korea, he continued to move north and approached the Chinese border. The Chinese warned the United States not to advance farther, and when MacArthur continued his northern thrust, the Chinese entered the fighting and pushed American and United Nations troops back to the old border between the two Koreas. MacArthur hoped that Truman would permit him to use atomic weapons against the Chinese Communists and publicly criticized the President when weapons of total war were denied. Truman removed MacArthur from his command, and a military stalemate lasted until General Dwight Eisenhower was elected President in 1952.

It was easier for Eisenhower as a Republican to make a compromise peace with the Communists than it had been for Truman as a Democrat. "Liberal" Republicans, like Wendell Willkie and Thomas E. Dewey, the Republican presidential candidates in 1940, 1944, and 1948, had accepted the welfare provisions of Roosevelt's New Deal and his foreign policy of military internationalism. In 1952, the "liberal" Republicans had again defeated the "conservatives" led by Senator Taft and nominated the war hero Eisenhower. At the same time as Eisenhower promised to preserve the framework of the New Deal and to continue the foreign policy of "containment," he accused the Democrats of being politically irresponsible. He linked the legislative program of the New Deal with un-American radicalism and spoke of the "creeping socialism" during "the last twenty years," which had corrupted the United States. Eisenhower also blamed the "loss" of China on the Democrats because they had been soft on communism.

In attacking the New Deal, Eisenhower especially criticized the academic intellectuals in government. For Eisenhower, the "long-haired academic men in Washington" were lacking in the masculinity necessary to defend their country. Franklin Roosevelt and Harry Truman had persuaded blue-collar and lower-middle-class voters that corporate leaders lacked the vitality to save America. In 1952, the Republicans generated the aura of vital executive leadership. They disparaged the Democratic candidate, Adlai Stevenson, as an "egghead" intellectual who could not understand the masses of voters.

Roosevelt had ignored civil liberties during World War II and had placed Americans of Japanese ancestry in concentration camps. Truman had instituted the Federal Employee Loyalty Program because "subversive elements must be removed from the employ of the government." In 1948, when Truman faced the opposition of another Progressive party, headed by Henry A. Wallace, he sought to identify Wallace in the public mind with the Communists. "I do not want and will not accept the support of Henry Wallace and his Communists," stated the President. But the Republicans nevertheless linked Truman and the New Deal with communism. Senator Joseph McCarthy of Wisconsin declared that "the issue between Republicans and Democrats is clearly drawn by those that have been in charge of twenty years of treason." And Senator Richard M. Nixon of California announced that the Communists had "infiltrated the very highest councils" of the Truman administration.

A prolonged "Red Scare" rolled across America from 1945 to 1955. The U.S. Chamber of Commerce demanded that all "Communists, fellow-travelers and dupes" be barred from jobs in "newspapers, radio, television, book and magazine publishing, and research institutions" as well from schools, libraries, and "large manufacturing plants." The House Un-American Activities Committee (HUAC), supported by many in the Catholic hierarchy, including Cardinal Spellman, came to Hollywood, where its investiga-

tions of Communist influence in the movie industry led to the
blacklisting of four hundred actors, writers, and directors. Members
of Congress, including John F. Kennedy, Richard M. Nixon, and
Lyndon B. Johnson, helped to pass the McCarran Act in 1950,
which set up six concentration camps across the country to hold
political prisoners. Thirty states established loyalty oaths for
teachers.

Despite his military background, President Eisenhower relieved
some of the tensions of the cold war. His secretary of state, John
Foster Dulles, had called for the building of many long-range
rockets armed with atomic warheads to serve as "the deterrent of
massive retaliatory power" in a world where "the forces of good and
evil are massed and armed and opposed as rarely before in history."
But faced with the rapid success of the Soviets in developing atomic
warheads and long-range rockets, Eisenhower decided to meet with
the Russian leader, Nikita Khrushchev, to negotiate a limit to the
arms race.

As the Russians placed Sputnik, an earth satellite, into orbit in
1957, jumping ahead of America in the race to pioneer the exploration of space, it looked as if Lenin's prophecy in 1917 might come
true. The United States had not led the world into a new urban-
industrial era in 1918 and, in 1941, it had fought against Germany
and Japan to restore the status quo of 1939. Herbert Hoover's fears
that another civil war among the capitalist nations would allow
communism to expand out of Soviet Russia had been fulfilled.
Many American cultural leaders were interpreting the experience of
World War II as marking the end of the American commitment to
the idea of progress, the end of the belief that an environment of
rational space and linear time could be achieved.

To justify Roosevelt's permanent intrusion of political power into
the domestic marketplace and the permanent intrusion of military
power overseas, these men declared that a major revolution had
taken place in America's cultural identity. Reinhold Niebuhr, a
Protestant theologian, who had been the most important critic of
isolation between 1937 and 1941, became the leading interpreter of
this cultural revolution. Born in 1892, Niebuhr was a convert to
liberal Protestantism and a believer that World War I would usher
in the kingdom of God on earth. After 1919, a disillusioned Niebuhr moved to isolation and pacifism. A Detroit minister, Niebuhr
shared the views of the "lost generation" novelists that industrialism

was irrational and destructive of human beings. "Here manual labor is a drudgery and toil is slavery; the lowliest peasant of the dark ages had more opportunity for self-expression than the highest paid employee in the Ford factory." Briefly, at the beginning of the 1930s, he turned toward Soviet Russia as he hoped that industrialism under communism could be a rational and constructive force. "The workers control the vast machinery of modern civilization," he said. "The future belongs to the workers." And as the capitalist nations of Europe seemed headed for another civil war, Niebuhr urged, "Let America hold out as an island of sanity in an insane world."

As he lost faith in the rationality of a proletarian revolution in the mid-1930s, Niebuhr began to create a "neo-orthodox" theology that denied the possibility of earthly harmony for mankind. Niebuhr criticized his former faith, liberal Protestantism, for believing that history was progressive. And he criticized communism for holding that same faith. Niebuhr used this Christian "realism" as the basis of his criticism of the isolationists. Arguing the need for the United States to fight the evil represented by Nazi Germany, Niebuhr denied that America was a virtuous New World that needed to be segregated from an evil Old World. "Every nation has its own form of spiritual pride," he wrote. "Our version is that our nation turned its back upon the vices of Europe and made a new beginning."

If Americans were part of the same sinful brotherhood of mankind as Europeans, Niebuhr continued, then "the tragic element in a human situation is the conscious choice of evil for the sake of good." Americans must choose the lesser evil of war to defeat the greater evil of Nazism. For Niebuhr, America had no rational space to preserve from European chaos, and the defeat of Nazism would not lead Europe and the rest of the world out of a perpetually compromised human history. The human choice, Niebuhr insisted, is always that of relative good and relative evil.

Niebuhr was trying, between 1939 and 1941, to influence the majority of Protestant leaders away from pacifism. Polls taken during the depression indicated that a majority of Protestant ministers had lost faith in the capitalist system. And many, as Niebuhr had much earlier, had turned toward pacifism.

Growing throughout the 1920s, the pacifist movement reached its strongest expression between 1933 and 1937. In 1933, 75 percent of Protestant ministers declared themselves opposed to any war, and in 1937, 95 percent of Americans voiced their opposition to participation in a European war. Writing in 1933, William Allen White, a Kansas editor and strong political supporter of Theodore Roosevelt, declared, "Fifteen years ago came the Armistice and we all thought it was to be a new world. It is! But a lot worse than it was before." Harry Emerson Fosdick, a Protestant leader, confessed his "increasing agony" with "the anti-Christian nature of the war's causes, processes, and results." And a Jewish leader, Rabbi Stephen Wise, joined the confession: "I committed a sin when I blessed war banners and I will never again commit that sin." Dorothy Day and Peter Maurin brought the Catholic Worker Movement into the peace coalition. With 40 percent of college students identifying themselves as pacifists, college strikes against war were organized in 1934 and 1935, efforts were made to drive ROTC off campuses, and many students took the Oxford Oath, pledging to refuse to serve in the armed forces.

From 1937 to 1941, however, there were increasing defections from the isolationist and pacifist movements. The key factor in this shift was a growing recognition that industrialism was not liberating the individual from the corruption of bureaucracies as Beard and Dewey had prophesied. President Roosevelt was willing to preserve and work with the large corporations. The political rhetoric in the 1936 election campaign seemed as absurd and irrelevant as that of the Harding-Coolidge years. And the Russian worker, under Marxism, seemed to be just as much a captive of bureaucracies run by capricious and evil men as was the American worker. The erratic and oppressive role of Communists in the Spanish Civil War had disillusioned many young Americans about communism. Final disillusionment came in the form of political purges in Russia and the willingness of Soviet Russia to enter into diplomatic negotiations with Nazi Germany.

The heart of Niebuhr's new theology was his argument that the individual was not able to separate his rational mind from his unconscious mind, that the individual could not escape the biological cycle of the body, and therefore could not escape death. Given these necessary conditions of human existence, it seemed that there was no way for Americans to live only in the realm of rational space and linear time. For Niebuhr in 1940, both the modern capitalist and the Marxist theories of revolution were based on false and unrealizable principles.

He did not see this theological position, however, as a novel and revolutionary challenge to the whole modern American cultural identity. His emphasis on biological cycles seemed to be closer to the views of Native Americans than to those of Anglo-Americans, and his dismissal of the idea of progress brought him closer to the Afro-American sense of time. But Niebuhr did not make these connections; instead he used his new theology in defense of the status quo both in the United States and on the international scene.

Rejecting the isolationist position as sinful, Niebuhr had insisted that it did not represent the true American tradition. The seventeenth-century Puritans and the eighteenth-century Founding Fathers, according to Niebuhr, were aware of the sinfulness of man and the need, therefore, for political humility. These wise elders had wanted "to preserve some relative decency and justice in society against the tyranny and injustice into which society may fall." Like the great English conservative Edmund Burke, they were "intent upon developing politics as the art of the possible, being cautious not to fall into worse forms of injustice in the effort to eliminate old ones."

"The demonic fury of fascist politics," for Niebuhr, came from the dictators' rejection of divine judgment of human actions. In their cynicism the dictators denied the existence of any values other than those they personally created. Having defeated this heresy by 1945, the United States faced the even more dangerous heresy of Soviet Russia, which insisted that the human and the divine could become one. "This tendency of playing God to human history," Niebuhr insisted "is the cause of communist malignancy."

Rejecting the progressive intellectual idea that America needed a strong President who was not frustrated by the checks and balances of the Constitution, Niebuhr now celebrated the Founding Fathers for creating those checks and balances that preserved the liberties of a pluralistic society from any temptation of centralized power. The United States, in its pluralism, was like the community of nations in the Free World. The United States must save that international pluralism from the threat of Communist centralization.

From this position, it was easy for Niebuhr and other neo-orthodox theologians to move to a justification of the cold war against Soviet Russia in 1945 because, for them, communism was committed to the messianic redemption of the world. Unfortunately, with the expansion of Communist influence into Eastern Europe and the victory of the Communists in China, half the world lived under the control of this "false religion." For Niebuhr and many Protestant leaders, this situation created an unprecedented need for a peacetime military strength to contain communism within its boundaries. Though the Free World could not destroy communism where it existed, it could not allow further expansion.

John Dos Passos had moved in parallel lines with Niebuhr, as had many other secular intellectuals. At the end of the 1930s, Dos Passos published another fictional trilogy, *District of Columbia,* in which he attacked Communists, New Deal reformers, and labor leaders. He also saw a pluralistic American history full of liberty for the individual, liberty that might be lost not to the corporations as he had believed in the 1920s, but to political radicals, liberals, and labor unions. The defenders of American liberty, for Dos Passos in 1945, were big businsssmen and the leaders of the armed forces.

By 1950, Dos Passos was articulating a "new conservatism," which he shared with an aggressive group of young intellectuals including Russell Kirk, Peter Viereck, Clinton Rossiter, and James Burnham. These writers considered the major American political tradition to be conservative, embodying the principles of the political philosopher Edmund Burke, who had written in opposition to the French Revolution of 1789. And they saw the Republican party as the vehicle of this conservatism.

But Niebuhr in 1950 linked Burke to a "new liberalism," identified with the Democratic party. Younger historians like Richard Hofstadter, Arthur Schlesinger, Jr., and Oscar Handlin joined Niebuhr in rejecting the vision of Charles Beard, who remained a bitter isolationist until his death at the end of World War II. They dismissed the distinction that Beard had made between the productive middle class and the parasitical Robber Barons. They discredited Beard by linking him with Karl Marx. They argued that it was the perspective of the French visitor Alexis de Tocqueville, who had described a homogeneous, classless, middle-class society in his classic of 1840, *Democracy in America,* which was the appropriate vehicle for contemporary scholars.

These "consensus" historians found allies among sociologists and political scientists, among them Daniel Bell and Seymour Lipset. Bell described the conversion of many young progressive and socialist scholars of the 1930s, like himself, away from the hope of a purified world. "For the radical intellectual who had articulated the revolutionary impulses of the past century and a half," he wrote, "there was now an end to chiliastic hopes, to millenarianism, to apocalyptic thinking—and to ideology."

These self-defined liberal scholars, many of whom had helped form Americans for Democratic Action (ADA) in 1947, seemed to apologize for having earlier been progressives or socialists by pointing out the salutory contributions of the business elite. Called Robber Barons in the 1920s and 1930s, they were described in the scholarly books of the 1940s and 1950s as constructive captains of industry. The liberal economist John Kenneth Galbraith promised in his book of 1952, *American Capitalism,* that the individual was still free in a United States of big business organizations, big government organizations, and big labor organizations because, according to his theory of countervailing power, each of these organizations restrained the influence of the others.

Many of the leading intellectuals of the "consensus" and "end of ideology" schools were Jewish: Daniel Bell, Seymour Lipset, Daniel Boorstin, Oscar Handlin, Louis Hartz, Richard Hofstadter, and others. Until World War II, it had been almost impossible for Jews to gain tenure at the major universities. Although the mainstream white Protestant establishment had lowered its barriers to Jews in academic life only in the 1940s, and although Jews continued to be barred from leadership in the large corporations, these scholars argued that it was traditional WASP elites who had preserved and nurtured the democratic tradition in America. They also wrote, in their scholarly books, that it was the lower middle class that had been antidemocratic and anti-Semitic. Richard Hofstadter in *The Age of Reform* (1955) had identified anti-Semitism with the Populists of the late nineteenth century. In *Anti-Intellectualism in America,* he argued that this traditional hostility to educated leadership was "founded in the democratic institutions and egalitarian sentiments of this country." It followed, he continued, that professors must look to social and economic elites for support since the "intellectual class is of necessity an elite in its manner of thinking and functioning."

These intellectuals also identified isolationism with the lower middle class, while they related internationalism to the "democratic" social and economic elites. And they cooperated with those elites in creating a cold-war ideology that involved our overseas allies. The CIA subsidized the Congress for Cultural Freedom, which published its major journal, *Encounter,* in England. Sidney Hook, a philosophy professor who had converted from the radicalism of the 1930s, told a meeting of the Congress at Berlin in 1950 that soon all "references to 'right,' 'left,' and 'center' will vanish from common usage as meaningless." Fulfilling his prophecy, a "new liberal,"

Arthur Schlesinger, Jr., and a "new conservative," James Burnham, joined with others to build the American Committee for Cultural Freedom as a branch of the Congress.

These intellectuals were writing to persuade the youth of America not to be seduced by Marxist perfectionism. They also feared that young people might be seduced by reactionaries, the radical right, into believing that it was possible to return to the perfectly rational space that supposedly characterized nineteenth-century agrarian America. These scholars identified a search for perfection with adolescence and the acceptance of a desanctified world with maturity. An explosion of scholarly books praised the Founding Fathers as such models of maturity able to live in an imperfect, an ironic, even a tragic world.

James Gould Cozzens' novel *By Love Possessed,* published in 1957, marked the climax of this effort at cultural redefinition. Hailed as "a masterpiece" in the *New Yorker,* as "delicate and subtle" in the *Saturday Review,* and as "magnificent" by the *New York Times,* it had as its hero Arthur Winner, who at the age of fifty-four is finally initiated into manhood. Winner, described by reviewers as "intelligent," "tolerant," "the quintessence of our nation's best qualities," had reached middle age without the ability to understand or accept the advice given him by his father. His father had warned him that it was impossible to improve the world and that it was a sign of maturity and responsibility to work to sustain the status quo.

Three million hard-cover copies of the novel were sold to readers who appreciated Winner's slow and painful growth into an understanding of his inability to make the world fit his dreams. He was bitterly disappointed by his first wife and his sons. Practicing law as part of the WASP establishment in a small Pennsylvania town, Winner came to realize that his social group had been too concerned with its own purity and that social stability depended upon the admission of a Jewish and a Catholic lawyer to the town's legal profession. In questioning traditional symbols of purity, Winner was even willing to permit the black janitor of the Episcopal Church to take communion with the white congregation, the janitor waiting to be the last recipient of the communion cup.

The final test of Winner's manhood comes when he is faced with the fact that the most elderly member of his law firm has stolen church funds from the trust he administered. Julius Penrose, another older member of the firm, persuades Winner that the responsible course is for him not to accept financial responsibility for his partner's actions. To hold to the letter of the law would mean humiliation for an old man and financial ruin for Winner's family. Winner accepts Penrose's advice that "as a wise old man once said to me: 'Boy—never try to piss up the wind.' " That night, Winner can tell his wife: "It's all right. Nothing has to be changed."

In 1957, WASP cultural leaders and the Jewish intellectuals who had been incorporated within the establishment were insisting that the Anglo-Americans of the seventeenth and eighteenth centuries had not believed in the myth of a New World where young people could escape from the traditions of Old World elders. They were insisting that fathers had wisdom, which was more relevant than the frontier experiments of young people. But, like Arthur Winner, they saw no immediate conflict between this philosophy of limits and their capitalist institutions, institutions that assumed that the marketplace was an endless frontier. And this infinite space for limitless growth was supposed to be capable of rational, mathematical description. The progressive development of the marketplace was also described by the regular increments of linear time. But younger dissidents who were forming a counterculture, as well as scientists within the academic community, began by the 1950s to insist that a world of limits was totally incompatible with the capitalist institutions of the Founding Fathers.

"Who will find peace with the lands?"

★ ★ ★ ★ ★ ★ ★ ★ ★ ★ ★ ★ ★ ★ ★ ★ ★ ★ ★

16

New Visions, New Ethics,
1950–70

Voices of the beatnik poets

Ecology: "a counterculture" science

Children in the counterculture

Changing sex and social roles: women's liberation

Lifting taboos on aging and death

TV: mirror of modern times

Just as the collapse of the Progressive prophecy of a better future resulted in a youthful "lost generation" in the 1920s, so the paradoxical rejection of progress by the cultural leaders of the 1950s resulted in another lost generation of dropouts and hippies. Again there was a sense of being trapped by a meaningless bureaucracy. Allen Ginsberg, one of a group of poets centered in San Francisco, wrote of America as

> Moloch! Solitude! Filth! Ugliness! Ashcans and unobtainable
> dollars! Children screaming under the stairways! Boys
> sobbing in armies! Old men weeping in the parks! . . .
> Moloch whose mind is pure machinery! Moloch whose blood is
> running money! . . .
> Moloch whose breast is a cannibal dynamo! Moloch whose
> ear is a smoking tomb!*

But in rejecting progress, the Beat poets did not repeat the "lost generation's" agony about the plight of the individual hero. Looking west from San Francisco, they saw hints in Asian thought of another way of perceiving the world. Asian philosophies and religions enjoined the individual to perceive reality from the inside, to find meaning from within. Man was not a seeker, as in modern Western thought, looking at reality from the outside, learning to analyze and map the external rationally. If man understood from within, then it was not tragic that the self-conscious mind could never free itself from the unconscious, as Niebuhr had said in 1940. It was the feeling, the intuition, the imagination flowing from the unconscious that made it possible to know the cosmos that surrounded the self. Perhaps man was intended to live within his personal body and within the earth as a body. Perhaps the individual was not tragically trapped within those bodies, with their inevitable cycles leading to death. Perhaps to live and die, to experience fully the cycles of existence, was to be in harmony with the universe.

* Allen Ginsberg, from "Howl," in *Howl and Other Poems* (San Francisco: City Lights Books, 1956), p. 17.

Ginsberg wrote of his mother,

One night, sudden attack—her noise in the bathroom—like croaking up her soul—convulsions and red vomit coming out of her mouth—diarrhea water exploding from her behind . . . urine running between her legs— left retching on the tile floor smeared with her black feces—

He wrote of her degenerating body,

Too thin, shrunk on her bones—age come to Naomi—now broken into white hair—loose dress on her skeleton—face sunk, old! withered—cheek of crone—

And he wrote of her beauty,

O Russian faced, woman on the grass, your long black hair is crowned with flowers, the mandolin is on your knees—

He wrote of her rebirth,

holy mother, now you smile on your love, your world is born anew, children run naked in the field spotted with dandelions—*

Unlike the "lost generation," he could write in exaltation,

> Come, sweet lonely Spirit, back
>   to your bodies, come great God
>   back to your only image, come
>   to your many eyes & breasts,
>   come thru thought and
>   motion up all your
>   arms the great gesture of
>   Peace & acceptance . . .†

Norman Podhoretz of *Commentary* magazine summed up the liberal establishment's view of the Beat poets when he wrote, "In America, we are witnessing the revolt of all the forces hostile to civilization itself." They represented, he continued, "a movement of brute stupidity and know-nothingism." Podhoretz was correct that these poets were challenging the fundamental attitudes toward space and time in modern civilization. He was mistaken, however, in thinking that they stood for no alternative principles and represented no alternative disciplines.

* Allen Ginsberg, from "Kaddish," in *Kaddish and Other Poems* (San Francisco: City Lights Books, 1961), pp. 22, 29.

† Allen Ginsberg, from "The Change," in *Planet News* (San Francisco: City Lights Books, 1968), p. 61.

Another of the San Francisco poets, Gary Snyder, spent three years learning Oriental languages before he went to Japan, where he remained for a decade, to study Zen Buddhism. Zen gave him the power of discipline necessary to cleanse his mind of the untruths he had learned in American culture. He had to unlearn the separation of matter and spirit. He had to learn that nature is matter and spirit. Climbing out of modern society in his pilgrimage to find meaning, he of necessity had come to stand alone. Now free, standing as on a mountaintop, he wrote

> I cannot remember things I once read
> A few friends, but they are in cities.*

Once having found meaning, however, Snyder could begin to descend from his aloneness:

> Pressure of sun on the rockslide
> Whirled me in a dizzy hop-and-step descent,
> Pounded by heat raced down the slabs to the creek
>
> . . .
>
> Whole head and shoulder in the water:
> Stretched full on cobble—ears roaring
> Eyes open aching from the cold and faced a trout.†

Baptized, he was within nature, one with the rich multitude of living things. Now he could share in life, ecstatic in escaping the loneliness of the "lost generation." He was one with the cycles of nature:

> Eating the living germs of grasses
> Eating the ova of large birds
>
> . . .
>
> Eating each other's seed
> eating
> ah, each other.
> Kissing the lover in the mouth of bread:
> lip to lip.‡

* Gary Snyder, from "Mid-August at Sourdough Mountain Lookout," in *Riprap, and Cold Mountain Poems* (San Francisco: City Lights Books, 1965), p. 1.

† Gary Snyder, "Water," ibid., p. 10.

‡ Gary Snyder, from "Song of the Taste," in *Regarding Wave* (New York: New Directions, 1968), p. 17.

"I am convinced a time will come when the physiologist, the poet, and the philosopher will all speak the same language and mutually understand each other," declared Garrett Hardin, a biologist writing in 1972. "That language is proving to be the language of ecology." Hardin had just written a science-fiction fable, *The Voyage of the Space Ship Beagle,* in which men attempted to colonize the planets they were certain must exist around the star closest to our sun. They found no such planets. Hardin's moral was the need for men to recover the sense of the earth as the center of their existence and meaning. Another major biologist, Barry Commoner, also used medieval symbolism to criticize the modern when he entitled his 1971 book *The Closing Circle.* Citing Earth Week in April 1970, he stated that "the environment has just been rediscovered by the people who live in it." Rediscovered, he added, because we saw the evidence all around us of the disintegration of the ecosphere, "the thin skin of air, water, and soil which sustains life." We had caused an ecological crisis, he said, because we had forgotten that "all living things must fit into the ecosphere or perish." For Commoner, as for Hardin, modern perception was Newtonian, or mechanical, not Darwinian or biological. "We have become accustomed to think of separate, singular events each dependent upon a unique singular cause." Commoner was trying to educate people into the laws of the ecosystem. The first law of ecology, he wrote, was "Everything is connected to everything else"; the second was "Everything must go somewhere"; the third was "Nature knows best"; and the fourth was there is "no such thing as a free lunch."

By the early 1970s, few intellectual and political leaders challenged either the scientific validity or the philosophical implications of the ecology movement. This consensus had not always existed. A few scientists and laymen had responded to the desanctification of space and progress in the 1940s in ways similar to the Beat poets. They had emphasized the idea of limits, of being within the cycles of the earth, and had questioned the ability of the economic system to continue to progress and expand. Fairfield Osborn, in *Our Plundered Planet,* and William Vogt, in *Road to Survival,* both published in 1948, raised the questions later explored by Commoner and Hardin in 1970. They had been dismissed, however, as fearmongers by the intellectual establishment.

But a slowly growing number of physical scientists and social scientists were willing to listen to these heretics, as was evidenced by a major scholarly conference in 1955 on "Man's Role in Changing the Face of the Earth." The experience of atomic fallout had shocked some scholars into accepting the premodern notion of life as a chain of interrelationships. Atomic bombs had been tested in the far Pacific, thousands of miles distant from the United States. But much to the dismay of the government, Strontium 90 had been carried across the ocean, across the United States, precipitated into the ground by rain, absorbed by grasses, eaten by cows, and finally drunk in milk by infants, in whose bones it had caused degeneration.

But the idea of nature as a living chain of interrelationships had not yet been accepted at the level of the popular press. In 1962, Rachel Carson's *Silent Spring* brought together evidence that described how DDT had entered into food chains and threatened the health of mankind. *Time* identified her concept of a chain with unscientific mysticism and emotionalism: "Many scientists sympathize with Miss Carson's love of wildlife, and even with her mystical attachment to the balance of nature," *Time* concluded, "but they fear her emotional and inaccurate outburst in *Silent Spring*" may do harm. By the end of the 1960s, however, intellectual orthodoxy had come to accept concepts of chains and balance and interdependence. Many business, labor, and political leaders continued to fight the application of ecological principles to specific environmental and economic issues. But their arguments, in the 1970s, were pragmatic, not scientific. No longer could these groups call on science to undermine the credibility of the ecologists.

"The subversive science" was a name applied to ecology, and its subversiveness was accompanied in the 1950s and 1960s by the development of a "counterculture" of white American youth searching for alternative lifestyles. In 1970, polls indicated that a majority of American adults rated the problem of dissident youth above all other problems: war, the environment, race relations, the economy. The adult fear and anger revealed by these polls came from the recognition that the pattern of "adolescence" established between 1880 and 1914 was breaking down. The counterculture adolescents of the 1960s were rejecting conventional virtues such as militant masculinity, competitiveness and aggressiveness, emphasis on bodily cleanliness and self-discipline in order to channel energy into economic achievement. Parents were confronted by "loose" young people, resisting the armed forces and the world of work.

Ironically, sociologists suggested that these adolescents had learned many of their "dropout" characteristics from their "straight" parents. "Parents lack not only the self-assurance that successful inner-direction brings," wrote David Riesman in his study of American culture in the 1940s, *The Lonely Crowd,* but "the loss of old certainties in the spheres of work and social relations is accompanied by doubt as to how to bring up children."

For Riesman, "inner-direction" was the character taught to children in the nineteenth century when production was the most important social aim. In a society of many small producers, the necessary virtues for success were self-reliance and self-assurance: a narrow, deeply held, inflexible set of principles. But since 1920, machines owned by giant corporations had taken over much of the productive process. Job opportunities moved into large private and public corporations, and success in these jobs demanded a more flexible and compromising personality. These social pressures to create an "other-directed" personality were reinforced by economic pressures to consume what the machines produced. To learn to be a good consumer, the individual had to be sensitive to his neighbors. To keep up with the Joneses was to keep up with whatever new consumer product brought status. Because advertising was constantly redefining which product was most prestigious, the consumer had to be able to respond flexibly to shifting styles.

The infancy of the consumer was the subject of Dr. Benjamin Spock and his best-selling book *Baby and Child Care.* In his view, there were no problem children, only problem parents. Spock rejected the rigid schedules that previous child-care books had advised. Children should be fed according to their own rhythms and not by the clock, he claimed. Children varied in the age in which they were ready to read. These "new" parents, therefore, pushed for the replacement of "inner-directed" schools with "open" classrooms where children developed their personalities in a relaxed and friendly atmosphere and teachers were opinion leaders.

Riesman quoted a twelve-year-old girl in 1948 talking about comic-book heroes to illustrate the shift away from an emphasis on competitive academic achievement which might separate the individual from the group. "I like Superman better than the others because they can't do everything Superman can do. Batman can't fly and that is very important." But when she was asked if she would like to fly, her reply was, "I would like to be able to fly if everybody else did, but otherwise it would be kind of conspicuous."

Riesman also used the Little Golden Book *Tootle the Engine* to illustrate other changes in childhood heroes. When most young people went to work within established corporations, it was no longer socially functional to encourage children to be independent. In engine school, Tootle was taught to "always stay on the track no matter what." When he had trouble learning to be perfectly adjusted to the system, the whole town of friendly people helped him learn to be socially responsible.

These parents of the 1940s, however, were establishing a major dissonance in their children. In their crucial first years with their mothers, they were being raised permissively. In schools they were also free, in a limited way at least, from rigid timetables. But they nevertheless would be expected to join an economic system that was rigidly defined, that ran by timetables. They would have to accept the uniform clock time of an economy where everyone went to work at eight o'clock and came home at five o'clock.

This dissonance was intensified by other lessons learned at home. Hard liquor, along with cigarettes, had become legally and morally acceptable as bodily pleasures by the 1930s. The appreciation of good food and wine were added to the list of acceptable bodily pleasures. The consuming culture of the late 1940s encouraged the consideration of meals as artistic and sensual events. The elegance and variety of European food and the European use of wine was to be imitated. Enjoyment of the body in lovemaking also became more important to the "new" middle class. Admitting female sexuality by 1920, the middle class had attempted to contain that sexuality within the home. A wife could learn from sex manuals how to express herself sexually and be more pleasing to her husband. These women had learned only to be concerned with being good mothers and homemakers. These were their areas of skill, while men expended their energies in the conflicts of the marketplace.

In the 1940s, however, fathers were members of a company team rather than warriors in the marketplace, and they had the responsibility of teaching the skills of cooperation and teamwork to their sons while they were still young. The division between the home as woman's domain and work as man's domain began to be questioned. And if fathers had social skills learned on the job to teach to their sons, did they also have the responsibility to develop an artful social relationship with their wives, including the art of lovemaking?

The idea of the relationship between men and women as a cooperative one challenged the cultural tradition of competitiveness between the sexes. In that tradition an adult male was free and independent. Someday he would be caught by a woman and trapped into marriage. In his home, he returned to his childhood dependence on his mother. In popular culture, in the movies, radio serials, the comic strips, women ruled the home. In the comic strip "Blondie," for instance, the husband, Dagwood, was a bumbling child who depended upon his wife-mother to provide the guidance necessary for his survival. The appearance of the successful TV series "Father Knows Best" in the 1950s reflected the effort to make fathers more relevant in the home situation. Sons, taught the importance of social interdependence by their fathers, could no longer reject their fathers in the name of becoming independent, self-made men.

Beginning to feel in the 1950s that their bodies were important and that they should be noncompetitive in their social relationships, middle-class teen-agers began to reject the prototypical boy-girl relationship that had been dominant from World War I to World War II. According to the traditional rules, the boy developed a skillful line to persuade the girl that he was seriously interested in her. The girl simultaneously developed the ability to persuade the boy that she believed him and that she, in turn, was interested in him. If the girl was *really* interested in the boy, she might let him get to first base, perhaps to second. The boy was the object of peer pressure to advance as far as possible and finally to "score," so that he could return to his friends and boast of his conquest. To be equally successful at the game, the girl had to give up as little as possible and not surrender her virginity. At the same time she had to keep the boy interested in her. With a steady boy friend and her virginity, she had proved herself a winner at the game.

Rejecting this covert and competitive sexuality in favor of a more open and cooperative attitude toward sex, the adolescents of the 1950s began to respond to displays of emotion. They applauded singers like Johnny Ray, who cried when he sang sad songs. They made a cult hero of Elvis Presley, who augmented the sexuality of the lyrics with body movement. They danced the Twist, with its explicit body language. They shared in the renewed influence of Afro-American rhythm with its sense of present time.

Social and cultural attitudes toward women had been changing gradually since the 1920s. Although Hollywood continued to present the cultural convention of the normal woman as a housewife throughout the 1930s, a few women, among them Mary Pickford and Clara Bow, became powerful stars. They became rich and famous. Their wealth, social position, and authority blatantly contradicted the cultural convention of the good woman as a passive, sexless homebody. Greta Garbo, Marlene Dietrich, and Mae West went much further in the 1930s in attacking the convention itself as they portrayed strong, intelligent, and self-reliant women in their roles. Katharine Hepburn, Bette Davis, Joan Crawford, and Barbara Stanwyck continued this tradition through the 1930s and into the next decade.

As men began to realize that their traditional domination of the public world was being threatened by the changing definitions of male and female roles, as there was a tremendous rise in the number of working wives and another dramatic increase in the divorce rate, male fears began to find expression in certain films of the 1940s. These movies generally portrayed women as monsters, scheming to destroy men. Rita Hayworth, Mary Astor, Barbara Stanwyck, Ava Gardner, Lana Turner, and Dorothy Malone all appeared in such roles. By the 1950s, films would present less powerful and less "dangerous" stars like Debbie Reynolds and Doris Day.

Mickey Spillane, one of the best-selling novelists in American history, expressed this cultural hostility toward women who were not passively dependent on men. Middle-class men in the 1950s bought Spillane's detective stories by the millions. All these books centered on the effort of women to tempt the hero, Mike Hammer, away from self-reliance, a self-reliance that was necessary, according to Spillane, to Hammer's task of purging the city of its criminal element. Although he was often close to being seduced by women with such serpentine characteristics as a stomach with "smooth parallel rows of light muscles" or "ripply muscles in her naked thighs," Hammer always saved himself by brutally and happily killing the seductress. " 'How could you,' she gasped. I only had a moment before talking to a corpse, but I got it in. 'It was easy,' I said." Norman Mailer also presented woman as a source of evil in his writings, especially in *An American Dream,* where the hero had to kill his wife in order to become free.

Almost hysterically, leading magazines like *Life* and the *Ladies' Home Journal* presented the figure of the contented housewife. "I'm so grateful for my blessings: wonderful husband, handsome sons with dispositions to match, big comfortable house," declared a heroine of a story in a woman's magazine. "I'm thankful for my good health and faith in God and such material possessions as two cars, two TVs, and two fireplaces," it continued. Leading anthropologists such as Margaret Mead, and sociologists such as Talcott Parsons, reassured women that they were happiest in the home, as did the psychologists Marynia Farnham and Ferdinand Lundberg in their book *Modern Women.* "Feminism was at its core a deep illness," they wrote in 1947, and "the more educated the woman is, the greater chance there is of sexual disorder."

The dynamic women's liberation movement that emerged in the 1960s simply brought to consciousness nearly a half-century of doubt about the traditionally aggressive male role and the passive female role. Women's Liberation as a movement was precipitated by the generation of middle-class children born at the end of the 1940s who were coming of age in the 1960s. Not only had they been raised more permissively, but also their special experience at the end of the 1950s and the early 1960s gave them such a strong sense of the present as to constitute the basis of a generation gap with their parents. They had grown up under the shadow of the atomic bomb. They had been drilled in school on how to react to an atomic attack from Russia; they had been encouraged to go home and ask their parents to build bomb shelters. With this giant threat the specter of death entered the conversation of everyday life.

Another deep cultural taboo seemed to be broken in the 1960s as people began to speak openly about death and dying. Many barriers between the sacred and the profane had been broken in this revolutionary decade. The words "piss," "shit," and "fuck" were brought into polite conversation. But the discussion of death was probably the most profound violation of the establishment commitment to an expanding society which was perpetually young. Psychologists like David Gutmann, who were doing cross-cultural research on attitudes toward death, reported that the attitudes of counterculture adolescents were similar to those of elders in premodern cultures. According to these psychologists, these elders expressed a tender, affectionate outlook toward life; they disliked competition; they avoided provocation; they entered conflict only as peacemakers. They approached the universe that fed them with humility. The psychologists called this attitude of elders in traditional societies "religious." Seeing themselves close to death at the end of the life cycle, they rejoiced in the symbols of plants, animals, and children, which reassured them that they were part of the larger life cycles of the universe and that their deaths would be meaningful within these cycles.

Counterculture adolescents in the 1960s seemed to be opting for the same sense of religious interdependence with natural cycles that characterized premodern culture. They were rejecting stereotyped adolescent behavior rooted in the past. They also were rejecting stereotyped ideas about sex roles: that men must suppress their caring, loving instincts (so-called feminine characteristics) from public view and that women must control their aggressive qualities and remain pliant and subordinate in their caretaker roles. Counterculture adolescents accepted the idea that it was all right for men to allow their feminine characteristics to become stronger and for women to become more masculine.

For psychologists studying aging and death, the counterculture children of the middle class represented a revolutionary shift away from behavioral models of their parents' modern culture. They were more like premodern elders in their attitudes than they were like their peers, those adolescents who kept modern values. They accepted the polymorphous sensuality of the traditional premodern society. They would not limit sensuality to their genitals, where it could be quickly and briefly satisfied. They enjoyed the lingering satisfaction of considering the entire skin of their bodies as a source of sensual pleasure, as well as their ears, their noses, their eyes, and their mouths. Taking a religious attitude toward the environment, they desired to be fed. Not surprisingly, many counterculture musical groups provided symbolic food—"The Cream," "The Lovin' Spoonful"—as did counterculture books—*Watermelon Sugar, The Strawberry Statement, The Naked Lunch.*

The antiheroism of the counterculture, therefore, like Beat poetry, was not nihilistic. It expressed values that could be compared to those held by the elders of premodern societies.

Television had mirrored social values from its inception. In 1948 children were reassured by a variety of western programs that there still was an American frontier. "The Lone Ranger," "The Cisco Kid," and "Hopalong Cassidy" all were fulfilling, in fantasy, the hope of the historian Frederick Jackson Turner that there was a West which allowed the individual to step outside the area of eastern settlement. These heroes, operating by their own personal codes, provided justice in a way that establishment lawmen could not. The children observed that this independence was related to the freedom of these heroes from women, who were literally presented as intellectually inferior to the hero's horse.

The children's horse operas, however, were replaced after 1955 by adult westerns. With the gun as an important symbol, "The Rifleman," "Colt .45," "Restless Gun," "Have Gun, Will Travel," "Yancey Derringer," and twenty-five other adult westerns expressed a high level of violence. Often they dealt with men trying to fight their way out of a trap. The area of open space was receding. The irony of the trap, however, was that these killers were not enforcing a personal code; they were being paid for doing a job—they were institutional men trying to preserve individual autonomy. In this masculine world women usually appeared as prostitutes. But there were no good women to trap men into a community where feminine characteristics were important.

As the adult westerns moved into the 1960s, they changed into male communities that were in motion, as in "Wagon Train" and "Rawhide." Paralleling the unprecedented popularity of professional football, the western hero became a member of a team, where the orders were given by the captain of this overland ship. But this all-male community soon reached a final destination and began to defend the boundary lines of its property. In "Bonanza," "High Chaparral," "The Big Valley," and "The Men from Shiloh," the open space of the West was replaced by large parcels of property. The virtues of masculine aggressiveness, of normal adolescent violence were still necessary to the protection of this property. The most popular TV western, "Gunsmoke," made the transition from gun western to property western. Its original opening focused on Marshall Matt Dillon and his gun. In a series of subsequent openings, the camera came to spend more and more time on the town setting. Finally, a totally different opening had Dillon riding across the prairie toward the town. Reversing Turner's frontier hypothesis, the town had become the center of virtue that Dillon protected against evil, which hid within the open spaces of the prairie. The major Hollywood directors of the 1950s and 1960s also had expressed in a more bitter way the end of the West, of a frontier of space and new opportunities. Sam Peckinpah in *The Ballad of Cable Hogue* and *McCabe and Mrs. Miller,* and Monte Hellman in *Ride the Whirlwind,* presented a West in which all traditional heroes must find ironic or tragic defeat.

From the 1890s to the 1960s, Anglo-Americans had tried to escape the prophecy that their historian, Frederick Jackson Turner, had given them in 1893. But in a major, prize-winning book of 1972, *A Religious History of the American People*, Sydney E. Ahlstrom reasserted that the sacred hoop of the Anglo-Americans indeed was broken. From 1600 to 1960, a Puritan Protestantism had been dominant in America, Ahlstrom wrote, but no longer. A new religious era had begun in the 1960s, Ahlstrom argued, a post-Protestant era.

Simultaneously, the Native American writer Vine Deloria, Jr., published his book *God Is Red*. He explained the collapse of the intellectual and religious structure of white Protestant America by reminding the reader of the ways in which twentieth-century physics and biology contradicted Anglo-American assumptions of rational space and linear time. The fundamental building block of the universe, the atom, was now defined as a dynamic and energetic complex constantly receding into mystery as scientists learned to analyze it more deeply. Equally mysterious was twentieth-century biology with its emphasis on the web of life, the living interrelationships of all things. Had not all of us come to accept a cyclical cosmology, that the solar system had been born and ultimately was to die? For Deloria, the logic of these twentieth-century sciences then led inexorably to a "relinquishment of temporal attitudes, an acknowledgement of the reality of places, and the reformation of social and political ideas around communal rather than individual considerations." And he argued that the conversion of the Anglo-Americans to these attitudes would mark their recovery of Native American wisdom. He quoted Chief Luther Standing Bear: "The white man does not understand America. The roots of the tree of his life have not yet grasped the rock and soil. But in the Indian, the spirit of the land is still vested, it will be until other men are able to meet its rhythm. Men must be born and reborn to belong. Their bodies must be formed of the dust of their forefathers' bones."

"Who will find peace with the lands? Who will listen to the trees, the animals and birds, the voices of the places of the land?" Deloria asked. And then he answered confidently, "As the long-forgotten peoples of the respective continents rise and begin to reclaim their ancient heritage, they will discover the meaning of the lands of their ancestors. That is when the invaders of the North American continent will finally discover that for this land, God is Red."

"The endless horizon no longer exists"

★ ★ ★ ★ ★ ★ ★ ★ ★ ★ ★ ★ ★ ★ ★ ★ ★ ★ ★

17

Patterns of Economic Change, 1960–76

The Kennedy-Rostow economy

Economic change and the black community

The growth of space technology

Lyndon Johnson's War on Poverty

International corporate growth

Inflation and recession

Nixon faces the economic crunch

Oil crisis

Curbing environmental exploitation

Limits to growth

Toward the end of the 1950s, many cultural leaders began to reject the new national identity of realism and restraint that they had helped to create and that was symbolized by the elderly and cautious President Eisenhower. They were reacting to the emerging counterculture, which denied that capitalism could continue to exist when people lived within the circle of nature. They were also reacting to Soviet Communism, which boasted that it alone represented the progressive march of history toward ever greater rational control of nature. "We find ourselves as a nation on the defensive," declared the president of Princeton University, "and as a people seemingly paralyzed in self-indulgence." "We must acknowledge that the loss of faith in our world, our destiny, our religion, is the cloudy and dark climate which most of America finds itself living in today," added the president of Yale. And the president of Harvard agreed that America is "adrift with little sense of purposeful direction, lacking deeply-held convictions, wandering along with no more stirring thought in the minds of the people than the desire for diversion, personal comfort, and safety."

In 1960, academic leaders rejoiced at the nomination of a youthful John F. Kennedy by the Democratic party. Since 1928, it seemed as if the white Protestant leaders of the corporate establishment needed to tap new sources of vitality to keep the economic structure from crumbling. Kennedy was to be the first Catholic President in the nation's history. Despite his religious background, however, Kennedy's childhood recalled the older Anglo-American emphasis on militant adolescence. Kennedy's father, a self-made millionaire, had been, according to the President, "very tough when we failed to meet those standards. The toughness was important." "Coming in second was just no good," Kennedy remembered. "The important thing was to win."

Kennedy came to the Presidency using the same metaphor of politics as war that Franklin Roosevelt had used from 1933 to 1945. "I think to be an American in the next decade will be a hazardous experience. We will live on the edge of danger." That was Kennedy's promise in 1961. His Inaugural Address emphasized foreign policy. "I believe that Americans are ready to be called to greatness," he declared, and that greatness was to be defined as victory in the cold war. "We must challenge the enemy in fields of our own choosing. We must indeed take the initiative again—we must start moving forward again—at home and abroad." He placed himself in the tradition of the Democratic commanders-in-chief, Wilson, Roosevelt, and Truman. "It is a fact that in those administrations, the vitality of the American system was mostly developed." "We stand on the edge of a New Frontier. I am asking each of you to be new pioneers on that New Frontier," he concluded, "and so, my fellow Americans, ask not what your country can do for you, ask what you can do for your country."

Much of Kennedy's confidence that the United States could overcome Communist Russia and Communist China in the battle for world leadership came from his academic advisers, especially the economist Walt Whitman Rostow. During the 1950s, Rostow had developed a theory of modernization. Like the idea of progress, which seemed to have disintegrated in the 1940s, modernization theory insisted that human history moved inexorably in a single direction from primitive societies to higher forms of civilization. In his book of 1960, *The Stages of Economic Growth,* Rostow described the upward drive of modernization as moving from "traditional societies" to "pre-conditions for take-off" to "take-off" to "drive to maturity" and finally to the "age of high mass-consumption." The crucial factor in breaking humanity loose from the intellectual darkness of traditional societies was the scientific revolution of the seventeenth century. "Newton is a symbol for that watershed in history," Rostow wrote, "when men came widely to believe that the external world was subject to a few knowable laws and was systematically capable of productive manipulation." Rostow offered his book as "an alternative to Karl Marx's theory of modern history," which saw the progressive sequence of stages as feudalism, bourgeois capitalism, socialism, and communism. Under normal conditions, Rostow declared, the whole world should develop along the patterns first experienced in Western Europe and the United States. The Great Depression of 1929, for Rostow, indicated no major flaw of Western capitalism. A slight difficulty had appeared in moving from the stage of "maturity" to the final state of "high mass-consumption." The theories of Keynes, however, had clarified the way in which governments could manipulate spending to help societies into "high mass-consumption." For Rostow, "the technical tricks of that trade are widely understood," and government expenditures during World War II had brought the United States,

Western Europe, and Japan safely into this happy era of constantly growing standards of living.

Rostow argued that the Communist revolution in Russia had stopped the normal pattern of modernization in that country. Unfortunately, he continued, "societies in the transition from traditional to modern status are peculiarly vulnerable to such a seizure of power." Communists, committed to the use of military power to force modernization, were keeping Russia from moving to the final stage of high mass-consumption by restricting the normal working of the marketplace. Only under capitalism, declared Rostow, could countries totally fulfill the evolutionary patterns of modernization. Communism was tempting many nations in Asia, Africa, and Latin America to begin to move away from traditional society. Communism, Rostow insisted, "is a kind of disease which can befall a transitional society if it fails to organize effectively those elements within it which are prepared to get on with the job of modernization."

Faced with 8 percent unemployment in 1960, the result of the slow rate of economic growth during the Eisenhower administration, Kennedy and his advisers decided to use those "technical tricks" of Keynesian economics to make the economy grow. The budget for national defense was increased dramatically, and another $25 billion was budgeted for the National Aeronautics and Space Administration. Kennedy also asked Congress for a tax cut, which was not enacted into law until Lyndon Johnson became President in 1964. Under this pump priming, the Gross National Product (GNP) grew from 1961 to 1968 at twice the rate of the 1950s.

With the increase of industrial production in the 1960s, average income also increased by 18 percent, but corporate profits, as in the 1920s, expanded even more rapidly, by 65 percent. Defense contracts, especially for the new complex technology of rockets and nuclear weapons, were not competitive and, again as during the war, made allowances for cost overruns. By the end of the 1960s, the job of one of every ten Americans was tied into the Department of Defense budget. Two-thirds of the income of aircraft companies and a third of the income of radio and television companies came from the government. More than 40 percent of the work force in Seattle and Los Angeles depended on government contracts. Half the scientists and engineers in private enterprise also depended upon such government contracts, as did many university scientists and engineers. Academic departments had become directly involved in the war economy in the 1940s, and this relationship intensified during the cold war. Resources put into research and development before 1940 were negligible, but after 1945 a significant part of the GNP was invested in this area, much of it in major universities. By the 1960s, more than half the annual budgets of the twenty most important private and state universities came from the federal government.

Much of this research involved weapon systems, and much of the expenditure arising from the application of this research by the Department of Defense was overseas. This investment of billions of dollars in research and development, therefore, did not benefit the entire American economy. The Japanese economy grew three times as fast, the German economy at twice the American rate, and even the French and Italian economies grew more rapidly. While these nations experienced labor shortages, the United States had a continuing unemployment rate of 5 to 7 percent through the 1950s. There were several ironic causes of this unemployment beyond the distortion given the economy by the Department of Defense. During the years 1941–45, much of the deficit spending had gone into the South, where the massive fourteen-million-man army was trained. Southern income jumped from one-half to two-thirds the national average, and white southerners were able to buy farm machinery and mechanize their farms. As a result, millions of black sharecroppers were driven off the land and into southern and northern cities.

Between 1950 and 1970, black populations dramatically increased in major northern cities. Black population went from 10 to 30 percent in New York, from 14 to 33 percent in Chicago, from 16 to 40 percent in Detroit, from 35 to 70 percent in Washington, D.C. By 1970, half of the blacks in the United States lived in the North. They arrived in northern cities when job opportunities for unskilled workers were declining. A million and a half factory jobs disappeared between 1950 and 1960 as production became more automated. Even worse for the blacks who filled the central cities, much industry was in the process of moving to the suburbs.

Government policy in the late 1940s and 1950s had subsidized the building of bridges and highways, which encouraged the flight of the white middle class to the suburbs. Federal mortgage policy also enabled middle-income people to build new homes outside the city limits. Most federal funds available for urban renewal were spent on tearing down slums, which were replaced by office build-ings, luxury apartments, theaters, and stadiums. Business leaders, searching for ways to strengthen the tax base of their cities, con-cluded that there was no profit in building public housing. And at the end of the 1960s, only 2 percent of city dwellers lived in hous-ing provided by the federal government. As the result of this urban renewal, which destroyed slum housing without providing new dwellings for the poor, low-income groups, especially blacks, were forced into even more crowded and rundown housing. In 1960, blacks, as 23 percent of the population of Chicago, occupied only 4 percent of the physical space of the city. Black unemployment was twice that of whites throughout the 1950s and 1960s. But besides the 10 percent unemployment rate in 1970, another 25 percent worked only part-time or were paid below the poverty level. Unem-ployment for teen-age blacks increased throughout the 1960s and had reached 50 percent during the recession of 1974–75.

Blacks had made some economic gains during World War II. Black leaders had forced Roosevelt to establish a committee on Fair Employment Practices. The prejudice it was designed to combat was expressed by the hiring instructions of North American Aviation: "The Negro will be considered only as janitors and in other similar capacities. Regardless of their training as aircraft workers, we will not employ them." The percentage of black workers did increase from 3 to 8 percent in war industries and from 60,000 to 200,000 in the federal civil service. The CIO had welcomed black production workers, and there were more than a million in unions in the 1950s. The average wage for blacks had increased from 50 percent of whites in the 1930s to 60 percent in the 1950s. But the decline of the number of production workers in the country and the slowdown of union growth in the 1950s because of automation closed this avenue of economic progress. The skilled trade unions, which had explicitly barred blacks from membership before World War II, bent slowly and reluctantly under government pressure in the 1960s. In 1960, 1 percent of apprentices were black, but this figure rose to only 3 percent by 1970.

The problems of deterioration of central-city slums, with large unemployed or underemployed black populations, were intensified by the continual flow of poor whites from the cotton and mountain South into urban areas. Several cities, especially New York, had hundreds of thousands of Puerto Ricans added to their slum popu-lations. These migrants had fled the overcrowded conditions of their

native land. Texas, New Mexico, Arizona, and California also experienced the influx of a Spanish-speaking population from Mexico.
They too had a very high birthrate, and these Chicanos also sought
opportunity in the cities, especially Los Angeles. The final irony was
the explosion of Native American population, which doubled in the
generation after World War II. There was no space for these young
Native Americans on the impoverished reservation lands, and they
came by the tens of thousands into the slums of Los Angeles, San
Francisco, Chicago, St. Paul, and Minneapolis.

Native Americans, who had had their hunting and agricultural
economies destroyed in the 1880s and had been forced to survive on
government welfare for a century on the reservations, were entering
city slums where they found themselves caught up in the same
welfare patterns as the blacks, poor whites, Puerto Ricans, and
Chicanos, for whom there also was no functional place in an economy dominated by the corporations of the Anglo-American elites.

The deterioration of the cities in the 1960s, the poverty, the
broken families, the rising crime rate, and the flight to the suburbs
of the middle class contradicted the prophecy of the Kennedy-
Johnson administrations that rational urban planning directed from
Washington could make the cities the showcase of Rostow's final
stage of modernization, high mass-consumption. It also shattered
the hopes of liberal Protestant theologians who had abandoned
Reinhold Niebuhr's critique of progress and had accepted the theory
of modernization put forward by Rostow and other social scientists.
Harvey Cox, a Baptist theologian at Harvard University Divinity
School, embraced modernization in his book *The Secular City*
(1964), which proved to be the most influential theological statement published during the Kennedy-Johnson years of 1961–68.
"Secularization and urbanization," Cox wrote, "do not represent
sinister curses to be escaped, but epochal opportunities to be embraced." Modern Protestantism, he continued, the religion of secularization and urbanization, represents the final "liberation" of
humanity from "ancient oppressions." It represents "the disenchantment of nature," "the desocialization of politics," and "the deconse-
cration of values." Seeing history as moving necessarily through
stages of tribal and town life before the final stage of urban civilization, Cox rejoiced in "the fact that urban-secular man is incurably
and irreversibly pragmatic," "that he is less and less concerned with
religious questions" and "that he is shedding the lifeless cubicles of
the mythical periods and stepping into the functional age."

By 1969, as the Kennedy-Johnson policies to renew the city seemed to have failed and the policies to regulate the economy were resulting in an unpredicted inflation to be followed by an unpredicted recession, Cox reversed his thinking completely. In his book of 1969, *The Feast of Fools,* Cox insisted that to be human is to live by myths. "We have forgotten," he wrote, "that before man made tools, he made myths and rituals." Converting to the counterculture, he asserted that "ritual provides both the form and the occasion for the expression of fantasy" and that "it is through ritual movement, gesture, song and dance that man keeps in touch with the sources of creativity." As Cox wrote these words, the Kennedy-Johnson administration was celebrating its one great ritual success, putting a man on the moon.

In NASA's publication, *Space: The New Frontier,* it was asserted that "If there has been a single factor responsible for our success over the past two hundred years, it has been the characteristic American confidence in the future." And President Kennedy had insisted that "No single space project will be more impressive to mankind" than putting a man on the moon. "In a very real sense, it will not be one man going to the moon, it will be an entire nation." For Kennedy, success in the mission would "demonstrate to a watching world that America is first in the field of technology and science."

This mobilization of American "know-how," "can-do," and "will-do" seemed to demonstrate the validity of the WASP commitment to modern definitions of space and time. John Glenn, who first orbited the earth in 1962, and Neil Armstrong and Edwin Aldrin, who first landed on the moon in 1969, were youthful, clean-cut, male Anglo-Americans; they seemed much like the heroes of the western frontier. For John Glenn in 1969, the success of Project Apollo proved that "if we could develop in only eight years the means of landing men on the moon, we could do just about anything we set our minds to. We could solve the problems of poverty in the midst of plenty, correct racial injustice, and ease social tensions." Everything was possible, Glenn continued, because "in Project Apollo, we learned how to organize teams of experts in government, industry, and the universities to define objectives, plan programs, and solve difficult technical problems."

In 1969, the WASP elite, in spite of failures in the cities and in Vietnam, still seemed to control the process of economic modernization.

Eighty percent of the top executives of manufacturing corporations were WASPs, as were 95 percent of the top executives of the major insurance and banking institutions. The prestigious Ivy League universities and a number of other private colleges were providing three-fourths of the recruits for corporate leadership. Episcopalians and Presbyterians controlled more than half the large fortunes in the country, although they were less than 6 percent of the population. For them, the 1950s and 1960s had been rewarding. And there was no significant organized dissent to the affirmation that the capitalist system was working splendidly. The two major parties were totally committed to the status quo and faced no serious third-party threats. The universities, integrated into the economy, were producing scholars who overwhelmingly praised the system. And George Meany, head of the AFL–CIO, said labor believed "in the capitalist system. We are dedicated to the preservation of this system, which rewards the workers." But the Kennedy-Johnson management of the economy through Keynesian principles had shown increasing signs of weakness throughout the 1960s.

When Lyndon Johnson became President in 1963, the problems of the inner cities were so obvious that he declared "unconditional war on poverty." The sweeping Democratic victories in the elections of 1964 gave Johnson a substantial majority in Congress, which rapidly passed many bills to support his economic policy. One of these was the Economic Opportunity Act, which promised "to eliminate the paradox of poverty in the nation." This legislation would create, according to Johnson, a "Great Society," which rested on "abundance and liberty for all." He called, too, for an immediate "end to poverty and racial injustice."

A bill reducing taxes was passed. Two percent of the taxpayers who had incomes of more than $20,000 a year received 30 percent of the reduction. Federal funds to subsidize urban mass transit largely benefited the middle classes who commuted into the city from their suburban homes. Funds for universities and hospitals also largely benefited the middle class, as did Medicare, which provided medical care for the elderly under social security.

Direct aid to the poor came in the form of a Food Stamp Program and rent supplements and grants to the states for health service for the poor through a Model Cities Program. But most of the legislation was designed to send middle-class employees or volunteers into the slums to teach the poor how to succeed in the marketplace (Vista). These efforts reached from a Head Start Program for preschool children to an Upward Bound program for college students. The program also established a Job Corps for school drop-outs and a Neighborhood Youth Corps. The assumptions of the Johnson administration blended the conventional wisdom of Herbert Hoover, that education could provide an equality of opportunity, enabling the individual to compete in the marketplace, with the conventional wisdom of Franklin D. Roosevelt, that the marketplace could be made to expand by increasing government spending. Only the major breakdown of the economy between 1929 and 1933 had forced the establishment to provide a minimum of federal aid to the poor.

In the midst of apparent plenty, the inability of the economy to employ at least a fifth of the population at a livable wage led to terrifying riots in the cities during the mid 1960s. The establishment responded by dramatically expanding funds available to the poor through Aid to Families with Dependent Children (AFDC). During the quiet years of the Eisenhower administrations, as the urban crisis was taking shape, the number of families receiving AFDC had risen from 635,000 to 745,000. Even in the more prosperous 1960s, the worsening condition of the poor forced the number of welfare families to double, totaling 1,545,000 households. Kennedy-Johnson increases for defense spending, tax cuts, and the drafting of millions of young men for the war in Vietnam temporarily had increased the rate of economic growth and had reduced the rate of unemployment.

But the rapid rate of inflation after 1968 began to cause serious trouble in the economy, followed by a major recession in 1973 and 1974, which sent the rate of unemployment soaring over 9 percent. To avoid social unrest, the number of families receiving AFDC doubled to stand at 3,500,000 families with more than 8,000,000 children. Since 1950, the work situation for black men had deteriorated. Those who could not find employment or were underemployed had difficulty committing themselves to the expected cultural role as father and husband. "I've been scuffling for five years," a young black husband said. "I've been scuffling for five years from morning till night. And my kids still don't have anything, my wife don't have anything, and I don't have anything." Like many young males who felt defeated, he abandoned his family and looked for a woman to support him. "She's not pretty, but she's got a beautiful job. She just got herself a government job. She never misses a day's work. She's a real mule." When another young male friend asked, "Hell, who wants to live with a mule?" he answered, "Man, that's the best thing to live with. When you got somebody who can pull that wagon, you really got something." As a result of this demoralization, black women had to take the responsibility for heading their households. By 1973, 35 percent of black families were headed by women, and these families had more than half the young black children.

A major reason for the national shortage of jobs in the 1960s and 1970s was the decision of the largest corporations to invest much of their huge profits overseas. Between 1950 and 1974, $100 billion had been invested in Canada, Latin America, Europe, Asia, and Africa. During the decade of the 1960s, major manufacturers increased their industrial production in the United States by 70 percent while their overseas production increased by 500 percent. In 1972, while they exported $50 billion worth of goods from the United States, their overseas plants were producing $180 billion worth of goods and they received 40 percent of their profits from these sales.

When the corporations left the central cities for the suburbs, or left New England for the South, they were following the same logic that motivated them to leave the United States to go overseas—the pursuit of profits. "Few trends could so thoroughly undermine the very foundations of our free society," wrote the conservative economist Milton Friedman, "as the acceptance by corporate officials of a social responsibility other than to make as much money for the stockholders as possible." And Carl A. Gerstacker, the chairman of Dow Chemical Company, expressed the corporate desire to operate in a pure marketplace situation without any social responsibility when he confessed that "I have long dreamed of buying an island owned by no nation, and of establishing the world headquarters of the Dow Company on the truly neutral ground of such an island, beholden to no nation or society."

The production of almost all TV sets, radios, and other electronic equipment in Asian countries was an example of the way American companies went abroad to strengthen profits by using cheaper labor. The increase of the proportion of Americans with incomes above the poverty level depended, therefore, on the growth of service industries. A "baby boom" at the end of the 1940s had briefly reversed the long-term decline of the birthrate. As fifteen million

whites fled the central cities and headed for the suburbs, they created a great demand for new houses, new appliances, new furniture,
new cars. The "baby boom" also created a demand for many more
schoolteachers, and the new affluence encouraged the rapid expansion of colleges and universities. The proportion of high-school
students going on to college increased constantly from 1945 until
the late 1960s, when it passed 50 percent.

The postwar "baby boom" did not last. The birthrate plunged
until by 1975, for the first time in the history of white people in
America, it supported a zero growth or even a declining population.
Housing costs had reached a point where many young married
couples had to think in terms of apartments rather than suburban
homes. And the rising prices of cars and gasoline had started a
trend among younger Americans to buy European and Japanese
compact cars.

As the psychology of the suburban frontier disintegrated in the
1960s and Americans in jobs like teaching no longer were able to
see themselves moving away from a blue-collar past, they lost much
of their contempt for organized labor. The production and craft
unions either had managed to bargain for escalator clauses to tie
their wages to increases in the cost of living or they had organized
the power to engage in successful strikes. Public-school teachers
began to unionize to protect themselves against inflation, and there
was even a trend among college teachers toward collective bargaining. In 1970, most professors had seen themselves as independent
professionals, but when their salaries fell drastically in proportion to
the organized high-school teachers and when their job security was
threatened by declining enrollments, they began to reconsider the
need for collective bargaining. Unions also spread among government employees, including firemen and policemen.

Government jobs at the federal, state, and local level had provided the major new opportunity for employment throughout the
1950s and 1960s. While federal expenditures increased at the rate of
8 percent a year, rising from $37 billion in 1948 to $246 billion in
1972, state and local expenditures increased at the rate of 10 percent a year, leaping from $18 billion in 1948 to $180 billion in
1972. In the four years between 1967 and 1971, state taxes increased on the average of 67 percent and local taxes by 50 percent.
Laboring under the burden of increasing inflation, the federal government ran deficit budgets every year after 1964 with the exception

of one. After a deficit of $44 billion in 1975, it anticipated a deficit of $66 billion in 1976 as a result of increased expenditures for welfare and a major tax cut designed to stimulate the economy and bring it out of the worst recession since the 1930s. Many states and cities also had engaged in deficit spending as they worked with the same assumption that future growth would bring increased taxes to pay off the debt.

All of these economic trends emerged in exaggerated form in New York City, creating a major financial crisis in the spring of 1975, when the city admitted it could not pay the interest on its debts. Between 1963 and 1973, New York had increased the number of city employees by 50 percent. These workers, by organizing, had won significant pay increases. Average salaries for police, for example, had increased from $12,000 to $17,000 between 1971 and 1975. Out of a city population of eight million, one million were on welfare, necessitating payments of more than $2 billion a year. There were 91,000 retired city workers whose pensions required $1 billion a year from the city budget. City officials had begun borrowing in 1964 to balance the budget, and in 1975 the interest on the debt had reached about $2 billion a year, more than the entire city budget had been in 1960. New York, like the nation, seemed caught in a vicious cycle. As taxes had risen to meet public payrolls, debt, and welfare costs, business and middle-class people had left the city, removing 400,000 jobs in the early 1970s. This forced the city to go further in debt and to raise taxes still higher. By 1976, economic experts were predicting a crisis for the national government in meeting the increasing financial obligations of the social security system.

As city indebtedness paralleled the rise in the national debt, so did private deficit spending. Commercial bank loans doubled from $198 billion in 1965 to $445 billion in 1973, and consumer installment credit more than doubled from $8 billion to $21 billion during those same years, as did indebtedness for new mortgages from $29 billion to $63 billion. Despite this increased indebtedness, which magnified the rate of inflation, despite all this pump priming, the national economy had begun to slide into recession in 1973 and suffered a 10 percent decrease in the GNP by 1975. Economists and government leaders were baffled by the unprecedented combination of inflation and recession. "This has been the worst slump of all," wrote the columnist Sylvia Porter, "for in 1929–32, prices at least fell along with incomes—but this time they galloped at the start of the decline and even now, 18 months later, are still climbing at an intolerable rate."

A medium rate of inflation had been useful to the average American through the 1950s and 1960s. Most wages had kept up with the rate of inflation. Long-term debts, especially mortgages, diminished because of inflation and higher wages. But this steady pattern of inflation was undermining the value of the dollar in international finance and trade. The United States had been even more dominant economically at the end of World War II than in 1918. Japan and Germany, its chief competitors, were captive nations, and England and France were severely impoverished. America, therefore, had been able to establish an international financial community which included the western European nations and Japan. Within this community, the dollar was the unit of exchange, convertible to gold at the price of $35 an ounce.

The expenses of the Korean war and the Vietnam war as well as the cost of large numbers of troops, airplanes, and naval vessels deployed at bases throughout the world caused a balance-of-payments deficit in which the United States sent more dollars abroad than it received. As the value of the dollar shrank because of inflation, American leaders were able to coerce the European military allies to continue to accept the dollar at its old value. Nevertheless, American economic power was diminishing. In 1948, the United States controlled 71 percent of the money in the "free world"; by 1962, it controlled only 40 percent. Between 1956 and 1966, its gold reserves fell from $23 to $13 billion, while foreign reserves increased from $12 billion to $30 billion. Then in 1971, the country had its first trade deficit since the 1890s, importing goods worth more than American exports.

President Nixon, faced with trade deficits and balance-of-payments deficits combined with steep inflation in 1971, devalued the dollar by 9 percent and then again by 10 percent in 1973. He tried desperately to deal with the economic crisis in 1971 by using the Keynesian technique of cutting taxes and imposing a ninety-day freeze on all wages, rents, and prices. He placed a 10 percent tariff on all imports and suspended the convertibility of dollars into gold. With the collapse of American financial domination of the free world and the collapse of the value of the dollar, the price of gold on the world market leaped overnight from $35 an ounce to $120 and continued to climb.

Then in 1973, the major oil-exporting nations of the world (OPEC) organized to raise the price of the precious fuel dramatically and further weaken the American economic situation. As oil reserves in the United States were depleted (it was predicted in 1975 that only a twenty-year supply of U.S. oil reserves remained at the current rate of use), the nation became increasingly dependent upon foreign producers. An even greater trade deficit resulted as billions of dollars a year flowed out to pay for the ever more expensive oil from abroad. The government of Libya, recognizing the deteriorating American economic situation, would not accept dollars for its oil. The dollar had lost its value, the Libyans insisted, and they wanted a currency that was convertible to gold.

The skyrocketing cost of oil endangered the whole system of American agriculture in which 5,000,000 farmers fed 200,000,000 Americans and exported food to the rest of the world. The use of gasoline on farms had quadrupled between 1940 and 1970, and the use of fertilizer had increased eight times. The manufacture of fertilizer consumed oil. So too did the generation of electricity, which was being consumed in 1970 at seventy times the rate of 1940. Indeed, the farmers in 1970 were expending twelve calories of energy to get back one calorie of food. The rapidly rising cost of oil, therefore, inevitably meant rising food prices.

As the country became aware of the limits of its resources, it was also becoming aware of the limits of space—the air, the land, and the water—into which it could pour its industrial and agricultural wastes. It was also becoming aware of the living complexity of those spaces. A Clean Air Act in 1970 hoped to end industrial and automobile pollution by 1975. The health hazards of industrial and other kinds of pollution had been accepted. But the complexity of the interrelationships of the economy with the environment had been vastly underestimated in 1970, and the air had not been made much cleaner by 1975.

It also had been accepted by the end of the 1960s that economic exploitation of natural resources took place within a complex and delicate biological environment, and Congress had passed a National Environmental Policy Act in 1969 asking that environmental-impact studies be made before new economic exploitation began. In 1975, however, the administration of President Ford was pressing for speedy development of coal strip mining and the rapid building of nuclear electricity-generating plants despite the warnings by many scientists that both would have a disastrous impact on the environment.

When President Nixon cut back federal aid to universities and to space projects in 1969, he accelerated the doubts that had been growing in the academic establishment about the inevitability of expansion and growth. The federal government had been expanding its commitment to research from $3 billion in 1959 to $17 billion in 1969. This had enabled educational institutions to expand at twice the rate of the GNP. Many expected this expansion to last forever, and futurism, the science of a future without work or poverty in which automation made a life of creative leisure possible for everyone, became a respectable academic subject. But with major unemployment among engineers and scientists by 1970, Philip Handler, the president of the National Academy of Sciences, reported that "our national apparatus for the conduct of research and scholarship is not yet dismantled, but it is falling into shambles." And for Bentley Gates, retiring president of the American Association for the Advancement of Science, "We are like the explorers of a great continent who have penetrated to its margins in most points of the compass and have mapped the major mountain chains and rivers. There are still innumerable details to fill in, but the endless horizons no longer exist."

On university campuses, there were scientists and social scientists, like Professor Jay Forrester of the Massachusetts Institute of Technology, who were using the computer to predict a future which was the absolute opposite of that of the futurists. Arguing that all scientific principles pointed to the reality of limits, Forrester declared that he saw "no solution for urban problems until cities develop the courage to plan in terms of maximum population, a maximum number of housing units, a maximum permissible building height and a maximum number of jobs."

Orthodox economists, committed to a mechanistic model of the world, seemed to be discredited by the failure of Keynesian economics to predict the combination of inflation and recession that plagued the country from 1969 onward. This situation of "stagflation" made it possible for the few heretical economists to begin to win converts to their biological definition of nature. Important books, *Small Is Beautiful* by E. F. Schumacher, *The Entropy Law and the Economic Process* by Nicholas Georgescu-Roegen, and *Toward a Steady-State Economy* by Herman Daly, reached increasing audiences of economists and lay people with their messages of the necessity to limit growth, decentralize economic and social life, and use renewable sources of energy that came from the cycles of nature.

Even the leaders of the great corporations were talking about the limits to growth. "You can bet that for the next generation we're going to have to live with the conditions we've seen over the past couple of years," reported one. And another declared that the limited availability of energy "puts constraints on the rate of economic growth, constraints that were not apparent in the preceding twenty years." At a seminar in 1975, sponsored by the Chamber of Commerce, a stockbroker declared, "I would think it unlikely my kids will live as well as I have and I would doubt that your kids will either." The increasing reluctance of the children of the upper middle class to choose business careers had reached some of their fathers. "Well, I made it," reminisced a corporate dropout, "but I wasn't happy. I felt the need for some kind of renewal."

The prophecies of Frederick Taylor and Henry Ford had failed by 1975. The discipline of the machine had not kept either management or workers loyal to linear time and to the vision of the factory as rational space. Union leaders, recognizing the unhappiness of assembly-line workers, insisted that "workers are not seeking self-fulfillment on the job. They are looking for a pay check. The job is the means by which they can support their families. And if it pays enough, they can seek self-fulfillment in other ways." But older workers spoke of the need to escape the pain of meaningless work. "You dream, you think of things you've done. I drift back continuously to when I was a kid and what me and my brothers did. The things you love most are the things you drift back into."

Younger workers increasingly were in rebellion against the gospel of Frederick Taylor. "What I demand of the worker is not to produce any longer by his own initiative," Taylor had declared, "but to execute punctiliously the orders given, down to their minutest details." Refusing to accept a speed-up of the assembly line at the new General Motors plant at Lordstown, Ohio, the young workers sabotaged the work process. "Occasionally, one of the guys will let a car go by," was the cheerful description given by one employee. "At that point, he's made a decision: 'Aw, fuck it. It's only a car.' It's more important to just stand there and rap. With us, it becomes a human thing. It's the most enjoyable part of my job, that moment. I love it."

"We have concealed our true circumstances even from ourselves"

★ ★

18

American Foreign Policy and Domestic Politics, 1960–76

John F. Kennedy and Cuba

Escalating involvement in Vietnam

Johnson's Vietnam war

Civil-rights activism and change

Native Americans and "Red Power"

Political women

Nixon reunites the Republican party, 1968

Abuses of the Presidency: Watergate

On the November day in 1963 when he was assassinated at the end of a thousand days in office, President Kennedy was planning to deliver a speech on the "painful, risky, and costly effort" that was being made in Southeast Asia. He was going to ask Americans to be good soldiers and to make the sacrifices necessary to win the cold war because "we dare not weary of the task." Kennedy and his advisers were sure that they could stop a Communist revolution in South Vietnam. They had confidence in Rostow's model that the normal evolution of a traditional society was toward capitalism. They believed that communism was abnormal, a disease that could strike a society in transition. But if the United States applied temporary force to contain the Communist malignancy, then countries such as South Vietnam would continue their normal development.

When Kennedy had taken office, he was so certain of capitalist strength and Communist weakness that he endorsed a CIA plan to invade Cuba to topple the new regime of the Communist leader, Fidel Castro. It was assumed that the Communist disease had no strength among the Cuban people and that a small force of anti-Castro Cubans supplied and trained by the United States in Florida could spark a massive anti-Castro uprising. The invasion at the Bay of Pigs proved a total disaster. Kennedy was deeply embarrassed by the fiasco and he became distrustful of his military advisers. He also was angry at the press for discussing the abortive invasion. "Details of this nation's covert preparations," he criticized, "have been available to every newspaper reader." Without consulting the public, Kennedy went on to make decisions in October 1962 that threatened nuclear war if Russia did not withdraw missiles it had placed in Cuba. Khrushchev removed them under this threat of all-out war.

Kennedy, however, was opposed to a policy of "brinkmanship." He believed that the rigid commitment to a policy of massive deterrence—the threat of total atomic war—in the Eisenhower administration had made it impossible for American leaders to use the small but necessary amount of conventional military force that could have kept Cuba out of Communist control. The mistake must not be repeated in Vietnam.

In 1954, the Eisenhower administration had paid 80 percent of the cost of the French effort to retain its colony in Indo-China in the face of a national revolution for independence. When the French finally withdrew, Vietnam was divided. The revolutionary group of Ho Chi Minh, identifying itself with Marxism, held the north. The United States encouraged an anti-Communist military group in the south. The instability of the South Vietnamese government, its unpopularity in the countryside, and the strength of South Vietnamese rebels forced the Kennedy administration to increase financial and military aid. Kennedy and his advisers proposed an increase of conventional ground forces and air power with an emphasis on special troops, Green Berets, skilled in guerrilla warfare. Kennedy informed the public only that he was increasing the number of military advisers. He doubted whether he had public support for the overt use of armed forces to suppress a national revolution.

In the 1964 presidential election campaign, the Republican candidate, Barry Goldwater, took the position that the United States should not get involved in another stalemate like the Korean war. He declared that he was even willing to use atomic weapons to win decisively. President Lyndon Johnson bitterly criticized Goldwater's threat of total war and reassured the people that there was no possibility of large-scale American involvement. "We are not about to send American boys nine or ten thousand miles away from home," Johnson declared during the campaign, "to do what Asian boys ought to be doing for themselves."

While making these public declarations, Johnson informed Congress that American ships had been attacked by North Vietnamese torpedo boats in the Bay of Tonkin. Although no firm evidence of North Vietnamese aggression was presented, Congress voted 416 to 0 in the House and 88 to 2 in the Senate to give President Johnson full authority to use all necessary military power to defend Americans from attack. Johnson used this power to move hundreds of thousands of troops into South Vietnam and to begin heavy bombing of North Vietnam. "I am not about to lose South Vietnam," Johnson told his advisers.

Johnson had accepted Rostow's advice that "it is on this spot that we have to break the liberation war. If we don't break it here, we shall have to face it again in Thailand, Venezuela, elsewhere." Johnson had Kennedy's confidence in the ability of the economists to manage the war as they managed the economy. It was expected that Secretary of Defense Robert McNamara, the former president

of the Ford Motor Company, could efficiently mobilize the resources necessary to suppress the rebellious forces. Careful calculations of infantry and artillery firepower, of electronic devices for
detecting the enemy, of numbers of air strikes and weight of bombs
dropped, all would add up to produce a "body-count" of the enemy
and indicate the disappearance of an effective Communist fighting
force.

McNamara's attempt to define Vietnam as the rational space of
the marketplace where "every quantitative measurement we have
shows we're winning this war" crumbled by 1967. American generals kept promising that one more army division would tip the
balance until five hundred thousand troops were committed. They
promised that another wave of bombing would cause the collapse of
the Viet Cong until, by the end of 1967, more tons of bombs had
been dropped than in World War II. McNamara confessed failure
and urged President Johnson to negotiate peace. McNamara was
relieved of his position; Johnson was not ready to accept the failure
of American planning. But the steady escalation of the war during
1965, 1966, and 1967 led to massive criticism within American
borders. Johnson, his Cabinet, and the generals responded to critics
with reassurances that the last increase in troop strength had finally
pacified the countryside and the most recent increase in bombing of
North Vietnam had finally broken their will to wage war. But in
January 1968, Viet Cong operating in the South and Communists in
the North launched a major attack during the season of Tet. The
Tet offensive, in the words of Senator Robert Kennedy, "shattered
the mask of official illusion with which we have concealed our true
circumstances, even from ourselves." Defecting from his brother's
commitment to sustain South Vietnamese generals at any cost, Kennedy joined Senator Eugene McCarthy of Minnesota in challenging
Johnson's leadership of the Democratic party. On March 31, 1968,
Johnson announced his withdrawal from the presidential race and
curtailed the bombing of North Vietnam.

A major reason for President Johnson's withdrawal from national
politics in 1968 was his sense that the legislation of his Great
Society program had failed to provide domestic stability. Johnson
had created the National Advisory Commission on Civil Disorders
(the Kerner Commission) to study the cause of the ghetto riots of
the 1960s. The commission's report found "white racism" to be the
major cause and warned that "our nation is moving toward two

societies, one black, one white—separate and unequal." To overcome the economic and social plight of blacks caused by endemic
racism, the commission recommended that the federal government
create two million jobs and build six million housing units. It also
recommended a massive attack on school segregation and "a national system of income supplementation." But Johnson turned his
back on the commmission's report because he was sure that the majority of white southerners and northern Catholics, who were essential parts of the Democratic party's national majority, would not
support such a legislative program.

As early as World War II white southerners had become fearful
that an effective policy of racial integration would be implemented,
even though Roosevelt had preserved segregation in the armed services. When the Democratic party advocated civil rights in 1948, a
States' Rights party appeared throughout the South to oppose it.
The party had its greatest membership in South Carolina, Georgia,
Alabama, Mississippi, and Louisiana. More than the President or
Congress, the Supreme Court was free from immediate political
pressures and therefore could better express symbolic changes in the
national identity. The white Protestant business and political elite
tried to change its image during World War II in order to separate
itself from its racist profile. In future patriotic ceremonies the Protestant chaplain would be flanked by a Catholic and a Jewish chaplain. Jews were admitted into major universities. In 1944, the
Supreme Court reversed an older Court decision and ruled that
blacks could not be barred from primaries in the southern states on
racial grounds. This decision permitted blacks to participate in the
elections in those states where the Democrats had one-party control.
A small number of blacks began to vote, especially in southern
cities and the border states, and the number grew steadily throughout the 1950s. Then in 1954, the Court again reversed a decision of
1900 and ruled that legal segregation in school systems was unconstitutional. The southern states refused to comply. But moderates
within the South, supported by the presence of federal troops,
effected some measure of compliance with the Supreme Court decision. In 1957, however, Eisenhower was forced to send troops into
Little Rock, Arkansas, to desegregate a high school.

Southern blacks sensed the inability of whites to maintain rigid
racial discrimination. In Montgomery, Alabama, Mrs. Rosa Parks,
an elderly black woman, refused to obey the law and move to the
back of the bus. Her arrest led to a spontaneous mass protest of

Montgomery blacks in which Martin Luther King, Jr. a Baptist minister, emerged as a major leader. From Montgomery, protests spread throughout black communities everywhere in the South. All aspects of the Jim Crow caste patterns were being challenged.

King established the Southern Christian Leadership Conference (SCLC), dedicated to a philosophy of nonviolent protest in an effort to overthrow the caste system. Black college and high school students initiated "sit-ins" at lunch counters and other areas of public segregation and formed the Student Non-Violent Coordinating Committee (SNCC) in 1960. In the North, the Congress of Racial Equality (CORE) picketed businesses that supported segregation. Violence between black demonstrators in the South and police was not infrequent. But nonviolent sit-ins, "Freedom Marches," and "Freedom Rides" against public segregation continued nevertheless. These demonstrations eventually penetrated the conscience of white liberals, who began to join the southern marches. Some were beaten and even killed. As northern whites were attacked by southern mobs, President Kennedy and his brother Robert, the attorney general, were forced to extend protection to the protestors and to sanction a massive March on Washington for Jobs and Freedom in August 1963. Surrounded by a crowd of two hundred thousand, Martin Luther King, Jr., described his apocalyptic dream "that one day the sons of former slaves and the sons of former slave-owners will be able to sit together at the table of brotherhood."

Under massive pressure from black and white liberals, President Kennedy called for civil-rights legislation in 1963. After Kennedy's death, President Johnson maneuvered a Civil Rights Act through Congress in 1964. According to the law, racial, religious, and sexual discrimination were barred in public accommodations as well as in employment. The law also provided for the enforcement of the desegregation of schools and public accommodations. Congress also passed a Voting Rights Act, which authorized sending federal registrars into counties where the majority of persons were not registered. By 1970, nearly 70 percent of blacks had registered to vote, in contrast to the 2 or 3 percent in 1944 when blacks began their re-entry into southern politics.

The triumph of civil-rights legislation in 1964 coincided, however, with a new kind of black activism. Spontaneous riots exploded in black ghettos throughout the North and West. Led by young unemployed blacks, these rebellions were an expression of dissatisfaction with economic and social conditions, and they spotlighted the disastrous condition of the black community. Achieving integration in the political system, blacks discovered the limitations of economic and social opportunity. Disillusionment came to Stokely Carmichael, a leader of SNCC, for whom "this nation, from top to bottom is racist, and does not function by morality, love, and nonviolence, but by power." "Black Power" became the cry of many young black leaders after 1965. Even Martin Luther King, Jr., redirected his emphasis toward a search for jobs and economic justice. He was in Memphis to support a strike of black sanitation workers when he was assassinated in April 1968. Radical groups such as the Black Panthers urged economic revolution and a coalition of poor blacks with poor whites.

Most black leaders, however, continued to hope that the exercise of political power within the system would achieve social and economic justice. In 1965, blacks were still vastly underrepresented in the political life of northern cities. In Chicago, for example, fewer than 5 percent of governmental positions were held by blacks although more than 20 percent of the city's population was black. After 1965, blacks struggled to gain a fair share of political leadership. They began to win the mayorships of cities like Cleveland, Ohio; Gary, Indiana; Newark, New Jersey; Detroit, Michigan; and even Atlanta, Georgia. But the flight of white population to the suburbs, which made these victories possible, also left black mayors facing segregated school systems. They also inherited deteriorating tax situations as white middle-class taxpayers and white-owned industry moved to the suburbs.

A similar pattern of increasing political power coupled with the absence of economic power described the situation of Native Americans. In 1924, the government had ruled that Indians were citizens even if they were not landholders. This "toleration" of Native Americans culminated in the Indian Reorganization Act of 1934, which recognized tribal cultures and permitted the establishment of tribal governments. As the morale of the Native Americans strengthened, they formed the National Congress of American Indians (NCAI), which pressured Congress to respect the treaty rights of Indians. By 1961, a national Indian Youth Council had been established to express the growing militancy of young Native Americans.

"Red Power" developed in the 1960s as young Native Americans worked to develop a sense of cultural pride. No longer was it necessary to think themselves and their culture inferior to whites, and young Sioux danced their Sun Dance for the first time since the defeat of Sitting Bull. Radical Native Americans like Dennis Banks, Russell Means, and Clyde and Vernon Bellecourt helped to form the American Indian Movement (AIM) to pressure the government to provide social and economic justice for their people, whose average income was $1,500 a year, whose unemployment rate was 40 percent in 1970, whose infant-mortality rate was three times the national average, and whose teen-age suicide rate was a hundred times that of whites. In November 1972, Native Americans briefly seized the Bureau of Indian Affairs building in Washington, D.C., to protest the corruption and inefficiency of the government's Bureau of Indian Affairs. And in February 1973, AIM warriors occupied Wounded Knee, South Dakota, and fought FBI forces for more than two months.

A recurring theme in the Native American movement in the twentieth century was colonial rebellion. "We have more in common with the Africans and Vietnamese and all the non-Western people than we do with the Anglo-Saxon culture of the United States," declared Vine Deloria, Jr. "We are a tribal people with tribal sympathies. An Indian doesn't have to know, or understand, anything about Kenya, or Burma, or Peru, or Vietnam. He feels the way they feel."

Chicanos, too, had lost their deference for Anglo-Americans in the 1960s. They were no longer "grateful" for the right to vote, to citizenship, without the accompanying social and economic power. Their population swelled in the Southwest and the West as the exodus from Mexico continued. A high birth rate also contributed to the growth of the Chicano communities. In 1960, their income was less than half that of the whites among whom they lived, and they enjoyed vastly inferior public services. The struggle for political and economic power continued throughout the 1960s. Cesar Chavez led an effort to unionize farm workers, while José Angel Gutierrez was beginning a LaRaza Unida party in Texas as a vehicle for Chicanos to take political power where they were a majority of the population. Newspapers like *La Raza,* published in Los Angeles, and *El Guito: A Journal of Contemporary Mexican-American Thought* encouraged young Chicanos to reject Anglo-American culture and participate in a revival of their native heritage. Leaders like Rudolfo Gonzales of the Denver Chicano community were working to have the people take over the schools to see that Spanish was taught as a language along with Spanish-American culture. The militancy of the movement was expressed by the formation of the paramilitary Brown Berets, committed to the defense of their people against police brutality and interference with Chicano autonomy.

As other groups grappled for economic and political power, so too women stirred to action during the 1960s. The gradual increase since 1900 in the number of women working outside the home, including working mothers, accelerated drastically during World War II. Despite the hope of business leaders that "too many should not stay in the labor force" after the war because "the home is the basic American institution," women continued to become a larger part of the work force, and by 1970 more than 50 percent of mothers were employed. Most of this increase was in "traditional" women's work—clerical, sales, and domestic-service jobs. The percentage of women in the professions had decreased between 1920 and 1970, and between 1950 and 1970, the median wage of women had slipped from 65 percent to 59 percent of that of male workers. In 1963, Betty Friedan published *The Feminine Mystique*, which bitterly pointed to the contradiction between the social ideal of the woman as "young and frivolous, almost childlike; fluffy and feminine; passive, gaily content in a world of bedroom and kitchen, sex, babies, and home" and the reality of most women working at dull and poorly paid jobs.

Women in 1960, like blacks and Chicanos and other groups at the bottom of the economy, had little influence in politics. Like them, women were dissatisfied with the status quo. Polls indicated an almost universal desire on the part of mothers that their daughter have a different lifestyle. Pressure from women forced President Kennedy to create a National Commission on the Status of Women, and by 1967 every state had followed suit in creating such commissions. But male leaders throughout the country, as represented by the Equal Employment Opportunity Commission (EEOC), had no intention of enforcing the equal-employment section of the Civil Rights Act of 1964, considering it, as one commission member said, "a fluke, conceived out of wedlock."

Frustration with male apathy and hostility led to the formation in 1966 of the National Organization of Women (NOW) to force change. NOW lobbied for the passage of the Equal Rights Amendment (ERA) to the Constitution (prohibiting discrimination in government on the basis of sex), enforcement of laws on sex discrimination in employment in private industry, maternity-leave rights for working women, tax deductions for child care, child-care centers, equal and unsegregated education, equal job-training opportunities and allowances for women below the poverty level, and the right of women to control their reproductive lives. Special-interest groups also organized, such as the Women's Equity Action League (WEAL) to represent women in higher education and the Federally Employed Women (FEW).

These groups largely represented moderate women activists. But radical feminist groups apeared in reaction to the sexism of male radicals. Jo Freeman and Shulamith Firestone helped to form a National Conference for a New Politics to express feminist radicalism. Small journals appeared across the country such as *Off Our Bodies, Ain't I a Woman,* and *Majority Report;* feminist leaders exhorted women to see themselves as a group that had been successfully colonized and to see their need to break from the subordinate cultural identity given them by their male colonizers. By 1972, the movement had gained such strength that it was able to support a major national magazine, *Ms.*

A national Women's Political Caucus led by Congresswomen Shirley Chisholm and Bella Abzug had forced much greater representation by women in the conventions of the major political parties in 1972, and there was a dramatic increase in the number of women elected to public office. Women took seats in state legislatures as well as in the United States Congress. This trend was even stronger in the 1974 elections, which also saw the election of Ella Grasso to the governorship of Connecticut, the first woman in American history elected to a governorship in her own right.

Radical political groups proliferated on college campuses in the early 1960s. Students for a Democratic Society (SDS) was one of the major ones. Polls indicated, however, no significant shift of students toward the political left between 1960 and 1972. The polls did indicate dramatic shifts in cultural values and a tremendous loss of faith in established political, economic, and social institutions. Students widely engaged in premarital sex; abortion became a conventional method of contraception to some; marijuana was as available as cigarettes; and homosexuality was tolerated. At the same time students shrank from the idea of fighting wars for national honor, and in general they eschewed the use of violence. Students expressed growing distrust of business corporations, the national government, and established churches, and skepticism about the modern work ethic.

It was within this context of student alienation that blacks, Native Americans, Chicanos, and women succeeded in helping to form new college departments or programs in their respective ethnic cultures, areas once defined as worthless by educational leaders. College students, supported by high-school students, wanted to grow up and erase the definition of adolescence established earlier in the century. Colleges responded by ending their *in loco parentis* role. Congress and the states responded by passing a constitutional amendment lowering the voting age to eighteen. Many states lowered the permissible age for alcohol consumption and were easing their penalties for the possession of marijuana.

Many of these pressures for social change sought political expression at the Democratic Convention meeting in Chicago in 1968. But young people protesting against "politics as usual" were met by massive police violence directed by Mayor Richard Daley, who represented the power of the old politics within the Democratic party.

Richard Nixon won the Republican nomination in 1968 because party leaders believed he could reunite their party. Vice-president under Eisenhower, Nixon had been the Republican presidential candidate in 1960 and lost to Kennedy. He then ran for the governorship of California in 1962 and lost. He was on the political sidelines in 1964 when a rebellion against "liberal" control of the party took place. Many Republicans throughout the country had never accepted the "liberal" Republican compromises with welfare capitalism and the cold war. In 1964, these conservatives organized at the local level to take control of the selection of delegates to the national convention, where they nominated Senator Barry Goldwater to express their views. Goldwater lost disastrously to Johnson, however, and Nixon faced the difficult task of building a new coalition in 1968. The number of Americans identifying themselves as Republicans had continued to shrink during the 1950s and 1960s. But the Democratic party did not benefit from these defections. Many people, especially the young, were turning away from politics completely. Many others were defining themselves as "independents." Nixon's strategy for election in this unprecedented situation of party weakness was to de-emphasize his relationship with the Republican party and to appeal to independents and dissatisfied Democrats.

Large numbers of white southern Democrats had voted for Eisenhower in 1952 to express their discontent with the national party's commitment to civil rights. But they continued to vote for local Democrats and to send Democrats to Congress. They also worried that Republican control of the legislative process might change the pattern of government intervention in the economy established since 1933, a pattern that had provided benefits and subsidies for the middle-class and blue-collar workers. A similar political outlook had developed among many northern lower-middle-class and blue-collar Catholic voters. They continued to vote as Democrats except at the presidential level, where they expressed their anger at civil-rights programs that affected northern cities and at welfare legislation for the poor. They had expected the work ethic to provide avenues of upward mobility for their children. The public support of large numbers of permanently unemployed people called into question the validity of the competitive system. It also challenged the sacrifices they were making in hopes that their children would have better lives. "Those lazy sluts having kids like it was a factory. You don't work, you don't live, right?" was the way in which a blue-collar worker expressed his fear and anger at the increase of welfare in the 1960s.

Although Nixon was a wealthy Wall Street lawyer when he became President he was a model for many who admired the self-made man. Born into a poor California family, Nixon associated his rise to the White House with the Lincoln tradition. "I believe in the American dream because I have seen it come true in my own life." Wilson was Nixon's greatest hero because he had spoken so eloquently for the Protestant work ethic. "The way to assure maximum growth is not by expanding the function of government," Nixon wrote, "but by increasing the opportunities for investment for millions." Competition in the marketplace, he declared, was still the American way. "I never in my life wanted to be left behind," he said, and "When you have won one battle is the time you should step up your effort to win another."

The average voters showed at the polls their resentment of the privileged upper class. This upper class called into question the belief in a classless society of self-made men. Nixon had never been comfortable with leaders from the eastern establishment, and as President, he chose two self-made millionaires from the South and West as his closest friends. Every President from Theodore Roosevelt to John F. Kennedy had heard political, educational, and church leaders of the eastern establishment preach the virtues of the militant and competitive life. Suddenly, after 1965, these leaders seemed to have capitulated to the permissiveness and pacifism of the college students. As the resentment of the lower-middle-class and blue-collar workers turned to anger, so it seemed did the attitudes of Richard Nixon. He saw a "great spiritual crisis" in the nation because there was "a breakdown in, frankly, what I would call the leadership of this country." Because "the Establishment is dying," he saw signs of national collapse. "Drugs, crime, campus revolts, racial discord, draft resistance—on every hand, we find old standards violated and old values discarded."

Nixon won the Presidency in 1968 by the slimmest of margins as the third-party candidacy of Governor George Wallace of Alabama split off a number of southern and northern Democrats. In his Inaugural Address, however, he asked the people of the United States to see him as a strong President who, like Kennedy, would fulfill the goal of Woodrow Wilson to Americanize the world. We will have, Nixon affirmed, "a crusading zeal, not just to hold our own but to change the world—including the Communist world—and to win the battle for freedom and true economic progress without a hot war."

Nixon knew that Wilson's dream had been put on the defensive in the 1930s by Germany and Japan and in the 1940s by Soviet Russia. Under Eisenhower, the United States had tried to create the image of invincible power through massive nuclear armaments, and then Kennedy had tried to create an image of strength through conventional armed forces. But the threat of nuclear weapons had not stopped a Communist revolution in Cuba, and the use of conventional weapons had not been able to destroy such a revolution in Vietnam.

Having struggled from poverty to the White House, having paid the price of tremendous inner discipline, which repressed all impulses to relax or play, Nixon could not admit that he had taken over a Presidency that had lost its meaning to the American people. He could not admit that it was his destiny to be the first President who commanded the retreat of American armies. "For the United States," he declared, "the first defeat in our nation's history would result in a collapse of confidence in American leadership not only in Asia but throughout the world."

During the four years of his first administration, he withdrew hundreds of thousands of troops committed to Vietnam by Lyndon Johnson. He conducted this retreat, however, within the illusion of an America on the military offensive. In the tradition of Franklin Roosevelt, Truman, Kennedy, and Johnson, Nixon, as commander-in-chief, made secret decisions that threw the enemy off balance. He ordered the bombing of Cambodia, the invasions of Cambodia and Laos, the mining of Haiphong harbor, and the Christmas bombing of Hanoi in 1972. Nixon praised professional football as the perfect embodiment of the American spirit. Under his quarterbacking, the American team was not "a pitiful and helpless giant." Under his direction, the nation moved with quickness and precision, with power and deception. His play-calling was unpredictable and successful.

Nixon's leadership, however, brought the country ever closer to his own goal line, not the enemy's. For Nixon, it was disastrous for the individual to stop expanding, and it was disastrous for the nation to stop expanding. "We stand at a crossroad in our history," he proclaimed. "We shall reaffirm our destiny for greatness or we shall choose to withdraw into ourselves." He reacted against those who advocated peace for a price in Asia: "North Vietnam cannot defeat or humiliate the United States," he cried out. "Only Americans can do that." Nor was Vice-President Agnew silent on the subject of the eastern establishment, calling them an "effete corps of impudent snobs," given to "sniveling, hand-wringing, and fawning." But Nixon continued to direct the retreat of American power.

Nixon saw himself standing alone as President in his commitment to the preservation of American power. The Supreme Court encouraged cultural permissiveness. Congress refused to support further war. Academic intellectuals, churchmen, and media leaders had renounced their 1964 position as cold-war warriors. The press especially infuriated Nixon. It had supported the military secrecy of Johnson, Kennedy, Eisenhower, and Truman. He thought it was undermining "respect for the office of President of the United States." Alone in the White House, without the support of a powerful party, without the support of the establishment figures who had traditionally shaped public opinion, Nixon believed that "the press is the enemy" and that "a full-fledged drive should be put against the media." Public relations was brought to a fine art within the

White House to manipulate the hostile media. Nixon's public-relations experts were supposed to create images to the public that were favorable to the administration. "When we have our public relations discussion Saturday," Nixon ordered, "I think we ought to put down five or six public relations goals that we want to impress on public consciousness."

Nixon was outraged that the power to use the FBI, the CIA, or Army Intelligence to harass his enemies (as Johnson had used them against the peace movement in 1967 and 1968) had been taken from him. He knew of J. Edgar Hoover's FBI program, COINTELPRO, which since 1956 had disrupted the personal lives of radicals, but Hoover would no longer cooperate with the President. Nixon began his own undercover activities: wiretapping members of the press as well as officials in his own administration. An undercover team was sent into Democratic party headquarters at the Watergate complex in Washington, D.C., to place wiretaps in telephones. Nixon seemed to think the Democrats were among the domestic enemies against whom he must wage war because they no longer believed in the image of invincible American international strength. Without the assurance of a viable Republican party to support his bid for re-election in 1972, the President and his men initiated a series of political "dirty tricks" to be played against the strongest Democratic candidates, especially Senator Edmund Muskie of Maine. "We ought to go down to the kennels and turn all the dogs loose on Ecology Ed," Nixon remarked. Secret money was sent into Alabama to undermine Governor Wallace.

When White House burglars were caught at the Watergate on June 17, 1972, Nixon endorsed a cover-up. He later advised Attorney General John Mitchell "I don't give a shit what happens, I want you to stonewall it, let them plead the Fifth Amendment, or anything else, if it'll save it—save the plan." With the White House connection to the burglars successfully hidden for the moment, Nixon advanced to a great personal triumph in the November election. He successfully identified the Democratic candidate, Senator George McGovern, with the social revolution of "amnesty, abortion, and acid" feared by so many voters. His advisers put pressure on corporations to contribute $60,000,000, much of which was illegal, to the President's campaign. But his smashing victory had no institutional base. The Republican party made few gains at the local level or in Congress. "Let's face it," Nixon told an aide, "nobody is a friend of ours."

Unable to cope with the disintegrating economy or the deep social divisions, Nixon continued to manufacture the image of great presidential power. He received huge media coverage during his trips to Russia and China, where he seemed to achieve détente with the great Communist powers, and he made a peace with North Vietnam that permitted North Vietnamese troops to remain in South Vietnam. By concentrating on the President's role in foreign policy, by traveling abroad, by flying constantly from the White House to his mansions in Florida and California and to Camp David in Maryland, he presented the illusion of active leadership. But he found no personal security in his role as national leader. Instead, he enriched himself as a private citizen, arranging for the expenditure of $17,000,000 of government funds for his estates at Key Biscayne and San Clemente, and falsifying his income tax to retain $400,000. His fears that there was no substance to his Presidency began to be fulfilled when Vice-President Agnew had to resign because of tax evasion and bribery charges and when one of the Watergate burglars, James McCord, decided to inform Judge John Sirica that the burglary was part of a larger conspiracy. "But the point is that everything is a crisis," Nixon reassured an aide. "I mean, Christ, it'll be mainly a crisis among the upper intellectual types. You know, the soft heads."

A Senate investigation of the Watergate break-in was initiated in addition to the grand jury investigation, and suddenly it was revealed that Nixon taped all conversation in his Oval Office at the White House. Throughout the spring of 1974, Nixon provided carefully edited transcripts of the White House tapes. But even with the most incriminating evidence of the President's role in the Watergate cover-up repressed, the circumstantial evidence was great enough for the House Judiciary Committee to bring several articles of impeachment against him. And when the Supreme Court ruled that he must give the tapes containing the incriminating evidence to the grand jury, his aides persuaded him to resign rather than face conviction by the Senate.

In his second Inaugural Address, Nixon had called for a rewriting of American history because "our children have been taught to be ashamed of their country, ashamed of their parents, ashamed of America's record at home and its role in the world." One reason he taped all conversations in the Oval Office might be that he wanted to be assured control over the materials he would use when he wrote the history of his administration in the hopes of proving that the system that he had learned at his mother's knee was still valid. In his resignation speech, he affirmed that "I have tried to remain in control of the Presidency." Only the President had the power to define the American past and the American future. But on August 9, 1974, Richard Nixon was a "pitiful and helpless giant."

★ ★ ★ ★ ★ ★ ★ ★ ★ ★ ★ ★ ★ ★ ★ ★ ★ ★

Epilogue

He had come a long way . . . and his dream must have seemed so close that he could hardly fail to grasp it. He did not know that it was already behind him, somewhere back in that vast obscurity beyond the city, where the dark fields of the republic rolled on under the night.

Gatsby believed in the green light, the orgiastic future that year by year recedes before us. It eluded us then, but that's no matter —tomorrow we will run faster, stretch out our arms farther. . . . And one fine morning—

So we beat on, boats against the current, borne back ceaselessly into the past.

—F. Scott Fitzgerald, *The Great Gatsby*

In 1976, the year of the nation's Bicentennial, the Republican party nominated Gerald Ford of Michigan as its presidential candidate and the Democrats nominated Jimmy Carter of Georgia. Unlike 1876, when Americans had celebrated the future and progress, Americans in 1976 celebrated the past and nostalgia. Both Ford and Carter presented themselves as representatives of an older and simpler America and emphasized rural and small-town strengths and virtues. Both promised, if elected, to restore purity to the Republic. Each was certain that he could end the scandals and corruption in the nation's capital and stop corruption abroad. American corporations not only had deliberately broken American laws on a massive scale in making illegal campaign contributions in 1972, but through their bribes they had also damaged the careers of leaders in such widely separate areas as Japan and the Netherlands. Polls in the summer of 1976 indicated that less than 19 percent of the electorate saw Ford or Carter as a candidate of heroic stature in comparison to American leaders of preceding generations—Franklin Roosevelt, Dwight Eisenhower, John and Robert Kennedy, and Martin Luther King, Jr. Political analysts reported that ten million Americans had stopped voting since the 1960s, and another ten million, who had come of voting age at the end of the 1960s and early 1970s, had never voted because they found no relevance in the platforms of the two major parties and were not taken with the leaders representing them. A number of political scientists pointed out that this decline in voter participation, from 63 percent of eligible voters casting ballots in 1960 to 53 percent in 1976, was evidence that only a dwindling number of Americans would define America's future in traditional terms.

The mythic geography of the English who left Europe to come to America in the early seventeenth century was one that defined the Old World as home and the New World as a frontier. Gerald Ford and Jimmy Carter are self-made men, men who left homes in small American towns to make their careers on the frontier of the market-place. The small-town and rural America that they represent is not a place to live and grow in, but a home to be left. Ironically, then, the identity of America as a frontier is an identity given to us by Europeans. As long as we continue to define America as a frontier,

we will not be a people who live in America. We will continue the
negative perception of ourselves as the descendants of ancestors who
left Europe.

One hope for a positive American future is to redefine America
as a home. Since World War II, we have been engaged in just such
a struggle to redefine ourselves as dwellers within the boundaries of
America. This may be the logic that links ecology with our redis-
covery of the Native Americans. Ecologists tell us that the earth is
our home, that we cannot treat it as a frontier. Pioneers are not
aware of pollution or limited resources. People acknowledge responsibility for the cleanliness and supplies in their homes, but they deny
responsibility for the frontier that they only pass through. If, since
the 1960s, Native Americans are entering our historical consciousness, does this mean that we are learning to appreciate their sense of
America as home and not as a frontier of Europe?

Is this the shared logic that also has brought us a new perception
of Afro-Americans, a people who did not choose to leave home?
For WASPs, the New World frontier was sacred because the Old
World center was profane. Like Afro-Americans, Jews and Catholics have never been able to share totally in this negative identity.
For a Jew, America has a sacred relationship to Israel. For a Catholic, America has a sacred relationship to Rome. WASPs have always
known that Jews and Catholics have never spiritually left home in
the same way that the original Puritans did. In contrast to the
frontiers of the WASP, ecology means home. Native Americans are
home. Afro-Americans are home. Catholics and Jews are home.

If a hopeful American future is as a home for Americans and not
a frontier, then we may unashamedly name Native Americans, Afro-
Americans, and Catholic and Jewish Americans among our American heroes. Until the present, of course, our heroes have been
soldiers or have had soldierly characteristics. Frontiers were the
domain of soldiers, of the strongest young men. Old people and the
sick and the weak were left at home as were children and women.
Mothers, wives, sweethearts, daughters were left at home when the
young men went to war. They were largely ignored by history.

But our historical perceptions have changed radically in the last
fifteen years to include these home dwellers, these nonsoldiers, these
civilians. What significance can be attached to this widened percep-
tual field? What does it mean when Carolyn Heilbrun in her book
of 1973, *Toward a Recognition of Androgyny,* can visualize a
future without the aggressive masculinity of self-made men on the

frontier or the passive femininity of women who remain at home?
Do all these changes of historical consciousness indicate the possibility of women as heroes, not as frontierswomen, but in a new America
without the distinction between frontier and home? Elizabeth Janeway in her book of 1971, *Man's World, Woman's Place: A Study in
Social Mythology,* described this dualistic mythic pattern and called
for a new mythology where women and men would be equal to each
other. Surely roles for men as well as women would be different if
the world were seen as a home and not a frontier. Surely America
would be dramatically different if we saw it as a home and not a
frontier.

There is hope in 1976 that we may take better care of this
"home." Biologists and physicists have offered another definition of
nature than that of rational space and linear time which contradicts
the notion of endless expansion. Heretical economists have used
these new scientific principles to challenge marketplace economics
and to urge responsibility to the environment. Heretical poets, mystics, and religious prophets have asked us to see ourselves within the
body of the earth, which is an expression of the body of God.

The hope for the future, therefore, may be this shared logic of
the peoples whose American citizenship has only recently been
recognized. If there is a shared logic of home and body that links
twentieth-century biology and physics and ecology to the appearance of the liberation movements of the once considered worthless
and useless Americans—black and red liberation, ethnic liberation,
women's liberation—then one can hope that we are at the beginning
of a new era in America. A beginning, of course, shares the moment with an ending. There is sadness at an ending. There is pain
but joy at a beginning. The leaders of this painful beginning may
seem strange to many of us. But if Native Americans are some of
those leaders, they are not strangers to America. Afro-American
leaders are no strangers to a continent to which they arrived in
1619. And although some have thought it amusing to consider
women as "strangers" in America, it is no longer amusing to consider them as leaders for the future.

As we read this, each of us will be choosing our personal understanding of American history. Some of us will choose to believe that
the patterns that began to become dominant in the seventeenth
century have the strength and vitality to continue to dominate the
future. Some of us, however, will have chosen to believe that these
patterns have been losing their power since the end of the geo-

graphic frontier at the end of the nineteenth century. We can believe, therefore, that since the 1880s we have had almost a century
of culture in America, a culture with sciences, painting, music,
theater, poetry, novels, and social institutions that are not based on
the concepts of rational space and linear time. For us, there is an
alternative future, which is growing out of an alternative view of
history.

Selected References

The following books, arranged chapter by chapter, have been especially valuable in preparing *The Free and the Unfree,* and they are also good introductions for readers who wish to pursue the subject further. Most of them are secondary works that contain full bibliographies and additional references.

CHAPTER 1. Native Americans Meet Native Europeans

Bindoff, S. T. *Tudor England.* London, 1950.

Crosby, Alfred W., Jr. *The Columbian Exchange: Biological and Cultural Consequences of 1492.* Westport, Conn., 1972.

Eccles, W. J. *France in America.* New York, 1972.

Elliott, J. H. *The Old World and the New: 1492–1650.* Cambridge, England, 1972.

Farb, Peter. *Man's Rise to Civilization as shown by the Indians of North America.* New York, 1968.

Gibson, Charles. *Spain in America.* New York, 1966.

Huizinga, J. *The Waning of the Middle Ages.* London, 1924.

Josephy, Alvin M., Jr. *The Indian Heritage of America.* New York, 1968.

Morison, Samuel Eliot. *Admiral of the Ocean Sea: A Life of Christopher Columbus.* Boston, 1942.

———. *The European Discovery of America.* 2 vols. New York, 1971–74.

Nash, Gary B. *Red, White, and Black: The Peoples of Early America.* Englewood Cliffs, N.J., 1974.

O'Gorman, Edmundo. *The Invention of America.* Bloomington, Ind., 1961.

Parry, J. H. *The Age of Reconnaissance.* New York, 1963.

Quinn, David Beers. *Raleigh and the British Empire.* London, 1947.

Rowse, A. L. *The Expansion of Elizabethan England.* New York, 1955.

Washburn, Wilcomb E., ed. *The Indian and the White Man.* Garden City, N.Y., 1964.

———. *The Indian in America.* New York, 1975.

CHAPTER 2. The Transplantation

Bailey, Chris. *Two Hundred Years of American Clocks and Watches*. Englewood Cliffs, N.J., 1975.

Bindoff, S. T. *Tudor England*. London, 1950.

Carroll, Peter N. *Puritanism and the Wilderness: The Intellectual Significance of the New England Frontier*. New York, 1969.

Collinson, Patrick. *The Elizabethan Puritan Movement*. Berkeley, 1967.

Cowing, Cedric B. *The Great Awakening and the American Revolution: Colonial Thought in the 18th Century*. Chicago, 1971.

Craven, Wesley Frank. *The Colonies in Transition: 1660–1713*. New York, 1968.

deMause, Lloyd, ed. *The History of Childhood*. New York, 1974.

Demos, John. *A Little Commonwealth: Family Life in Plymouth Colony*. New York, 1970.

Dickens, Arthur G. *The English Reformation*. London, 1964.

Erikson, Kai T. *Wayward Puritans: A Study in the Sociology of Deviance*. New York, 1966.

George, Charles H., and George, Katherine. *The Protestant Mind of the English Reformation, 1570–1640*. Princeton, N.J., 1961.

Greven, Philip J., Jr. *Four Generations: Population, Land, and Family in Colonial Andover, Massachusetts*. Ithaca, N.Y., 1970.

Hansen, Chadwick. *Witchcraft at Salem*. New York, 1969.

Heimert, Alan, and Miller, Perry, eds. *The Great Awakening*. Indianapolis, 1967.

Jordan, Winthrop D. *White Over Black: American Attitudes Toward the Negro, 1550–1812*. Chapel Hill, 1968.

Laslett, Peter. *The World We Have Lost*. New York, 1965.

Lockridge, Kenneth A. *A New England Town: The First Hundred Years*. New York, 1970.

McLoughlin, William G. *Isaac Backus and the American Pietistic Tradition*. Boston, 1967.

Miller, Perry. *The New England Mind: From Colony to Province*. Cambridge, Mass., 1953.

Morgan, Edmund S. *American Slavery, American Freedom: The Ordeal of Colonial Virginia*. New York, 1975.

———. *The Puritan Dilemma: The Story of John Winthrop*. Boston, 1958.

———. *The Puritan Family*. New York, 1966.

————. *Roger Williams: The Church and the State*. New York, 1967.

Nash, Gary B. *Red, White, and Black: The Peoples of Early America*. Englewood Cliffs, N.J., 1974.

New, John F. H. *Anglican and Puritan: The Basis of Their Opposition*. Stanford, Calif., 1964.

Notestein, Wallace. *The English People on the Eve of Colonization*. New York, 1954.

Tillyard, E. M. W. *The Elizabethan World Picture*. New York, 1943.

Vaughan, Alden T. *American Genesis: Captain John Smith and the Founding of Virginia*. Boston, 1975.

Ver Steeg, Clarence L. *The Formative Years*. New York, 1964.

Walzer, Michael. *The Revolution of the Saints: A Study in the Origins of Radical Politics*. New York, 1968.

Wright, Louis B. *Religion and Empire: The Alliance between Piety and Commerce in English Expansion*. Chapel Hill, 1943.

CHAPTER 3. Colonial Economy and Social Structure

Bailyn, Bernard, ed. *The Apologia of Robert Keayne: The Self-Portrait of a Puritan Merchant*. New York, 1965.

————. *The New England Merchants in the Seventeenth Century*. Cambridge, Mass., 1955.

Bushman, Richard L. *From Puritan to Yankee: Character and the Social Order in Connecticut, 1690–1765*. Cambridge, Mass., 1967.

Grant, Charles S. *Democracy in the Connecticut Frontier Town of Kent*. New York, 1961.

Hofstadter, Richard. *America at 1750: A Social Portrait*. New York, 1971.

Jordan, Winthrop D. *White Over Black: American Attitudes Toward the Negro, 1550–1812*. Chapel Hill, 1968.

Kammen, Michael. *Empire and Interest: The American Colonies and the Politics of Mercantilism*. Philadelphia, 1970.

Morgan, Edmund S. *American Slavery, American Freedom: The Ordeal of Colonial Virginia*. New York, 1975.

Mullin, Gerald W. *Flight and Rebellion: Slave Resistance in Eighteenth-Century Virginia*. New York, 1972.

Nash, Gary B. *Red, White, and Black: The Peoples of Early America.* Englewood Cliffs, N.J., 1974.

Rawick, George P. *From Sundown to Sunup: The Making of the Black Community.* Westport, Conn., 1972.

Tolles, Frederick B. *Meeting House and Counting House: The Quaker Merchants of Colonial Philadelphia.* Chapel Hill, 1948.

Vaughan, Alden T. *New England Frontier: Puritans and Indians, 1620–1675.* Boston, 1965.

Ver Steeg, Clarence L. *The Formative Years.* New York, 1964.

CHAPTER 4. Politics and the American Revolution

Bailyn, Bernard. *The Ideological Origins of the American Revolution.* Cambridge, Mass., 1967.

———. *The Origins of American Politics.* New York, 1968.

Brodie, Fawn M. *Thomas Jefferson: An Intimate History.* New York, 1974.

Brown, Wallace. *The King's Friends: The Composition and Motives of the American Loyalist Claimants.* Providence, R.I., 1966.

Ernst, Joseph Albert. *Money and Politics in America: 1755–1775.* Chapel Hill, 1973.

Gipson, Lawrence Henry. *The Coming of the Revolution, 1763–1775.* New York, 1954.

Greene, Jack P. *The Quest for Power.* Chapel Hill, 1963.

Henretta, James A. *"Salutary Neglect": Colonial Administration Under the Duke of Newcastle.* Princeton, N.J., 1972.

Higginbotham, Don. *The War of American Independence: Military Attitudes, Policies, and Practice.* New York, 1971.

Jensen, Merrill. *The Articles of Confederation.* Madison, Wis., 1940.

———. *The New Nation.* New York, 1950.

———, ed. *Tracts of the American Revolution: 1763–1776.* Indianapolis, 1967.

Kammen, Michael. *Deputyes and Libertyes: The Origins of Representative Government in Colonial America.* New York, 1969.

Kurtz, Stephen G., and Hutson, James H., eds. *Essays on the American Revolution.* Chapel Hill, 1973.

Maier, Pauline. *From Resistance to Revolution: Colonial Radicals and the Development of Opposition to Britain.* New York, 1972.

Main, Jackson Turner. *Political Parties Before the Constitution*. Chapel Hill, 1973.

—————. *The Upper House in Revolutionary America, 1763–1788*. Madison, Wis., 1967.

Morgan, Edmund S., and Morgan, Helen. *The Stamp Act Crisis: Prologue to Revolution*. Chapel Hill, 1953.

Nelson, William H. *The American Tory*. Oxford, England, 1961.

Sydnor, Charles S. *Gentlemen Freeholders*. Chapel Hill, 1952.

Wood, Gordon S. *The Creation of the American Republic: 1776–1787*. Chapel Hill, 1969.

Zemsky, Robert. *Merchants, Farmers, and River Gods: An Essay on Eighteenth-Century American Politics*. Boston, 1971.

Zuckerman, Michael. *Peaceable Kingdoms: New England Towns in the Eighteenth Century*. New York, 1970.

CHAPTER 5. The Constitution and American Identity

Boorstin, Daniel J. *The Lost World of Thomas Jefferson*. New York, 1948.

Brodie, Fawn M. *Thomas Jefferson: An Intimate History*. New York, 1974.

Henretta, James A. *The Evolution of American Society, 1700–1815*. Lexington, Mass., 1973.

Hofstadter, Richard. *The American Political Tradition*. New York, 1948.

Jordan, Winthrop D. *White Over Black: American Attitudes Toward the Negro, 1550–1812*. Chapel Hill, 1968.

Main, Jackson Turner. *The Antifederalists: Critics of the Constitution*. Chapel Hill, 1961.

—————. *The Social Structure of Revolutionary America*. Princeton, N.J., 1965.

McDonald, Forrest. *We the People: The Economic Origins of the Constitution*. Chicago, 1958.

Nye, Russel B. *The Cultural Life of the New Nation, 1776–1830*. New York, 1960.

Robinson, Donald L. *Slavery in the Structure of American Politics*. New York, 1971.

Sheehan, Bernard W. *Seeds of Extinction: Jeffersonian Philanthropy and the American Indian*. Chapel Hill, 1973.

Wood, Gordon S. *The Creation of the American Republic: 1776–1787*. Chapel Hill, 1969.

CHAPTER 6. Social Patterns, North and South

Bailey, Chris. *Two Hundred Years of American Clocks and Watches*. Englewood Cliffs, N.J., 1975.

Barker-Benfield, G. J. *The Horrors of the Half-Known Life: Male Attitudes Toward Women and Sexuality in Nineteenth-Century America*. New York, 1976.

Blassingame, John W. *The Slave Community: Plantation Life in the Antebellum South*. New York, 1972.

Flexner, Eleanor. *Century of Struggle: The Woman's Rights Movement in the United States*. Cambridge, Mass., 1959.

Fogel, Robert William, and Engerman, Stanley L. *Time on the Cross: The Economics of American Negro Slavery*. Boston, 1974.

Fredrickson, George M. *The Black Image in the White Mind*. New York, 1971.

Genovese, Eugene D. *The Political Economy of Slavery*. New York, 1965.

———. *Roll Jordan Roll: The World the Slaves Made*. New York, 1974.

Handlin, Oscar, and Handlin, Mary. *Commonwealth: A Study of the Role of Government in the American Economy*. New York, 1947.

Hansen, Marcus L. *The Atlantic Migration, 1607–1860*. Cambridge, Mass., 1940.

Hareven, Tamara K., ed. *Anonymous Americans: Explorations in Nineteenth-Century Social History*. Englewood Cliffs, N.J., 1971.

Hartz, Louis. *Economic Policy and Democratic Thought: Pennsylvania, 1776–1860*. Cambridge, Mass., 1948.

Henretta, James A. *The Evolution of American Society, 1700–1815*. Lexington, Mass., 1973.

Katz, Michael. *The Irony of Early School Reform*. Cambridge, Mass., 1968.

Miller, Perry. *The Life of the Mind in America: From the Revolution to the Civil War*. New York, 1965.

Pessen, Edward. *Riches, Class, and Power Before the Civil War*. Lexington, Mass., 1973.

Rozwenc, Edwin C., ed. *Ideology and Power in the Age of Jackson.* Garden City, N.Y., 1964.

Sklar, Kathryn Kish. *Catherine Beecher: A Study in American Domesticity.* New Haven, 1973.

Taylor, George R. *The Transportation Revolution, 1815–1860.* New York, 1951.

Taylor, William R. *Cavalier and Yankee: The Old South and American National Character.* New York, 1961.

Temin, Peter. *The Jacksonian Economy.* New York, 1969.

Thernstrom, Stephan. *Poverty and Progress: Social Mobility in a Nineteenth Century City.* Cambridge, Mass., 1964.

Wishy, Bernard. *The Child and the Republic.* Philadelphia, 1968.

CHAPTER 7. The Organization of Space

Billington, Ray Allen. *America's Frontier Heritage.* New York, 1966.

————. *The Protestant Crusade, 1800–1860.* New York, 1938.

Dangerfield, George. *The Awakening of American Nationalism, 1815–1828.* New York, 1965.

Filler, Louis. *The Crusade Against Slavery, 1830–1860.* New York, 1960.

Foner, Eric. *Free Soil, Free Labor, Free Men: The Ideology of the Republican Party Before the Civil War.* New York, 1970.

Knights, Peter R. *The Plain People of Boston, 1830–1860.* New York, 1971.

Merk, Frederick. *Manifest Destiny and Mission in American History.* New York, 1963.

————. *The Monroe Doctrine and American Expansionism: 1843–1849.* New York, 1966.

Moquin, Wayne, ed. *Great Documents in American Indian History.* New York, 1973.

Nye, Russel Blaine. *Society and Culture in America, 1830–1860.* New York, 1974.

Richards, Leonard L. *"Gentlemen of Property and Standing": Anti-Abolition Mobs in Jacksonian America.* New York, 1970.

Rogin, Michael Paul. *Fathers and Children: Andrew Jackson and the Subjugation of the American Indian.* New York, 1975.

Rothman, David J. *The Discovery of the Asylum: Social Order and Disorder in the New Republic.* Boston, 1971.

Sheehan, Bernard W. *Seeds of Extinction: Jeffersonian Philanthropy and the American Indian*. Chapel Hill, 1973.

Smith, Henry Nash. *Virgin Land: The American West as Symbol and Myth*. Cambridge, Mass., 1950.

Sorin, Gerald. *Abolitionism: A New Perspective*. New York, 1972.

Starr, Kevin. *Americans and the California Dream: 1850–1915*. New York, 1973.

Sweet, Leonard I. *Black Images of America: 1784–1870*. New York 1976.

Tyler, Alice Felt. *Freedom's Ferment: Phases of American Social History*. Minneapolis, 1944.

Washburn, Wilcomb E. *The Indian in America*. New York, 1975.

Weinberg, Albert K. *Manifest Destiny: A Study of National Expansionism*. Baltimore, 1935.

CHAPTER 8. Politics and Power

Banner, James M., Jr. *To The Hartford Convention*. New York, 1970.

Barney, William. *The Road to Secession: A New Perspective on the Old South*. New York, 1972.

Brown, Roger H. *The Republic in Peril: 1812*. New York, 1964.

Chambers, William. *Political Parties in a New Nation*. New York, 1963.

Channing, Steven A. *Crisis of Fear: Secession in South Carolina*. New York, 1970.

Current, Richard N. *Daniel Webster and the Rise of National Conservatism*. Boston, 1955.

Curtis, James C. *Andrew Jackson and the Search for Vindication*. Boston, 1976.

Eaton, Clement. *Henry Clay and the Art of American Politics*. Boston, 1957.

Fischer, David Hackett. *The Revolution of American Conservatism: The Federalist Party in the Era of Jeffersonian Democracy*. New York, 1965.

Foner, Eric. *Free Soil, Free Labor, Free Men: The Ideology of the Republican Party Before the Civil War*. New York, 1970.

Freehling, William W. *Prelude to Civil War: The Nullification Controversy in South Carolina*. New York, 1966.

Hofstadter, Richard. *The Idea of a Party System: The Rise of Legitimate Opposition in the United States, 1780–1840*. Berkeley, 1969.

Meyers, Marvin. *The Jacksonian Persuasion*. Stanford, Calif., 1957.

Miller, John C. *The Federalist Era, 1789–1801*. New York, 1960.

Nichols, Roy Franklin. *The Disruption of American Democracy*. New York, 1948.

Remini, Robert V. *Andrew Jackson and the Bank War*. New York, 1967.

Sydnor, Charles. *The Development of Southern Sectionalism, 1819–1848*. Baton Rouge, 1948.

Ward, John William. *Andrew Jackson: Symbol for an Age*. New York, 1962.

CHAPTER 9. The Civil War and American Identity

Barney, William L. *Flawed Victory: A New Perspective on the Civil War*. New York, 1975.

Catton, Bruce. *This Hallowed Ground*. New York, 1956.

Cornish, Dudley. *The Sable Arm: Negro Troops in the Union Army, 1861–1865*. New York, 1956.

Current, Richard N., ed. *The Political Thought of Abraham Lincoln*. Indianapolis, 1967.

Donald, David, ed. *Why the North Won the Civil War*. Baton Rouge, 1960.

Eaton, Clement. *A History of the Southern Confederacy*. New York, 1954.

Fehrenbacher, Don E. *Prelude to Greatness: Lincoln in the 1850's*. Stanford, Calif., 1962.

Fredrickson, George M. *The Inner Civil War: Northern Intellectuals and the Crisis of the Union*. New York, 1965.

———, ed. *A Nation Divided: Problems and Issues of the Civil War and Reconstruction*. Minneapolis, 1975.

Hofstadter, Richard. *The American Political Tradition*. New York, 1948.

McPherson, James M. *The Negro's Civil War*. New York, 1965.

Pressly, Thomas J. *Americans Interpret Their Civil War*. New York, 1954.

Washburn, Wilcomb E. *The Indian in America*. New York, 1975.

CHAPTER 10. The Collapse of Nineteenth-Century Culture

Andrist, Ralph. *The Long Death*. New York, 1964.

Barker-Benfield, G. J. *The Horrors of the Half-Known Life*. New York, 1976.

Brown, Dee. *Bury My Heart at Wounded Knee*. New York, 1971.

Fredrickson, George. *The Black Image in the White Mind*. New York, 1971.

Gillis, John. *Youth and History*. New York, 1974.

Handy, Robert. *A Christian America*. New York, 1971.

Higham, John. *Strangers in the Land*. New Brunswick, N.J., 1955.

Hoover, Dwight. *The Red and the Black*. Chicago, 1976.

Jackson, John B. *American Space*. New York, 1972.

Jaher, Frederic. *Doubters and Dissenters*. New York, 1964.

Kraditor, Aileen. *The Ideas of the Woman Suffrage Movement*. New York, 1965.

Kern, Stephen. *Anatomy and Destiny*. Indianapolis, 1975.

Kirby, Jack. *Darkness at the Dawning*. Philadelphia, 1972.

Marty, Martin. *Righteous Empire*. New York, 1970.

Marx, Leo. *The Machine in the Garden*. New York, 1964.

Miner, H. Craig. *The Corporation and the Indian*. Columbia, Mo., 1976.

Nash, Gary, and Weiss, Richard, ed. *The Great Fear*. New York, 1970.

Nash, Roderick. *Wilderness and the American Mind*. New Haven, 1967.

Newby, I. A. *Jim Crow's Defense*. Baton Rouge, La., 1965.

Paulson, Ross. *Women's Suffrage and Prohibition*. Glenview, Ill., 1973.

Pivar, Donald. *Purity Crusade*. Westport, Conn., 1973.

Salomon, Roger. *Twain and the Image of History*. New Haven, 1961.

Smith, Henry Nash. *Virgin Land*. Cambridge, Mass., 1950.

Solomon, Barbara. *Ancestors and Immigrants*. Cambridge, Mass., 1956.

Weiss, Richard. *The American Myth of Success*. New York, 1969.

Wissler, Clark. *Red Man Reservations*. New York, 1938.

CHAPTER 11. The New Industrial Economy

Chandler, Alfred. *Strategy and Structure*. Garden City, N.Y., 1961.

Cross, Robert. *The Emergence of Liberal Catholicism in America*. Cambridge, Mass., 1954.

Diamond, Sigmund. *The Reputation of the American Businessman*. Cambridge, Mass., 1955.

Fite, Gilbert. *The Farmer's Frontier*. New York, 1966.

Hays, Samuel P. *The Response to Industrialism*. Chicago, 1957.

Hidy, Ralph, and Hidy, Muriel. *Pioneering in Big Business*. New York, 1955.

Karson, Marc. *American Labor Unions and Politics*. Carbondale, Ill., 1958.

Kirkland, Edward C. *Industry Comes of Age*. New York, 1961.

Logan, Rayford. *The Betrayal of the Negro from Rutherford Hayes to Woodrow Wilson*. New York, 1965.

McAvoy, Thomas. *The Great Crisis in American Catholic History*. Chicago, 1957.

Meier, August. *Negro Thought in America, 1880–1915*. Ann Arbor, 1963.

Messbarger, Paul. *Fiction with a Parochial Purpose: Social Use of American Catholic Literature, 1884–1900*. Brookline, Mass., 1970.

Passer, Harold. *The Electrical Manufacturers*. Cambridge, Mass., 1953.

Rischin, Moses. *The Promised City: New York's Jews, 1870–1914*. Cambridge, Mass., 1962.

Spear, Allan. *Black Chicago*. Chicago, 1967.

Taylor, George. *The Transportation Revolution*. New York, 1951.

Thernstrom, Stephen. *Poverty and Progress*. Cambridge, Mass., 1964.

Unger, Irwin. *The Greenback Era*. Princeton, N.J., 1964.

Warner, Sam. *Streetcar Suburbs*. Cambridge, Mass., 1962.

Weinstein, James. *The Corporate Ideal in the Liberal State*. Boston, 1968.

Wiebe, Robert. *The Search for Order*. New York, 1967.

Woodward, C. Vann. *The Strange Career of Jim Crow*. New York, 1957.

Wyllie, Irvin. *The Self-Made Man in America*. New Brunswick, N.J., 1954.

CHAPTER 12. Politics in the Late Nineteenth Century

Bullough, William. *Cities and Schools in the Gilded Age*. Port Washington, N.Y., 1974.

Cox, Lawanda, and Cox, John. *Politics, Principle, and Prejudice*. New York, 1963.

Donald, David. *Charles Sumner and the Rights of Man*. New York, 1970.

Durden, Robert. *The Climax of Populism*. Lexington, Ky., 1965.

Glad, Paul. *McKinley, Bryan, and the People*. Philadelphia, 1964.

Grimes, Alan. *The Puritan Ethic and Woman Suffrage*. New York, 1967.

Gusfield, Joseph. *Symbolic Crusade: Status Politics and the American Temperance Movement*. Urbana, Ill., 1961.

Hoogenboom, Ari. *Outlawing the Spoils: A History of the Civil Service Reform Movement, 1865–1880*. Urbana, Ill., 1961.

Kleppner, Paul. *The Cross of Culture: A Social Analysis of Midwestern Politics, 1850–1900*. New York, 1970.

Kousser, J. Morgan. *The Shaping of Southern Politics: Suffrage Restriction and the Establishment of the One-Party South, 1880–1910*. New Haven, 1974.

Morgan, David. *Suffragists and Democrats: The Politics of Woman Suffrage in America*. East Lansing, Mich., 1972.

O'Neill, William. *Everyone Was Brave: The Rise and Fall of Feminism in America*. Chicago, 1969.

Paul, Arnold. *Conservative Crisis and the Rule of Law*. Ithaca, N.Y., 1960.

Rose, Willie Lee. *Rehearsal for Reconstruction*. Indianapolis, 1964.

Rothman, David. *Politics and Power: The United States Senate, 1869–1901*. Cambridge, Mass., 1966.

Sproat, John. *The Best Men: Liberal Reformers in the Gilded Age*. New York, 1966.

Stampp, Kenneth. *The Era of Reconstruction*. New York, 1965.

Williamson, Joel. *After Slavery, the Negro in South Carolina During Reconstruction*. Chapel Hill, 1965.

Wood, Forrest. *Black Scare: The Racist Response to Emancipation*. Berkeley, 1968.

Woodward, C. Vann. *Reunion and Reaction*. New York, 1951.

———. *Tom Watson*. New York, 1938.

Youngdale, James. *Populism: A Psychohistorical Perspective*. Port Washington, N.Y., 1975.

CHAPTER 13. The End of Isolation, 1898–1920

Bailey, Thomas. *Woodrow Wilson and the Lost Peace*. New York, 1944.

Blum, John. *The Republican Roosevelt*. Cambridge, Mass., 1956.

Burton, David. *Theodore Roosevelt, Confident Imperialist*. Philadelphia, 1968.

Cuff, Robert. *The War Industries Board*. Baltimore, 1973.

Davis, Allen. *Spearheads for Reform: The Social Settlements and the Progressive Movement, 1890–1914*. New York, 1967.

George, Alexander, and George, Juliette. *Woodrow Wilson and Colonel House*. New York, 1956.

Grubbs, Frank, Jr. *The Struggle for Labor Loyalty: Gompers, the AFL, and the Pacifists, 1917–1920*. Durham, N.C., 1968.

Hays, Samuel P. *Conservation and the Gospel of Efficiency*. Cambridge, Mass., 1959.

Healy, David. *U.S. Expansionism: The Imperialist Urge in the 1890s*. Madison, Wis., 1970.

Kolko, Gabriel. *The Triumph of Conservatism*. Chicago, 1963.

Kuehl, Warren. *Seeking World Order: The United States and International Organizations to 1920*. Nashville, Tenn., 1969.

LaFeber, Walter. *The New Empire*. Ithaca, N.Y., 1963.

Levin, N. Gordon. *Woodrow Wilson and World Politics*. New York, 1968.

Link, Arthur. *Woodrow Wilson and the Progessive Era*. New York, 1954.

Livermore, Seward. *Politics Is Adjourned: Woodrow Wilson and the War Congress, 1916–1918*. Middletown, Conn., 1966.

Noble, David W. *The Progressive Mind*. Chicago, 1968.

Penick, James. *Progressive Politics and Conservation*. Chicago, 1968.

Perkins, Bradford. *The Great Rapprochement: England and the United States, 1895–1914*. New York, 1968.

Preston, William. *Aliens and Dissenters: Federal Suppression of Radicals, 1903–1933*. New York, 1963.

Shannon, David. *The Socialist Party of America*. New York, 1955.

Stone, Ralph. *The Irreconcilables: The Fight Against the League of Nations*. Lexington, Ky., 1970.

Thelen, David. *The New Citizenship*. Columbia, Mo., 1972.

Tishler, Hace Sorel. *Self-Reliance and Social Security, 1870–1917*. Port Washington, N.Y., 1971.

Weston, Rubin. *Racism in U.S. Imperialism*. Columbia, S.C., 1972.

Williams, William Appleman. *The Roots of the Modern American Empire*. New York, 1969.

CHAPTER 14. Prosperity and Depression, 1920–40

Bernstein, Irving. *The Lean Years: A History of the American Worker, 1920–1933*. Boston, 1960.

———. *Turbulent Years: A History of the American Worker, 1933–1941*. Boston, 1970.

Cooperman, Stanley. *World War I and the American Novel*. Baltimore, 1970.

Flynn, George. *American Catholics and the Roosevelt Presidency*. Lexington, Ky., 1968.

Fullinwider, S. P. *The Mind and Mood of Black America*. Homewood, Ill., 1969.

Haber, Samuel. *Efficiency and Uplift*. Chicago, 1964.

Handlin, Oscar. *Al Smith and His America*. Boston, 1958.

Heald, Morrell. *The Social Responsibities of Business*. Cleveland, 1970.

Hoffman, Frederick. *The Twenties: American Writing in the Post-War Decade*. New York, 1955.

Huggins, Nathan. *Harlem Renaissance*. New York, 1972.

Huthmacher, J. Joseph. *Senator Robert Wagner and the Rise of Urban Liberalism*. New York, 1968.

Israel, Jerry, ed. *Building the Organizational Society: Essays on Association Activities in Modern America*. New York, 1972.

Lemons, J. Stanley. *The Woman Citizen: Social Feminism in the 1920's*. Urbana, Ill., 1973.

Leonard, Neil. *Jazz and the White Americans*. Chicago, 1962.

Leuchtenburg, William. *Franklin D. Roosevelt and the New Deal*. New York, 1963.

———. *The Perils of Prosperity*. Chicago, 1958.

Lubove, Roy. *The Struggle for Social Security*. Cambridge, Mass., 1968.

Dale,

If you'll send
this back to me *
when you've finished
with it, I'll take
the next step —
whatever that might
be.

Thanks for your time.

T.

* St. #19

with it I'll take

Meyer, Leonard. *Music, the Arts, and Ideas.* Chicago, 1967.

Miller, Robert. *American Protestantism and Social Issues, 1919–1937.* Chapel Hill, 1958.

Nash, Roderick. *The Nervous Generation: American Thought, 1917–1930.* Chicago, 1970.

Pleasants, Henry. *Serious Music and All That Jazz.* New York, 1969.

Sidran, Ben. *Black Talk.* New York, 1971.

Sternsher, Bernard, ed. *Hitting Home: The Great Depression in Town and Country.* Chicago, 1970.

Vincent, Theodore. *Black Power and the Garvey Movement.* Berkeley, 1971.

Warren, Frank. *Liberals and Communism.* Bloomington, Ind., 1966.

Wolters, Raymond. *Negroes and the Great Depression.* Westport, Conn., 1970.

Zieger, Robert. *Republicans and Labor, 1919–1929.* Lexington, Ky., 1969.

CHAPTER 15. War, Economic Prosperity, and Consensus, 1936–60

Ambrose, Stephen. *The Rise to Globalism: American Foreign Policy Since 1938.* Baltimore, 1971.

Blum, John M. *V Was for Victory: Politics and American Culture During World War II.* New York, 1976.

Broder, David. *The Party's Over: The Failure of Politics in America.* New York, 1971.

Daniels, Roger. *Concentration Camps, U.S.A.: Japanese Americans and World War II.* New York, 1971.

Divine, Robert. *The Reluctant Belligerent: American Entry into World War II.* New York, 1968.

Donaldson, Scott. *The Suburban Myth.* New York, 1969.

Fleming, D. F. *The Cold War and Its Origins.* New York, 1961.

Freeland, Richard. *The Truman Doctrine and the Origins of McCarthyism.* New York, 1972.

Galbraith, John K. *The New Industrial State.* Boston, 1967.

Gardner, Lloyd C. *Economic Aspects of New Deal Diplomacy.* Madison, Wis., 1964.

Goldman, Eric. *The Crucial Decade.* New York, 1966.

Guttman, Allen. *The Wound in the Heart: America and the Span-ish Civil War*. New York, 1962.

LaFeber, Walter. *America, Russia, and the Cold War*. New York, 1967.

Lubell, Samuel. *The Future of American Politics*. New York, 1965.

Meyer, Donald. *The Protestant Search for Political Realism*. Berke-ley, 1960.

Morton, Marian. *The Terrors of Ideological Politics*. Cleveland, 1972.

Newman, William. *The Futilitarian Society*. New York, 1961.

Rogin, Michael Paul. *The Intellectuals and McCarthy*. Cambridge, Mass., 1967.

Wenk, Michael, et al. *Pieces of a Dream: The Ethnic Workers' Crisis with America*. New York, 1972.

Wise, Gene. *American Historical Explanations*. Homewood, Ill., 1973.

Wittner, Lawrence. *Rebels Against War: The American Peace Movement*. New York, 1969.

Wood, Robert. *Suburbia: Its People and Their Politics*. Boston, 1958.

———. *The Necessary Majority: Middle America and the Urban Crisis*. New York, 1972.

CHAPTER 16. New Visions, New Ethics, 1950–70

Berman, Ronald. *America in the 'Sixties*. New York, 1968.

Benthall, Jonathan, and Pothemus, Ted, eds. *The Body as a Me-dium of Expression*. New York, 1975.

Braden, William. *The Age of Aquarius*. New York, 1970.

Brauer, Ralph. *The Horse, the Gun, and the Piece of Property: Changing Images of the TV Western*. Bowling Green, Ohio, 1975.

Burnshaw, Stanley. *The Seamless Web*. New York, 1970.

Carden, Maren Lockwood. *The New Feminist Movement*. New York, 1974.

Commoner, Barry. *The Closing Circle*. New York, 1971.

Cottrell, Fred. *Energy and Society*. New York, 1955.

Deckard, Barbara. *The Woman's Movement*. New York, 1975.

Deloria, Vine, Jr. *God Is Red*. New York, 1973.

Diggins, John P. *The American Left in the Twentieth Century*. New York, 1973.

Gordon, Michael, ed. *The American Family in Social-Historical Perspective.* New York, 1973.

Hardin, Garrett. *Exploring New Ethics for Survival: The Voyage of the Spaceship Beagle.* New York, 1972.

Hunter, Robert. *The Storming of the Mind.* New York, 1972.

Keniston, Kenneth. *Youth and Dissent.* New York, 1971.

———. *The Uncommitted.* New York, 1965.

King, Richard. *The Party of Eros: Radical Social Thought and the Realm of Freedom.* Chapel Hill, 1972.

Mack, Arien, ed. *Death in American Experience.* New York, 1973.

Roszak, Theodore. *The Making of a Counter Culture.* New York, 1969.

Shepard, Paul, and McKinley, Daniel, eds. *The Subversive Science: Essays Toward an Ecology of Man.* Boston, 1969.

Slater, Philip. *The Pursuit of Loneliness.* Boston, 1970.

Stannard, David, ed. *Death in America.* Philadelphia, 1975.

Vernon, John. *The Garden and the Map: Schizophrenia in Twentieth-Century Literature and Culture.* Urbana, Ill., 1973.

Wright, Will. *Six Guns and Society.* Berkeley, 1976.

Yorburg, Betty. *The Changing Family.* New York, 1973.

CHAPTER 17. Patterns of Economic Change, 1960–76

Baltzell, E. Digby. *The Protestant Establishment: Aristocracy and Caste in America.* New York, 1964.

Barber, Richard. *The American Corporation.* New York, 1970.

Commoner, Barry. *The Poverty of Power: Energy and the Economic Crisis.* New York, 1976.

Daly, Herman, ed. *Toward a Steady-State Economy.* San Francisco, 1973.

Ferkiss, Victor. *The Future of Technological Civilization.* New York, 1974.

Georgescu-Roegen, Nicholas. *The Entropy Law and Economic Process.* Cambridge, 1971.

Harrington, Michael. *The Twilight of Capitalism.* New York, 1976.

Heath, Jim. *John F. Kennedy and the Business Community.* Chicago, 1969.

Lodge, George C. *The New American Ideology.* New York, 1975.

Logsdon, John. *The Decision to Go to the Moon.* Cambridge, 1970.

O'Neill, William. *Coming Apart.* Chicago, 1972.

Parker, Richard. *The Myth of the Middle Class.* New York, 1972.

Piven, Frances Fox, and Cloward, Richard. *Regulating the Poor.* New York, 1971.

Radosh, Ronald. *American Labor and United States Foreign Policy.* New York, 1969.

Ridgway, James. *The Closed Corporation: American Universities in Crisis.* New York, 1968.

Rothschild, Emma. *Paradise Lost: The Decline of the Auto-Industrial Age.* New York, 1973.

Russett, Bruce. *What Price Vigilence: The Burden of National Defense.* New Haven, 1970.

Schumacher, E. F. *Small Is Beautiful.* New York, 1973.

Seligman, Ben, ed. *Permanent Poverty.* Chicago, 1968.

Sexton, Patricia, and Sexton, Brendon. *Blue Collars and Hard Hats.* New York, 1971.

Tanzer, Michael. *The Sick Society.* New York, 1968.

Toffler, Alvin, ed. *The Futurists.* New York, 1972.

Warren, Donald. *The Radical Center: Middle Americans and the Politics of Alienation.* Notre Dame, Ind., 1976.

Willhelm, Sidney. *Who Needs the Negro?* New York, 1970.

CHAPTER 18. American Foreign Policy and Domestic Politics, 1960–76

Acuna, Rudolfo. *Occupied America: The Chicano's Struggle Toward Liberation.* San Francisco, 1972.

Branden, Henry. *The Retreat of American Power.* New York, 1972.

Chafe, William. *The American Woman: Her Changing Social, Economic, and Political Roles, 1920–1970.* New York, 1972.

Fairlie, Henry. *The Kennedy Promise.* New York, 1972.

Fitzgerald, Frances. *Fire in the Lake: The Vietnamese and the Americans in Vietnam.* New York, 1972.

Geyelin, Philip. *Lyndon B. Johnson and the World.* New York, 1966.

Halberstam, David. *The Best and the Brightest.* New York, 1972.

Haskell, Molly. *From Reverence to Rape: The Treatment of Women in the Movies.* New York, 1974.

Hertzberg, Helen. *The Search for an American Indian Identity.* Syracuse, N.Y., 1971.

Krickus, Richard. *Pursuing the American Dream: White Ethnics and the New Populism.* New York, 1976.

Ladd, Everett, and Hadley, Charles. *Transformations of the American Party System.* New York, 1975.

Lasch, Christopher. *The Agony of the American Left.* New York, 1969.

Levine, Stuart, and Lurie, Nancy. *The American Indian Today.* Deland, Fla., 1965.

Lewis, David. *King.* New York, 1970.

Mazlish, Bruce. *In Search of Nixon.* New York, 1972.

Meier, Matt, and Rivera, Feliciano. *The Chicanos.* New York, 1972.

Miroff, Bruce. *Pragmatic Illusions: The Presidential Politics of John F. Kennedy.* New York, 1976.

Murphy, Reg, and Buliver, Hal. *The Southern Strategy.* New York, 1971.

Muse, Benjamin. *The American Negro Revolution: From Non-Violence to Black Power.* Bloomington, Ind., 1968.

Novak, Michael. *The Rise of the Unmeltable Ethnics.* New York, 1971.

Schlesinger, Arthur, Jr. *The Imperial Presidency.* Boston, 1973.

Schrag, Peter. *The Decline of the WASP.* New York, 1970.

Skolnick, Jerome. *The Politics of Protest.* New York, 1969.

Steiner, Sam. *The New Indians.* New York, 1968.

Yates, Gayle Graham. *What Women Want: The Ideas of the Movement.* Cambridge, Mass., 1975.

Index